DEFENDING
SIN

DEFENDING

SIN

A RESPONSE

TO THE CHALLENGES OF EVOLUTION

AND THE NATURAL SCIENCES

HANS MADUEME

B

Baker Academic

a division of Baker Publishing Group

Grand Rapids, Michigan

Published by Baker Academic
a division of Baker Publishing Group
Grand Rapids, Michigan
BakerAcademic.com

Printed in the United States of America

Library of Congress Cataloging-in-Publication Data
Names: Madueme, Hans, 1975– author.
Title: Defending sin : a response to the challenges of evolution and the natural sciences / Hans Madueme.
Description: Grand Rapids, Michigan : Baker Academic, a division of Baker Publishing Group, [2024] | Includes bibliographical references and index.
Identifiers: LCCN 2023035148 | ISBN 9780801098000 (paperback) | ISBN 9781540967787 (casebound) | ISBN 9781493446148 (ebook) | ISBN 9781493446155 (pdf)
Subjects: LCSH: Sin—Christianity. | Sin—Biblical teaching. | Bible—Theology.
Classification: LCC BT715 .M128 2024 | DDC 241/.3—dc23/eng/20230914
LC record available at https://lccn.loc.gov/2023035148

Baker Publishing Group publications use paper produced from sustainable forestry practices and postconsumer waste whenever possible.

24   25   26   27   28   29   30   7   6   5   4   3   2   1

To Shelley,
my partner in all things
and the love of my life

Contents

Contents

Acknowledgments

This book has been cooking in the oven a long time, far longer than planned. Doubtless, part of the problem is that writing at the interface of science and theology is just daunting. Christian doctrine is enough to handle all on its own; what fool would deign to take on another discipline as complex and multifaceted as natural science? How many times did I find myself going to bed at night only to wake up the next day to discover that ten new books relevant to my research had just been published? Worse yet, as I was writing, my theological convictions were changing—or, rather, crystallizing—in unexpected ways. For instance, at the outset of this project, I firmly resolved to steer clear of the most controversial issues swirling around the origins debate: Why tempt fate? Yet it became clear in time that I could not ignore those questions and instead had to face them head-on, which meant that the argument was not only expanding but would often strike off suddenly into hazardous terrain. Mind your step.

Now that the monograph is done, I have incurred many debts along the way. Pride of place goes to Bob Hosack, whose patience I can say with some authority is seemingly bottomless—I am definitely unworthy. My thanks to Bob, Melisa Blok, and their fantastic team at Baker Academic for being so helpful and such a pleasure to work with. My research began in earnest during a two-year summer grant at Oxford University in 2015–16 under the auspices of SCIO (Scholarship and Christianity in Oxford) and the Bridging the Two Cultures of Science and the Humanities program. I am grateful to the program director, Stan Rosenberg, as well as the many science-and-religion scholars I interacted with during those two memorable summers.

My most productive time was in the following spring semester of 2017 while serving as a Residential Fellow at the Carl F. H. Henry Center for

Theological Understanding at Trinity Evangelical Divinity School (TEDS). This fantastic opportunity was made possible by a generous three-year grant from the Templeton Religion Trust (later extended by another three years with a grant from the John Templeton Foundation). Given that the other residential fellows were none other than Jack Collins, John Hilber, and Clinton Ohlers, there was never a dull moment. I miss the lively lunch banter! I should also mention that the Dabar conference at TEDS, which happened every year of the Creation Project grant, was always a summer highlight and left me with fresh insights relevant to the book I was writing. My deep thanks to Tom McCall, who was director at the time, and especially to the Henry Center staff—Geoff Fulkerson, Joel Chopp, and Matt Wiley—the trio of expert friends that any scholar would wish for. Speaking of TEDS, I am also indebted to Kevin Vanhoozer, who supervised my early attempts at tackling these questions during my doctoral research over a decade ago.

I work at Covenant College on a holy mountain among the most fearless people on the planet. It may not be New Jerusalem, but while the Lord tarries, there is no other place in the world I'd want to be. I'm grateful to the administration that made much of my research possible, including Derek Halvorson and Jeff Hall. Several generous colleagues helped me with questions that I had and even read drafts of one or two chapters, among them John Wingard, Bill Davis, Phill Broussard, and Don Petcher. I also recognize my former students Jonathan Blackmon, Makayla Payne, John Bush, Chandler Kelley, and Sarah Bozarth, who helped me at various stages in the writing process. And special thanks to my colleagues in the Biblical and Theological Studies department, who have supported my work: Jeff Dryden, Scott Jones, Kelly Kapic, Luke Irwin, Clift Ward, Herb Ward, and (now retired) Dan MacDougall and Ken Stewart. We've been through thick and thin together—what a privilege to work with such first-rate scholars and friends.

Many friends and colleagues from other institutions in the US and around the world were kind enough to read parts of the manuscript and offer insightful critique and feedback, including Rob Allen, Bill Barrick, Mark Crago, Morgan Crago, Ted Davis, Travis Dumsday, Mike Emlet, Donald Fairbairn, Brad Gundlach, Brian Hecker, Joshua Hill, Danny Houck, Lydia Jaeger, Jonathan King, Ken Keathley, B. Kyle Keltz, Robert Larmer, Andrew Leslie, Stephen Lloyd, Marcus Mininger, Flavien Pardigon, Keith Plummer, Del Ratzsch, Jill Ross, Blair Smith, Richard Tison, Gijsbert van den Brink, Jitse van der Meer, Theodore Van Raalte, Aku Visala, Matthew Warnez, Michael Wittmer, and Todd Wood (I hope I haven't missed anyone—if so, mea culpa!).

I am especially grateful to my dear friends who dedicated their time to reading the entire manuscript and providing invaluable feedback. That noble company includes Charles Anderson, Robert Erle Barham, Jeremy Blaschke, Travis Hutchinson, Paul Gesting, C. Ben Mitchell, Michael Radmacher, Marcus Ross, Henry B. Smith Jr., and Stephen Williams. While they will not agree with every point in this book, their feedback improved it beyond measure.

In many respects, this book is a meditation on what sin is in view of the world as rendered by most scientists, the sin that I continue to grapple with and for which Jesus made atonement—alleluia! I am profoundly grateful to my Father in heaven for the family he blessed me with. To my two children, Caleb and Zoë, who eventually tired of asking me how the "big book on sin" was coming along, and to my patient and long-suffering wife, Shelley, to whom I dedicate this book: your unwavering support has been my greatest encouragement. As God helps us navigate the challenges of sin together, I anticipate the glorious day when all things will be made new and sin will be no more. Come, Lord Jesus!

Setting the Stage

Changing Conceptions of Sin

Christianity is most thoroughly a *practical* system in the highest and most intimate sense. . . . Everything in it relates to the great contrast between sin and redemption. . . . It is impossible to understand the doctrine of redemption, which is its very essence, until we have a thorough knowledge of sin. Christian theology here, if anywhere, *wages war, pro aris et focis.*

—Julius Müller[1]

James Orr (1844–1913) had served in pastoral ministry for seventeen years before publishing his bestseller, *The Christian View of God and the World,* which launched his academic career.[2] He took his first post at the United Presbyterian College in Edinburgh (1891–1900) and then transitioned to United Free Church College in Glasgow, Scotland, where he served as professor of apologetics and systematic theology until his death in 1913. In the fall of 1903, when invited to give a series of lectures at Princeton Theological Seminary, the Scottish theologian was evidently concerned about changing conceptions of sin in his day. He worried that "vital aspects of Christian doctrine" were being surrendered on the altar of "the modern view of the world."[3] He said that the Christian perspective

1. Julius Müller, *The Christian Doctrine of Sin,* trans. William Urwick, 5th ed., 2 vols. (Edinburgh: T&T Clark, 1868), 1:xix, emphasis original.

2. James Orr, *The Christian View of God and the World, as Centring in the Incarnation* (Edinburgh: Andrew Elliot, 1893). The book has gone through at least ten editions.

3. James Orr, *God's Image in Man and Its Defacement in the Light of Modern Denials* (Grand Rapids: Eerdmans, 1948), vi (originally published 1905).

on reality stood in stark contrast to the modern one. "We ought to have the courage to avow this," he wrote, "and take the consequences."[4]

Others disagreed. They were fellow Christians and keenly aware of what they perceived as the undeniable findings of natural science.[5] "If Christianity is to survive," they insisted, "it must undergo an entire transformation and re-interpretation in harmony with modern theories, and must part with many of the doctrines hitherto regarded as distinctive of it."[6] Despite their admonitions, Orr discounted this perspective as a road to perdition. Any extrabiblical theories that threatened the doctrines of God, humanity, and sin could only bring ruin to genuine faith.

Orr was particularly worried that acceptance of the idea that humans were the product of evolution would have devastating repercussions throughout hamartiology (the doctrine of sin). For starters, if humans evolved "from the state of animalism," then there could never have been an original state of righteousness. And, worse yet, grafting modern theories of human origins onto the body of theology only led to "defective and inadequate views of sin."[7] It is not surprising that Orr was in no conciliatory mood: these new ideas, he thought, were eviscerating the doctrines of sin, atonement, and salvation. High stakes indeed.

The Scotsman was no relic of twentieth-century fundamentalism.[8] He was a leading theologian in his day who was asking prescient questions— indeed, I share Orr's concerns. The Christian doctrine of sin has been under pressure from multiple disciplines in the natural sciences. Evolutionary biology, human genetics, and the neurosciences (to name just three) are raising difficult questions about human sinfulness. Alistair McFadyen once remarked about the doctrine of original sin: "The various points of conflict between the traditionally expressed doctrinal corpus of the Christian faith and the natural sciences raise a series of pressing issues concerning the relationship between science and Christian doctrine."[9] Those same questions were troubling Orr a century earlier. These issues, McFadyen insisted,

---

4. Orr, *God's Image in Man*, vi.

5. In this preface and the rest of the book, I use the terms "science" and "natural science" when referring to disciplines in the hard sciences like biology, chemistry, physics, geology, and astronomy.

6. Orr, *God's Image in Man*, 6.

7. Orr, *God's Image in Man*, 11.

8. Orr contributed four articles to twelve pamphlets known as *The Fundamentals*, published between 1910 and 1915 and circulated to about 250,000 church leaders across the transatlantic English-speaking world. Many of the articles (including Orr's) were reprints from earlier publications, and the pamphlets generally reflected "mainstream nineteenth-century evangelical orthodoxy." Glen G. Scorgie, *A Call for Continuity* (Macon, GA: Mercer University Press, 1998), 150.

9. Alistair McFadyen, *Bound to Sin: Abuse, Holocaust and the Christian Doctrine of Sin* (Cambridge: Cambridge University Press, 2000), 19.

"have yet adequately to be addressed either at the methodological or the substantive level."[10] This book is an attempt to engage these core issues in the encounter between the doctrine of sin and natural science.

Some Background

My interest in questions surrounding science and theology has been percolating for some time. Growing up as a Nigerian, I knew I wanted to be a physician—all African adolescents go through that phase (an inside joke for Africans). My undergraduate degree at McGill University in Montreal was in science, specifically anatomy. I went on to four years of medical school at Howard University in Washington, DC, and then I completed a three-year residency in internal medicine at the Mayo Clinic (Rochester, MN).

As a first-year medical student in 1996, I vividly recall sitting through psychiatry lectures and wrestling with questions about the human person and why people do the things they do. In retrospect, I was trying to understand the biblical teaching of sin in light of a wild landscape of scientific conundrums. I was a relatively new believer back then and did not have the intellectual or theological categories to frame the right questions. However, I knew in my bones that there was a story worth pursuing.

These questions haunted me throughout my medical training. Any breaks I could catch from hospital rounds or studying for board exams were spent reading any Christian reflections on psychiatry that I could get my hands on, and this pursuit morphed into a growing interest in theology. I reached out to senior physicians and seminary professors with questions (God bless them all for their patience and generosity!). Around that time, I came across a well-known story told by Peter Kramer in *Listening to Prozac*. The psychiatrist and author introduces us to one of his patients, Sam, who was suffering from depression related to poor business decisions and the death of his parents. Sam was also dealing with conflict in his marriage from "his interest in pornographic videos."[11] Since a traditional antidepressant had been ineffective, Kramer prescribed Prozac because Sam's symptoms were suggestive of obsessive-compulsive disorder (in those days, Prozac was thought to help with compulsiveness).

The results were dramatic. Sam was feeling "better than well," and "he no longer had any interest in pornography."[12] The antidepressant had virtually

---

10. McFadyen, *Bound to Sin*, 19.

11. Peter D. Kramer, *Listening to Prozac: The Landmark Book about Antidepressants and the Remaking of the Self*, rev. ed. (New York: Penguin Books, 1997), ix.

12. Kramer, *Listening to Prozac*, x.

eliminated this man's struggle with the sin of pornography. This case of "cosmetic psychopharmacology" (a term coined by Kramer) is just one of many examples in psychiatry, neuroscience, and other medical fields that raise difficult questions for the doctrine of sin.[13] The Christian tradition had always taken sin to be fundamentally spiritual rather than a biological or neurological problem.

By the time I had moved on from medicine to pursue a calling in theology, the doctrine of sin was under pressure on multiple fronts. Among North American and British evangelicals, scholars crossed swords over interpretations of the early chapters of Genesis, Adam's historicity, the fall, original sin, and so on. Some of the books narrowly focused on the historical Adam.[14] Others rethought several aspects of theology in light of evolution.[15] Much of this research was being sponsored by the Templeton Foundation, BioLogos, and affiliated groups. Evangelicals were taking the natural sciences seriously and thinking through their many implications for Christian doctrine. This flood of research activity, which seemed to have no end, intensified the questions I had been pondering ever since medical school. Jumping into the fray was almost a foregone conclusion.

Books on the interface between science and theology come in all shapes and sizes. Some are eager to present a picture of theology that is scientifically appealing and will not be rejected by non-Christians, but such motivations can end up merely reshaping theology in the image of its cultured despisers. Not always, however. Christians can also engage theological questions in a scientifically informed way that is at once orthodox, winsome, accessible, and able to build bridges across theological differences. Others adopt strategies such as intentionally de-emphasizing confessional commitments in order to reach more people or engaging in hypothetical thought experiments to open up fruitful insights and allow dialogue with different perspectives.[16] While I have learned from many of these

13. For a probing meditation on cosmetic psychopharmacology and other facets of modern medicine that help people feel "better than well," see Carl Elliott, *Better Than Well: American Medicine Meets the American Dream* (New York: Norton, 2003).

14. For examples, see Peter Enns, *The Evolution of Adam: What the Bible Does and Doesn't Say about Human Origins* (Grand Rapids: Baker Academic, 2012); John Walton, *The Lost World of Adam and Eve: Genesis 2–3 and the Human Origins Debate* (Downers Grove, IL: IVP Academic, 2015); Dennis Venema and Scot McKnight, *Adam and the Genome: Reading Scripture after Genetic Science* (Grand Rapids: Brazos, 2017).

15. See, inter alia, the essays in R. J. Berry and T. A. Noble, eds., *Darwin, Creation and the Fall: Theological Challenges* (Nottingham, UK: Apollos, 2009); Michael S. Northcott and R. J. Berry, eds., *Theology after Darwin* (Milton Keynes, UK: Paternoster, 2009).

16. S. Joshua Swamidass, *The Genealogical Adam and Eve: The Surprising Science of Universal Ancestry* (Downers Grove, IL: IVP Academic, 2019).

approaches, the present work is an explicitly confessional argument that engages natural science theologically.

I write as a theologian and trained physician with the highest respect for the natural sciences. In my judgment, science is precisely the kind of cultural activity we would expect when considering who God is and what he has called humans to be and do within his glorious creation. Scientific investigation depends on distinct theological assumptions, including the fact that humans are made in God's image, that the orderliness of creation reflects the wisdom of the creator, and that creation itself is inherently good and thus worthy of study. Natural science as we know it today was born in Judeo-Christian medieval Europe, and many of the earliest scientists were deeply pious believers.[17] Natural science as such would be an inferior enterprise without its underlying theological judgments about creation.

I also write as someone with a stake in this matter. I am a Reformed theologian hailing from the Presbyterian Church in America (PCA), a small, orthodox, theologically conservative segment of the larger church catholic. As a ruling elder in my denomination, I subscribe to the seventeenth-century Westminster Standards, including the Westminster Confession of Faith and the Westminster Shorter and Larger Catechisms. The most pointed scientific challenges to the classical doctrine of sin are far from esoteric or merely theoretical; if they hold up to scrutiny, then the PCA and other denominations are no longer theologically viable. They should reinvent themselves or close up shop. This book is a sustained account of the doctrine of sin with an eye to these post-Darwinian challenges—and spoiler alert: it is also my caution against anything so drastic as the end of Protestantism.

Sketching the Argument

Defending Sin lays out a doctrine of sin that pays attention to the challenges from the natural sciences, especially biological evolution. My thesis is that the classical notion of sin reflected in Scripture, the ecumenical creeds, and the Protestant confessions remains enduringly true, even in our post-Darwinian context, and offers the most compelling and theologically coherent account of the human predicament.

17. For a popular account, see Rodney Stark, *For the Glory of God: How Monotheism Led to Reformations, Science, Witch-Hunts, and the End of Slavery* (Princeton: Princeton University Press, 2004), esp. 121–97. But see the tempering remarks in Noah J. Efron, "Myth 9: That Christianity Gave Birth to Modern Science," in *Galileo Goes to Jail: And Other Myths about Science and Religion*, ed. Ronald Numbers (Cambridge, MA: Harvard University Press, 2009), 79–89.

The argument begins with part 1, two chapters on the authority of Scripture and the role that it should play in the interaction between science and theology. Chapter 1 tells the story of how the Western church gradually lost confidence in Scripture's ability to speak with any epistemic authority on the origins of the natural world. The history of the relationship between early scientists and the Christian faith is complex, but I call attention to one consistent thread: creative yet unsatisfying strategies by Christians to avoid the perception of deep conflicts between science and Holy Scripture. In chapter 2, I develop a constructive proposal called *biblical realism* outlining how Christians can address substantial conflicts between mainstream scientific theories and theological doctrines. The five commitments of biblical realism—(1) supernaturalism, (2) inerrancy, (3) scientific fallibilism, (4) doctrinal confidence, and (5) eclecticism—clarify my position on contentious issues in the science-theology dialogue and lay down methodological guidelines for the rest of the book.

The three chapters in part 2 engage a range of questions on human origins that need resolution before we can start addressing the doctrine of sin proper. In chapter 3, I make the case that skepticism about the historicity of Adam and Eve naturally follows from skepticism that the early chapters of Genesis are reliable sources of historical knowledge. I argue, therefore, that we should recover the biblical chronology implied in the genealogies of Genesis 5 and 11; furthermore, I develop a theological interpretation of ancient Near Eastern religious perspectives that illuminates rather than undermines the internal witness of Scripture. In chapter 4, I review the scientific reasons for thinking that Adam and Eve must have been part of an already existing population of multiple thousands. After critiquing this idea for exegetical and theological reasons, I show why Adam and Eve are indeed the first and only two human beings from whom the entire human race descends. In chapter 5, I argue that creation was once unfallen and that this original goodness was lost with the disobedience of Adam and Eve. Given that many scholars think this doctrine of a primordial goodness is no longer believable, I spend time in dialogue with church history and the arguments of recent critics.

The main course is served up in part 3. Here I articulate the doctrines of the fall, original sin, and the human person in dialogue with the scientific claims that have led many theologians to make radical revisions to the received doctrine of sin. Chapter 6 is an account of the fall that clarifies why human mortality is a consequence of Adam's sin and therefore foreign to God's original creation in Genesis 1–2; furthermore, I argue that the fall functions as a theodicy in the logic of Christianity and is thus central to the fundamental shape of the biblical story. Chapter 7 moves on to a constructive proposal for relating original sin and biology, where I take embodiment seriously without reducing sin to a biological problem. I also explain my theological reservations with recent proposals by theistic evolutionists to revise the doctrine of original sin in light of genetics and evolutionary biology. In chapter 8, I compare the two main Christian theories of the human person and how well they account for the human experience of sin. Christian physicalists picture human beings as ontologically physical, while their dualist counterparts picture them as ontologically physical *and* nonphysical—body and soul. I contend that the dualist anthropology offers a more plausible account of *sinners*, men and women who are blameworthy before the living God.

Although I write as a Reformed theologian, I hope this book appeals to a wide range of readers from different church traditions. In the first place, Scripture is the norming norm and holds authority over all Reformed doctrines; the Westminster Confession of Faith describes "the Holy Spirit speaking in the Scripture" as the supreme authority over "all decrees of councils, opinions of ancient writers, doctrines of men, and private spirits."[18] Other Protestant traditions share this high view of the Bible.[19] In the second place, parts 1 and 2 engage issues that are central to Christian theology and are therefore ecumenical in spirit; the explicitly Reformed elements of my thesis are largely limited to part 3. I welcome my non-Reformed readers to engage these latter chapters with special scrutiny, especially if at some points it looks like my Presbyterian perspective is occluding a fair reading of Scripture. Yet I think the overall questions that I will be wrestling with throughout will interest Christians from all traditions. The Christian doctrine of sin handed down to us from our theological forebears not only is faithful to the theological system of Christianity and resilient to the searching questions from biology but remains the most perceptive diagnosis of the human condition.

Final Caveats

Let me close with two qualifications. First, throughout the book I will often use the phrase "theistic evolution" even though some Christian evolutionists have criticized this terminology. They object that young-earth and

18. The Westminster Confession of Faith 6.2, in *The Book of Confessions* (Louisville: Office of the General Assembly, Presbyterian Church [USA], 2002), 124.
19. Needless to say, I do not claim to speak for the entire Reformed tradition! Good friends and colleagues, even from my own small PCA denomination, will undoubtedly have reservations about parts of my argument.

old-earth creationists do not have a monopoly on creationism; as such, *all* Christians are creationists. Moreover, when "theistic" is an adjective modifying the noun "evolution," it gives the impression that evolution is the controlling idea and the Christian element a mere qualifier; by contrast, "evolutionary *creation*" puts the emphasis in the right place—namely, God's creation. As Jim Stump remarks, "The label 'evolutionary creation' has increasingly been used to refer to those theistic evolutionists who hold to the traditional Christian creeds that the creator God is a personal being."[20] Thus, using the self-designation of "evolutionary creationism" helps distinguish their position from more theologically progressive versions of evolution like process theism and panentheism.[21] However, while all these points are well taken, I have chosen to continue using the designation "theistic evolution" because it remains the most frequently used term in published literature.[22] At the same time, I shall try to fairly portray how particular theistic evolutionists define their own positions.

Second, this monograph deals with controversial issues facing the doctrine of sin today. (*Caveat lector*: every chapter steps into sometimes treacherous, contested territory.) My audacious hope is that everyone reading this book will agree with its main argument and all the ancillary points too, but any systematic theologian who accomplished that would likely win the next Nobel Prize! In reality, readers will find plenty to disagree with in a book like this. My more humble hope is that the Spirit will use it to prompt further dialogue, sharper insights, and deeper faithfulness. Nevertheless, regardless of any faults in my argument, I remain convinced that the divine and supernatural power of God's Word turns the world upside down, changes lives, and unveils the true contours of reality with its radiant light. I present the following account of sin with as much conviction and humility as I can muster. Of course, holding together these twins—grace and truth—is easy in theory but notoriously difficult in practice. God help me.

---

20. J. B. Stump, introduction to *Four Views on Creation, Evolution, and Intelligent Design*, ed. J. B. Stump (Grand Rapids: Zondervan, 2017), 12.

21. Denis Lamoureux, "Intelligent Design Theory: The God-of-the-Gaps Rooted in Concordism," *Perspectives on Science and Christian Faith* 70, no. 2 (2018): 114.

22. For example, in books published between 1800 and 2019, the Google Books Ngram Viewer indicates that the term "theistic evolution" is used over forty times more frequently than "evolutionary creation" (see https://books.google.com/ngrams).

PART 1

AUTHORITY

The authority of the Holy Scripture, for which it ought to be believed, and obeyed, dependeth not upon the testimony of any man, or church; but wholly upon God (who is truth itself) the author thereof: and therefore it is to be received, because it is the Word of God.

—Westminster Confession of Faith 1.4

1

Science, Theology, and Biblical Authority

The Scriptures were not viewed as simply a religious book which was thereby limited to human salvation and conduct. The Bible was considered a source of truth about history, geography, nature, human origins, and whatever else its words happened to touch. . . . This meant that it carried an authority far greater than even the most expert treatises in many fields.

—Kenneth Howell[1]

The basis of Christian doctrines, or the ground for belief in them— for example, creation, the fall, the election of Israel, the Incarnation, eternal life, and so on—had for most of Protestantism been the infallible inspiration of scripture. This basis, however, had dissipated due to the developments of science which had demonstrated the error of important aspects of the traditional forms of these doctrines.

—Langdon Gilkey[2]

The relationship between faith and reason has a long history fraught with chronic quarreling and occasional high drama. Some pit faith and reason against each other as mortal enemies; others praise

1. Kenneth Howell, "The Hermeneutics of Nature and Scripture in Early Modern Science and Theology," in *Nature and Scripture in the Abrahamic Religions: Up to 1700*, ed. Jitse M. van der Meer and Scott Mandelbrote (Leiden: Brill, 2008), 275.
2. Langdon Gilkey, *Naming the Whirlwind: The Renewal of God-Language* (Indianapolis: Bobbs-Merrill, 1969), 74.

them as close friends.[3] As far back as the early church, reason and faith have been like two lovers caught in a delicate on-again, off-again relationship. The apostle Paul, for instance, parleyed with Stoic and Epicurean thinkers (Acts 17:16–34) and was no stranger to Greek philosophy. He famously cited the Epimenides paradox: "One of the Cretans, a prophet of their own, said, 'Cretans are always liars, evil beasts, lazy gluttons'" (Titus 1:12). But Paul also drew a sharp line between human wisdom and the power of God (1 Cor. 2), and he warned against "philosophy and empty deceit, according to human tradition, according to the elemental spirits of the world, and not according to Christ" (Col. 2:8). Brief and undeveloped as Paul's remarks are, they foreshadow tensions between theology (faith) and philosophy (reason) that are still with us.

By the following century, early Christians were actively engaging pagan philosophers. Justin Martyr, Theophilus of Antioch, Athenagoras, and Clement of Alexandria, all second-century Christian apologists, heard echoes of divine truth in the writings of Plato and other non-Christian philosophers.[4] One of Origen's students reported that "there was nothing forbidden, nothing hidden, nothing inaccessible. We were allowed to learn every doctrine, non-Greek and Greek, both spiritual and secular, both divine and human."[5] Yet Tertullian and other dissenting voices distrusted extrabiblical philosophy: "What indeed has Athens to do with Jerusalem?"[6]

The tensions between theology and philosophy persisted in the medieval period. Theology ruled as the queen of the sciences, and philosophy—including the study of nature and its laws—played the dutiful handmaiden. As Edward Grant explains, "Science was not pursued for its own sake but only for the aid it could provide in the interpretation of Holy Scripture."[7] This asymmetrical relationship prevailed in the West until the twelfth century when Aristotle's writings, which had been previously unavailable, were translated into Latin. These works, along with those of Aristotle's

3. For a range of perspectives, see Steve Wilkens, ed., *Faith and Reason: Three Views* (Downers Grove, IL: IVP Academic, 2014).

4. Hamilton Timothy, *The Early Christian Apologists and Greek Philosophy: Exemplified by Irenaeus, Tertullian and Clement of Alexandria* (Assen, Netherlands: Royal Van Gorcum, 1973).

5. Gregory Thaumaturgus, *In Origenem Oratio*, quoted in David Lindberg, "Science and the Early Church," in *God and Nature: Historical Essays on the Encounter between Christianity and Science*, ed. David Lindberg and Ronald Numbers (Berkeley: University of California Press, 1986), 24.

6. Tertullian, *De Praescriptione Haereticorum* 7.9, quoted in *A New Eusebius: Doctrines Illustrative of the History of the Church to A.D. 337*, ed. J. Stevenson (London: SPCK, 1963), 178.

7. Edward Grant, "Science and Theology in the Middle Ages," in Lindberg and Numbers, *God and Nature*, 50. However, Grant overstates the case; for example, medieval medical manuals surely aimed at goods besides interpreting Scripture.

Greek and Arabic commentators, opened up a new world of learning that was vastly more sophisticated than anything Western Christians had seen before.[8]

Two views prevailed at the University of Paris in the thirteenth century. On the one side were traditionalists who feared that philosophy's extrabiblical claims often contradicted Holy Scripture, and on the other side were open-minded arts masters and theologians who embraced the insights of non-Christian philosophy.[9] For the traditionalists, Aristotle was a thorn in the flesh who propounded positions inimical to biblical teaching, and the university leadership was forced more than once to ban his works on natural philosophy (inevitably, that only made Aristotle more enticing to students!).[10] Eventually, on March 7, 1277, Étienne Tempier, then bishop of Paris, handed down a formal condemnation of 219 propositions, many of them relating to Aristotle's philosophy. Positions defended by arts masters like Boethius of Dacia and Siger of Brabant were now forbidden knowledge. Thomas Aquinas's integration of medieval theology and Aristotelian philosophy was also in the crosshairs. These debates were the latest skirmish in the lovers' quarrel between faith and reason.

In this chapter, I argue that the historical interactions between theology and natural science intensified chronic tensions between faith and reason; the main attempts at resolving these conflicts undermine the classical notion of biblical authority. First, I chronicle how Galileo's arguments for heliocentrism introduced a radical way of negotiating conflicts between Scripture and extrabiblical (scientific) knowledge. Second, I argue that Galileo's assumptions persisted in later thinkers as they tried to shield Scripture and Christian faith from any direct conflict with emerging scientific theories surrounding earth's geological history and the origins of species populating it. Although such thinkers often had good intentions, their attempts at relieving deep tensions between science and theology ultimately undermine the authority of Scripture.

---

8. Aristotle's rediscovered works included his *Posterior Analytics*, *On the Soul* (*De anima*), *On the Heavens* (*De caelo*), *Nicomachean Ethics*, *Metaphysics*, *Physics*, *Poetics*, and *Politics*. For a comprehensive list, see Edward Grant, ed., *A Source Book in Medieval Science* (Cambridge, MA: Harvard University Press, 1974), 39–40.

9. John Wippel, "The Parisian Condemnations of 1270 and 1277," in *A Companion to Philosophy in the Middle Ages*, ed. Jorge Gracia and Timothy Noone (Malden, MA: Blackwell, 2002), 65.

10. In the ancient and medieval eras, the investigation of the natural world was termed "natural philosophy" or "philosophy of nature" and involved "questions of material causation, as opposed to mathematical analysis" (David Lindberg, *The Beginnings of Western Science*, 2nd ed. [Chicago: University of Chicago Press, 2007], 3). In this chapter, I will sometimes use "natural philosophy" and "science" interchangeably.

Galileo and the Authority of Science

Geocentrism had a long reign as the default position in medieval Christianity.[11] Classical astronomy incorporated Aristotle's view that the earth was the center of the universe with heavenly bodies circulating in perfect uniformity. Building on Aristotle, the second-century astronomer Ptolemy laid out a geocentric system in his book *The Almagest*. His updated view addressed the most obvious problems with Aristotle's cosmology, such as the irregular motion of planets, by introducing theoretical models, like eccentric orbits. Additionally, Ptolemy appealed to concepts like epicycles to refine his model based on careful observations. This Aristotelian-Ptolemaic natural philosophy was the best available cosmology and dominated Western thought for about two millennia (roughly 350 BCE to 1650 CE).[12]

Heliocentrism, on the other hand, was almost entirely absent in antiquity. Aristarchus of Samos (310–230 BCE), a mathematician and astronomer, was the lone exception that we know of, but his views contradicted the science of his day and were universally rejected.[13] It was not until 1543 that a new defense of heliocentrism appeared when the Polish astronomer Nicolaus Copernicus published his book, *On the Revolutions of the Heavenly Spheres*.[14] His arguments were highly technical; only fellow astronomers had even read the work, and most of them disagreed with heliocentrism. They had good reasons to demur because at the time there was little empirical evidence for the theory. Copernicanism was counterintuitive to the pretheoretical experience of a static earth with daily sunrises and sunsets.[15]

The situation changed with Galileo Galilei. Born in 1564 in the city of Pisa, Italy, he was a mathematician by training. Galileo had been skeptical of the Copernican theory until the invention of the telescope finally allowed him, in 1609, to identify features of the solar system inconsistent with Aristotelian cosmology. He published his observations in two books, *The Starry Messenger* (1610) and *History and Demonstrations Concerning Sunspots*

11. I am drawing on Gregory Dawes, *Galileo and the Conflict between Religion and Science* (New York: Routledge, 2016), 27–42. See also Klaus Scholder, *The Birth of Modern Critical Theology: Origins and Problems of Biblical Criticism in the Seventeenth Century*, trans. John Bowden (London: SCM, 1990).

12. See the exegetical examples in Edward Grant, *Planets, Stars, and Orbs: The Medieval Cosmos, 1200–1687* (Cambridge: Cambridge University Press, 1994), 83–105.

13. James McClellan III and Harold Dorn, *Science and Technology in World History*, 2nd ed. (Baltimore: Johns Hopkins University Press, 2006), 82–84.

14. David Lindberg, "Galileo, the Church, and the Cosmos," in *When Science and Christianity Meet*, ed. David Lindberg and Ronald Numbers (Chicago: University of Chicago Press, 2003), 35–41.

15. Other examples included the (apparent) absence of stellar parallax, which counted against heliocentrism. Harald Siebert, "The Early Search for Stellar Parallax: Galileo, Castelli, and Ramponi," *Journal for the History of Astronomy* 36, no. 3 (2005): 251–71.

and Their Phenomena (1613).[16] From that point on, Galileo's heliocentrism became public enemy to the Catholic hierarchy.

For one thing, Aristotelian natural philosophy—including medieval geocentrism—had been fully integrated into the Roman Catholic tradition; changing the one would threaten the other. Furthermore, the Reformation had prompted a new hypervigilance among Roman Catholic gatekeepers who blamed Luther's Reformation on ecclesiastical policies that they felt had been unduly lax. They reacted by consolidating Catholic tradition, centralizing its structures, and thus bolstering its authoritarian scope (hence the Council of Trent and the Counter-Reformation).[17] Indeed, Cardinal Robert Bellarmine—a leading theologian and one of Galileo's main critics—appealed to Trent when he ruled against Galileo that only interpretations of Scripture with the unanimous consensus of the holy fathers are lawful. The relevant wording from the council is in the second decree:

> Furthermore, to control petulant spirits, the Council decrees that, in matters of faith and morals pertaining to the edification of Christian doctrine, no one, relying on his own judgment and distorting the Sacred Scriptures according to his own conceptions, shall dare to interpret them contrary to that sense which Holy Mother Church, to whom it belongs to judge of their true sense and meaning, has held and does hold, or even contrary to the unanimous agreement of the Fathers, even though such interpretations should never at any time be published. Those who do otherwise shall be identified by the ordinaries and punished in accordance with the penalties prescribed by the law.[18]

As Galileo recognized, the decree's pronouncement was limited to "matters of faith and morals pertaining to the edification of Christian doctrine." He concluded that astronomy had no bearing on faith and morals and that the fathers never addressed such questions in their writings. But Bellarmine pushed back by saying that *everything* in Scripture concerns faith: "Thus that man would be just as much a heretic who denied that Abraham had two sons and Jacob twelve, as one who denied the virgin birth of Christ, for both are declared by the Holy Ghost through the mouths of the prophets and apostles."[19] Bellarmine thought it was inconceivable that heliocentrism would ever be demonstrated given the contrary biblical witnesses like

16. The full text of *The Starry Messenger* and excerpts from *History and Demonstrations* are available in *Discoveries and Opinions of Galileo*, trans. Stillman Drake (Garden City, NY: Doubleday Anchor, 1957).

17. Lindberg, "Galileo, the Church, and the Cosmos," 45.

18. Quoted in Richard Blackwell, *Galileo, Bellarmine, and the Bible* (Notre Dame, IN: University of Notre Dame Press, 1991), 11–12.

19. Drake (trans.), *Discoveries and Opinions of Galileo*, 163.

Ecclesiastes 1:5 ("The sun rises and the sun sets, / and hurries back to where it rises" [NIV])—a text written under divine inspiration. As one historian comments on Bellarmine's logic, "If God is the author of Scripture, everything in the Bible is true, whether it is essential to salvation or merely a piece of accidental historical information."[20] In retrospect, Galileo's fate was sealed, and on February 24, 1616, theologians of the Holy Office issued a decree banning Copernicanism.[21]

The Triumph of Reason and the Eclipse of Scripture

Unfortunately for Galileo, his heliocentrism was a ticking time bomb. Aside from Aristotle's cosmology, several passages in the Old Testament seem to describe the sun moving around a stationary planet. In Joshua's military defeat of the Amorites, God answers his prayer for the sun to stand still: "And the sun stood still, and the moon stopped, / until the nation took vengeance on their enemies" (Josh. 10:13 NRSV). Scripture goes on to say: "The sun stopped in the midst of heaven and did not hurry to set for about a whole day. There has been no day like it before or since, when the LORD heeded the voice of a man, for the LORD fought for Israel" (10:13–14). Other passages appear to corroborate this geocentric picture: in Psalm 19:6, the sun rises at one end of the heavens and makes its circuit to the other; in Psalm 93:1, the earth is described as fixed and immovable; Ecclesiastes reports the sun rising and setting (1:5; see also Matt. 5:45); and the list goes on (see also Ps. 104:5; Isa. 38:8; and Hab. 3:11). In light of such passages, it was only a matter of time before Galileo's heliocentrism would blow up in his face.

Galileo's critics accused him of denying the divine authority of Scripture. In a letter to the Grand Duchess Christina—penned in 1615—he responded to his critics and explained why Scripture does not contradict heliocentrism. Galileo's arguments showed nuanced hermeneutical judgment and drew freely on the early fathers (especially Augustine).[22] He never wavered in proclaiming the inerrancy of Scripture. "Holy Scripture," he wrote in one of his letters, "can never lie or err, and . . . its declarations are absolutely

20. Blackwell, *Galileo, Bellarmine, and the Bible*, 32.

21. They specifically banned two propositions entailed by the Copernican theory. See Petrus Lombardus et al., "Consultants' Report on Copernicanism (24 February 1616)," in *The Galileo Affair: A Documentary History*, ed. and trans. Maurice Finocchiaro (Berkeley: University of California Press, 1989), 146–47.

22. For analysis, see Ernan McMullin, "Galileo on Science and Scripture," in *The Cambridge Companion to Galileo*, ed. Peter Machamer (Cambridge: Cambridge University Press, 1998), 271–347, esp. 302–25.

and inviolably true."[23] The problem is that readers misinterpret Scripture. Rightly understood, he argued, Scripture could never contradict a legitimate scientific conclusion since God is the author of both Scripture and creation.[24] Galileo assumed the unity of all truth and that only Scripture—not one's interpretations of Scripture—is inerrant.[25] When a scientific theory conflicts with biblical teaching, the church must privilege the Bible over science if the theory has not been proven; yet if the literal sense of Scripture contradicts a proven scientific theory, then we must reinterpret Scripture.

Galileo was a heliocentrist, but it is not clear whether he thought his arguments were demonstrably true,[26] nor does he make clear how one should distinguish "demonstrative" scientific proofs from merely speculative theories. The ambiguity lies in the fact that Galileo and his critics falsely believed that investigating nature could yield absolute certainty when, in reality, natural science is inductive and generates arguments with different degrees of strength.[27] Galileo and his critics accepted Aristotelian epistemology—namely, that the physical sciences secure "conclusions [that] are *true* and *necessary* and have nothing to do with human will."[28] If true science yields certainty, this leaves "undemonstrated scientific claims (including heliocentrism at that time) in a sort of epistemological limbo."[29]

Interestingly, while Galileo raised challenges to the accepted Aristotelian-Ptolemaic view, his observations were consistent with other models of the universe. For example, responding to Galileo, the Danish astronomer Tycho Brahe (1546–1601) developed a new theory using his own observational data. His system had the planets revolving around the sun, but the sun carried the rest of the solar system around the motionless earth. The compromise was a stroke of genius—partly heliocentric, partly geocentric—built on very precise and accurate observations, and, best of all, able to explain everything Galileo saw in the skies but without putting the earth

23. Galileo Galilei, "Letter to Castelli (1613)," in Finocchiaro, *Galileo Affair*, 49.
24. Galileo Galilei, "Galileo's Letter to the Grand Duchess (1615)," in Finocchiaro, *Galileo Affair*, 91.
25. Galilei, "Galileo's Letter to the Grand Duchess," 105.
26. See the helpful remarks in McMullin, "Galileo on Science and Scripture," 286–87; and Jean Dietz Moss, "Galileo's *Letter to Christina*: Some Rhetorical Considerations," *Renaissance Quarterly* 36, no. 4 (1983): 547–76, esp. 563–65.
27. Edward Davis and Elizabeth Chmielewski, "Galileo and the Garden of Eden: Historical Reflections on Creationist Hermeneutics," in *Nature and Scripture in the Abrahamic Religions: 1700–Present*, ed. Jitse M. van der Meer and Scott Mandelbrote (Leiden: Brill, 2008), 446.
28. Galileo Galilei, *Dialogue concerning the Two Chief World Systems, Ptolemaic and Copernican*, trans. Stillman Drake, rev. ed. (Berkeley: University of California Press, 1967), 53, my emphasis (originally published 1632).
29. Blackwell, *Galileo, Bellarmine, and the Bible*, 85.

in motion. Jesuit astronomers found Brahe's model more compelling than the Copernican alternative.

Nevertheless, Galileo defended heliocentrism in spite of the seemingly geostatic biblical texts surveyed earlier. His mantra was that the Bible has nothing to do with astronomy; Scripture's main purpose is religious, not scientific. In his letter to the Duchess, he clarified his hermeneutical approach: "In the Scripture one finds many propositions which look different from the truth if one goes by the literal meaning of the words, but which are expressed in this manner to accommodate the incapacity of common people; likewise, for the few who deserve to be separated from the masses, it is necessary that wise interpreters produce their true meaning and indicate the particular reasons why they have been expressed by means of such words."[30] He was invoking the principle of accommodation, the idea that God's communication in Scripture is adapted to the finite capacities of human beings. God is infinite and transcendent, while humans are finite and fallen, so that his ways are ultimately unknowable to us (Isa. 55:8–9). In accommodation, God expresses his kindness by bridging the conceptual and linguistic chasm between heaven and earth. However, Galileo was also convinced that the book of nature suffers no such limitations since it is written in the divine language of mathematics. For him, the precision of mathematics had none of the vulgarities and imperfections of human discourse:

> I think that in disputes about natural phenomena one must begin not with the authority of scriptural passages but with sensory experience and necessary demonstrations. . . . To accommodate the understanding of the common people it is appropriate for Scripture to say many things that are different (in appearance and in regard to the literal meaning of the words) from the absolute truth; on the other hand, nature is inexorable and immutable, never violates the terms of the laws imposed upon her, and does not care whether or not her recondite reasons and ways of operating are disclosed to human understanding.[31]

In appealing to divine accommodation, Galileo joined a long line of Christian interpreters with similar views.[32] Jewish and Christian interpreters believed that we only know anything about the infinite God because he

30. Galilei, "Galileo's Letter to the Grand Duchess," 50.

31. Galilei, "Galileo's Letter to the Grand Duchess," 93.

32. I am drawing from Stephen D. Snobelen, "'In the Language of Men': The Hermeneutics of Accommodation in the Scientific Revolution," in van der Meer and Mandelbrote, *Nature and Scripture in the Abrahamic Religions: Up to 1700*, 691–732.

condescended to our finite human capacities. The anthropomorphisms of Scripture that attribute physical features and emotions to God were identified as accommodations to ordinary human understanding. In the words of John Chrysostom, "God condescends whenever he is not seen as he is, but in the way one incapable of beholding him is able to look upon him. In this way God reveals himself by accommodating what he reveals to the weakness of vision of those who behold him."[33] Among interpreters of late antiquity, Augustine used accommodation as a hermeneutical tool to reconcile astronomy and Scripture. In one of his familiar quotes, he warns against well-meaning Christians presumptuously reading philosophical ideas into the biblical text:

> There is knowledge to be had, after all, about the earth, about the sky, about the other elements of this world, about the movements and revolutions or even the magnitude and distances of the constellations, about the predictable eclipses of moon and sun, about the cycles of years and seasons, about the nature of animals, fruits, stones and everything else of this kind. And it frequently happens that even non-Christians will have knowledge of this sort in a way that they can substantiate with scientific arguments or experiments. Now it is quite disgraceful and disastrous, something to be on one's guard against at all costs, that they should ever hear Christians spouting what they claim our Christian literature has to say on these topics, and talking such nonsense that they can scarcely contain their laughter.[34]

Augustine's accommodation theology became influential and served as a model for later Catholic and Protestant thinkers—not just Galileo but men like Martin Luther, John Calvin, Georg Joachim Rheticus, Tommaso Campanella, and Johannes Kepler.[35] Clearly, parts of Galileo's hermeneutical argument for accommodation had precedent in church history.

But Galileo took things in a radical direction. The issue was not merely about the use of accommodation but the deeper question about the epistemic relation between science and Scripture. One detects the shift in his remark to the Duchess: "I would say that the authority of Holy Scripture aims chiefly at persuading men about those articles and propositions which, surpassing all human reason, could not be discovered by scientific

33. John Chrysostom, *On the Incomprehensible Nature of God*, trans. Paul Harkins (Washington, DC: Catholic University of America Press, 1984), 101–2.

34. Augustine, *The Literal Meaning of Genesis* 1.19.39, in *The Works of Saint Augustine: On Genesis*, trans. Edmund Hill (Hyde Park, NY: New City, 2002), 186.

35. See Snobelen, "'In the Language of Men.'" On Calvin, see Arnold Huijgen, *Divine Accommodation in John Calvin's Theology: Analysis and Assessment* (Göttingen: Vandenhoeck & Ruprecht, 2011).

research or by any other means than through the mouth of the Holy Spirit himself."[36] Galileo limits biblical authority to supernatural realities that are not scientifically accessible. One might wonder whether the word "chiefly" in the quotation mitigates the damage, but Galileo is unambiguous in another letter two years earlier: "The authority of the Holy Writ has merely the aim of persuading men of those articles and propositions which are necessary for their salvation and surpass all human reason, and so could not become credible through some other science or any other means except through the mouth of the Holy Spirit itself."[37] Galileo thinks we should deny that "the same God who has furnished us with senses, language, and intellect would want to bypass their use and give us by other means the information we can obtain with them."[38] This strategy in effect erects a wall between biblical exegesis and the investigation of nature.[39]

This broader context sheds light on Galileo's famous words: "The intention of the Holy Spirit is to teach us how one goes to heaven and not how heaven goes."[40] The aphorism can be taken innocently as a reminder that Scripture's main purpose is not to teach astronomy but to make us wise for salvation through faith in Christ Jesus (2 Tim. 3:15). However, Galileo intended something less benign, which Ernan McMullin dubs the principle of scriptural limitation: "Since the primary concern of Scripture is with human salvation, we should not look to Scripture for knowledge of the natural world."[41] In other words, as Klaus Scholder writes, "the authority of the Bible may no longer be asserted in scientific questions. On this point its answers are no longer binding. But the reverse now suddenly becomes

---

36. Galilei, "Galileo's Letter to the Grand Duchess," 93–94.

37. Galilei, "Letter to Castelli," 51.

38. Galilei, "Letter to Castelli," 51.

39. Maurice Finocchiaro, *Defending Copernicus and Galileo: Critical Reasoning in the Two Affairs* (Dordrecht, Netherlands: Springer, 2010), 85. As we shall see, Galileo is not consistent. Although he clearly downplays the relevance of the Bible to strictly scientific questions, he also expects theologians interpreting the Bible to be mindful of what science has to say so that their exegesis does not contradict demonstrated scientific claims. In short, theologians should interpret the Bible with proven science, a principle that is inconsistent with his claim that science and religion occupy separate spheres of knowledge. On this point, see Craig Boyd, "Using Galileo to Teach Darwin: A Developmental and Historical Approach," *Perspectives on Science and Christian Faith* 59, no. 4 (2007): 283, 287n2.

40. Galilei, "Galileo's Letter to the Grand Duchess," 96. He credits the quote to Cardinal Baronio. Johannes Kepler echoed the sentiment when he argued that readers of Scripture should "regard the Holy Spirit as a divine messenger and refrain from wantonly dragging Him into physics class." Johannes Kepler, *New Astronomy*, trans. William Donahue (Cambridge: Cambridge University Press, 1992), 62 (originally published 1609).

41. Ernan McMullin, "Galileo's Theological Venture," *Zygon* 48, no. 1 (2013): 199.

conceivable: that the results of the exact sciences are binding on the exegesis of scripture."[42]

Galileo thought Augustine's writings offered patristic precedent for his view. For instance, in *The Literal Meaning of Genesis*, Augustine remarks that "our [biblical] authors knew about the shape of the sky whatever may be the truth of the matter. But the Spirit of God who was speaking through them did not wish to teach people about such things *which would contribute nothing to their salvation*."[43] At first glance he seems to endorse a limited view of biblical authority—and Galileo interprets him precisely that way. Likewise, McMullin has suggested that Augustine endorsed something like the principal of scriptural limitation.[44] But this interpretation strains credulity.

It is true that Augustine's perspective on extrabiblical natural philosophy was rich and multilayered—he exploited it to elaborate a desacralized view of nature rooted in Scripture, used it to shore up and defend Christian doctrine, and even allowed his understanding of natural philosophy to influence his exegesis of Scripture (and vice versa).[45] Nonetheless, like other churchmen in his day, Augustine accepted the biblical assertions about the natural world as binding.[46] Even if the Bible's redemptive message was primary, he took its claims about the physical world seriously. And besides, there are obvious counterexamples to McMullin's contention.

First, reflecting on Genesis 1, Augustine considers the extent to which the brightness of the sun, the moon, and the stars depends on how "their different distances from the earth appear to our eyes." He thinks that one's position on this question must comport with 1 Corinthians 15:41: "One is the glory of the sun and another the glory of the moon and another the glory of the stars; for star differs from star in glory."[47] Augustine as-

---

42. Scholder, *Birth of Modern Critical Theology*, 60.

43. Augustine, *Literal Meaning of Genesis* 2.9.20 (*On Genesis*, 202), my emphasis (quoted in "Galileo's Letter to the Grand Duchess," 95).

44. McMullin makes this case in "Galileo on Science and Scripture," 298–99, and more circumspectly, in Ernan McMullin, "From Augustine to Galileo," *Modern Schoolman* 76, no. 2/3 (1999): 176–77. In both instances, however, McMullin is tempered in his judgment.

45. See Stephen A. Bradley, "Augustine on Science and the Bible" (PhD diss., Southwestern Baptist Theological Seminary, 2002).

46. David Lindberg concedes that, for Augustine, "ultimate authority rests with revelation." But Augustine's interaction with science was more nuanced than our modern categories: "Augustine viewed faith not as a taskmaster to which reason must submit but as the condition that makes genuine rational activity possible." David Lindberg, "Science and the Early Church," in Lindberg and Numbers, *God and Nature*, 28.

47. Augustine, *Literal Meaning of Genesis* 2.16.33 (*On Genesis*, 211).

sumes that biblical assertions about the physical world have epistemic force.[48]

Second, while interpreting Genesis 1:7, he accepts the reliability of Scripture's statements about the waters above the expanse. Despite the critics "who assert that there can be no waters above the heaven of the constellations on account of the weights of the elements," Augustine thinks differently: "Let us have no doubts at all that that is where they are; the authority of this text of scripture, surely, overrides anything that human ingenuity is capable of thinking up."[49] We find no hint of a limitation principle in Augustine's exegetical reasoning.

Third, while mapping out the history of God's redemptive work in *The City of God*, Augustine devotes much time to defending Scripture from the aspersions of critics. He usually interprets the primeval accounts of Genesis 1–11 literally—and thus historically—knowing full well that his stance invites incredulity from unbelievers. The African bishop could do no other because of "the reliability of our sacred history."[50] He interprets the chronology of Scripture literally against the claims of Egyptian chronologies and other extrabiblical sources: "These people are also led astray by certain wholly fallacious writings which cover, so they tell us, many thousands of years in their recording of history. On the basis of Sacred Scripture, however, we calculate that not even six thousand years have passed since the origin of humankind."[51] Augustine's belief in the authority of Scripture also leads him to defend the long antediluvian ages of the patriarchs and the primeval account of Nephilim giants (Gen. 6:4).[52]

Evidently, Augustine appeals to divine accommodation as the need arises, but—unlike Galileo—he does not limit the scope of biblical authority. In Augustine's epistemology, the Word of God has authority over any relevant domain of reality, whether spiritual or physical. Conversely, Galileo denies that the authority of Scripture covers anything crossing into the sphere of natural philosophy; but, of course, once you accept

48. Gregory Dawes, "Could There Be Another Galileo Case? Galileo, Augustine and Vatican II," *Journal of Religion & Society* 4 (2002): 7. Dawes proposes a principle of *differing purpose* as truer to Augustine's thinking than the limitation principle defended in McMullin (McMullin, "Galileo on Science and Scripture," 298).

49. Augustine, *Literal Meaning of Genesis* 2.5.9 (*On Genesis*, 195–96).

50. Augustine, *The City of God* 15.9, in *The Works of Saint Augustine: The City of God XI–XXII*, trans. William Babcock (Hyde Park, NY: New City, 2013), 151.

51. Augustine, *City of God* 12.10 (*City of God*, 47).

52. Augustine, *City of God* 15.9. Augustine often tried to vindicate the biblical account by appealing, apologetically, to pagan historians and the science of his day.

this epistemology, the boundaries inevitably get pushed as science keeps expanding.[53]

In fact, the seeds of Galileo's radical turn were sown centuries earlier. Natural philosophy had long been a servant to theology, especially in the early medieval period.[54] But new ideas were sprouting everywhere in the twelfth century through the influence of Platonic and Neoplatonic natural philosophy. By the thirteenth century, after the rediscovery of many of Aristotle's works, Aristotelian philosophy had completely transformed Western intellectual discourse. Human reason and sense experience became the barometer of rational inquiry. As Grant explains, "It was the obligation of philosophy, not Holy Scripture, to teach about nature and its regular causes and events."[55] Medieval natural philosophers were now confident in natural philosophy and saw its objective as providing "natural explanations for natural phenomena."[56] The same attitude could be found with arts masters and theologians like Thomas Aquinas, Albertus Magnus, and Nicole Oresme. Medieval thinkers often set aside theological questions when engaging in natural philosophy: "Even the Bible, especially the creation account of Genesis, had to conform to the demands of physical science."[57]

Galileo's hermeneutical arguments in the early seventeenth century were the culmination of the growing separation of natural philosophy from Scripture, a drama that had been unfolding for centuries at the hands of medieval philosophers. While he was clearly right about heliocentrism, he was wrong in how he reconciled that conclusion with Scripture. Building on his predecessors, Galileo's theological legacy was to curtail the scope of biblical authority, a move that would embolden his intellectual heirs to exclude Scripture from any area over which natural science claimed

---

53. Historians disagree on whether Galileo was a traditionalist or a radical innovator. For Galileo as a traditionalist, see Hoon Lee, "'Men of Galilee, Why Stand Gazing Up into Heaven': Revisiting Galileo, Astronomy, and the Authority of the Bible," *Journal of the Evangelical Theological Society* 53, no. 1 (2010): 103–16. For a recent defense of Galileo as an innovator, see Maurice Finocchiaro, "The Galileo Affair," in *The Warfare between Science and Religion: The Idea That Wouldn't Die*, ed. Jeff Hardin, Ronald Numbers, and Ronald Binzley (Baltimore: Johns Hopkins University Press, 2018), 27–45.

54. My comments on medieval natural philosophy draw from Grant, "Science and Theology in the Middle Ages," 49–52.

55. Grant, "Science and Theology in the Middle Ages," 51.

56. Edward Grant, *God and Reason in the Middle Ages* (Cambridge: Cambridge University Press, 2001), 191.

57. Grant, "Science and Theology in the Middle Ages," 52. According to Michael Shank, "Bringing scriptural or theological arguments into the discussion violated the standard rules for doing natural philosophy." Michael H. Shank, "Naturalist Tendencies in Medieval Science," in *Science without God? Rethinking the History of Scientific Naturalism*, ed. Peter Harrison and Jon Roberts (Oxford: Oxford University Press, 2019), 56.

expertise. Whenever the scientific consensus might conflict with the biblical witness, Galileo has given scientists and theologians the hermeneutical license to bypass the epistemic relevance of Scripture.

Science and Whig Theology

Galileo was the herald; more was coming. In the post-Reformation era, Scripture still had a privileged status, but its glory days were fading. As natural philosophy turned its focus to empirical data, the older patristic and medieval epistemology was losing hegemony. Europeans explored new lands teeming with strange animal species and unknown people groups. Christian chronologists grappled with pagan histories from Egypt, China, and other ancient civilizations, all of them suggesting that the human race was vastly older than the standard biblical computations. The data from these voyages of discovery and the conflicting chronologies were destabilizing the sacred geography and chronology of Scripture.[58]

Even the Reformation principle of *sola scriptura* could not hold the Protestant movement together. Polemical factions sparred acrimoniously over biblical interpretation, and each group was tethered to confessional statements that only magnified their differences. Luther, Calvin, and Ulrich Zwingli disagreed over the Lord's Supper; the Remonstrants and Contra-Remonstrants split over predestination; Anabaptists and Lutherans denounced each other as heretics. Soteriology and sacramentology were not the only flash points; heliocentrism was one too.[59] With everyone reading the same Bible but interpreting it differently, Europe staggered under doctrinal conflict and ecclesial division.[60]

Many blamed the endless discord on the Bible's linguistic ambiguity, casting doubt on its authority. Seventeenth-century natural philosophers turned instead to nature as the more reliable guide. As one historian observes, "The Book of Nature, once considered virtually inscrutable, is considered in the

58. Charlotte Methuen, "On the Threshold of a New Age: Expanding Horizons as the Broader Context of Scriptural Interpretation," in *Hebrew Bible/Old Testament: The History of Its Interpretation*, ed. Magne Sæbo, 2 vols. (Göttingen: Vandenhoeck & Ruprecht, 2008), 2:668–69; David Livingstone, *Adam's Ancestors: Race, Religion, and the Politics of Human Origins* (Baltimore: Johns Hopkins University Press, 2009), 8–11; Martin J. S. Rudwick, "The Shape and Meaning of Earth History," in Lindberg and Numbers, *God and Nature*, 301–4.

59. For the controversy in the Dutch Republic, see Rienk Vermij, *The Calvinist Copernicans: The Reception of the New Astronomy in the Dutch Republic, 1575–1750* (Amsterdam: Koninklijke Nederlandse Akademie van Wetenschappen, 2002).

60. Jitse M. van der Meer and Richard Oosterhoff, "The Bible, Protestantism and the Rise of Natural Science: A Response to Harrison's Thesis," *Science and Christian Belief* 21, no. 2 (2009): 144–45.

seventeenth century more coherent and legible than the Bible."[61] The ordinary language of Scripture was clumsy against the precision of the physical sciences: "The Bible was necessarily inaccurate and incomplete because its wording had been accommodated to the simple understanding of the vulgar."[62] By the end of the seventeenth century, philosophers claimed that physical data were easier to interpret than biblical discourse.[63] These shifts further demoted Scripture and paved the way for the biblical criticism of early Enlightenment figures like Baruch Spinoza and Thomas Hobbes.

Most seventeenth-century thinkers accepted the premodern understanding of Genesis, believing that the earth was roughly six thousand years old and the victim of a global flood. In time, however, the rock strata and emerging fossils rendered this received view increasingly suspect.[64] As geology gained ground in the eighteenth century, it was more difficult to harmonize the book of Scripture with the book of nature. In the face of these scientific developments, many Christians revised and sometimes discarded staid beliefs about creation, human origins, divine action, and so on—beliefs they once held as inviolable.[65] They justified these moves by appealing to Galileo's hermeneutic: the corrective insights of science, they reasoned, enabled Christians to upgrade their invalid doctrines to the sober truth ("truth," in this case, was defined by then-current science).[66]

61. Margreta de Grazia, "The Secularization of Language in the Seventeenth Century," *Journal of the History of Ideas* 41, no. 2 (1980): 323.

62. De Grazia, "Secularization of Language," 322. This attitude was common among English churchmen: "The basic historicity of the [biblical] narratives was not necessarily questioned; but it was assumed that behind the conventional or 'vulgar' interpretation lay a true or 'philosophical' interpretation, which could be discovered by the light of the latest natural philosophy." Rudwick, "Shape and Meaning of Earth History," 306.

63. This dynamic was in full bloom in the nineteenth century: "Natural science was a body of knowledge which grew by feeding on itself, which developed under the powerful influence of an internal drive, limitless energy within nature and the universe, within humanity, rendering the supernatural superfluous and demonstrating in concrete achievements what reason could accomplish when freed from the bonds of superstition." Peter Addinall, *Philosophy and Biblical Interpretation: A Study in Nineteenth-Century Conflict* (New York: Cambridge University Press, 1991), 17.

64. See, e.g., Davis Young and Ralph Stearley, *The Bible, Rocks and Time: Geological Evidence for the Age of the Earth* (Downers Grove, IL: InterVarsity, 2008), 47–70; and Roy Porter, "Creation and Credence: The Career of Theories of the Earth in Britain, 1660–1820," in *Natural Order: Historical Studies of Scientific Culture*, ed. Barry Barnes and Steven Shapin (Beverly Hills, CA: SAGE, 1979), 97–123. For a retrospective on seventeenth- and eighteenth-century theories of the earth, see Andrew Brown, "Reflecting on a Wreck: The Book of Genesis and the Marginalization of Christianity in the West," in *Proclaiming the Gospel, Engaging the World: Celebrating One Hundred Years of Melbourne School of Theology*, ed. Justin T. T. Tan, Michael Bräutigam, and Peter G. Riddell (Eugene, OR: Wipf & Stock, 2021), 204–28.

65. For historical background, see Ronald Numbers, "Science without God: Natural Laws and Christian Beliefs," in Lindberg and Numbers, *When Science and Christianity Meet*, 265–85.

66. For a similar argument, see Richard P. Tison, "Galileo's Ghost and the Haunting of the Protestant (and Scholarly) Mind," *American Nineteenth Century History* 20, no. 3 (2019): 249–72.

By the nineteenth century, we see the rise of what I call "Whig theology": the tendency to interpret past theology in light of the scientific assumptions of the present. Savants reinterpreted creation and other doctrines through the lens of current science instead of understanding them on their own terms.[67] The underlying logic was hard concordism—as we will see, hard concordists were believers who sought, and often thought they possessed, a definitive harmonization of scientific discoveries with the biblical text.[68] According to Richard Helmstadter's analysis of nineteenth-century views, "Whatever was true in geology must, by the very nature of truth, be true in the Bible as well." God's two truths of science and Scripture could not possibly contradict. "Everyone who participated in the Genesis-geology debate at the time," Helmstadter continues, "agreed that there could not be, in the end, more than one truth. The methods of discovering scientific truth and religious truth might be different, but their ultimate results must be in harmony."[69] Hard concordists were convinced that science was unearthing the true meaning of the Bible, and even *enhancing* scriptural authority by showing how such an ancient text anticipated modern discoveries.

Nineteenth-century geologists mapped out what they perceived to be detailed "coincidences" between the latest geological findings and the order of creation events in Genesis 1. For example, they found that the teeth and scales of fish from the Tilgate limestone correspond to the fish created in Genesis 1:20, and the diversity of reptile fossils from the Jura strata match

67. I am adapting Herbert Butterfield's notion of "Whig history" to the history of science and theology. Whig history, he wrote, is "the tendency in many historians to write on the side of Protestants and Whigs, to praise revolutions provided they have been successful, to emphasize certain principles of progress in the past and to produce a story which is the ratification if not the glorification of the present" (Herbert Butterfield, *The Whig Interpretation of History* [London: G. Bell & Sons, 1951], v). See also Adrian Wilson and T. G. Ashplant, "Whig History and Present-Centred History," *The History Journal* 31, no. 1 (1988): 1–16.

68. In chap. 2, I will argue that soft concordism—the idea that God's Word and his works ultimately harmonize into one holistic, coherent picture—is implied in how God has revealed himself in the biblical story. For a broad survey of nineteenth-century concordism, see Young and Stearley, *Bible, Rocks and Time*, 120–31.

69. Richard Helmstadter, "Condescending Harmony: John Pye Smith's Mosaic Geology," in *Science and Dissent in England, 1688–1945*, ed. Paul Wood (Aldershot, UK: Ashgate, 2004), 172. The "scriptural" or "Mosaic" geologists, a group of primarily Anglican believers who criticized all hard concordist approaches by privileging the biblical narrative over geological science, were dwarfed intellectually and outmaneuvered professionally by members of the Geological Society of London. On these scriptural geologists, see Milton Millhauser, "The Scriptural Geologists: An Episode in the History of Opinion," *Osiris* 11 (1954): 65–86. For the North American dimension, see Rodney Stiling, "Scriptural Geology in America," in *Evangelicals and Science in Historical Perspective*, ed. David Livingstone, D. G. Hart, and Mark Noll (Oxford: Oxford University Press, 1999), 177–92; Richard P. Tison, "Lords of Creation: American Scriptural Geology and the Lord Brothers' Assault on 'Intellectual Atheism'" (PhD diss., University of Oklahoma, 2008).

how God created reptiles on the third day of creation (1:21), and so on. Likewise, geologists connected what they interpreted as evidence of a past seismic revolution in the earth's crust to the Genesis 7 account of Noah's flood.[70] While Galileo warned against precisely such a naive hermeneutic, these hard concordists were nonetheless legatees of Galileo's epistemology, according to which natural science offered the most reliable window into creation.

Geology prompted ingenious exegetical approaches to harmonizing Genesis with science. The "gap" and "day-age" theories were leading strategies in the nineteenth century.[71] The gap theory posits a long period between God's initial creation in Genesis 1:1 and the formless earth in Genesis 1:2. It was an idea supported by clergymen and early geologists, men like Thomas Chalmers, William Buckland, Edward Hitchcock, John Pye Smith, and Adam Sedgwick. On the other hand, the day-age theory, which takes the Genesis days not as literal twenty-four-hour days but as symbols of eons of time, boasted able champions, including Benjamin Silliman, James Dwight Dana, Robert Jameson, Hugh Miller, Arnold Guyot, and J. William Dawson.

An early day-age theorist was James Parkinson, an English surgeon and geologist, who published a three-volume work on geology. Although the first volume assumed a young earth, by the third volume he had become convinced of a gradualist, day-age framework. As Parkinson reports, "So close indeed is this agreement, that the Mosaic account *is thereby confirmed in every respect*, except as to the age of the world."[72] Similarly, Robert Payne Smith, a day-age theorist and one-time Regius Professor of Divinity at Oxford, claims that "the agreement of the Mosaic record with geology is so striking that there is no real difficulty in believing it to be inspired."[73] William Buckland was the author of the influential *Geology and Mineralogy Considered with Reference to Natural Theology*, in which he defends gap-theory concordism. He expresses confidence that "there is no inconsistency between our interpretation of the phenomena of nature

70. These examples are drawn from a harmonization table produced by Robert Jameson (1774–1854), a Scottish naturalist and mineralogist, and later reproduced in an appendix by Benjamin Silliman (1779–1864), a famous New England geologist. See Edward Davis, "The Word and the Works: Concordism and American Evangelicals," in *Perspectives on an Evolving Creation*, ed. Keith Miller (Grand Rapids: Eerdmans, 2003), 44.

71. For the shifting patterns in Old Testament exegesis, see Andrew Brown, *The Days of Creation: A History of Christian Interpretation of Genesis 1:1–2:3* (Blandford Forum, UK: Deo, 2014), 219–79.

72. James Parkinson, *Organic Remains of a Former World: An Examination of the Mineralized Remains of Vegetables and Animals of the Antediluvian World, Generally Termed Extraneous Fossils*, 3 vols. (London: J. Robson, 1804–11), 3:451, quoted in Brown, *Days of Creation*, 225, my emphasis.

73. Robert Payne Smith, "Genesis," in *An Old Testament Commentary for English Readers*, ed. Charles J. Ellicott, 5 vols. (London: Cassell and Company, 1897), 1:13.

and of the Mosaic narrative, but that the results of geological inquiry throw important light on parts of this history, which are otherwise involved in much obscurity."[74] Such testimonies proliferated everywhere, buoyed by the assumption that the new geological science was confirming the biblical material.

Hard concordist expectations also pervaded Roman Catholic circles. Richard Simpson, a former Anglican priest and literary scholar who converted to Catholicism, uses effusive language that was common in the nineteenth century on both sides of the Atlantic:

> Now, after ages of toil, science, approaching its perfection, announces to us as its own profound theories and brilliant discoveries, the same truths which Moses announced three thousand years ago. . . . Moses enjoyed the communion of a higher Spirit; and the spirit of the age, which is a spirit of hostility to Moses and to the Spirit that inspired him, has been forced hitherto, in spite of its repugnance, to confirm his account to the very minutest particular; for every advance that science has yet made is a fresh proof of his accuracy.[75]

In 1855, John Henry Newman appointed James Burton Robertson as professor of modern history and geography at the Catholic University of Ireland. Like other hard concordists at the time, Robertson was bursting with optimism:

> At no former time have the Christian evidences assumed a bolder front, occupied a wider field, or been in a more solid or compact array, than in the present age. The literary and scientific laborers of the nineteenth century have been overthrowing, in succession, all the Anti-Christian theories of the preceding age. The various sciences, physical as well as moral, have been returning, one by one, to their Divine Queen, from whom alone they can derive dignity and permanent support. Geology and Physics prove the order of creation as related by Moses; Physiology the descent of mankind from one couple; Philology the original unity and subsequent disrupture in human language. Ethnography in its progress testifies more and more to that primeval division of mankind into three great races, as recorded in the Mosaic genealogy of nations; while the labours of Archaeology in deciphering the mysterious monuments, and bringing to light the buried remains of primitive

---

74. William Buckland, *Geology and Mineralogy Considered with Reference to Natural Theology*, 2 vols. (Philadelphia: Carey, Lea and Blanchard, 1836), 1:22.

75. Richard Simpson, "Religion and Modern Philosophy, III," *Rambler* 6 (November 1850): 390, quoted in John Root, "Catholics and Science in Mid-Victorian England" (PhD diss., Indiana University, 1974), 62.

nations, more or less connected with the people of God, corroborate to a remarkable extent the historic and chronological statements of Holy Writ.[76]

Some thinkers were more reticent in their harmonization, but even they believed that hard concordism embodied *the* truth to which Scripture had been pointing. Scientific facts would always agree with the Bible properly understood. In the eighteenth and nineteenth centuries, each new physical discovery seemed to support Whig theology.[77]

From its earliest days, however, there were critics who questioned the methodological consistency of hard concordism.[78] They worried that science was placing undue limits on the meaning of Scripture. In a blistering essay, the British polymath Charles Goodwin argued that geology was the nineteenth century's heliocentrism forcing Christians to revise their understanding of divine revelation; it was clear to "geologists of all religious creeds . . . that the earth has existed for an immense series of years,—to be counted by millions rather than by thousands." The standard reading of Genesis, he wrote, "gives a view of the universe adverse to that of modern science."[79] Goodwin rejected the contorted harmonizations of hard concordism, saying, "these theories divest the Mosaic narrative of real accordance with fact," obliterating the meaning of Genesis and introducing "obscurity into one of the simplest stories ever told, for the sake of making it accord with the complex system of the universe which modern science has unfolded."[80] Such concordism is only plausible if one already presupposes geology during exegesis. And what happens when science moves on? As a later commentator concludes, "Ultimately, the harmonization program defeated itself—partly because of dissonance between the harmonizers, but also because the more successful the harmonization, the more trouble it

76. James Burton Robertson, "Philosophic Researches on Christianity," *Dublin Review* 32 (March 1852): 1, cited in Root, "Catholics and Science," 52. Robertson's article was originally published anonymously.

77. Hard concordist syntheses were not limited to the English-speaking world; for major contributions from Switzerland, the Netherlands, and Germany, see the literature cited in Nicolaas Rupke, "Geology and Paleontology," in *Science and Religion: A Historical Introduction*, ed. Gary Ferngren (Baltimore: Johns Hopkins University Press, 2002), 191. Comparatively speaking, however, hard concordism dominated the British and North American contexts.

78. E.g., see Moses Stuart's critique of Edward Hitchcock's gap-theory concordism: "The digging of rocks and the digging of Hebrew roots are not as yet precisely the same operation." Moses Stuart, "A Critical Examination of Some Passages in Gen. 1; with Remarks on Difficulties That Attend Some of the Present Modes of Geological Reasoning," *American Biblical Repository* 7 (1836): 103, cited in Davis, "Word and the Works," 46.

79. Charles Goodwin, "On the Mosaic Cosmogony," in *Essays and Reviews*, 2nd ed. (London: John W. Parker & Son, 1860), 209, 210.

80. Goodwin, "On the Mosaic Cosmogony," 249.

caused when the science moved on."[81] Theology that marries science today will file for divorce tomorrow.

Historical critics jettisoned hard concordism entirely. Since they rejected biblical infallibility, contradictions between the Bible and science did not provoke anxiety. The bishop of Natal in South Africa, John William Colenso (1814–83), is representative of this new historical-critical attitude. According to his reading of Genesis, the creation days were ordinary, twenty-four-hour days.[82] Genesis 1–11, he warned, "cannot be regarded as historically true, being contradicted in their literal sense, again and again, by the certain facts of modern Science."[83] Samuel Driver, a Hebrew professor at Oxford, similarly rejected the harmonizing impulse, conceding that the scientific facts contradicted the Bible: "Read without prejudice or bias, the narrative of Gen. i. creates an impression *at variance with the facts revealed by science*: the efforts at reconciliation which have been reviewed are but different modes of obliterating its characteristic features, and of reading into it *a view which it does not express*."[84] After the 1859 publication of Darwin's *On the Origin of Species*, the standard ways of harmonizing science with the Genesis text were no longer credible to critically minded theologians.

Although some conservative theologians gave up the hard concordist mentality, most still operated with those assumptions.[85] Charles Hodge at Old Princeton was typical when he argued, "The proposition that the Bible must be interpreted by science is all but self-evident. Nature is as truly a revelation of God as the Bible, and we only interpret the Word of God by the Word of God when we interpret the Bible by science."[86]

81. John Hedley Brooke, "Genesis and the Scientists: Dissonance among the Harmonizers," in *Reading Genesis after Darwin*, ed. Stephen Barton and David Wilkinson (Oxford: Oxford University Press, 2009), 106.

82. John William Colenso, *The Pentateuch and Book of Joshua Critically Examined* (London: Longmans, Green, 1865), 317.

83. Colenso, *Pentateuch and Book of Joshua*, 278. On the Colenso episode, see Brown, *Days of Creation*, 274–77.

84. Samuel Driver, *The Book of Genesis* (London: Methuen & Co., 1904), 26, emphasis original.

85. Asa Gray (1810–88), the American botanist and Calvinist evolutionist, rejected the methodological inconsistencies of hard concordism (Davis, "Word and the Works," 48–50). It was possible for a "conservative" to be a non-concordist evolutionist in the nineteenth and early twentieth century; such combinations were not uncommon before modern young-earth creationism reconfigured the landscape after the mid-twentieth century. For a striking rejection of hard concordism by an evangelical, see Davis Young, "Scripture in the Hands of Geologists (Part Two)," *Westminster Theological Journal* 49, no. 2 (1987): 290–91.

86. Charles Hodge, "The Bible in Science," *New York Observer*, March 26, 1863, 98. That Hodge conflated "revelation of God" and "science" is a telling slip; they are not coextensive. Hodge's hard concordism is representative of other Old Princetonians, including B. B. Warfield and James

Hodge's engagement with science was not naive by any stretch, but his writings sometimes betray an undue optimism about our scientific ability to understand the natural world and its history.[87] The ability to assimilate shifts in science by reinterpreting Scripture (à la Hodge), or by refashioning the nature of Scripture to circumvent the problem entirely (à la Driver), governed the shape of theology from the nineteenth century onward.[88]

Scripture was the putty that was constantly remolded by then-current scientific models. Anti-concordists rejected biblical infallibility and therefore had long given up the premise that Scripture was worth accommodating to the findings of science. Rather than falling back on hermeneutical creativity to resolve the challenges, they simply denied any epistemic status to the relevant biblical texts.[89] In either case, science was the needle pulling the thread and its asymmetry with Scripture would be stitched through the very fabric of modern theology.

Theology and the Authority of Scripture

Modern theology inherited the methodological assumptions shared by Galileo and his intellectual descendants. The recurring question was whether science would prompt reinterpretations of religious doctrine or whether

---

McCosh. For background on Hodge's and Warfield's theological attitudes to natural science, see Mark Noll and David Livingstone, "Charles Hodge and B. B. Warfield on Science, the Bible, Evolution, and Darwinism," in Miller, *Perspectives on an Evolving Creation*, 61–71; and, on the Old Princetonians more broadly, see Bradley Gundlach, *Process and Providence: The Evolution Question at Princeton, 1845–1929* (Grand Rapids: Eerdmans, 2013). "Old Princeton" refers to Princeton Theological Seminary from its founding in 1812 until the reorganization of its board by the General Assembly in 1929. See David VanDrunen, "Presbyterians, Philosophy, Natural Theology, and Apologetics," in *The Oxford Handbook of Presbyterianism*, ed. Gary Scott Smith and P. C. Kemeny (Oxford: Oxford University Press, 2019), 462.

87. For further evidence, see Jonathan Wells, "Charles Hodge on the Bible and Science," *American Presbyterians* 66, no. 3 (1988): 157–65.

88. Day-age concordism informs the writings of Hugh Ross and others at the Reasons to Believe organization. E.g., see Hugh Ross, *A Matter of Days: Resolving a Creation Controversy*, 2nd ed. (Covina, CA: RTB Press, 2015).

89. For a complementary observation, see Brown, *Days of Creation*, 277: "The most conservative and the most critical biblical interpreters tended to share a literal understanding of the days of creation, while those in the middle, who respected both the Bible and the fundamental soundness of sciences like geology, often resorted to more figurative interpretations of the creation week in the interest of achieving harmony between the two." See also Daniel K. Williams, "When Science Turned Secular: The Mainline Protestant Abandonment of Natural Theology and the Secularization of American Colleges in the Early Twentieth Century," *Fides et Historia* 51, no. 2 (2019): 1–12; and Frederick Gregory, "The Impact of Darwinian Evolution on Protestant Theology in the Nineteenth Century," in Lindberg and Numbers, *God and Nature*, 369–90.

Christian thinkers would devise ways of avoiding scientific problems altogether. Everyone felt the pressure to stand in line and not overstep the
canons of science.

The Rise of Modern Theology

Most thinkers before the 1800s, whether they were theologians, philosophers, artists, or scientists, believed that Bible doctrines were divine
accounts of actual events in the past and the future, including creation, the
fall, the origin of man, the history of the human race, and so on.[90] They believed that one of the key functions of doctrinal language is to *depict reality*,
meaning that Scripture reliably communicates states of affairs outside the
mind.[91] On this view, infallible Scripture establishes religious doctrines as
matters of fact and, as Langdon Gilkey says, potentially includes "divinely
revealed 'information' on almost any topic of interest."[92] Martin Luther, to
pick one example, reflects this cognitive world in his *Commentary on Genesis* when he tries to identify the rivers of Eden. He takes it as a given that
Scripture reveals infallible truths about our space-time reality.[93] As Gilkey
comments, "With all their debates about reason and revelation, neither the
Reformers, nor most of the Enlightenment theologians, ever doubted that
revelation was composed of objective propositions concerning matters of
fact, that it could therefore tell us what had happened in space and time,
and provide authoritative descriptions of the character, time, place, and
causes of such concrete events as were crucial to the meaning of significant
doctrines."[94]

Such was the received view; sometimes dubbed the "propositional" account of revelation, it held that Scripture discloses infallible truths about

90. Langdon Gilkey, *Nature, Reality, and the Sacred: The Nexus of Science and Religion* (Minneapolis:
Fortress, 1993), 17.

91. As Anthony Thiselton writes, "The terminology 'propositional' and 'non-propositional' sets
the discussion off in unhelpful directions, but what those who *use* this term generally seek to express is that some genres within the Bible authoritatively declare *the truth* of certain *states of affairs*"
(Anthony Thiselton, "Can 'Authority' Remain Viable in a Postmodern Climate? 'Biblical Authority
in the Light of Contemporary Philosophical Hermeneutics,'" in *Thiselton on Hermeneutics: Collected
Works and New Essays* [Grand Rapids: Eerdmans, 2006], 631). See also Rhyne Putman, *In Defense of
Doctrine: Evangelism, Theology, and Scripture* (Minneapolis: Fortress, 2015), 286–87.

92. Langdon Gilkey, *Religion and the Scientific Future: Reflections on Myth, Science, and Theology*
(New York: Harper & Row, 1970), 4.

93. Martin Luther, *Luther's Commentary on Genesis*, trans. J. Theodore Mueller, 2 vols. (Grand
Rapids: Zondervan, 1958), 1:48–49.

94. Gilkey, *Religion and the Scientific Future*, 7. Geerhardus Vos makes the same case at length
in his article "Christian Faith and the Truthfulness of Bible History," *Princeton Theological Review*
4, no. 3 (1906): 289–305.

the world outside the text.[95] At their best, recent defenders of this position do not abstract it from God's broader work of redemption—as J. I. Packer writes, "When this affirmation is not related to God's saving work in history and to the illuminating and interpreting work of the Spirit, it too is theologically incomplete."[96] For most of church history, Christian doctrines were of one piece with the historical events within our space-time universe.

However, as science changed our grasp of and control over nature, this premodern conception of Scripture lost plausibility. Building on the insights of natural science and historical criticism, theological liberals disconnected creation, fall, and redemption from concrete history, thus rejecting the propositional dimension of Scripture.[97] They accepted the Kantian antithesis in order to shield religious faith and piety (*noumena*) from the physical dimensions of redemptive history (*phenomena*). Adopting this Kantian framework, Friedrich Schleiermacher—the father of liberal theology—redefined Christian religion as the feeling of absolute dependence on God, and he made sure that his theological conclusions avoided conflict with the results of Enlightenment criticism.[98]

Although they opposed liberal theology, Karl Barth, Emil Brunner, and other neo-orthodox theologians contested the idea of propositional revelation. Scripture for them was the personal revelation of God, not cognitive information about him—revelation is *personal*, not *propositional*.[99] As William Abraham observes, this existential account of revelation swept

95. John Baillie, *The Idea of Revelation in Recent Thought* (New York: Columbia University Press, 1956), 3–5. See also Gary Dorrien, *The Making of American Liberal Theology: Imagining Progressive Religion, 1805–1900* (Louisville: Westminster John Knox, 2001), xv: "Before the modern period, all Christian theologies were constructed within a house of authority. All premodern Christian theologies made claims to authority-based orthodoxy. Even the mystical and mythopoetic theologies produced by premodern Christianity took for granted the view of scripture as an infallible revelation and the view of theology as an explication of propositional revelation." Avery Dulles is more hesitant: "Elements of the doctrinal, or propositional, model of revelation may be traced back to the rabbinic theories of inspiration in late Judaism and to the early church Fathers. . . . But it would be too much to claim that this theory was dominant in patristic times or in the Middle Ages, for during these periods revelation was often depicted in more dynamic and less verbal terms" (*Models of Revelation*, 2nd ed. [Maryknoll, NY: Orbis Books, 1992], 36).

96. J. I. Packer, "Scripture," in *New Dictionary of Theology*, ed. Sinclair Ferguson, D. F. Wright, and J. I. Packer (Leicester, UK: Inter-Varsity, 1988), 628.

97. Gilkey, *Nature, Reality, and the Sacred*, 17–18.

98. For example, see Friedrich Schleiermacher's second speech in *On Religion: Speeches to Its Cultured Despisers*, trans. John Oman (New York: Harper & Row, 1958), 26–118.

99. For a review of the debate with a mediating proposal, see Kevin Vanhoozer's works: e.g., "The Semantics of Biblical Literature," in *Hermeneutics, Authority, and Canon*, ed. D. A. Carson and John Woodbridge (Grand Rapids: Zondervan, 1986), 53–104; "God's Mighty Speech-Acts: The Doctrine of Scripture Today," in *A Pathway into the Holy Scripture*, ed. Philip Satterthwaite and David Wright

the field: "Indeed the reaction has been so successful in winning ad-
herents that outside fundamentalism it is difficult to find anyone who
espouses [propositional revelation]."[100] Barth, for example, refuses to
submit the Genesis creation narrative to extrabiblical scrutiny. He reads
the opening chapters of Genesis as "saga"—not myth—that is, as "an intuitive and poetic picture of a pre-historical reality of history which is
enacted once and for all within the confines of time and space."[101] This
approach avoids getting entangled with historical-critical or scientific
accounts of primordial history, not because Barth denies those modes
of knowledge—indeed he happily affirms them—but because he sees
the subject matter of Genesis as the transcendent Word of God. Barth's
postcritical and postconcordist doctrine of creation circumvents apologetic conflicts with scientific theories.[102] By mapping creation within covenant and Christology, he decouples his theology of Genesis from science: "The creation of the world by God can be known only in faith."[103]
Barth's approach protects theology from being falsified by future scientific
discoveries.[104]

Similar instincts prevailed among other neo-orthodox theologians. In
Brunner's judgment, "the Biblical view of the world is absolutely irreconcil-
able with that of modern science, just as the world view of Aristotle cannot
be reconciled with that of modern science."[105] The church could have avoided
conflicts between science and theology had she distinguished "between the
vessel and its content, between the view of the world and the statement of
faith."[106] Dietrich Bonhoeffer likewise laments the defensive apologetics of
Christians who reject the conclusions of natural science. He thinks that
well-meaning theologians "taking up arms" against evolution and other
scientific ideas are wasting time in such ill-fated rearguard efforts.[107] Bon-

---

(Grand Rapids: Eerdmans, 1994), 143–81; and *The Drama of Doctrine: A Canonical-Linguistic Approach
to Christian Theology* (Louisville: Westminster John Knox, 2005).

100. William James Abraham, *Divine Revelation and the Limits of Historical Criticism* (Oxford:
Oxford University Press, 1982), 9.

101. Karl Barth, *Church Dogmatics*, III/1, *The Doctrine of Creation*, ed. Geoffrey Bromiley and T. F.
Torrance (Edinburgh: T&T Clark, 1958), 81.

102. Barth, *Church Dogmatics*, III/1:ix–x.

103. Barth, *Church Dogmatics*, III/1:6.

104. Gijsbert van den Brink, *Philosophy of Science for Theologians* (Frankfurt am Main, Germany:
Peter Lang, 2009), 225.

105. Emil Brunner, *Dogmatics*, vol. 2, *The Christian Doctrine of Creation and Redemption*, trans.
Olive Wyon (Philadelphia: Westminster, 1952), 36.

106. Brunner, *Dogmatics*, 2:28.

107. Dietrich Bonhoeffer, letter to Eberhard Bethge, June 30, 1944, in *Letters and Papers from
Prison*, ed. Eberhard Bethge, trans. Reginald Fuller (New York: Macmillan, 1971), 341.

hoeffer accepts contemporary scientific knowledge, though not uncritically. The creation account, he writes, presents "the ancient world picture in all its scientific *naïveté*"; thus, Genesis 1 is not intended as a reliable scientific account of the origin of creation: "The biblical author is exposed as one whose knowledge is bound by all the limitations of the author's own time."[108] Thus, the six days of creation should be understood *theologically* rather than scientifically: "Whether the creation occurred in rhythms of millions of years or in single days, this does no damage to biblical thinking. We have no reason to assert the latter or to doubt the former; the question as such does not concern us."[109]

In sum, liberal theologians fixated on history, cosmology, and biology, while the neo-orthodox gave science a wide berth in their theologizing. Neo-orthodox thinkers never denied evolution or historical criticism, yet their doctrines of creation and providence conspicuously avoided those topics in order to steer clear of any conflicts with the scientific world-picture.[110] Barth and his allies gained a reputation for doing theology with complete autonomy from natural science, but it was all stagecraft:

> The neo-orthodox did not, as the liberals had done, deliberately or consciously refashion the Biblical Word to fit into the scientific world view they themselves accepted, nevertheless in their theological work they all presupposed important aspects of this modern view of things. Despite their protests to the contrary when they discussed hermeneutical *theory*, still the scientific world they lived in massively influenced their hermeneutic in *practice*. The theology that was ostensibly constructed solely on the Bible was in actual fact built upon and around certain basic assumptions of modern science and reflected in all its aspects this grounding in the modern scientific world view, though this dependence was never admitted and often denied. In much the same way one might build a house on some great rock hidden by the house, but still determining its structure and shape, and making it very different from a house built in another kind of place.[111]

108. Dietrich Bonhoeffer, *Creation and Fall: A Theological Exposition of Genesis 1–3*, ed. John W. de Gruchy, trans. Douglas Stephen Bax (Minneapolis: Fortress, 1997), 50.

109. Bonhoeffer, *Creation and Fall*, 49.

110. Gilkey, *Religion and the Scientific Future*, 25. See chap. 4 below for concrete examples in relation to the doctrine of Adam's fall.

111. Gilkey, *Religion and the Scientific Future*, 26, emphasis original. Bultmann and Tillich, also part of neo-orthodoxy, were exceptions to Gilkey's observation. Gilkey is emphatic: "The separation between factual propositions and religious statements, established by scientific development and liberal religion, was thus accepted and reformulated by neo-orthodoxy to express its own understanding of religious truth within the limits set by an increasingly secular culture" (Gilkey, *Religion and the Scientific Future*, 24). See also Langdon Gilkey, *On Niebuhr: A Theological Study* (Chicago: University of Chicago Press, 2001), 233–36.

In other words, the neo-orthodox writers approach the theological task already assuming the truth of modern cosmology, geology, and evolution—a kind of armistice with science is built into theology from the outset. These creative strategies to avoid conflict with science reflect the inner logic of post-Darwinian theology. Modern theology is difficult to understand outside the parameters laid down by scientific modes of thought, meaning that various theological positions were often specifically designed to coincide with the science of the day. The sensibility is so common in the literature that we often miss its significance: Genesis 1 reflects ancient cognitive habits and thus cannot conflict with modern science; Genesis 1–11 is not a historical genre—it is something else—and therefore cannot be falsified by historical science and archaeological discoveries. Since Christ alone is God's Word, Scripture is only a *witness* to that Word, which opens up space for the natural sciences or historical criticism to expose any mistakes in the biblical narrative.[112] With the possible exception of some early twentieth-century fundamentalists and their neo-evangelical heirs who tried to resist these forces (with varying degrees of success), modern theologians often revised their doctrines in deference to science, or they constructed their theological systems to avoid conflict altogether.[113]

Science and Theology after Barbour

Ian Barbour (1923–2013), the doyen of the academic field that explores questions at the interface of science and religion, was also allergic to conflict between the two disciplines.[114] He earned a physics doctorate from the University of Chicago and a bachelor of divinity degree from Yale Divinity School, both indispensable for his later interdisciplinary work. In his groundbreaking 1966 book, *Issues in Science and Religion*, Barbour ponders

112. I recognize, of course, that these examples are streamlining complex and long-standing theological debates and controversies. My intention here is simply to clarify some of the typical neo-orthodox strategies that I think were prompted, at least in part, by scientific developments.

113. Kirsopp Lake, *The Religion of Yesterday and To-morrow* (Boston: Houghton Mifflin, 1926), 61–62: "It is a mistake . . . to suppose that Fundamentalism is a new and strange form of thought. It is nothing of the kind: it is the partial and uneducated survival of a theology which was once universally held by Christians. . . . The Fundamentalist may be wrong; I think he is. But it is we who have departed from the tradition, not he, and I am sorry for the fate of anyone who tries to argue with a Fundamentalist on the basis of authority. The Bible and the *corpus theologicum* of the church is on the Fundamentalist side." Conservative theologians, however, were hardly immune to these forces (see, for example, my earlier remarks about Whig theology).

114. I have chosen Barbour over other important thinkers (e.g., Arthur Peacocke, John Polkinghorne, Alister McGrath) because, arguably, he is the chief architect of the academic field of science-and-religion. Most scholars in the discipline appropriate his methodological assumptions.

the question whether faith is still viable after the rise of science in the seventeenth and eighteenth centuries.[115] He identifies four models for relating science and religion: independence, integration, dialogue, and conflict. The *integration* and *dialogue* views are mediating positions between science and theology; the *independence* view conceives science and theology as moving along independent tracks, while the *conflict* view posits an adversarial relation between the two.

Barbour rejects the conflict model because he feels it brings disrepute to Christians.[116] He sees inerrancy as the root problem; by his lights, it not only is to blame for needlessly generating conflict between the Bible and science but is also untenable in the aftermath of Copernicus, geology, and historical criticism.[117] The seeming failure of Scripture to stand up to the findings of natural science conditions Barbour to scrupulously avoid defending any theological position potentially falsifiable by science. Geoffrey Cantor and Chris Kenny agree that this avoidance of conflict dominates Barbour's thinking. As they explain, "Our pilgrim starts with the familiar conflict thesis. In an important sense the other three positions are developed out of criticism of that foundational thesis. To put the matter another way, although ultimately rejected, *the conflict thesis has set Barbour's agenda* for categorizing the ways in which science and religion interrelate. This point applies not only to Barbour but also to many other religious writers whose understanding of science-religion relationships have been forged in the furnace of their enemies."[118]

Reflecting Barbour's aversion to conflict, dialogue and integration are the dominant strategies in the literature.[119] Even those who try to move beyond this aversion usually share its impulses to erase, or tone down, any deep discord between science and Scripture.[120] The overall effect of such

115. Ian Barbour, *Issues in Science and Religion* (Englewood Cliffs, NJ: Prentice Hall, 1966). Some years later, he maintains that "science seems to provide the only reliable path to knowledge." Ian Barbour, *Religion in an Age of Science* (New York: Harper & Row, 1990), 3.

116. Barbour, *Religion in an Age of Science*, 3–30.

117. Barbour, *Issues in Science and Religion*, 96.

118. Geoffrey Cantor and Chris Kenny, "Barbour's Fourfold Way: Problems with His Taxonomy of Science-Religion Relationships," *Zygon* 36, no. 4 (2001): 768, my emphasis.

119. As one scholar of science and religion writes, "Even a brief and cursory glance at contemporary work by Christian theologians, scientists, and philosophers of religion shows that dialogue and integration are their favored models." Helen De Cruz, "The Relationship between Science and Christianity: Understanding the Conflict Thesis in Lay Christians," in *Global Dialogues in the Philosophy of Religion: From Religious Experience to the Afterlife*, ed. Yujin Nagasawa and Mohammad Saleh Zarepour (Oxford: Oxford University Press, 2024).

120. Ted Peters, for instance, outlines eight ways for relating science and theology—his own preference for "hypothetical consonance" and "ethical overlap" rules out any possibility of conflict. See his "Science and Theology: Toward Consonance," in *Science and Theology: The New Consonance*, ed.

moves is to downplay the epistemic relevance of Scripture and thus betray the effects of scientism on modern plausibility structures.[121] Modern science is so definitive of reality—that which is *really* real—that Barbour and his allies find it inconceivable that the witness of Holy Scripture can stand on its own integrity with, *but sometimes against*, the conclusions of science.

A Chastened Conflict Thesis

Playing down conflict is also a trademark move for historians of science. They typically cite John Draper's *History of the Conflict between Religion and Science* and Andrew White's *A History of the Warfare of Science with Theology in Christendom*, two nineteenth-century polemical tracts, as the main source of the "warfare" myth.[122] Thomas Huxley, a contemporary of Draper and White, relishes this imagery at every turn: "Extinguished theologians lie about the cradle of every science as the strangled snakes beside that of Hercules, and history records that whenever science and dogmatism have been fairly opposed, the latter has been forced to retire from the lists, bleeding and crushed, if not annihilated; scotched, if not slain."[123] Huxley and other

Ted Peters (Boulder, CO: Westview, 1998), 11–39. So, too, with J. Wentzel van Huyssteen, who rejects foundationalism in part because it exacerbates conflict between science and theology. See his "Post-foundationalism in Theology and Science: Beyond Conflict and Consonance," in *Rethinking Theology and Science: Six Models for the Current Dialogue*, ed. Niels Henrik Gregersen and J. Wentzel van Huyssteen (Grand Rapids: Eerdmans, 1998), 13–49.

121. Mikael Stenmark shows that "scientism" has been understood in several different ways. Here I take scientism to be "the attempt to expand the boundaries of science in such a way that all genuine (in contrast to apparent) knowledge must either be scientific or at least be able to be reduced to scientific knowledge." Mikael Stenmark, *Scientism: Science, Ethics and Religion* (Aldershot, UK: Ashgate, 2001), 4.

122. John William Draper, *History of the Conflict between Religion and Science*, 8th ed. (New York: D. Appleton, 1884); Andrew Dickson White, *A History of the Warfare of Science with Theology in Christendom*, 2 vols. (New York: D. Appleton, 1896). Of the countless historians who single out Draper and White, see, for example, James Moore, who writes,

Clever metaphors die hard. . . . Through constant repetition in historical and philosophical exposition of every kind, from pulpit, platform, and printed page, the idea of science and religion at "war" has become an integral part of Western intellectual culture. Like other clever metaphors, this one shows few signs of dying out. . . . A study of the origins of the military metaphor and of its influence over the past one hundred years inspires little confidence in its utility as an historiographic device. Rather, this captivating idea remains the one best guide to the sentiments of its embattled founders, John William Draper and Andrew Dickson White. (James Moore, *The Post Darwinian Controversies: A Study of the Protestant Struggle to Come to Terms with Darwin in Great Britain and America, 1870–1900* [Cambridge: Cambridge University Press, 1979], 19–20)

123. Thomas H. Huxley, "Darwin on the Origin of Species," *Westminster Review* 17 (1860): 556. For additional context on Huxley and the warfare metaphor, see Colin Russell, "The Conflict Metaphor and Its Social Origins," *Science and Christian Belief* 1, no. 1 (1989): 3–26.

nineteenth-century thinkers weaponized the conflict metaphor—the idea that science and theology always oppose each other—a trope that infects the popular imagination.[124]

The historian John Hedley Brooke challenges this conflict narrative in a now classic critique.[125] He argues that science and Christianity have always had a complex and surprising relationship, such that simple depictions of conflict are poor witnesses to the historical record. "To portray the relations between science and religion as a continuous retreat from theological dogma before a cumulative and infallible science," warns Brooke, "is to overlook the fine structure of scientific controversy, in which religious interests intruded, but often in subtle rather than overtly obstructive ways."[126] He also cautions against the secularization thesis— the claim that science was instrumental in secularizing modern society. According to Brooke, such judgments rely on the conflict thesis and are misleading. Fine-grained historical case studies reveal a messier picture in which science always has built-in religious presuppositions and religion often informs scientific theories, sometimes even shaping the scientific content itself.[127] Scholars have dubbed Brooke's argument the "complexity thesis."[128]

Although the hawkers of the conflict narrative are the ones in Brooke's crosshairs, he also faults the "harmony" side. Critics of the conflict thesis, reacting to the bad history of Draper and White, sometimes overcompensate in the opposite direction.[129] Many Christian apologists, for example, like pointing out that the origins of science in Judeo-Christian Europe reveal an underlying harmony between Christianity and science. However, such pacifying narratives neglect the fact that ancient Greeks and medieval Muslims were also instrumental in the emergence of science. Rather than weaponizing narratives of conflict and harmony, Brooke urges us to recognize the complexities of the historical protagonists. "To my knowledge,"

---

124. See the important essays in Jeff Hardin, Ronald Numbers, and Ronald Binzley, eds., *The Warfare between Science and Religion: The Idea That Wouldn't Die* (Baltimore: Johns Hopkins University Press, 2018).

125. John Hedley Brooke, *Science and Religion: Some Historical Perspectives* (Cambridge: Cambridge University Press, 1991). On his significance, see Thomas Dixon, Geoffrey Cantor, and Stephen Pumfrey, eds., *Science and Religion: New Historical Perspectives* (Cambridge: Cambridge University Press, 2010).

126. Brooke, *Science and Religion*, 6.

127. For one example, see Jeremy Blaschke, "Parasite Soup: Faith and Science in the History of Parasitology," *Zygon* 57, no. 2 (2022): 344–67.

128. Ronald Numbers was the first to do so in his review of Brooke, *Science and Religion*, in *Metascience* 1 (1992): 35–39.

129. Brooke, *Science and Religion*, 12.

Ronald Numbers writes, "no reputable historian of science and religion now doubts the truth of this tangled view of the past."[130] Peter Harrison even claims there was no conflict between "science" and "religion" prior to the nineteenth century; the conceptual categories implied in such conflict did not yet exist. "Science" and "religion" are not timeless entities but modern and socially constructed terms.[131] In short, the complexity thesis is the reigning paradigm.

These helpful perspectives should discipline any dialogue between science and theology. Systematic, atemporal categories always risk distorting the richness and ambiguity in the historical interaction between scientists and theologians.[132] I happily affirm the contributions of complexity narratives and concede that "science" and "religion" are partially constructed categories. However—from the perspective of historic Christian orthodoxy—reliance on complexity alone prevents us from seeing the forest for the trees. The conceptual language of "science" and "theology," whatever its limitations, does pick out genuine aspects of reality and helps crystallize what is at stake theologically when scientific claims impinge on Christian doctrine.[133]

The warfare narrative is flawed, but that fact alone does not negate real instances of conflict between scientific understanding and the knowledge of faith. Ironically, in much of the literature, the complexity thesis has become the new reductionism.[134] Thomas Dixon asks the right question: "Does that mean that conflict needs to be written out of our story altogether? Certainly not. The only thing to avoid is too narrow an idea of the kinds of

130. Ronald Numbers, *Science and Christianity in Pulpit and Pew* (Oxford: Oxford University Press, 2007), 4–5.

131. Peter Harrison, *The Territories of Science and Religion* (Chicago: University of Chicago Press, 2015), 5: "The idea of a perennial conflict between science and religion must be false." Harrison argues that modern religion did not exist before the seventeenth century, nor modern science before the nineteenth—so applying those categories to the more distant past is anachronistic. See John Hedley Brooke and Geoffrey Cantor, *Reconstructing Nature: The Engagement of Science and Religion* (Oxford: Oxford University Press, 1998), 43–72. Claude Welch laments "the hypostatization of 'science' and 'religion'" represented by Draper, White, and their disciples. See Claude Welch, "Dispelling Some Myths about the Split between Theology and Science in the Nineteenth Century," in *Religion and Science: History, Method, Dialogue*, ed. W. Mark Richardson and Wesley Wildman (New York: Routledge, 1996), 29.

132. For an argument that favors using local instead of global methodologies in science and religion, see Josh Reeves, *Against Methodology in Science and Religion: Recent Debates on Rationality and Theology* (New York: Routledge, 2018).

133. As Thomas Dixon writes, "The fact that the phrase 'science and religion' names an academic field, as well as conjuring up vivid if historically debatable cultural stereotypes, is enough, I think, to justify its continued use as a category of thought." Thomas Dixon, *Science and Religion: A Very Short Introduction* (Oxford: Oxford University Press, 2008), 17.

134. Brooke anticipates this problem. Brooke, *Science and Religion*, 12, 49–50.

conflicts one might expect to find between science and religion."[135] Dixon's judgment seems right to me and tempers the tendency that I see among many (usually Christian) scholars to leverage the legitimate insights of the complexity thesis to erase the significance of conflict in the history of science and theology.[136]

On one level, the desire for a more congenial relationship between science and faith is salutary given how often New Atheists and others mischaracterize them as enemies. Yet one wonders whether adamant critics of the warfare narrative are straining at gnats while swallowing the camel. The defective narratives of Draper and White have inoculated many historians against taking seriously how conflict plays an important—even central—role in the encounter between science and faith.[137]

Conflict is possible because of the different epistemic norms of science and faith. Scientific and theological disciplines handle knowledge claims in fundamentally different ways.[138] For one thing, modern science doesn't appeal to divine revelation or any other instances of special divine action. Scientific theories can appeal only to forces within the natural, causal nexus of the world, data accessible to everyone. By contrast, Christian theology that has any claim to orthodoxy accepts the witness of Scripture as genuine knowledge. These contrasting epistemic norms open up the possibility of conflict between the investigation of nature and divinely warranted knowledge. Even worse, the secularization of science and its allegiance to methodological (and metaphysical) naturalism make conflicts with classical Christianity virtually inevitable. Therefore, a nuanced or *chastened* conflict thesis better describes the long relationship between science and theology while also avoiding the flawed conflict narratives of the nineteenth century.[139]

135. Dixon, *Science and Religion*, 3. See also his comments in "Religion and Science," in *The Routledge Companion to the Study of Religion*, ed. John Hinnells, 2nd ed. (London: Routledge, 2010), 509: "Religion and science share an interest in the same fundamental questions about the origins and nature of the physical universe in general, and of human beings in particular. *It is when religion and science have found themselves giving different answers to these questions, whether in Renaissance Italy or in modern-day America, that conflicts have arisen*" (my emphasis).

136. See Geoffrey Cantor, "What Shall We Do with the 'Conflict Thesis'?," in *Science and Religion: New Historical Perspectives*, ed. Thomas Dixon, Geoffrey Cantor, and Stephen Pumfrey (Cambridge: Cambridge University Press, 2010), 283–98.

137. In an interesting revisionist monograph, James Ungureanu lays the blame for the conflict thesis not on Draper or White but—centuries earlier—on sixteenth- and seventeenth-century Protestant-Catholic polemics. James Ungureanu, *Science, Religion, and the Protestant Tradition: Retracing the Origins of Conflict* (Pittsburgh: University of Pittsburgh Press, 2019).

138. Dawes, *Galileo and the Conflict*, 16.

139. Although his concerns are different from mine, I agree with Maurice Finocchiaro: "The idea to which I am attributing considerable truth is a more nuanced and moderate thesis: that there

Conclusion

As we survey the terrain we have covered in the long shadow of Galileo,
we can see how judgments about the epistemic scope of God's Word have
changed remarkably over the centuries and were often the bellwether of
the evolving relationship between science and theology. Scientific developments slowly compromised the classical notions of Scripture; this in
turn transformed the shape of the dogmatic tradition in the modern academy. Constant attempts to eliminate deep conflicts between scientific and
theological disciplines eventually sidelined Scripture as a reliable guide to
primeval history and the natural world.

Some scholars give the impression that the relationship between science
and Scripture is a settled issue, but that is not true. The persistence of un-
resolved questions is one reason believers still disagree on a wide range of
doctrinal matters, including the fall and original sin. Such disagreements
often reflect fundamentally different judgments about the epistemic status
of God's Word, the relative authority of catholic tradition, and the evidential
strength of scientific theories. Given the modern infatuation with natural
science, the fabric of theology will continue unraveling unless we engage
these prolegomena with conceptual tools that illuminate rather than obscure the Bible's own self-understanding. To that task we now turn.

---

is often actual conflict between science and religion, and almost always potential conflict between
them." Finocchiaro, "Galileo Affair," 43.

2

Biblical Realism

A Dogmatic Proposal

To prefer to err with scripture than be right with the innovators: that is the pathos of orthodoxy.

—Klaus Scholder[1]

But what men consider reasonable or unreasonable alters. At certain periods men find reasonable what at other periods they found unreasonable. And vice versa. But is there no objective character here?

—Ludwig Wittgenstein[2]

Scripture has a special status because it is God-breathed. Like no other book, it is fully human and preeminently divine. What then should we do when a mainstream scientific claim contradicts a doctrine the church has held for millennia? Suppose that the doctrine is not a trivial inference from a random passage in Habakkuk but is rooted firmly in the Old and New Testaments—what then? Perhaps, in the kindness of God's providence, science is prompting us to recognize exegetical mistakes inherited from church history. If we simply reinterpret the

1. Klaus Scholder, *The Birth of Modern Critical Theology: Origins and Problems of Biblical Criticism in the Seventeenth Century*, trans. John Bowden (Philadelphia: Trinity Press International, 1990), 120.

2. Ludwig Wittgenstein, *On Certainty*, ed. G. E. M. Anscombe and G. H. Wright, trans. Denis Paul and G. E. M. Anscombe (New York: Harper & Row, 1969), para. 336.

offending biblical texts, we resolve the science-theology conflict and restore the peace. All's well that ends well.

Yet this hermeneutical instinct may be a sign of bad faith hiding the fact that Scripture no longer functions as a lamp to our feet and a light for our path. As Joseph McKenna points out, "Modern theology has always risked intellectual dishonesty and self-deception in the very act of modernizing theology. Nineteenth-century Liberal theologians and twentieth-century Revisionist theologians have reinterpreted most Christian ideas, believing that modernity's new knowledge and scholarly methodologies—in the natural sciences, social sciences, history, literature, philosophy and ethics—are largely correct and that therefore the only solution to the cognitive crisis facing modern Christianity is to revise traditional doctrines in terms suitable to contemporary learning and credible to contemporary sensibilities."[3] However, we should take issue with McKenna singling out "liberals" and "revisionists." They were the worst offenders, but the "conservative" faction is hardly immune to these trends. They just tend to lag behind a few decades. *All* Christians face the same predicament. We are all wrestling with how to be biblical—and what that would even mean—in a world saturated with scientific perspectives.

There is no easy way forward, but we must try to cut through the brambles of controversy. If we are to defend a doctrine of sin attentive to scientific questions, our methodological house must be in good order. In the previous chapter, after reviewing a long history of Christians responding to conflicts between science and theology, I suggested that many of their strategies undermine the integrity of Scripture. In this chapter, I offer my own proposal, called *biblical realism*, that lays down clear tracks for the rest of the book.[4] Our attention to conflict, we should remember, is not meant to negate the many positive aspects of the relationship between theology and science. That rich story is simply not our focus here. However, since conflict is not the whole story, we must constantly guard against a distorted picture.

In what follows, I will sketch out biblical realism as five core commitments:

(1) *Supernaturalism* contends that the natural sciences should be open to supernatural realities when seeking to understand God's world. (2) *Dogmatic inerrancy* sees biblical authority not as an evidential or apologetic argument but as a presupposition of faith. (3) *Scientific fallibilism* recognizes

---

3. Joseph McKenna, "Honesty in Theology?," *Heythrop Journal* 42, no. 1 (2001): 53.

4. I am updating my earlier account of "scriptural realism" in "'The Most Vulnerable Part of the Whole Christian Account': Original Sin and Modern Science," in *Adam, the Fall, and Original Sin: Theological, Biblical, and Scientific Perspectives* (Grand Rapids: Baker Academic, 2014), 240–45.

the inevitable fallibility of science and places it within a larger eschatological framework. (4) *Doctrinal confidence* reminds us that central doctrinal beliefs receive their epistemic warrant from Scripture and should
therefore not be revised (or abandoned) in the face of conflicting scientific
theories. (5) An *eclectic method* holds that no single method should regulate how Christians ought to engage with scientific theories, but that we
should instead evaluate such theories on a case-by-case basis. I will take
each commitment in turn.

Supernaturalism

Let us start with definitions. A "metaphysical naturalist" believes that God
and other supernatural entities do not exist; by contrast, a "methodological naturalist" may believe in supernatural realities but stipulates that only
natural explanations are permissible in scientific research.[5] In methodological naturalism, scientists approach nature *as if* metaphysical naturalism were true.[6] George Frederick Wright, a nineteenth-century Christian
evolutionist, agrees that science pursues "known secondary causes as far
as they will go in explanation of facts. We are not to resort to an unknown
cause for explanation of phenomena till the power of known causes has
been exhausted. If we cease to observe this rule there is an end to all science and all sound sense."[7] In Wright's view, supernatural explanations
impede scientific discovery.

Ever since Paul de Vries coined the term in 1986, methodological naturalism has been a disputed concept.[8] One of its strengths is that it protects
scientists from the "God-of-the-gaps" fallacy—something Wright also cau-
tioned against. Just because we currently lack a natural explanation doesn't
mean we will not have one in the future. Critics also charge supernatural
explanations with being intellectually lazy and science-stoppers. While

---

5. Paul de Vries, "Naturalism in the Natural Sciences: A Christian Perspective," *Christian Scholar's Review* 15, no. 4 (1986): 388–96. For a stimulating account of "theological naturalism" that I cannot engage here, see Sarah Lane Ritchie, *Divine Action and the Human Mind* (Cambridge: Cambridge University Press, 2019).

6. Del Ratzsch, "Science and Religion," in *The Oxford Handbook of Philosophical Theology*, ed. Thomas Flint and Michael Rea (Oxford: Oxford University Press, 2009), 58.

7. George Wright, "Recent Works Bearing on the Relation of Science to Religion: No. II," *Bibliotheca Sacra* 33, no. 131 (1876): 480.

8. For defenses of methodological naturalism, see Patrick McDonald and Nivaldo Tro, "In Defense of Methodological Naturalism," *Christian Scholar's Review* 38, no. 2 (2009): 201–30; and Kathryn Applegate, "A Defense of Methodological Naturalism," *Perspectives on Science and Christian Faith* 65, no. 1 (2013): 37–46.

these concerns have some merit, methodological naturalism suffers from remarkable weaknesses. By artificially limiting the beliefs we can appeal to when investigating creation, it can only yield a truncated picture. But if science is the pursuit of truth, then why limit its theoretical terms to natural entities only?

Alvin Plantinga argues that Christians should pursue "science using *all that we know*: what we know about God as well as what we know about his creation, and what we know by faith as well as what we know in other ways."[9] Natural science should include supernatural entities when they apply to the domain under investigation. Practicing science *as if* metaphysical naturalism is true will only yield results consistent with metaphysical naturalism.[10] As Robert Larmer explains,

> Insisting that methodological naturalism be adopted, implicitly commits one either to the claim that supernatural agents do not exist or to the claim that if they do they never intervene on the natural order. This, however, begs the important question of whether such claims are justified. Insofar as it guarantees that no matter what the evidence is it cannot be thought to lead to a supernatural cause, methodological naturalism makes the claim that all physical events have natural causes unfalsifiable.[11]

In other words, if the natural sciences are always limited to methodological naturalism, then this approach can generate a *metaphysical* bias among scientists about the kinds of entities that exist in the world.[12]

Mikael Stenmark argues that religious or ideological considerations should play no role in the evaluation of scientific theories.[13] Assessing scien-

9. Alvin Plantinga, "Methodological Naturalism?," in *Facets of Faith and Science: Historiography and Modes of Interaction*, ed. Jitse M. van der Meer, 4 vols. (Lanham, MD: University Press of America, 1996), 1:213–14, my emphasis.

10. Perhaps that explains why methodological naturalism was instrumental in secularizing the American academy. See Jon Roberts and James Turner, *The Sacred and the Secular University* (Princeton: Princeton University Press, 2000).

11. Robert Larmer, *The Legitimacy of Miracle* (Lanham, MD: Lexington Books, 2014), 92.

12. Gregory Dawes, "In Defense of Naturalism," *International Journal for Philosophy of Religion* 70, no. 1 (2011): 11. See Evan Fales, *Divine Intervention: Metaphysical and Epistemological Puzzles* (New York: Routledge, 2010), 1: "Methodological naturalism should not be embraced by any sane theist. Consistently applied, it would not only spell the end of natural theology, but also count as irrelevant to theology historical scholarship concerning the past that (insofar as it purports to verify the occurrence of miracles) is critically important to historical religions such as Judaism and Christianity."

13. Mikael Stenmark endorses methodological naturalism in his *Scientism: Science, Ethics and Religion* (New York: Routledge, 2001), 96–97: "Methodological naturalism lays down which sort of study qualifies as scientific. Naturalists, Christians, Buddhists and Marxists alike must in pursuing science be satisfied with this kind of explanation. . . . It is sufficient that only natural entities and

tific theories based on theological criteria threatens the integrity of science. He writes, "Theories should be accepted by the scientific community only in the light of considerations that involve empirical data, other accepted theories, and cognitive values such as consistency, simplicity, and explanatory power."[14] But Stenmark's methodological naturalism fails to persuade. He claims that science falsifies any religious arguments for geocentrism or young-earth creationism.[15] Furthermore, he writes, "science has the potential to undermine (or support, for that matter) *any* religious or ideological idea that has *empirical content*."[16] Tellingly, science can refute the empirical claims of religious traditions, but theology must *never* adjudicate scientific theories. Stenmark seems to think it is self-evident that scientific empirical claims are more reliable than theological empirical claims; the asymmetry smacks of scientism.[17] What's more, science is already religiously laden; for example, the lawfulness and intelligibility of nature are assumptions that turn on theological commitments.[18]

The fundamental problem with methodological naturalism is that it assumes a neat division of labor: science on the physical side of the ledger and Scripture on the supernatural side. Christians who accept this framework can practice methodological naturalism as scientists while, in other parts of their lives, remaining committed to a larger reality of supernatural things. However, Scripture rejects this hard line between the "material" and the "spiritual"—both of them are inseparably linked in the historical events of the exodus, the incarnation, Christ's resurrection, and countless other miracles. By adopting methodological naturalism in the historical sciences, Christians deny that Scripture offers any relevant revelation for our knowledge of primeval history.

---

processes will enter into the theories and explanations given by science for this enterprise to be successful; no further commitments about whether or not there exist objects and properties other than natural ones is required."

14. Mikael Stenmark, *How to Relate Science and Religion: A Multidimensional Model* (Grand Rapids: Eerdmans, 2004), 231.

15. Stenmark, *How to Relate Science and Religion*, 180.

16. Stenmark, *How to Relate Science and Religion*, 180, emphasis original.

17. See Del Ratzsch, "Stenmark, Plantinga, and Scientific Neutrality," *Faith and Philosophy* 21 (2004): 358.

18. For example, the empirical nature of science depends on the *contingency* of creation, which itself depends on creation as a free act of the divine will. Cf. Michael B. Foster, "The Christian Doctrine of Creation and the Rise of Modern Natural Science," *Mind* 43, no. 172 (1934): 446–68; John Henry, "Metaphysics and the Origins of Modern Science: Descartes and the Importance of Laws of Nature," *Early Science and Medicine* 9, no. 2 (2004): 73–114. Ironically, the empiricism that Stenmark privileges arose, in part, from Christian beliefs about the fall of Adam and Eve—see Peter Harrison, *The Fall of Man and the Foundations of Science* (Cambridge: Cambridge University Press, 2007).

To make matters worse, once scientists accept methodological naturalism, conflict between science and theology is *inevitable*. If Scripture attests
to supernatural events in our space-time reality (and it does), and if the standard canons of science exclude the supernatural from the physical-material
nexus (and they do), then conflict between science and faith becomes *en-
demic* because such partitions are inimical to Scripture. At least since Ian
Barbour, the discipline of science-and-theology has exhausted itself with
arguments designed to marginalize or eliminate conflict between the two
disciplines, but the conflicts will not go away; ironically, methodological
naturalism itself generates and sustains them.

In defense of methodological naturalism, some historians point out
its ancient pedigree. As far back as the high medieval period, Christian
philosophers were committed to the search for natural causes.[19] For natural philosophers in the twelfth and thirteenth centuries, reason without
revelation was the only legitimate tool for studying natural phenomena.
Medieval universities founded between 1200 and 1500 enshrined methodological naturalism as the dominant approach to understanding God's creation (largely by commenting on Aristotle's books on nature). Using pagan
sources, arts masters taught logic, mathematics, and natural philosophy
but left theological questions to the faculty of theology. As Michael Shank
states, "The mandate, self-understanding, and curriculum of the faculty of
arts thus enshrined as its modus operandi an approach that was effectively
functioning as methodological naturalism."[20] Theologians like Albertus
Magnus and Thomas Aquinas received their master of arts degrees before
becoming theologians—"They not only advocated treating natural philosophy separately from theology, but did so in practice."[21] The same goes for
their contemporaries Siger of Brabant (ca. 1240–84) and, by the following
century, John Buridan (ca. 1300–62) and Nicole Oresme (1320–82)—all of
them openly defending something like methodological naturalism.[22] But
this conclusion does not tell the whole story, because almost all medieval
theologians held to divine concurrence, believing that God was causally

19. This paragraph draws from Michael Shank, "Naturalist Tendencies in Medieval Science,"
in *Science without God? Rethinking the History of Scientific Naturalism*, ed. Peter Harrison and Jon
Roberts (Oxford: Oxford University Press, 2019), 37–57. See my introductory remarks in chap. 1 on
the thirteenth-century controversies over Aristotle at the University of Paris.

20. Shank, "Naturalist Tendencies in Medieval Science," 46.

21. Shank, "Naturalist Tendencies in Medieval Science," 47.

22. Edward Grant, "Jean Buridan and Nicole Oresme on Natural Knowledge," *Vivarium* 31, no. 1
(1993): 84–105; Tiddy Smith, "Methodological Naturalism and Its Misconceptions," *International
Journal for Philosophy of Religion* 82, no. 3 (2017): 326.

involved in and through all natural processes.[23] Absent this qualification, it is somewhat misleading and anachronistic to label their approach to the natural world "methodological naturalism."

The boundaries between natural philosophy and theology blurred in the wake of the Reformation. In the seventeenth and eighteenth centuries, for example, natural philosophers routinely invoked God in their scientific treatises.[24] But by the nineteenth century, this "godly natural philosophy" had morphed into naturalistic modern science, and that move was endorsed by believers and nonbelievers.[25] Pious believers were already naturalizing the study of creation long before geology and Darwin's evolutionary theory. Ronald Numbers concludes that "virtually all scientists . . . , whether Christians or non-Christians, came by the latter nineteenth century to agree that God talk lay beyond the boundaries of science."[26] Christians contributed to the naturalization of meteorology, medicine, physics, chemistry, biology, physiology, psychiatry, and the like.[27] Believers embraced methodological naturalism as the best way to study God's creation, deeming the Bible irrelevant to the empirical study of nature and to the content of scientific theories. Since the twelfth century, this strategy has allowed Christians to insulate theology from the encroaching claims of extrabiblical philosophy.

Methodological naturalism's rise to prominence belongs to the longer story I have been telling of pious thinkers feeling the pressure to deflect, de-emphasize, or deny conflicts between the judgments of science and classical readings of Scripture. While I agree that aspects of modern science raise difficult questions for the authority of God's Word, methodological naturalism was not then, nor is it now, the best way to resolve these challenges (largely because it artificially prevents scientists from accessing all the available evidence for understanding the natural world).

23. See Peter Harrison, "Naturalism and the Success of Science," *Religious Studies* 56, no. 2 (2020): 279.

24. Edward Grant, *God and Reason in the Middle Ages* (Cambridge: Cambridge University Press, 2001), 204: "When Newton wrote, it was regarded as wholly appropriate for a natural philosopher to discourse about God."

25. Ronald Numbers, "Science without God: Natural Laws and Christian Beliefs," in *When Science and Christianity Meet*, ed. David Lindberg and Ronald Numbers (Chicago: University of Chicago Press, 2003), 272.

26. Numbers, "Science without God," 272.

27. E.g., on the naturalization of physiology, see Alison Winter, "The Construction of Orthodoxies and Heterodoxies in the Early Victorian Life Sciences," in *Victorian Science in Context*, ed. Bernard Lightman (Chicago: University of Chicago Press, 1997), 24–50; and for a similar process in other disciplines, see the discussion and bibliography in Harrison and Roberts, *Science without God?*; and Numbers, "Science without God."

Biblical realism is more expansive and situates science within a *super-naturalist* framework.[28] The evidence base for a believing scientist should include everything he or she knows about reality.[29] Del Ratzsch demonstrates why it is ultimately self-defeating to limit the evidence base if we want to exegete God's creation: "If (perhaps for overwhelmingly good reasons) science is restricted (even just methodologically) to 'natural' explanatory and theoretical resources, then if there is a supernatural realm which does impinge upon the structure and/or operation of the 'natural' realm, then the world-picture generated by even the best science will unavoidably be either incomplete or else wrong on some points. Unless one assumes philosophical naturalism (that the natural constitutes the whole of reality) that will be the inescapable upshot of taking even mere methodological naturalism as an essential component of scientific procedure."[30]

A Christian's evidence base will include the supernatural doctrines of faith that testify to God's action in redemptive history—doctrines like special creation, the global flood, the fall, original sin, the soul, regeneration, sanctification, glorification, and more.[31] Scientific theories should not contravene any of these doctrines, for they are the clearest windows we have into the nature of reality. Scripture is awash in cases of special divine action, preeminently Christ's resurrection.[32] According to the classical Reformed tradition, God is not limited to secondary causes—"for he often exercises his providence without regard to them, and operates thus contrary to what we call the course of nature, and hence arises the difference between *ordinary* and *extraordinary* providence."[33] Supernatu-

---

28. Some worry that the term "supernatural" is implicitly dualistic, deistic, or just unbiblical (e.g., recent Roman Catholic debate has been shaped by Henri de Lubac, *The Mystery of the Supernatural* [New York: Crossroad, 1998]). Those are fair concerns. Although Scripture makes no hard distinction between "natural" and "supernatural," I use the term advisedly and following tradition to signal God's miraculous presence and activity, but without excluding or minimizing God's immanence and ordinary providence. I endorse the supernaturalism as laid out in Larmer, *Legitimacy of Miracle*; and C. John Collins, *The God of Miracles: An Exegetical Examination of God's Action in the World* (Wheaton: Crossway, 2000).

29. According to Alvin Plantinga, the "evidence base" is "the set of beliefs I use, or to which I appeal, in conducting an inquiry." Alvin Plantinga, *Where the Conflict Really Lies* (Oxford: Oxford University Press, 2011), 167.

30. Del Ratzsch, "Design Theory and Its Critics: Monologues Passing in the Night," *Ars Disputandi* 2 (2002): 4.

31. By "special creation," I mean that Genesis 1 describes many instances of God creating things directly, instantaneously, and without any protracted evolutionary development.

32. For a rich analysis, see Collins, *God of Miracles.*

33. Heinrich Schmid, *The Doctrinal Theology of the Evangelical Lutheran Church*, trans. Charles A. Hay and Henry E. Jacobs, 5th ed. (Philadelphia: Lutheran Publication Society, 1876), 193, emphasis original.

ralism still champions the empirical investigation of creation but insists that science be practiced in light of *everything* the Christian knows.[34] This "theistic science," as Plantinga dubs it, offers a richer empirical approach to the natural world.

Methodological naturalism is theologically problematic because it is a totalizing approach that imposes its methodology on *all* the natural sciences. However, I have no problems with a methodological naturalism that is limited to a narrow scientific pursuit.[35] This approach restricts the scope of scientific inquiry for largely pragmatic rather than ontological reasons—thus, it denies any form of scientism.[36] Furthermore, this limited methodology provides a system of justification that allows practitioners to validate claims externally—and, in principle, knowledge acquired from the framework of a limited naturalism can then be integrated with knowledge from other spheres (including other natural sciences and disciplines like theology).[37] Finally, in the day-to-day *practice* of science, supernaturalism and methodological naturalism largely overlap.[38] Supernaturalism agrees that God's presence is usually not physically detectable in the laboratory since the world generally operates according to God-sustained secondary causes. Thus, the scientific investigation of the orderly universe usually relies on natural causes—call this *nomological* science.[39] At the level of nomological science, the functional difference between supernaturalism and methodological naturalism is slim. In the *historical* sciences, however, the situation is different since the canonical witness reveals that God in times

34. My position is compatible with the argument in Andrew Torrance, "Should a Christian Adopt Methodological Naturalism?," *Zygon* 52, no. 3 (2017): 691–725.

35. This suggestion has similarities to what Alvin Plantinga labels "Duhemian" science (in honor of the Catholic physicist Pierre Duhem). See Alvin Plantinga, "Science: Augustinian or Duhemian?," *Faith and Philosophy* 13, no. 3 (1996): 368–94, esp. 380–83.

36. Scientism, J. P. Moreland explains, is "roughly the view that the hard sciences alone have the intellectual authority to give us knowledge of reality. Everything else—especially ethics, theology, and philosophy—is, at least according to scientism, based on private emotions, blind faith, or cultural upbringing." J. P. Moreland, *Scientism and Secularism: Learning to Respond to a Dangerous Ideology* (Downers Grove, IL: Crossway, 2018), 21.

37. Jonathan Bartlett, "Philosophical Shortcomings of Methodological Naturalism and the Path Forward," in *Naturalism and Its Alternatives in Scientific Methodologies*, ed. Jonathan Bartlett and Eric Holloway (Broken Arrow, OK: Blythe Institute, 2017), 13–37, esp. 32–33.

38. For a historical example of this dynamic, see Jeremy Blaschke, "Parasite Soup: Faith and Science in the History of Parasitology," *Zygon* 57, no. 2 (2022): 344–67.

39. For the distinction between "nomological" and "historical" science, see Robert Larmer, "The Many Inadequate Justifications of Methodological Naturalism," *Organon F* 26, no. 1 (2019): 5–24, esp. 16–21; and Stephen C. Meyer, "The Methodological Equivalence of Design and Descent," in *The Creation Hypothesis: Scientific Evidence for an Intelligent Designer*, ed. J. P. Moreland (Downers Grove, IL: InterVarsity, 1994), 67–112. In my analysis of scientific fallibilism below, I discuss epistemic questions surrounding historical science.

past acted miraculously in creation. If we limit historical science to natural explanations, we will miss much of the truth.

Dogmatic Inerrancy

In the nineteenth and twentieth centuries, both liberal and conservative theologians tried to avoid conflicts between science and theology. On the liberal side, science was a key reason that they rejected the authority of Scripture, downplayed its supernatural elements, and reinterpreted many of its classical doctrines. Although conservatives tended to "conserve" the received tradition, they, too, adjusted certain doctrines in light of science, but in a more subtle and protracted way. When science compelled them to reinterpret Scripture, they did so under the constraints of inerrancy. But over time their avoidance of conflict with established science shifted the grounds of inerrancy from dogmatic to evidential criteria (that is, the inerrancy of Scripture was always upheld without in any way contradicting the scientific consensus).[40] Biblical passages could only speak authoritatively to domains that did not conflict with current science; when conflicts arose, the biblical passages had to be reinterpreted.

The crisis over Scripture in nineteenth-century Britain is worth revisiting because the patterns that played out among historical critics and theologians then are resurfacing today.[41] In the early part of that century, virtually all churchmen held to the inerrancy of the Bible.[42] Holy Scripture was considered a supernatural, divine revelation, without epistemic rival. This high bibliology prevented German higher criticism from gaining any traction in Britain.[43] For the British mind, the Bible was "a volume inspired throughout from cover to cover, whose statements, whether they related to science, or history, or religion, were to be accepted without questioning.

40. In what follows, I have no time to defend but will simply assume that inerrancy is a classical and very biblical doctrine. See Mark Thompson, "The Divine Investment in Truth: Toward a Theological Account of Biblical Inerrancy," in *Do Historical Matters Matter to Faith? A Critical Appraisal of Modern and Postmodern Approaches to Scripture*, ed. James Hoffmeier and Dennis Magary (Wheaton: Crossway, 2012), 71–97; D. A. Carson, ed., *The Enduring Authority of the Christian Scriptures* (Grand Rapids: Eerdmans, 2016).

41. My account draws on Nigel Cameron, *Biblical Higher Criticism and the Defense of Infallibilism in 19th Century Britain* (Lewiston, ME: Edwin Mellen, 1987).

42. Some distinguish between "inerrancy" and "infallibility"—for discussion, see Daniel Treier, "Scripture and Hermeneutics," in *The Cambridge Companion to Evangelical Theology*, ed. Timothy Larsen and Daniel Treier (Cambridge: Cambridge University Press, 2007), 38–40.

43. The English deists certainly raised problems in the eighteenth century, but their unorthodox beliefs would never overturn the received Scripture doctrine. See Henning Graf Reventlow, *The Authority of the Bible and the Rise of the Modern World*, trans. John Bowden (Philadelphia: Fortress, 1985).

The Bible was treated as something apart from all other writings. Its various books were regarded as being all on the same level of inspiration, and as having been produced under a divine superintendence, which protected them from any material error."[44]

This consensus began to unravel with the 1860 publication of *Essays and Reviews*, a controversial collection of essays by Anglican churchmen defending the new German higher criticism. In one of the essays, Benjamin Jowett sets the terms of the coming debate when he describes the work of the exegete as recovering "the meaning . . . of the words as they first struck on the ears or flashed before the eyes of those who heard and read them. He has to transfer himself to another age; to imagine that he is a disciple of Christ or Paul; to disengage himself from all that follows. The history of Christendom is nothing to him; but only the scene at Galilee or Jerusalem. . . . All the after-thoughts of theology are nothing to him. . . . His object is to read Scripture *like any other book*."[45] Jowett and his fellow critics read the Bible without theological constraints, interpreting it like any other book, and they implied that historical, moral, and other errors were real textual possibilities. This was in stark contrast to the classical side, for whom inerrancy was an antecedent standpoint from which exegesis proceeds.[46]

Most believers at the time dismissed *Essays and Reviews* as spiritually destructive, but pious examples of historical criticism would arise in subsequent decades. In the field of New Testament studies, the "Cambridge Trio"—B. F. Westcott, J. B. Lightfoot, and Fenton A. J. Hort—developed "believing criticism," a new style of critical scholarship. They adopted the critical method cautiously, "arriving at markedly conservative conclusions on almost every matter, so much so as to arouse the particular ire of liberal commentators."[47] Their devout scholarship brought publicity to the principles of higher criticism, as did the infamous trial of the Old Testament scholar W. Robertson Smith (1846–94), who was dismissed from the Free Church of Scotland but acquitted of heresy. As a new generation of British evangelicals entered the fray, it became clear that historical-critical arguments deserved a more rigorous response.

44. Vernon Storr, *The Development of English Theology in the Nineteenth Century, 1800–1860* (London: Longmans, Green, 1913), 177. Storr's position is representative.

45. Benjamin Jowett, "On the Interpretation of Scripture," in *Essays and Reviews: The 1860 Text and Its Reading*, ed. Victor Shea and William Whitla (Charlottesville: University Press of Virginia, 2000), 481–82, my emphasis.

46. Nigel Cameron, "Inspiration and Criticism: The Nineteenth-Century Crisis," *Tyndale Bulletin* 35 (1984): 141.

47. Cameron, *Biblical Higher Criticism*, 40.

The problem was that the older tradition held to inerrancy on *dogmatic* grounds; inerrancy was a presupposition that conditioned exegesis. Let us call their position "dogmatic inerrancy." In nontheological and colloquial discourse, "dogmatic" is a derogatory word, a flawed character trait, a lack of virtue: "Dogmatism is a property of people, not beliefs; that somebody is dogmatic about some belief is a demerit of the person, not of the belief."[48] The "dogmatic" in dogmatic inerrancy signals something wholly different, a virtue rooted in the right appraisal of Scripture. As Herman Bavinck notes, "Over against all human beings, Scripture occupies a position so high that, instead of subjecting itself to their criticism, it judges them in all their thoughts and desires. And this has been the Christian church's position toward Scripture at all times. . . . For a dogma is not based on the results of any historical-critical research but only on the witness of God, on the self-testimony of Holy Scripture."[49] Far from being a demerit of the person, holding the inerrancy of Scripture dogmatically is a function of *humility*. It is faith seeking understanding and holding as true all that God has revealed to us in Scripture (see Heidelberg Catechism, answer 21). Pride and hubris are antithetical to the real meaning of dogmatic inerrancy.

The new generation of scholars, however, were no longer satisfied with this approach. Although they were still convinced on dogmatic grounds that Scripture was wholly true, even on matters of history, they strategically chose to engage the critics on their own terms. At first, they only engaged historical-critical scholarship apologetically *with no intention of changing their own prior assumptions about the truthfulness of Scripture,* but

> what began as an [apologetic] debating ploy had the unintended effect of withdrawing the conservatives from their commitment to the relevance of doctrine to the debate. That is, in their concern to engage the "critics" on the merits of their historical-critical arguments, the conservatives unwittingly evacuated their own distinctive position. They engaged in detailed historical discussion as they sought to establish the unreasonableness of critical reconstructions. Sometimes they succeeded, sometimes they did not; but the net result of their tactical decision to abandon the defence of distinctive theological warrants for their view of Holy Scripture was the collapse of their position.[50]

48. Robert Roberts and W. Jay Wood, *Intellectual Virtues: An Essay in Regulative Epistemology* (Oxford: Oxford University Press, 2007), 194.

49. Herman Bavinck, *Reformed Dogmatics*, ed. John Bolt, trans. John Vriend, 4 vols. (Grand Rapids: Baker Academic, 2003–8), 1:441.

50. Nigel Cameron, "Scripture and Criticism: Evangelicals, Orthodoxy and the Continuing Problem of Conservatism," in *A Pathway into the Holy Scripture*, ed. Philip Satterthwaite and David F. Wright (Grand Rapids: Eerdmans, 1994), 244.

In order to refute the critics, the traditionalists set aside dogmatic axioms and appealed to narrowly historical arguments. Dogmatic inerrancy became passé and the evidential approach became the new norm—let us call this position "evidential inerrancy." By the end of the nineteenth century, "the remaining conservatives found themselves marooned in a new consensus in which appeal to dogmatic or traditional considerations was no longer possible."[51]

So much for the history lesson, but the fallout from this episode still haunts us. The central question, Nigel Cameron writes, "was about whether what the Bible said was to be believed *because the Bible said it*, or whether it should be believed, or disbelieved, on the grounds of critical historical investigation"[52]—and, we might add, on the grounds of *scientific* investigation. Recent debate in science and theology follows the same script. For instance, evangelical scholars who are trying to "rescue" the Bible from the historical Adam usually assume evidential inerrancy; biblical authority is maintained on evidential, not dogmatic, grounds.[53] The tendency is to privilege arguments that do not violate historical or empirical findings, while dogmatic claims rooted in revelational testimony are ruled out as fideistic.

Evidential inerrantists follow a typical pattern. They inherit doctrinal formulations that overlap with mainstream scientific theories. For a time, any conflicts between the two are usually ignored or tolerated without quibble. Then, at some point, a later generation emerges that has changed its assessment of the science; they now judge it to be epistemically secure and will not accept any doctrinal formulations that conflict with said science. The only way to avoid conflict between the book of Scripture and the book of nature, within the constraints of inerrancy, is to reassess the relevant biblical texts, perhaps by invoking some kind of accommodation, reinterpreting the text, or, more radically, downgrading biblical authority. This process leaves doctrines like the Trinity or the parousia unaffected because they are not, and perhaps cannot be, affected by science. But the tendency of this evidential tradition is to distort and eventually dismantle the doctrine of inerrancy itself.[54]

51. Cameron, "Scripture and Criticism," 245.

52. Nigel Cameron, "The Logic of Infallibility: An Evangelical Doctrine at Issue," *Scottish Bulletin of Evangelical Theology* 1 (1983): 42, emphasis original.

53. E.g., see Christopher Hays and Stephen Lane Herring, "Adam and the Fall," in *Evangelical Faith and the Challenge of Historical Criticism*, ed. Christopher Hays and Christopher Ansberry (Grand Rapids: Baker Academic, 2013), 24–54. For another positive assessment of believing criticism, see Mark Noll, *Between Faith and Criticism: Evangelicals, Scholarship, and the Bible in America*, 2nd ed. (Grand Rapids: Baker, 1991).

54. See Peter Enns, *The Evolution of Adam: What the Bible Does and Doesn't Say about Human Origins* (Grand Rapids: Baker Academic, 2012); Hays and Ansberry, *Evangelical Faith*. In later chapters, I will engage with concrete examples of evidential inerrancy.

Dogmatic inerrancy is a horse of a different color. God's essential attributes of faithfulness and truth are the warrant for the utter trustworthiness of Scripture. As divine discourse, Scripture is vested with divine authority. God cannot lie (Num. 23:19; Heb. 6:18), and therefore scientific theories will always be epistemically inferior to the canonical words of God; the text absorbs the world, rather than the world the text.[55] Sometimes the scientific or historical consensus will conflict with firmly held doctrinal positions—which poses a challenge to Christian belief and demands an apologetic response—but scientific and historical inquiry are usually not the ultimate reason Christians have those doctrinal beliefs in the first place.[56] Since it is infallible Scripture that authorizes doctrinal beliefs, they are warranted on dogmatic—not scientific—grounds.[57]

Scientific Fallibilism

Natural science stands on holy ground. Science by its very nature investigates God's works of creation and providence. Secular habits encourage us to think of "nature" as something abstract, objective, and value neutral, as if disconnected from the triune God. But, as Bavinck reminds us, what we call nature is already a function of God revealing himself throughout his creation: "The world itself rests on revelation; revelation is the presupposition, the foundation, the secret of all that exists in all its forms. The deeper science pushes its investigations, the more clearly will it discover that revelation underlies all created being."[58] The deeper we go scientifically, the more the truth of general revelation confronts us, not only in its objectivity but also in its mystery, both of which mirror the creator.

But the question is whether science can ever discover genuine knowledge about the world. Antirealists and realists disagree. Antirealism denies that

55. I am co-opting George Lindbeck's famous remark: "It is the text, so to speak, which absorbs the world, rather than the world the text" (George Lindbeck, *The Nature of Doctrine* [Philadelphia: Westminster, 1984], 118). While I have fundamental quarrels with his cultural-linguistic approach, this line evokes the core difference between evidential and dogmatic inerrancy.

56. I agree with Plantinga, *Where the Conflict Really Lies*, 120: "If Christian belief is true, the warrant for belief in special divine action doesn't come from quantum mechanics or current science or indeed any science at all; these beliefs have their own independent source of warrant. That means that in case of conflict between Christian belief and current science, it isn't automatically current science that has more warrant or positive epistemic status; perhaps the warrant enjoyed by Christian belief is greater than that enjoyed by the conflicting scientific belief."

57. In response to the worry that I am guilty of circular reasoning—i.e., I appeal to Scripture's infallibility in order to justify a dogmatic sense of inerrancy—see John Frame, *The Doctrine of the Knowledge of God* (Phillipsburg, NJ: Presbyterian & Reformed, 1987), 130–33.

58. Herman Bavinck, *The Philosophy of Revelation* (London: Longmans, Green, 1909), 27.

scientific theories are ultimately true, that science is ever able to discern the world's underlying ontology, especially those entities that we cannot see. Antirealists justify this view on the grounds that scientific theories are only empirically adequate, or instrumentally effective, or underdetermined by the data—but not ontologically *true*.[59] Realism, by contrast, emphasizes the intelligibility of creation, that scientific theories can be accurate descriptions of the natural world. While we are typically expected to choose between these two positions, biblical realism instead combines insights from both antirealism and realism.

Let us begin with antirealism. Just because a scientific theory makes testable predictions that are confirmed empirically does not mean it is true or approximately true. The historical record shows many theories that were effective in their day but are mistaken by current standards.[60] Based on what we now know, we dismiss those theories as patently false. Antirealists infer from these past failures that our *current* theories are also very likely false.[61] This striking conclusion, otherwise known as a "pessimistic induction," relies on the dismal record of past theories like caloric theory or the Rankine vortex theory of thermodynamics.

Caloric theory was the eighteenth-century idea that heat is a fluid that moves from one body to another. The theory successfully predicted the adiabatic process and the speed of sound in air. Past scientists used caloric theory to predict that all gases have the same rate of expansion, that pressure lowers the freezing point, and that steam engines with higher pressures are more efficient. Scientists had similar success in the nineteenth century with William Rankine's thermodynamic theory, which described heat as vortices rotating in gas. Rankine made accurate predictions, including the entropy function, the cooling effect of carbon dioxide, and the behavior of air under constant pressure. The caloric theory and the Rankine vortex theory made specific and confirmed predictions, yet by present standards both theories have been shown to be false.

This pattern is repeated with phlogiston theory, Fresnel's theory of light and the luminiferous ether, Kekulé's theory of the Benzene molecule, Bohr's 1913 model of the atom, and the list goes on.[62] In fairness, however, we

59. For a helpful discussion of realism and antirealism, see Del Ratzsch, *Science and Its Limits: The Natural Sciences in Christian Perspective*, 2nd ed. (Downers Grove, IL: IVP Academic, 2000), 73–91.

60. Thomas Kuhn blew the whistle in *The Structure of Scientific Revolutions* (Chicago: University of Chicago Press, 1962).

61. For an important argument along these lines, see Larry Laudan, "A Confutation of Convergent Realism," *Philosophy of Science* 48, no. 1 (1981): 19–49.

62. My specific examples are drawn from Peter Vickers, "A Confrontation of Convergent Realism," *Philosophy of Science* 80, no. 2 (2013): 189–211; and Timothy Lyons, "Scientific Realism and the

should note that many of these theories—though incomplete in various ways—were superior to caloric theory. Sometimes theories are considered "false" because they are only valid under certain conditions, but they are still "true" as approximations (e.g., Kekulé's work opened up the whole field of organic chemistry). Nevertheless, as one scholar remarks, "the history of science seems to provide compelling inductive evidence that the successful theories we accept today are also apt to be discarded in the future."[63]

Realists dispute this pessimistic induction by noting that current theories are far more successful and mature than older theories ever were.[64] However, P. Kyle Stanford has bolstered the antirealist argument with *the problem of unconceived alternatives*. According to the historical record, Stanford explains, "We have repeatedly found ourselves encouraged or even forced under the impetus provided by recalcitrant phenomena, unexpected anomalies, and other theoretical pressures to discover *new theories that had remained previously unconceived despite being well confirmed by the evidence available to us*."[65]

Past scientists believed that their theories were the best explanations of the data, but we now know retrospectively that better alternatives existed. Scientists at the time just didn't know it because those theories were unconceived. According to Stanford, scientists today are in the same epistemic boat.[66] And the problem is deeper still: unconceived theories are just the tip

Pessimistic Meta-Modus Tollens," in *Recent Themes in the Philosophy of Science: Scientific Realism and Commonsense*, ed. Steve Clarke and Timothy Lyons (Dordrecht, Netherlands: Kluwer Academic, 2002), 63–90. Vickers and Lyons choose theories that were not merely successful but made *novel* predictions (a criterion used by many realists).

63. K. Brad Wray, "The Pessimistic Induction and the Exponential Growth of Science Reassessed," *Synthese* 190, no. 18 (2013): 4321.

64. E.g., see Stathis Psillos, *Scientific Realism: How Science Tracks Truth* (New York: Routledge, 1999); and Anjan Chakravartty, *A Metaphysics for Scientific Realism: Knowing the Unobservable* (Cambridge: Cambridge University Press, 2007).

65. P. Kyle Stanford, *Exceeding Our Grasp: Science, History, and the Problem of Unconceived Alternatives* (Oxford: Oxford University Press, 2006), 19, my emphasis. See also Stanford, "Unconceived Alternatives and the Strategy of Historical Ostension," in *The Routledge Handbook of Scientific Realism*, ed. Juha Saatsi (New York: Routledge, 2017), 212–24.

66. For responses to Stanford's new induction argument, see Anjan Chakravartty, "What You Don't Know Can't Hurt You: Realism and the Unconceived," *Philosophical Studies* 137 (2008): 149–58; and Emma Ruttkamp-Bloem, "Re-enchanting Realism in Debate with Kyle Stanford," *Journal of General Philosophy of Science* 44, no. 1 (2013): 201–24. But Stanford's argument is more resilient than the older pessimistic induction argument. As Peter Vickers argues, "Its inductive base is said to be stronger than that of the traditional pessimistic induction on the grounds that although scientific *theories* might be significantly different today compared with those advocated many years ago . . . there is no reason to suppose that current *theorists* are better able to come up with possible alternatives than past theorists were." Peter Vickers, "Historical Challenges to Realism," in *The Routledge Handbook of Scientific Realism*, ed. Juha Saatsi (New York: Routledge, 2018), 49, emphasis original.

of the iceberg since many other kinds of entities are similarly unconceived by scientists, including unconceived observations, models, predictions, explanations, methods, instruments, and experiments.[67] Some of these entities may even be *inconceivable*, not merely unconceived.

The problem of unconceived alternatives fits neatly with antirealism, but I shall defend a realist paradigm that I call *scientific fallibilism* that absorbs these antirealist insights. The realism of scientific fallibilism is rooted in the fact that the meaning of God's creation does not depend on human observers but on the creator, the divine Logos (John 1:1–3). We are also God's image bearers, and the rationality of science reflects the perfect wisdom of God who gave us the gift of human reason that can discern the order built into creation. God made the world freely, *ex nihilo*, and this contingency of creation inspired the empirical mode of science. As Barbour notes, "The details of the world must be found by observation rather than rational deduction because God is free and did not have to create any particular kind of universe."[68] Realism is consistent with the doctrine of creation.

One might therefore think that realism should compel Christians to revise or abandon core doctrines when they conflict with the canons of science, given that scientific theories are true descriptions of objective reality. But here we should incorporate the enduring insight of antirealism on the fallibility of science. Christians should be cautious when handling scientific judgments about creation and its history. I am not skeptical about aspects of the historical sciences because of their "subjectivity"; such a view would border on a reckless anti-science attitude at odds with the doctrine of creation.[69] Rather, my point is theological: science as such is fallible and conditioned by human finitude and fallenness. Scientific assessments of the primordial past are especially prone to our epistemic limitations and need the corrective witness of divine revelation.[70]

67. For further elaboration, see Darrell Rowbottom, "Extending the Argument from Unconceived Alternatives: Observations, Models, Predictions, Explanations, Methods, Instruments, Experiments, and Values," *Synthese* 196 (2019): 3947–59.

68. Ian Barbour, *Issues in Science and Religion* (New York: Harper & Row, 1966), 379.

69. As Jitse van der Meer states, "One strategy for dismissal of science appeals to the subjectivity of both the natural and the historical sciences as human enterprises. This fails because their subjectivity does not diminish their reliability" (Jitse van der Meer, "Genesis, Science, and Theories of Origins," in *The Cambridge Companion to Genesis*, ed. Bill Arnold [Cambridge: Cambridge University Press, 2022], 259). Van der Meer's argument is especially useful when responding to parochial anti-science rhetoric. But I note that his main insight applies *with even more force* to classical readings of Scripture that conflict with the historical sciences—namely, the "subjectivity" of these readings does not diminish their reliability. In my view, such conflicts signal the fallibility of mainstream science.

70. Stephen Moroney, *The Noetic Effects of Sin: A Historical and Contemporary Exploration of How Sin Affects Our Thinking* (Lanham, MD: Lexington Books, 2000).

Consider the biblical picture of divine providence unfolding in history. Few people ever grasp what God is really doing at any phase of history, and surface appearances often differ radically from his perspective—like how God orchestrated Joseph's trials to save Israel from famine (Gen. 37–50) or how Israel's captivity in Egypt set up the Lord to reveal himself as redeemer, the mighty warrior who conquers nations and their gods (Exod. 15:11). In the same way, Esther's improbable path to royalty is the means of God's deliverance, and Job (unlike the reader) is unaware of all the heavenly intrigue precipitating his many woes (Job 1:6–12; 2:1–7). In the New Testament, paradoxically, persecution is the seed for early church growth (Acts 8:1–8; 11:19–21). These examples only scratch the surface. God's real purposes, *obscured at the time*, only came to light later in redemptive history. Christ's work of atonement epitomizes this pattern, where we see a radical disconnect between real-time human judgments about the passion and what God was really doing in and through those events (Acts 2:23–24).

This paradox emerges in hindsight. Israelites saw loss, tragedy, and defeat, yet at the time they could not conceive the divine meaning of those very same events. So too for us. As Christians, we struggle to make sense of the loss, tragedy, and defeat in our own lives and the lives of those we love, all of which—apart from revelation—seem disconnected from God's good purposes. This side of the eschaton, we don't have the full picture, so we walk by faith and not by sight, trusting God (2 Cor. 5:7). From God's perspective, these disparate, perplexing events fit within a wider, coherent, *though presently inaccessible*, story.

This epistemology of providence also applies to the natural world. Our understanding of creation is limited by human finitude, the noetic effects of sin, and the fallenness of nature itself. Now we see through a glass darkly (1 Cor. 13:12). Many of the conflicts between Scripture and our best scientific theories are rooted in human fallenness and finitude. God himself allows us to misunderstand the physical data (cf. Isa. 55:8–9). However, since special revelation and creation have the same author, we know that the two must cohere despite present tensions between science and faith. In the face of deep conflicts between science and theology, the biblical realist confesses that the physical data cohere with one or more scientific theories that we are presently unable to conceive—and, perhaps, with theories that may be inconceivable until the eschaton.

The same logic applies to miracles like the exodus, the virgin birth, Jesus changing water to wine, and the resurrection. Naturalistic science is wrong to deny the very possibility of such miracles, for God can change the nature of physical things. But even setting aside the miraculous, our best scientific and historical narratives still rule out large segments of the biblical story that are not obviously miraculous (e.g., creation's original goodness, Adam and Eve as sole progenitors of the human race, and the Canaanite conquest). And yet orthodox Christians *continue* to affirm those parts of Scripture despite the countervailing scientific witness and often without having any plausible alternative theory. Surely there are alternative scientific models that naturalistic science has never dreamed of or imagined. In the face of science-theology conflicts, biblical realists are therefore warranted in believing that one or more unconceived theories exist that *do* explain the data and are compatible with Scripture, even if they presently have no idea what those theories are.[71]

Scientific fallibilism is not radically skeptical about scientific truth. Rather, consistent with realism, its default is to accept the scientific consensus provisionally. All things being equal, I gladly go along with the consensus *unless* it conflicts with a central tenet of Scripture. Biblical realism is obliged to revise or reject any scientific theory that violates a central biblical doctrine, but what counts as a "central" doctrine? A doctrine is central, I suggest, if it passes three tests—namely, if it is (1) clearly attested in Scripture, (2) central to the integrity of Scripture's redemptive-historical story, and (3) widely supported by the catholic tradition especially as it is expressed in the creeds, the major ecumenical councils, and later Protestant confessions.[72] Let us call this clarity-centrality-catholicity yardstick the *canonical criteria*. The clarity test underscores the perspicuity of Scripture and the authority of God's own words; God's clear words of special revelation are more reliable than scientific interpretations of the natural world. The centrality test emphasizes the importance of doctrines that are connected directly to the gospel or are essential to the coherence of the redemptive-historical narrative. The catholicity test recognizes that the Spirit has been working in and through the church down the ages and that the insights from the communion of saints correct our own limited understanding. Let us say that when science and Christian doctrine conflict, and when the doctrine satisfies the canonical criteria, then believers are warranted in rejecting (or revising) the offending scientific theory.

71. A potential rejoinder, using the logic of my argument, is that perhaps there are unconceived *naturalistic* theories that may explain such events without appealing to special revelation. Perhaps so, but the relevant point here is that *given* scientific fallibilism, appealing to special revelation is the most reliable option.

72. For my earlier defense of these three tests, see Madueme, "Most Vulnerable Part of the Whole Christian Account," 240–45.

At this point, some will accuse me of special pleading and complain that my earlier points on behalf of scientific fallibilism apply equally to theology—indeed to my *own* theologizing (sauce for the goose is sauce for the gander!). Human finitude and fallenness influence the theories of theologians just as much as they do the theorizing of scientists. Aspects of biblical realism may turn out to be wrong, and besides, God's common grace enables scientists to correct their errors, to monitor the ethical consequences of scientific research, and so on.

But more needs to be said. First, much Christian academic scholarship tends to privilege the insights of science over classical readings of Scripture. Since special revelation is authoritative over natural science, biblical realism resists that tendency. Special revelation and the Christian doctrine we derive from it are antecedent commitments that should shape theory construction in natural science.[73]

Second, God promised to help the church grow in its knowledge of Scripture, but while he may aid scientists in their work,[74] he never extends that particular promise to them. For example, Paul prays that the Holy Spirit will help the apostles (and, by implication, all believers) grow in their knowledge of God (Eph. 1:17–18).[75] He makes a similar point in 1 Corinthians 2:10–16: only the Spirit of God comprehends the things of God, and those with the Spirit gain understanding (v. 12). This knowledge mediated by the Spirit is the knowledge of Scripture rather than the natural world ("wisdom of God" [v. 7]). The psalmist often prays for God's help in understanding the truth of Scripture: "Open my eyes, that I may behold wondrous things out of your law" (Ps. 119:18). Indeed, Hebrews 11:3 suggests that without faith we lack true knowledge of creation: "By faith we understand that the universe was created by the word of God, so that what is seen was not made out of things that are visible."

Third, science-theology discourse (especially in evangelical settings) commonly equates general revelation with the physical data of creation.

73. On how religious doctrine shapes theory construction, see the different accounts in Roy Clouser, *The Myth of Religious Neutrality: An Essay on the Hidden Role of Religious Belief in Theories*, rev. ed. (Notre Dame, IN: University of Notre Dame Press, 2005); Nicholas Wolterstorff, *Reason within the Bounds of Religion*, 2nd ed. (Grand Rapids: Eerdmans, 1984); and Alvin Plantinga, *Warranted Christian Belief* (Oxford: Oxford University Press, 2000).

74. For the example of two scientists—Johannes Kepler (1571–1630) and George Washington Carver (ca. 1865–1943)—who believed that God played an instrumental role in their scientific discoveries, see Carola Baumgardt, *Johannes Kepler: Life and Letters* (New York: Philosophical Library, 1951); and Linda McMurry, *George Washington Carver: Scientist & Symbol* (Oxford: Oxford University Press, 1981).

75. Clinton Arnold, *Ephesians*, Zondervan Exegetical Commentary on the New Testament (Grand Rapids: Zondervan, 2010), 104.

In a 1987 article, David Diehl argues that the North American doctrine of general revelation is incomplete and needs expansion beyond its traditional boundaries.[76] His core thesis is that the nature and laws of creation that scientists discover are part of God's general revelation. He concedes that passages like Psalm 19:1, Romans 1:20, and Acts 14:17 concern the knowledge of God but then insists that this knowledge "comes by and with the knowledge of creation."[77] This knowledge of creation, he claims, is authoritative and infallible: "Not only does theology have a reliable and divinely authoritative source but so does science."[78] In this division of labor, theologians interpret special revelation (Scripture), scientists interpret general revelation (creation)—God is the author of both.

This approach has historical precedent in the patristic and medieval tradition of interpreting Scripture and nature as God's "two books."[79] For scholars in this tradition, however, the idea of nature as a metaphorical "book" had a more theological than empirical connotation. But by the time of the Scientific Revolution, leading thinkers (e.g., Francis Bacon, Johannes Kepler, Galileo Galilei, and Robert Boyle) were consistently using the metaphor to relate divine revelation to the empirical findings of natural science. God has written two texts—one physical, one linguistic—and we must interpret both of them correctly. The metaphor became a justification for harmonizing science and the Bible, which would eventually undermine the authority of Scripture. The historian G. Blair Nelson explains: "In practice, passages of the Bible bore the brunt of reinterpretation more often than scientific understandings of nature. Rarely did the process work in the other direction. Those who expressed discomfort at these exegetical changes might complain about that imbalance, but most writers in the religious press celebrated these new interpretations as a clear sign of the progress of religion in their day."[80]

By the lights of biblical realism, this equation of general revelation with the physical data of creation is a bridge too far. Here I concur with

76. David Diehl, "Evangelicalism and General Revelation: An Unfinished Agenda," *Journal of the Evangelical Theological Society* 30, no. 4 (1987): 441–55.

77. Diehl, "Evangelicalism and General Revelation," 448.

78. Diehl, "Evangelicalism and General Revelation," 449.

79. James J. Bono, *The Word of God and the Languages of Men: Interpreting Nature in Early Modern Science and Medicine* (Madison: University of Wisconsin Press, 1995); Peter M. J. Hess, "God's Two Books: Special Revelation and Natural Science in the Christian West," in *Bridging Science and Religion*, ed. Ted Peters and Gaymon West (Minneapolis: Fortress, 2003), 123–40.

80. G. Blair Nelson, "Ethnology and the 'Two Books': Some Nineteenth-Century Americans on Preadamist Polygenism," in *Nature and Scripture in the Abrahamic Religions: 1700–Present*, ed. Jitse M. van der Meer and Scott Mandelbrote (Leiden: Brill, 2008), 173–74.

G. C. Berkouwer: "It will not do simply to equate the knowledge of nature with the knowledge of God's general revelation, for this revelation deals with the knowledge of God *himself*. In our opinion, therefore, it is wrong to say, as is sometimes done, that the natural sciences 'investigate' God's general revelation."[81] Scripture regularly testifies that it is the knowledge of God (and his attributes)—*not* the empirical data of nature—that is mediated in and through creation.[82] The psalmist speaks of the sun in the heavens declaring the greatness of God (Ps. 19:1–6). Other nature psalms marvel at how creation is constantly displaying the attributes of God, his eternality, omnipotence, wisdom, and greatness (Pss. 8, 93, and 104). The vastness of the universe and the unimaginable variety within the animal kingdom remind us of God's infinite wisdom and power (Job 38 and 39). God is disclosing himself throughout the natural world: "For since the creation of the world God's invisible qualities—his eternal power and divine nature—have been clearly seen, being understood from what has been made, so that people are without excuse" (Rom. 1:20 NIV). In short, the content of general revelation is the knowledge of God, not the findings of science.

However, Richard Langer contends that this view of general revelation is overly restrictive. If "revelation" is always with reference to God, then this conclusion must apply equally to general *and* special revelation. "But certainly," writes Langer, "not every passage of Scripture (special revelation) is ostensibly about God."[83] As he goes on to note, Scripture covers a wide range of topics: "Some passages deal with the death of an evil queen, and others with a famine in Canaan. Still other passages describe a person committing adultery. On the surface, the content of these passages is certainly not about God. However, in such cases it is generally understood that the *proximate* object of the passage is a queen or a famine or an act of adultery, but the *ultimate* object of the passage is God in the sense that

<hr/>

81. G. C. Berkouwer, *General Revelation* (Grand Rapids: Eerdmans, 1955), 288–89, emphasis original. For a similar perspective, see Jason Van Vliet, "The Two Books Debate: What If Scripture and Science Seem to Say Different Things?," in *Correctly Handling the Word of Truth: Reformed Hermeneutics Today*, ed. Mees te Velde and Gerhard Visscher (Eugene, OR: Wipf & Stock, 2014), 1–16.

82. Nicolaas H. Gootjes, "General Revelation and Science: Reflections on a Remark in Report 28," *Calvin Theological Journal* 30, no. 1 (1995): 94–107. See also Nicholas H. Gootjes, "What Does God Reveal in the Grand Canyon?," in *Teaching and Preaching the Word: Studies in Dogmatics and Homiletics*, ed. Cornelis Van Dam (Winnipeg: Premier, 2010), 3–21; Bruce A. Demarest, *General Revelation: Historical Views and Contemporary Issues* (Grand Rapids: Zondervan, 1982), esp. 227–62; Mary Vanden Berg, "What General Revelation Does (and Does Not) Tell Us," *Perspectives on Science and Christian Faith* 62, no. 1 (2010): 16–24, esp. 18–21.

83. Richard Langer, "General Revelation, Science and Integration: Objections and Opportunities," *Christian Education Journal* 16, no. 3 (2019): 431.

the passage reveals something of God's character or purpose or actions in history."[84] According to the classical doctrine of inerrancy, even when Scripture makes assertions about the "proximate" object of a passage instead of the "ultimate" object—namely, God—those assertions are still considered infallibly true. In the same way, Langer argues, even if general revelation is ultimately about God, any relevant proximate realities are infallibly true as well.

Responding to Langer, I note that Scripture never describes general revelation as coming to know God in and through interpreting the *scientific* details of creation; in those instances when Scripture describes creation in relation to God, it is always creation in an ordinary, nontechnical, pretheoretical sense. More importantly, following the logic of Langer's proposal, just as the proximate details of special revelation are delimited *canonically*, so too the proximate details of general revelation are delimited *canonically*—authority should therefore apply, if at all, to those details about creation described *in Scripture*, not those derived extrabiblically by scientists. In any case, I propose that natural science should be theorized not in terms of general revelation at all but as an aspect of God's common grace, or better, of the *cultural mandate* (Gen. 1:26–28). The human capacity to study creation using all the tools of natural science lies in the astonishing fact that we are made in God's image. God's words are therefore essential for guiding us as we explore the world God has made; science should submit to Scripture, not compete with it.

Nevertheless, let us see what follows if—for the sake of argument—we take the more expansive view of general revelation that includes the physical facts of nature. In that case, we would construe both general and special revelation as equally authoritative modes of divine discourse.[85] Yet even then, scientific theorizing about creation is not on a level playing field with the exegesis of Scripture. There is a crucial asymmetry between Scripture and the natural world: creation has a kind of *ontological priority* to Scripture. As Vern Poythress explains, "[General revelation] comes prior to the special words in the Bible and forms the indispensable environment in which the Bible makes sense."[86] We can only read the Bible because God has already created the world and its creatures; God must first bring me into existence

84. Langer, "General Revelation," 431.

85. On creation as divine speech, see Vern Poythress, *Redeeming Science: A God-Centered Approach* (Wheaton: Crossway, 2006), 41. See also Kevin Vanhoozer, a former student of Poythress, who has defended creation as a form of divine *communicative* action. Kevin Vanhoozer, *Remythologizing Theology: Divine Action, Passion, and Authorship* (Cambridge: Cambridge University Press, 2010), 278.

86. Poythress, *Redeeming Science*, 44.

by creation before I can encounter Scripture as special revelation. Divine providence sustains my physical being (e.g., the eyes I need to read) and allows me to learn a language like English or Mandarin, all before I ever encounter Scripture.

Yet Scripture as a form of special revelation is in a different category because it is mediated *through words* and therefore has *epistemological priority* over creation.[87] Creation lacks the infallible *linguistic* form of the Bible. This epistemological priority of Scripture creates an asymmetry between creation and Scripture. Poythress clarifies the point:

> In this respect, the formulations by a human scientist are more like a commentary on the Bible than they are like the Bible itself. The commentary, as a human product, is fallible, whereas the Bible is infallible. But even this does not quite capture the differences. The human commentator on the Bible works from a starting message in the Bible that is already human language. Other commentators and ordinary people can compare the commentary with the original text and judge for themselves the value of the commentary. By contrast, when we formulate the laws of aerodynamics, there is no linguistically available original to which to compare the human formulations. It is as if we just had commentaries, with no known original text on which they are commenting. In fact, the analogy with commentaries breaks down completely, because commentaries depend in an essential way on interaction with an original text of human language.[88]

Although I believe we should not include the empirical details about nature within our concept of general revelation, even *if* one takes that view the epistemic authority of Scripture will always be more reliable than our best scientific interpretations of nature.

In summary, Scripture cannot be broken (John 10:35). The main purpose of Scripture is redemptive-historical, to make us "wise for salvation through faith in Christ Jesus" (2 Tim. 3:15). But this primary function of Scripture is not detached from what God has said and done in history and creation. Scientific fallibilism recognizes that the epistemological priority of Scripture functions on at least two levels for science. The spiritual virtues commended in Scripture, like honesty (Prov. 12:17), wisdom (Ps. 111:10; James

---

87. I am drawing on Poythress, *Redeeming Science*, 45–46, but I have modified his language.

88. Poythress, *Redeeming Science*, 45–46. For clarification, I take it that when Poythress compares scientific formulations to "commentaries" on the Bible, his point is that science offers *interpretations* of creation, just as Bible commentators offer *interpretations* of Scripture. In this view, science and exegesis are both therefore interpretative exercises, but the asymmetry lies in the fact that Scripture is *linguistic* while creation is not.

1:5), and love (1 Cor. 13), should frame the work of believing scientists.[89] Scripture also makes claims about creation, history, and human beings that should serve as an interpretative framework for scientific theorizing. On both fronts, scientific fallibilism receives the canonical testimony as a lamp to the feet and a light for the path. Consequently, the first three commitments of biblical realism—supernaturalism, dogmatic inerrancy, and scientific fallibilism—imply that believers should accept the central doctrines of the faith with confidence even if they contradict scientific orthodoxy.

Doctrinal Confidence

Before the rise of historical consciousness in the nineteenth century, doctrines were embraced as timelessly true and binding on everyone everywhere. This static view meshed well with the idea of a faith once for all delivered unto the saints (Jude 3), but it was also partly indebted to Hellenistic philosophy. Premodern Roman Catholic, Eastern Orthodox, and Protestant theologians would all have resisted the idea that doctrine evolves over time. The words of the First Vatican Council in 1870 captured this widespread sensibility: "That meaning of the sacred dogmas is ever to be maintained which has once been declared by holy mother church, and there must never be any abandonment of this sense under the pretext or in the name of a more profound understanding."[90] Vatican I officials were emphasizing the immutability of sacred doctrine. In the same conciliar document, they laid down this stark judgment: "If anyone says that it is possible that at some time, given the advancement of knowledge, a sense may be assigned to the dogmas propounded by the church which is different from that which the church has understood and understands: let him be anathema."[91] In other words, if doctrines are historically conditioned and constantly changing, is theology condemned to be tossed back and forth by the waves, blown here and there by every wind of teaching? Can tradition escape the fallibility of reason, ever learning and never able to come to the knowledge of the truth (2 Tim. 3:7)? The idea of doctrinal development seemed to jeopardize any notion of an enduring tradition.

89. Ordinary science incarnates many of these Christian virtues to an astonishing degree. Scientific research is (very often at least) an encouraging example of collaboration between humans, for the common good. My thanks to Lydia Jaeger for this reminder.

90. First Vatican Council, Session 3 (April 24, 1870), "Dogmatic Constitution on the Catholic Faith," in *Decrees of the Ecumenical Councils*, ed. Norman Tanner, 2 vols. (Washington, DC: Georgetown University Press, 1990), 2:809.

91. First Vatican Council, "Dogmatic Constitution on the Catholic Faith," 2:811.

Although premodern theology took static views of doctrine for granted, some church fathers did acknowledge implicitly that doctrine can (and does) develop. As far back as the fourth century, Gregory of Nazianzus remarked that truths like the Trinity, which the Spirit had hidden from the disciples, were gradually being revealed to the church.[92] In the same century, Hilary of Poitiers clarified how "the errors of heretics and blasphemers" drove the church to develop the doctrine of God and unfold the inner meaning of Scripture.[93] Vincent of Lérins, a Gallic monk, shaped premodern thinking about doctrinal stability when he famously said, "In the catholic church itself especial care must be taken that we hold to that which has been believed everywhere, always, and by all men."[94] His formula aimed to preserve central truths of the faith but also left room for doctrinal progress.[95] These early insights notwithstanding, a prevailing consciousness of doctrinal development only emerged after the Reformation.

Early Reformers like the Westminster divines showed some awareness of doctrinal development when they conceded the fallibility of their confessions (Westminster Confession of Faith 31.4). They believed in a permanent doctrinal truth expressed in Scripture and discerned in the fathers; they saw the Spirit guiding the church throughout history into a growing understanding of that truth (which implies progress at the level of dogmas). Later Protestant theologians Robert Rainy (1826–1906) and fellow Scotsman James Orr were more explicit about development from a Protestant perspective.[96] But the decisive shift came with John Henry Newman's *An Essay on the Development of Christian Doctrine*, published in 1845.[97] Newman, a former leader in the Anglican church, scandalized the Protestant community of Victorian Britain when he converted to Roman Catholicism. In his work on doctrinal development, he gave reasons for rejecting the view that true doctrines remain static. Instead, he proposed that Christian

92. Gregory of Nazianzus, *Orat.* 31.27, cited in J. Stevenson, ed., *Creeds, Councils and Controversies* (London: SPCK, 1966), 59.

93. Hilary, *De Trinitate* 2.2, cited in Maurice Wiles, *The Making of Christian Doctrine: A Study in the Principles of Early Doctrinal Development* (Cambridge: Cambridge University Press, 1967), 32–33. For the information on Hilary and Gregory of Nazianzus, I am drawing from Peter Toon, *The Development of Doctrine in the Church* (Grand Rapids: Eerdmans, 1979), xiiin2.

94. Vincent of Lérins, *The Commonitory* 2.3, in *Early Medieval Theology*, ed. and trans. George McCracken (London: Westminster John Knox, 1957), 38.

95. Thomas Guarino, *Vincent of Lérins and the Development of Christian Doctrine* (Grand Rapids: Baker Academic, 2013), xii.

96. Robert Rainy, *The Delivery and Development of Christian Doctrine* (Edinburgh: T&T Clark, 1874); James Orr, *The Progress of Dogma* (London: Hodder & Stoughton, 1901).

97. John Henry Newman, *An Essay on the Development of Christian Doctrine* (London: James Toovey, 1845).

dogmas such as the incarnation were more dynamic; such doctrines were already implicit in Scripture but then, over time, evolved through ecclesiastical tradition as the church grew in its understanding of divine revelation. As Kenneth Stewart remarks, "Up to and including the Newman era, the dominant Protestant outlook had been that medieval theology had departed from apostolic and patristic clarity; such development as there had been was therefore primarily by way of decline and departure."[98]

Those were growing pains. No theologian today would contest the fact of doctrinal development. The real issue, intensified by natural science, is how to distinguish faithful developments from sham corruptions. Over the past three centuries, scientific theories have put pressure on a range of doctrines, including special creation, the historicity of Adam and Eve, monogenism, the doctrine of original sin, and our soul-body constitution, to name a few.[99] To accept the present conclusions of science as binding implies that for almost two millennia Christians gravely misunderstood God's Word. If conventional science is correct, then generations of Christians entertained flawed ideas about human origins, our nature as creatures *and* as sinners, and the meaning of physical death. The same is true for millions of believers across the world today who are allegedly mistaken about core aspects of reality, including their knowledge of God. No doubt, well-meaning people are wrong on all kinds of things, but are we really saying the church had to wait eighteen centuries for the darkness to lift?

The problem is that if every new conflict between science and theology is always resolved in favor of science, then we will keep revising our doctrinal formulations, and those revisions will keep undermining the reality-depicting nature of Scripture. This dynamic, whatever we wish to call it, is not genuine doctrinal development. As David Yeago argues, doctrinal development happens when the stable *judgments* of Scripture are faithfully rendered using different *conceptual terms*, as when the implicit theology of Scripture in Isaiah 45:21–24 and Philippians 2:9–11 develops into Nicaea's *homoousios*.[100] If science always prompts the church to reinterpret Scripture, it is not clear that canonical judgments are being rendered in fresh conceptual terms. More often than not, science is downgrading Scripture, turning it into something less reality-depicting and thus limiting its epistemic reach to merely "spiritual" domains.

---

98. Kenneth Stewart, *In Search of Ancient Roots: The Christian Past and the Evangelical Identity Crisis* (Downers Grove, IL: IVP Academic, 2017), 66.

99. In later chapters of this book, I shall elaborate on these and other related matters.

100. David Yeago, "The New Testament and Nicene Dogma: A Contribution to the Recovery of Theological Exegesis," *Pro Ecclesia* 3, no. 2 (1994): 152–64.

Even the Protestant critique of late medieval Roman Catholicism was a call to recover *earlier* truths that had been lost to corrupt tradition. The Reformers did not think they were saying anything fundamentally new. It would therefore be surprising if God were to use natural science—a discipline with different epistemic norms from Scripture—to play such a radical and recurring role in shifting the church's understanding of doctrine, shifts that earlier believers would have rejected.[101] While science should correct misinterpretations of Scripture, can biblical doctrines ever challenge the interpretations of science? When a doctrine faces a conflicting judgment of science, believers have several options:

1. Abandon a long-held doctrine.
2. Revise the doctrine in light of science.[102]
3. Preserve the underlying *intent* of the doctrine while changing its particular conceptual formulation in light of science.
4. Reject the scientific theory in favor of the classical interpretation of Scripture.
5. Revise the scientific theory in order to reconcile it with the church's doctrine.

Depending on the particular conflict in view, each strategy has its time and place (and they are not mutually exclusive).[103] The real issue at the root of the conflicts between science and theology is the Christian conviction that Scripture reliably testifies to our space-time reality. Therefore, any doctrines that truly reflect what Scripture teaches are infallible and

---

101. I do not mean to gloss over the ambiguity of history or to ignore how complicated the historical development of doctrine and biblical interpretation really is, including the possibility that science offers common grace insights that correct faulty exegetical assumptions in the tradition. See the bracing, though overstated, argument in Francis Watson, "Genesis before Darwin: Why Scripture Needed Liberating from Science," in *Reading Genesis after Darwin*, ed. Stephen Barton and David Wilkinson (Oxford: Oxford University Press, 2009), 23–37.

102. Sometimes the scientific explanation is the (unstated) occasion for reinterpreting Scripture, but these scholars *justify* the new interpretation post facto as if they are merely engaged in "neutral" biblical exegesis.

103. In her book *Aquinas, Science, and Human Uniqueness: An Integrated Approach to the Question of What Makes Us Human* (Eugene, OR: Cascade Books, 2022), 99–106, Mary Vanden Berg suggests "paradox" as a model for relating science and Scripture in cases of deep conflict. While I accept that core doctrines like the incarnation and the Trinity can be seen as paradoxical from a human perspective, that's different from using the concept of "paradox" to resolve deep conflicts between science and Christian doctrine. The latter move may encourage believers to hold two *contradictory* truths, which is a problematic position reminiscent of the "double truth" notion that medieval theologians around the thirteenth century were accused of espousing. For example, see Richard Dales, "The Origin of the Doctrine of the Double Truth," *Viator* 15 (1984): 169–79.

share derivatively in the authority of Scripture.[104] Protestants will nevertheless insist that the trustworthiness of God's Word does not guarantee
that imperfect readers will interpret the Bible well. Doctrines are fallible
distillations and summaries of infallible Scripture. "Yet too much can be
made of this point," cautions Paul Helm. "For presumably the special revelation has what status it does have in the believing community because
that community believes that at least some of its interpretations admit of
no real debate. To suppose that all interpretations of the special revelation
might be overturned would call into question the whole status of the special
revelation in the community of believers, for it has this status because the
community holds that at least some of the expressions of the special revelation express certain propositions."[105]

The concept of dogmatic rank offers a preliminary way forward in distinguishing "essential" from "nonessential" doctrines. Scripture seems
to have an implicit sense of dogmatic rank—doctrines are not all created equal. Paul, for example, urges us to cherish sound doctrine (1 Tim.
1:8–11), warns against false teaching (4:1–3), and gives the resurrection
pride of place in the gospel (1 Cor. 15:1–8). John insists there is no gospel
without the incarnation (1 John 2:20–23). Here and elsewhere, Scripture
assumes that some doctrines are essential to the gospel, while others by
implication are not.[106]

In Reformational history, Lutheran and Reformed theologians clarified
three levels of doctrinal rank: Primary fundamental articles (articuli fundamentales primarii) include doctrines like the person and work of Christ, sin
and its consequences, and the authority of Scripture. Such doctrines are essential to Christianity and the preservation of faith. Secondary fundamental
articles (articuli fundamentales secundarii)—doctrines like the Lord's Supper
and baptism—are still vital to the faith but are not essential to salvation.
Finally, nonfundamental articles (articuli non-fundamentales)—such as the
nature of angels or the meaning of the antichrist—are biblical but are not

104. As Martin Chemnitz argues in Examination of the Council of Trent, Part I, trans. Fred Kramer
(St. Louis: Concordia Publishing House, 1971), 249, Christians should accept doctrines that "are
not set forth in so many letters and syllables in Scripture but are brought together from clear testimonies of Scripture by way of good, certain, firm, and clear reasoning." Or, as the Westminster
Confession of Faith puts it, "The whole counsel of God, concerning all things necessary for his
own glory, man's salvation, faith, and life, is either expressly set down in Scripture, or by good and
necessary consequence may be deduced from Scripture." Westminster Confession of Faith 1.6, in The
Book of Confessions (Louisville: Office of the General Assembly, Presbyterian Church [USA], 2002),
my emphasis.

105. Paul Helm, The Divine Revelation: The Basic Issues (Westchester, IL: Crossway, 1982), 113.

106. Kevin Vanhoozer, Biblical Authority after Babel: Retrieving the Solas in the Spirit of Mere Protestant Christianity (Grand Rapids: Brazos, 2016), 204–5.

fundamental to salvation.[107] Most Protestant doctrinal taxonomies adopt this tradition of classifying doctrines into primary, secondary, and tertiary levels.[108] Primary or first-order doctrines are fundamental to the faith and shape our lives at the deepest levels.

Aside from ranking doctrines from essential to nonessential, some scholars will also distinguish between the *substance* of a doctrine and its *form*. The way in which theologians conceptualize doctrines will often depend to some degree on their historical and cultural context. The substance of a doctrine is expressible in many linguistic forms.[109] Along these lines, Benno van den Toren tries to resolve the tension between evolutionary theory and Christian doctrine by making a conceptual distinction between *doctrine* and *theological theory*.[110] He takes "doctrine" to be a central teaching that guides the life of the church, while "theological theory" is our fallible attempt at explaining the meaning of the teaching. Doctrine is primary; theological theory is secondary. He gives the example of original sin, which as a *doctrine* teaches "that every human being is naturally prone to sin and depraved."[111] But over the millennia, theologians have formulated different *theological theories* to explain original sin, including Augustine's realist model and Francis Turretin's federalism. In conflicts between theology and science, van den Toren concludes, the church should retain its doctrines but find alternative theological theories that are consistent with the scientific picture.

Doctrinal taxonomies operate according to a *gospel* criterion. As Kevin Vanhoozer remarks, "Some doctrines are closer to the core events that make up the story of salvation, such that if we were to lose them, we could not tell the same story. Doctrines that are essential to the logic of the gospel story are thus of higher rank than doctrines that are not."[112] For Christians seeking common ground across ecclesial differences, it makes sense to

107. Richard Muller, *Dictionary of Latin and Greek Theological Terms: Drawn Principally from Protestant Scholastic Theology*, 2nd ed. (Grand Rapids: Baker Academic, 2017), 40–41.

108. For example, see R. Albert Mohler Jr., "Confessional Evangelicalism," in *Four Views on the Spectrum of Evangelicalism*, ed. Andrew Naselli and Collin Hansen (Grand Rapids: Zondervan, 2011), 68–96, at 77–80; Stanley J. Grenz and Roger E. Olson, *Who Needs Theology? An Invitation to the Study of God* (Downers Grove, IL: InterVarsity, 1996), 70–77; Kevin Vanhoozer and Dan Treier, *Theology and the Mirror of Scripture: A Mere Evangelical Account* (Downers Grove, IL: IVP Academic, 2015), 125–26; Gavin Ortlund, *Finding the Right Hills to Die On: The Case for Theological Triage* (Wheaton: Crossway, 2020).

109. M. James Sawyer, *The Survivor's Guide to Theology* (Grand Rapids: Zondervan, 2006), 148, 160.

110. Benno van den Toren, "Distinguishing Doctrine and Theological Theory—a Tool for Exploring the Interface between Science and Faith," *Science and Christian Belief* 28, no. 2 (2016): 55–73.

111. Van den Toren, "Distinguishing Doctrine," 57.

112. Vanhoozer, *Biblical Authority after Babel*, 204–5.

rank doctrines by how essential they are to salvation. This gospel criterion allows us to find biblical unity across denominations. However, when engaging conflicts between science and theology, the gospel criterion needs to be handled with care.[113] For a number of reasons, Christian scholars often mistakenly think that such conflicts are unrelated to the gospel. Let me explain.

A particular dogmatic ranking sometimes merely reflects the beliefs that Christians find scientifically plausible. Similarly, scientific concerns often motivate where theologians draw the line between form and substance or between theological theory and doctrine. Thus, an earlier generation gives a doctrine a high dogmatic ranking; then as scientific evidence against the doctrine grows, the next generation lowers its dogmatic rank and "ratchets" over to a new, less falsifiable interpretation of Scripture.[114] For instance, Genesis 1–11 is not historical; what matters is that God is creator. A historical Adam is no longer important; what matters is that humans are sinners—and so on. Doctrines that once enjoyed high dogmatic rank are demoted to the tertiary level.

More significantly, doctrinal taxonomies can mislead us. Just because Christians rank a doctrine as tertiary does not mean the doctrine is unimportant. Consider the historicity of Adam: on the one hand, many believers who hold a mythical view of Adam firmly believe in the Trinity, the gospel, justification, resurrection, and much else besides. It is wrong to denounce Christians who deny the historical Adam as abandoning the Christian faith. On the other hand, the material and physical reality of Adam is not insignificant. Theology is not an atomistic collection of unrelated doctrines but rather a coherent theological *system* of Christian doctrine. The doctrines of creation, the status of Adam, the fall, original sin, humanity, the flood, resurrection, and so on are not disconnected from each other but are interrelated and ultimately reflect the three persons

---

113. One should also note that how theologians and their traditions rank doctrines will vary widely. As Rhyne Putman notes, "It is important to remember that these taxonomies are human theological constructs, efforts on the part of fallible believers to make sense of what is most important in the word of God and the Christian tradition. Because Protestants and evangelicals have no magisterium for dictating doctrine, what counts as a primary, secondary, or tertiary issue may vary from person to person or tradition to tradition. These rankings are somewhat subjective, framed by the theological priorities of their authors." Rhyne Putman, *When Doctrine Divides the People of God: An Evangelical Approach to Theological Diversity* (Wheaton: Crossway, 2020), 218.

114. This dynamic has similarities to the "ratcheting concordism" described and criticized in Dennis Venema, "Genesis and the Genome: Genomics Evidence for Human-Ape Common Ancestry and Ancestral Hominid Population Sizes," *Perspectives on Science and Christian Faith* 62, no. 3 (2010): 166–78, here 176.

of the Trinity.[115] Bruce Ashford and Craig Bartholomew are correct to say that "perichoresis—the interwovenness of the acts of the Father, Son, and Spirit—applies not only to the acts of the persons of the Trinity but also to the doctrines of the faith."[116]

There are thus deep inner connections between so-called third-order and first-order doctrines—especially third-order doctrines that impinge on science. To deny the tertiary doctrine (or an orthodox understanding of the doctrine) can logically imply the denial of a core gospel truth. The apostle Paul made this precise point in response to some Corinthians who were denying the resurrection of the dead: denying the resurrection of the dead logically implies the denial of Christ's resurrection (1 Cor. 15:12–19). In his summary of Paul's reasoning, David Garland writes, "Paul correlates the tenet that Christ has been raised with the Corinthians' denial of the resurrection of the dead to expose the logical implications of this denial. He sets up, as it were, theological dominoes that fall, one after another, when the first domino—if Christ is not raised—is knocked over."[117] Core truths like the resurrection do not stand alone but interconnect with other lesser doctrines within the theological system embedded in Scripture.

The gospel criterion assumed by traditional taxonomies functions best as a guardrail to distinguish essential from nonessential doctrines and as a benchmark for ecclesial fellowship.[118] But it is less useful in conflicts between science and theology; in such cases, the *canonical criteria* that I introduced earlier are a more suitable taxonomy.[119] Recall the three-part clarity, centrality, and catholicity tests: in every instance of conflict between science and doctrine, we should ask whether the doctrine is clearly attested in Scripture, central to the integrity of the redemptive-historical story, and supported by the catholic tradition.[120] Doctrines that pass all three

115. For helpful analysis, see A. N. Williams, "What Is Systematic Theology?," *International Journal of Systematic Theology* 11, no. 1 (2009): 40–55.

116. Bruce Ashford and Craig Bartholomew, *The Doctrine of Creation: A Constructive Kuyperian Approach* (Downers Grove, IL: IVP Academic, 2020), 42–43.

117. David Garland, *1 Corinthians*, Baker Exegetical Commentary on the New Testament (Grand Rapids: Baker Academic, 2013), 696. For a similar judgment a century earlier, see Geerhardus Vos, "Christian Faith and the Truthfulness of Bible History," *Princeton Theological Review* 4, no. 3 (1906): 301–2.

118. For an insightful analysis of standard doctrinal taxonomies, based on what I call the gospel criterion, see Rhyne Putman's hermeneutical, gospel, and praxis tests in his *When Doctrine Divides the People of God*, 219–28.

119. The canonical criteria and the gospel criterion complement each other—indeed, the latter is implicit in the former. However, the canonical criteria can engage direct conflicts in science and theology in ways that the gospel criterion cannot.

120. I have listed them in order of priority: Scripture, doctrine, tradition.

tests are dogmatically weighty and should resist pressure from mainstream scientific theories. The second test (centrality) is, roughly, the gospel criterion but goes further to recognize that doctrines that seem to be less important often have a logical—or *theo-logical*—connection to core doctrines. The first test (clarity) hinges on *sola scriptura* and prompts the question: How do we know when science has definitively overturned a long-held interpretation of Scripture that touches on core aspects of the biblical story? This is a difficult question.

One answer, common among young-earth creationists, is to distinguish between "experimental" and "historical" science. Experimental (or operational) science deals with repeatable events observable in the present, whereas historical (or origins) science investigates singular events that happened only once—or infrequently—in the past.[121] The assumption here is that operational science is more reliable than origins science. Scientific theories that oppose young-earth creationism are typically instances of origins science (e.g., origin of the universe, origin of the planet, origin of humanity, origin of sin).

Although the distinction between experimental and historical sciences is well established,[122] some creationists have exploited it in overly simplistic ways. They pounce on the fact that historical science examines past events that are no longer observable, and thus they judge it as grossly inferior to experimental science's ability to repeat experiments and test theories under controlled conditions. However, these two modes of science are not so different. Archaeology and forensic science, for example, are both historical sciences, yet like experimental science they rely on regularities that can be tested.[123] Furthermore, experimental sciences like particle physics

121. John Byl, *God and Cosmos: A Christian View of Time, Space, and the Universe* (Carlisle, UK: Banner of Truth, 2001), 213–14. Although the origins-versus-operational distinction did not originate with young-earth creationists, they have since monopolized it—e.g., see Ken Ham, "Young-Earth Creationism," in *Four Views on Creation, Evolution, and Intelligent Design*, ed. J. B. Stump (Grand Rapids: Zondervan, 2017), 31–34; and Terry Mortenson, introduction to *Searching for Adam: Genesis and the Truth about Man's Origin*, ed. Terry Mortenson (Green Forest, AR: Master Books, 2016), 7–15.
122. See Carol Cleland and Sheralee Brindell, "Science and the Messy, Uncontrollable World of Nature," in *Philosophy of Pseudoscience: Reconsidering the Demarcation Problem*, ed. Massimo Pigliucci and Maarten Boudry (Chicago: University of Chicago Press, 2013), 183, 200n2.
123. See Ben Jeffares, "Testing Times: Regularities in the Historical Sciences," *Studies in History and Philosophy of Biology and Biomedical Sciences* 39, no. 4 (2008): 469–75; and Patrick Forber and Eric Griffith, "Historical Reconstruction: Gaining Epistemic Access to the Deep Past," *Philosophy & Theory in Biology* 3, no. 3 (2011): 1–19. See also Carol Cleland's seminal work "Historical Science, Experimental Science, and the Scientific Method," *Geology* 29, no. 11 (2001): 987–90; and her "Prediction and Explanation in Historical Natural Science," *British Journal for the Philosophy of Science* 62, no. 3 (2011): 551–82.

and forensic psychology are not immune to subjectivity, worldview bias, and other potential sources of error. Even under controlled conditions, experimental scientists often "employ highly artificial systems bearing only a passing resemblance to the whirling dervish that is nature."[124] In some cases, the epistemic disparities *within* the historical sciences, or *within* the experimental sciences, are greater than the epistemic disparities between historical and experimental science.[125] Epistemic arguments against historical science are therefore sometimes overstated.

Nevertheless, the claim that there are *no* noteworthy epistemological differences between historical and experimental science is equally overstated.[126] Epistemic access to the deep past presents a range of unique difficulties. (Thus, creationist worries are not just smoke and mirrors.)[127] The incompleteness of the fossil record and other physical data from the past lead to local underdetermination problems; that is, the physical evidence is equally consistent with different legitimate scientific theories. We often do not have enough evidence to know decisively what happened in the past.[128] In addition, when Scripture (or a doctrine derived from Scripture) makes assertions about primeval history that we have properly interpreted, we accept those assertions dogmatically because of their divine authority. It would make no theological sense to abandon such beliefs just because they conflict with some facet of the historical sciences (e.g., geology or evolutionary biology); at a minimum, any conflicting scientific hypothesis must meet a very high threshold before we would even consider revising our reading of Scripture.

Take evolutionary theory as a concrete example. People have epistemic confidence in evolution because of its multiple, independent lines of evidence. The evidence for common ancestry includes the fossil record, genetics, comparative anatomy, embryology, and geographical species distribution; natural selection is supported by natural and laboratory work, including computer simulations and mathematical models.[129]

124. Adrian Currie, *Scientific Knowledge and the Deep Past* (Cambridge: Cambridge University Press, 2019), 20.

125. Currie, *Scientific Knowledge*, 23–24.

126. Carol Cleland and Adrian Currie, for instance, seem to hold this view in the sources cited earlier.

127. For a discussion of these challenges in human evolution research, see Richard Smith and Bernard Wood, "The Principles and Practice of Human Evolution Research: Are We Asking Questions That Can Be Answered?," *Comptes Rendus Palevol* 16, nos. 5–6 (2017): 670–79.

128. For this argument, see Derek Turner, *Making Prehistory: Historical Science and the Realism Debate* (Cambridge: Cambridge University Press, 2007).

129. Kevin McCain and Brad Weslake, "Evolutionary Theory and the Epistemology of Science," in *The Philosophy of Biology: A Companion for Educators*, ed. Kostas Kampourakis (Dordrecht,

Yet it is daunting to determine the epistemic status of evolution comprehensively, since that would involve several subdisciplines and sub-subdisciplines. Elliott Sober discusses three statistical approaches for assessing the epistemic status of evolutionary claims: Bayesian, likelihood, and frequentist.

Bayesianism, a computational framework rooted in probability theory, enables researchers to adjust the strength of their beliefs in a scientific hypothesis as fresh data emerges. This process involves updating prior beliefs with new evidence, resulting in a refined degree of confidence. Thus Bayesian analysis allows scientists to quantitatively express how their initial convictions evolve in response to accumulating information. Likelihoodism, on the other hand, is an approach focused on evaluating the likelihood of observed data given various hypotheses. It allows researchers to gauge the plausibility of competing explanations by providing a nuanced understanding of how well each hypothesis aligns with the empirical observations. Meanwhile, model-selection theory, which falls under the frequentist framework, is a tool for evaluating competing hypotheses based on their predictive power. Models are fitted to existing data and their predictive performance is assessed. This approach helps scientists ascertain which model is better equipped to generalize its predictions beyond the dataset used for fitting.[130]

Sober underscores the significance of each of these approaches within specific scientific contexts. Collectively, these three methodologies are the main options in the evolutionary literature.[131] The evidence for evolution would seem to be a question of probabilities. Natural science is an abductive, not deductive, discipline, which means that inference to the best explanation will never reach certitude. "The evidence that scientists

---

Netherlands: Springer, 2013), 106. On the epistemic significance of independent lines of evidence, see Jitse van der Meer, "Background Beliefs, Ideology and Science," *Perspectives on Science and Christian Faith* 65, no. 2 (2013): 87–103, esp. 89–93.

130. Elliott Sober, *Evidence and Evolution: The Logic behind the Science* (New York: Cambridge University Press, 2008), 356–58. For my summary of Sober's work, I am grateful for conversations I had with Michael Radmacher.

131. For all three approaches, see Douglas Theobald, "A Formal Test of the Theory of Universal Common Ancestry," *Nature* 465 (2010): 219–22; for likelihood approaches, see Elliott Sober and Mike Steel, "How Probable Is Common Ancestry according to Different Evolutionary Processes?," *Journal of Theoretical Biology* 373 (2015): 111–16; and Elliott Sober and Mike Steel, "Similarities as Evidence for Common Ancestry: A Likelihood Epistemology," *British Journal for Philosophy of Science* 68, no. 3 (2017): 617–38. Two recent analyses from a Christian perspective reflect the likelihood perspective: Plantinga, *Where the Conflict Really Lies*, 186–90 ("the reduction test"); and Gijsbert van den Brink, Jeroen de Ridder, and René van Woudenberg, "The Epistemic Status of Evolutionary Theory," *Theology and Science* 15, no. 4 (2017): 454–72.

have for their theories," Sober remarks, "does not render those theories certain."[132] Nevertheless, while Sober concedes that evolutionary theory cannot achieve certainty, he levels a detailed critique of William Paley's likelihood argument for intelligent design (ID): Paley's problem is that he would need to have independent knowledge of the intelligent designer's goals and abilities, and he would also need to ensure that the created order accords with these goals and abilities.[133] Ironically, the classic ID argument hamstrings itself when it brackets out special revelation since, without it, the likelihood argument for a designer fails. Biblical realism, by contrast, incorporates background beliefs derived from special revelation when assessing the epistemic status of scientific theories. Background beliefs affect the plausibility we assign to any scientific explanation of a given set of data; such beliefs when functioning properly promote good interpretations of natural phenomena (but at other times they can distort and should be corrected by what we discover in the created order).[134] Most importantly, the background beliefs of Christians will include the sure declarations of Scripture and the doctrines they support.[135]

   Although biblical realism concedes that there is strong evidence for evolution, if mainstream evolution undermines classical readings of Scripture that satisfy the canonical criteria, then Christians should not accept evolutionary theory (or significant aspects of it), for the claims of Scripture are certainly true. Admittedly, Christians have become skittish about the language of "certainty," in reaction to the demise of classical foundationalism.[136] But there are more kinds of certainty than classical foundationalism. As Bavinck explains, "Certainty is a characteristic of faith throughout Scripture. Even in the midst of the most severe trials, when everything is opposed to them, hoping against hope, believers stand firm as seeing the Invisible (Job 19:25; Ps. 23; 32; 51; Rom. 4:20, 21; 5:1; 8:38; Heb. 11; etc.). Believers will sooner give up everything than renounce their faith. Nothing is more precious to them than faith, not their money, their goods, their honor, or even their lives."[137] Bavinck makes a similar point elsewhere:

132. Sober, *Evidence and Evolution*, 1.
133. Sober, *Evidence and Evolution*, 141–47.
134. As others have noted, naturalistic science already assumes a range of metaphysical and theological beliefs, including the intelligibility of nature and the reliability of our senses.
135. I disagree with Jitse van der Meer's argument that background beliefs, even *scriptural* background beliefs, should not function dogmatically in science lest one violate methodological naturalism—see his "Background Beliefs," 99.
136. E.g., Alvin Plantinga famously critiqued classical foundationalism in "Is Belief in God Rational?," in *Rationality and Religious Belief*, ed. C. F. Delaney (Notre Dame, IN: University of Notre Dame Press, 1979), 7–27, though he left room for more moderate kinds of foundationalism.
137. Bavinck, *Reformed Dogmatics*, 1:573.

Nevertheless, the kind of certainty that is valid and appropriate in science is wholly inadequate in religion. Scientific certainty, no matter how strong and fixed, always remains based on human argument and can, therefore, always be overturned by further and better investigation. Such a doubtful, fallible certainty is insufficient in the area of religion. Here we need an infallible, divine certainty, one that transcends all human doubt and can never let us down. We can count on it for time and eternity. Besides, scientific certainty transferred to the domain of religion would make religion a matter of reason.[138]

Christians should not apologize for their confidence in biblical doctrines. Of course, we will disagree about how to interpret disputed passages of Scripture. Some believe the evidence for evolution crosses the threshold and believers must reinterpret Scripture accordingly. Others believe that the Scriptures—and doctrines drawn from them—contradict mainstream evolution and that those doctrines have enough warrant on their own. While a doctrine may be improbable with respect to the evidence base of naturalistic science, it may enjoy an "intrinsic warrant" far greater than any potential challenge from science.[139] Whether a scientific theory successfully refutes a traditional interpretation depends on the strength of the scientific evidence weighed against the strength of the doctrine's intrinsic warrant.

Thankfully, at this stage of my argument I need not resolve this debate. My basic point is that Christians with a classical understanding of Scripture can be warranted in rejecting overwhelming scientific evidence if it conflicts with clear biblical teaching. If a claim in Scripture or a doctrine with a biblical basis has sufficient intrinsic warrant, incompatible scientific theories present no threat. Plantinga makes the point with a letter-filching analogy:

I am applying to the National Endowment for the Humanities for a fellowship; I write a letter to a colleague, trying to bribe him to write the Endowment a glowing letter on my behalf; he indignantly refuses and sends the letter to my chairman. The letter disappears from the chairman's office under mysterious circumstances. I have motive for stealing it; I have the opportunity to do so; and I have been known to do such things in the past. Furthermore

138. Herman Bavinck, *The Certainty of Faith*, trans. Harry der Nederlanden (St. Catherines, CA: Paideia, 1980), 24 (originally published 1901). For the argument that theological claims of certainty are regrettable post-Enlightenment developments within Protestant theology, see Carlos Bovell, *By Good and Necessary Consequence: A Preliminary Genealogy of Biblicist Foundationalism* (Eugene, OR: Wipf & Stock, 2010).

139. Alvin Plantinga, "Games Scientists Play," in *The Believing Primate: Scientific, Philosophical, and Theological Reflections on the Origin of Religion*, ed. Jeffrey Schloss and Michael Murray (Oxford: Oxford University Press, 2009), 167.

an extremely reliable member of the department claims to have seen me furtively entering the chairman's office at about the time when the letter must have been stolen. The evidence against me is very strong; my colleagues reproach me for such underhanded behavior and treat me with evident distaste. The facts of the matter, however, are that I didn't steal the letter and in fact spent the entire afternoon in question on a solitary walk in the woods; furthermore I clearly remember spending that afternoon walking in the woods.[140]

Knowledge of his own innocence has an intrinsic warrant that surpasses any evidence brought against him. So too with doctrines that are rightly derived from Scripture, even when there is strong scientific evidence against them. Fair enough, but can I specify exactly what level of warrant or positive epistemic status would allow me to privilege Scripture over scientific consensus? Here again I would appeal to the canonical criteria: doctrines have high warrant when they are clearly attested in Scripture, are central to Scripture's redemptive-historical narrative, and are supported by catholic tradition. Christians should reject scientific theories that conflict with such doctrines. According to Del Ratzsch, Abraham Kuyper agreed with this principle: "It may be that we will be called as scientists to hold to various views in the face of ridicule and in the face of our inability to justify them in terms of the secularly accepted canons of good science. We have no guarantees that our methodologies inevitably and ineluctably lead to physical truth, and . . . sometimes the sciences may seem to lead to results specifically contrary to Scripture, in which case we would have to reject those results."[141] This attitude reflects the logic of faith in a fallen, post-Christian, secular world.

Eclectic Method

According to biblical realism, how should we then characterize the relationship between science and theology?[142] Recall Barbour's taxonomy for the science-theology relationship: independence, conflict, dialogue, and integration. We can use this taxonomy heuristically to clarify our own position.[143]

140. Alvin Plantinga, "The Foundations of Theism: A Reply," *Faith and Philosophy* 3 (1986): 310.
141. Del Ratzsch, "Abraham Kuyper's Philosophy of Science," *Calvin Theological Journal* 27, no. 2 (1992): 300.
142. Although beyond the scope of this chapter, there is of course far more to say about the science-theology relationship. This chapter has focused on methodological issues of metaphysical and epistemic relevance.
143. I recognize that Barbour's taxonomy has imperfections. For example, see the more nuanced, multidimensional model in Stenmark, *How to Relate Science and Religion*, 250–69. Readers

Different scientific theories should invite a range of theological attitudes and responses; "science" is not a monolithic entity and thus demands an *eclectic* strategy, one that engages scientific theories on a case-by-case basis. For example, consider the fluid mosaic model of cell membrane structure, a hypothesis that does not directly interface with any core scriptural commitments; this non-interaction implies a relationship between science and theology of relative *independence*.[144] Alternatively, scientists and theologians can learn from each other while still acknowledging areas of tension and disagreement, a position that Barbour dubs as *dialogue*.[145] *Integration* happens when the two disciplines are brought into a tighter, more coherent synthesis. But the relationship between the two disciplines can also be one of *conflict*; in later chapters, I will argue that tensions between the doctrine of sin and evolution are largely intractable.

Biblical realism is happily eclectic and thus freely adopts any of these stances depending on the scientific issue at hand. This eclecticism assumes a basic concord between Scripture and science, not a hard concordism but, rather, a soft one. Hard concordists feel compelled to relieve any conflicts between Scripture and science; they are always trying to harmonize biblical exegesis and assured scientific results. The scientific consensus defines the sober truth and they then try to reconcile their interpretations of Scripture with *that*.[146] The tendency is to overvalue the trustworthiness of current scientific conclusions.

---

are free to substitute Barbour's fourfold scheme with their preferred taxonomy; my main point in this section remains unaffected.

144. Not that there is ever *complete* independence—even without any "direct" connection between Scripture and science, there are always deeper theological and metaphysical levels of contact. For an ambitious attempt to relate all the disciplines, including natural science, from a distinctly Christian philosophical perspective, see Herman Dooyeweerd, *A New Critique of Theoretical Thought*, rev. ed., 4 vols. (Lewiston, ME: Edwin Mellen, 1997). See also the proposal for a biblical social theory in Christopher Watkin, *Biblical Critical Theory: How the Bible's Unfolding Story Makes Sense of Modern Life and Culture* (Grand Rapids: Zondervan Academic, 2022).

145. I agree with Stenmark that Barbour's "dialogue" category is unhelpful: "It is . . . infelicitous to call one science-religion view the 'dialogue view' because it is desirable that people—regardless of whether they accept the conflict view, the contact view, or the independence view—should at least sometimes try to become involved in a dialogue with each other and listen carefully to what people with differing views think about these issues." Stenmark, *How to Relate Science and Religion*, 253.

146. I criticized hard concordism in chap. 1, which corresponds, roughly, to examples critiqued in John R. Schneider, "Recent Genetic Science and Christian Theology on Human Origins: An 'Aesthetic Supralapsarianism,'" *Perspectives on Science and Christian Faith* 62, no. 3 (2010): 197–200. See also Deborah Haarsma and Loren Haarsma, *Origins: A Reformed Look at Creation, Design, and Evolution* (Grand Rapids: Faith Alive Christian Resources, 2007), 82–84; and Denis Lamoureux, *Evolutionary Creation: A Christian Approach to Evolution* (Eugene, OR: Wipf & Stock, 2008).

Soft concordists assume that scientific theories and biblical texts sometimes describe the same, or overlapping, domains of reality. Conflict is possible when the two domains offer competing descriptions of creation or primeval history. But soft concordists take a longer, eschatological view. Scientific descriptions of reality will ultimately harmonize with Scripture when Christ returns and the noetic effects of sin are no more.[147] Until then, Christians should accept good science provisionally, engaging hypotheses on a case-by-case basis and sometimes rejecting (or revising) those that violate Scripture.

This eclectic method leaves me open to the charge that I do not take science seriously. A critic may object that I accept science as long as it does not collide with Scripture but reject it when it does; thus, I am not seriously accepting *science* at all, only certain *scientific conclusions*. The complaint is that my approach to science is ad hoc and fideistic.[148] This worry brings up complicated issues relating to the nature of Scripture, doctrine, and the scientific method: On what grounds can Christians be generally accepting of scientific conclusions while also reserving the right to demur in cases of conflict with doctrinal claims? Building on what I have said already in this chapter, let me sketch four reasons why Christian theology must be eclectic when engaging with natural science.

1. The goodness of the natural sciences. Science is one way in which we glorify God as his image bearers. Historians inform us that much of what we know as modern science grew out of the soil of Europe's Judeo-Christian heritage.[149] Several theological assumptions underlie the scientific method, among them the doctrines of creation (e.g., creation's goodness and coherence), humans as images of God, and the fall.[150] Furthermore, good scientific theorizing includes epistemic values like internal and external coherence, explanatory power, empirical accuracy, simplicity, fruitfulness, and scope—importantly, many of these values have deeply *Christian* justification.[151] In short, God made this world for us to enjoy to the fullest, and

147. The Reasons to Believe organization also defends "soft concordism," but its version is sometimes too confident in scientific conclusions. To the extent that scientific fallibility is based in human *finitude*, then natural science may never fully harmonize with Scripture. See Steve Lemke, John Walton, and Kenneth Samples, "Biblical Interpretation: What Is the Nature of Biblical Authority?," in *Old-Earth or Evolutionary Creation? Discussing Origins with Reasons to Believe and BioLogos*, ed. Kenneth Keathley, J. B. Stump, and Joe Aguirre (Downers Grove, IL: IVP Academic, 2017), 37–39.

148. I thank Stephen Williams for raising this objection in personal communication.

149. Reijer Hooykaas, *Religion and the Rise of Modern Science* (Edinburgh: Scottish Academic, 1972); Nancy Pearcey and Charles Thaxton, *The Soul of Science: Christian Faith and Natural Philosophy* (Wheaton: Crossway, 1994).

150. For example, see Harrison, *Fall of Man*.

151. Ratzsch, *Science and Its Limits*, 137–38.

science is one way of opening up the wonders of creation. For all these reasons, my default position is to accept well-reasoned scientific conclusions.

2. *The asymmetry between science and exegesis.* Despite the epistemic merits of science, however, biblical realism is also cognizant of the fallibility of the scientific disciplines. Scripture's account of primeval history and the natural world comes from the mind of God and is de facto more reliable than any scientific conclusions—indeed, not just more reliable, but *infallible*. Since Scripture is epistemologically ultimate, theology cannot avoid appearing arbitrary as it interacts with science since exegesis and science have an asymmetrical relationship. No doubt, we must distinguish the Bible's infallibility from our fallible exegesis of biblical texts. Sometimes conflicts between science and theology are rooted in bad exegesis; such conflicts can therefore prompt us to reexamine Scripture and improve our earlier exegesis. Nevertheless, when the *right reading* of the biblical witness contradicts some aspect of mainstream science, Christians should side with God's Word, always.

At this point, some will protest that science and exegesis are perfectly analogous: the scientist is interpreting general revelation in nature, just as the theologian is interpreting special revelation in Scripture. And since both special and general revelation are authoritative, the argument goes, then Scripture and nature should have equal epistemic authority. But this is mistaken. As I argued earlier, general revelation concerns the (nonsalvific) knowledge of God mediated through the created order (Rom. 1:18–20), not the physical facts of nature. Science is a human endeavor that originates in the cultural mandate and thus cannot have the authority of God's Word.

3. *Christian doctrine as a web of theological beliefs.* People often think that when Christian doctrine clashes with the scientific consensus, we should recalibrate our doctrinal understanding since we must have misunderstood Scripture. However, doctrines are not isolated dogmas that are infinitely malleable but exist as a web of beliefs—a noetic structure. No real harm is done if science causes a believer to revise or abandon a doctrine on the periphery of his noetic structure. For example, if I have always thought that rabbits chew cud based on Leviticus 11:6, my Christian faith is not threatened if I find out from scientists that rabbits technically do not chew cud. I will likely resolve this apparent conflict hermeneutically.[152] Such beliefs have a low *depth of ingression,* meaning that they have little impact on the rest of my noetic structure.[153]

152. E.g., see Gordon Wenham, *The Book of Leviticus* (Grand Rapids: Eerdmans, 1979), 171–72.
153. Alvin Plantinga, "Reason and Belief in God," in *Faith and Rationality: Reason and Belief in God,* ed. Alvin Plantinga and Nicholas Wolterstorff (Notre Dame, IN: University of Notre Dame Press, 1983), 50. For the original use of the depth of ingression image, see W. V. O. Quine, "The

But core doctrines of the faith function differently. Beliefs like the resurrection have a high depth of ingression, sometimes even a maximal depth of ingression. They are at the center, not the periphery, of the believer's noetic structure. My belief in such doctrines should be firm, not flaccid, even when they contradict the scientific consensus; indeed, such firmness of belief is an epistemic virtue.[154] This principle even holds for seemingly less important doctrines that are logically entailed by core doctrines; they, too, will have a high depth of ingression. For example, the apostle Paul defends the resurrection of the dead by connecting it to Christ's resurrection—denying the one implies denying the other (1 Cor. 15:12–20). Biblical realism will seem "arbitrary" when such doctrines—essential doctrines and the less central ones entailed by them—remain immune to scientific challenges, but the eclecticism reflects the interconnected nature of Christian doctrine.

4. *The epistemic status of scientific theories.* In conflicts between science and faith, Christians who find themselves disagreeing with the scientific consensus are often charged with fideism. The scientific evidence seems so compelling that anyone who denies it must be tilting at windmills. Here we should note in response that physical data are never self-interpreting; rather, scientists interpret the data. The problem we face is that scientists often interpret the same natural data from different, sometimes mutually exclusive, interpretative frameworks.

Take the example of *creatio ex nihilo*. Mainstream science adheres to methodological naturalism as it tries to infer truths about the origin of the universe from the available data. A biblical realist, however, has a wider evidence base that—in addition to the same empirical data—includes beliefs about God, his miraculous activity, and his words in Scripture. In the first two chapters of Genesis, we are told that God created everything in six days and then rested on day seven. After the creation week, God ceased these sorts of creation activities. "The seventh day," Ashford and Bartholomew explain, "alerts us to the theological distinction between creation and providence. Having ushered his creation into existence, God sustains it and remains fully engaged with it. But the fact that he finished creating on day seven draws a firm boundary between creation and providence."[155] After God's acts of creation in the first week, he now preserves the whole cosmos

Two Dogmas of Empiricism," in *From a Logical Point of View* (Cambridge, MA: Harvard University Press, 1953), 20–46.

154. Roberts and Wood, *Intellectual Virtues*, 209.

155. Ashford and Bartholomew, *Doctrine of Creation*, 169. On this distinction between creation and providence, see Nicolaas Gootjes, "Is Creation the Same as Providence?," in *Teaching and Preaching the Word: Studies in Dogmatics and Homiletics*, ed. Cornelis Van Dam (Winnipeg: Premier, 2010), 229–47.

by his providence. Given that the initial creation in Genesis 1 is from nothing, scientists have limited access to what happened during those first stages of created history. Even the best empirical tools of natural science cannot directly investigate the first six days of creation since God's original creative acts were supernatural and are therefore not empirically accessible. We need special revelation in order rightly to interpret those events.

Biblical realism is open to a wider evidence base that includes past events like Adam's fall, Noah's flood, the tower of Babel, the parting of the Red Sea, Christ's resurrection, and special revelation itself. Such epistemic openness will inevitably affect how the physical data are interpreted. This disparity between biblical realism and mainstream science is a key reason why conflicts between science and theology often arise from the historical rather than the experimental sciences. It is not that the historical sciences have no epistemic value, nor is it that the experimental sciences are inevitably superior. The real issue is that the commitment to methodological naturalism prevents the historical sciences from ever truly discerning the origin of the universe, earth, humanity, and the rest of God's creation. Therefore, my reasons for rejecting the standard scientific narrative about origins are not special pleading but reflect the epistemic disparity in the evidence available to biblical realists who are unhindered by methodological naturalism.

At this stage, some readers will ask whether biblical realism implies that sixteenth- and seventeenth-century Catholics and Protestants should have remained geocentrists in spite of the scientific evidence against it. Recall that geocentrism seems to be taught in several passages in the Old and New Testaments,[156] and the position was held across all sectors of Christendom going back to the church fathers. If Christians must be biblical realists, *then should they not also be geocentrists?* I answer no, for two reasons.

First, geocentrism does not implicate any core doctrines; it has a low depth of ingression. This judgment holds even though the geocentric Aristotelian-Ptolemaic cosmology had been fully integrated into the Roman Catholic worldview, which meant that rejecting geocentrism in that setting would have come at some cost. Geocentrism itself is not logically entailed by any core doctrines of the Christian faith.

Second, the main scientific arguments against geocentrism arise from the experimental, not historical, sciences. The evidence for geocentrism

156. Modern readers should not downplay the apparent biblical support for geocentrism: heliocentric hindsight is always twenty-twenty! Klaus Scholder is right to caution: "The charge which is often made, that from the beginning theology should have distinguished between a picture of the world and faith in scripture, is quite unhistorical. *For it presupposes that modern relationship to scripture which could only be the result of this process*" (*Birth of Modern Critical Theology*, 46, my emphasis).

became decisive in a way that (I would argue) does not apply to historical sciences like evolutionary biology or geology. Furthermore, none of the relevant experimental sciences violate any core exegetical or doctrinal commitments, whereas evolution and geology impinge on doctrines that have a far higher depth of ingression.[157]

For biblical realists who work professionally in the sciences, what follows from all this? Does holding such a position make life impossibly difficult for such scientists as religious minorities in their fields? It all depends. Recall that the eclectic method liberates just as much as it constrains; "resisting" consensus is not the only story. And besides, any realist position rooted in orthodox Christianity shares many of the same ideas that were instrumental in the emergence of science as we know it today.[158] Having said that, when a believer rejects a widely attested scientific theory for dogmatic reasons, he faces a dilemma. What to do?

These are not new challenges. Ancient Israelites and early Christians faced them in their own settings when pagan worldviews were dominant and animated all the plausibility structures in their world. Centuries later, Christians faced them during the Enlightenment and the progressive secularizing of the disciplines. We also know that intellectual consequences of sin impinge on a wide range of scientific (and nonscientific) disciplines. As Emil Brunner writes, "The more closely a subject is related to man's inward life, the more natural human knowledge is 'infected' by sin; while the further away it is, the less will be its effect."[159] The noetic effects of sin on disciplines like chemistry and physics are less evident than on biology and psychology.[160] The cultural dominance of science magnifies the urgency of these questions.

Biblical realism faces a situation not unlike the challenges Daniel and his three friends faced in Babylonian exile (Dan. 1:19–20). Our allegiance is to God come what may, regardless of what that means for our lives or our reputations. In our post-Christian context, we live out of the same faith that sustained the people of God in the Old and New Testament eras and throughout church history. The faith mediated by Scripture and its

157. See the essays in Hans Madueme and Stephen Lloyd, eds., *Young-Age Creationism: Restoring the Biblical Metanarrative* (Phillipsburg, NJ: P&R, forthcoming).

158. For a nuanced overview, see David Lindberg and Peter Harrison, "Early Christianity," in *Science and Religion around the World: Historical Perspectives*, ed. John Hedley Brooke and Ronald Numbers (New York: Oxford University Press, 2011), 67–91.

159. Emil Brunner, *Dogmatics*, vol. 2, *The Christian Doctrine of Creation and Redemption*, trans. Olive Wyon (Cambridge: James Clarke & Co., 1952), 27. Alvin Plantinga writes that "the closer the science in question is to what is distinctively human, the deeper the involvement." Alvin Plantinga, "When Faith and Reason Clash: Evolution and the Bible," *Christian Scholar's Review* 21, no. 1 (1991): 16.

160. Moroney, *Noetic Effects of Sin*.

revelational truths cannot be broken (John 10:35). Such faith will interact with ambiguous, sometimes competing narratives of science, and should always do so with gentleness, equanimity, and good cheer.

Conclusion

Even the most optimistic minds recognize that, at least sometimes, scientific theories have threatened biblical faith. Over time, this dynamic has led to a thousand different defensive moves, each creative in its own way, and all aimed at carving out a path for doctrinal truth in a scientific age. The doctrine of sin is merely one chapter in this story of twists and turns. The difficulty is that no agreement exists on the epistemic status of Scripture and its doctrinal teachings, much less on the scientific theories that forced us into this debate in the first place.

I have defended biblical realism as the approach I think should be taken. Natural science should favor supernaturalism over methodological naturalism as its modus operandi, insisting that what we know by faith is more important than what we know by reason alone. Dogmatic inerrancy is committed to Scripture as both truthful and depicting reality, although I recognize that Scripture is far richer than those categories. Natural science also attempts to depict reality truthfully, though it is an imperfect way of knowing in a fallen world. Scientific fallibilism assumes that science will only ever fully understand the book of nature in the new heaven and new earth, if at all; scientific knowledge on this side of the eschaton is fallible. Doctrines are also fallible, of course, but not in the same way, given the asymmetry between creation and the canonical text. Unlike creation, Scripture enjoys epistemological priority in that it is mediated through divine words; therefore, when doctrines are clearly attested in Scripture, central to Scripture's redemptive-historical narrative, and supported by catholic tradition—the three canonical criteria—they participate uniquely in the divine authority of Scripture.

None of these credos ignore the stubborn claims of science, nor do they preempt how those claims should interact with dogmatic truths informed by Scripture. Biblical realism is still obliged to engage science eclectically on a case-by-case basis. At any rate, confessing my own starting points is only a modest beginning; the real work lies ahead. As we take our leave of prolegomena and enter the hilly terrain of protology (first things), we had best roll up our sleeves and pray without ceasing.

PART 2

PROTOLOGY

Q. Did God create people so wicked and perverse?

A. No.

God created them good and in his own image, that is, in true righteousness and holiness, so that they might truly know God their creator, love him with all their heart, and live with God in eternal happiness, to praise and glorify him.

—Heidelberg Catechism

PART 2

PROLOGUE

3

Early Genesis and Extrabiblical Knowledge

The harm that has been done to souls, during the centuries of Christianity, first by the literal interpretation of the story of Adam, and then by the confusion of this myth, treated as history, with later speculations, principally Augustinian, about original sin, will never be adequately told.

—Paul Ricoeur[1]

The question of the antiquity of man has of itself no theological significance. It is to theology, as such, a matter of entire indifference how long man has existed on earth.

—B. B. Warfield[2]

One of the sharpest breaks with traditional Christian interpretation which the critical study of the Old Testament effected came in the handling of biblical chronology contained in the genealogies of Genesis. ... The collapse of this understanding of chronology came largely from the impact of the natural sciences in the early nineteenth century.

—Brevard Childs[3]

1. Paul Ricoeur, *The Symbolism of Evil*, trans. Emerson Buchanan (Boston: Beacon, 1967), 239.
2. B. B. Warfield, "On the Antiquity and the Unity of the Human Race," *Princeton Theological Review* 9, no. 1 (1911): 1.
3. Brevard S. Childs, *Introduction to the Old Testament as Scripture* (Minneapolis: Fortress, 1979), 152.

n the latter part of the nineteenth century, Charles Darwin's thesis about evolution was part of an avant-garde developmental perspective that was already reshaping, if not overturning, older creationist assumptions.[4] It is difficult to overstate the significance of evolutionary theory in supplanting the historical picture of Adam and Eve, but Darwin was not the only cause of Adam's demise. He was merely the latest chapter in a long story, one that included ancient debates over biblical chronology and competing non-Christian chronologies.

Medieval Christians were immersed in Scripture, and at the time of the Reformation most Europeans still considered Scripture the most reliable history of key world events. As Arthur McCalla reports, "The Bible was assumed to contain the complete history of the world. It was not a detailed history, to be sure, but all major events and peoples were present and accounted for."[5] According to classical chronology, the unbroken chain in the biblical genealogies of Genesis 5:3–32 and 11:10–26 allowed Christians to date God's creation of the world to around 4000 BCE and Noah's flood to around 2300 BCE.[6] By the end of the eighteenth century, however, the intellectual landscape had changed. Natural philosophers were doubting the Genesis chronology in favor of a deep-time creationism, the idea that "the history of life on earth was a sequence of periods in which new life forms were first specially created."[7] But everyone, even non-Christians, still felt obliged to think in terms of the biblical notion of creation. This progressive creationism fell away after Darwin published *On the Origin of Species* in 1859.

In this chapter, I contend that the historical plausibility of Adam and Eve and the events surrounding them recorded in Genesis are inseparable from Scripture's chronology. Reestablishing Adam and Eve within the canonical time frame is vital for a fully orbed doctrine of sin. My argument proceeds in three steps. First, I examine several factors that influenced early modern Christians to lose confidence in the scriptural chronology, and I discuss how that shift undercut the historical credibility of Adam and Eve. I give special attention to the arguments of Isaac La Peyrère. Second, I argue from the genealogies of Genesis 5 and 11 that we should recover the sacred history of early Genesis. Finally, after considering ancient Near

4. Peter Bowler, *The Non-Darwinian Revolution: Reinterpreting a Historical Myth* (Baltimore: Johns Hopkins University Press, 1988).

5. Arthur McCalla, *The Creationist Debate: The Encounter between the Bible and the Historical Mind* (New York: Bloomsbury Academic, 2006), 28.

6. As we shall see below, the Septuagint yielded earlier dates.

7. Philip Kitcher, *Living with Darwin: Evolution, Design, and the Future of Faith* (Oxford: Oxford University Press, 2007), 21.

Eastern (ANE) perspectives on Old Testament exegesis and their role in the eclipse of sacred history, I develop a theological account of ANE religions that privileges the internal witness of Scripture over extrabiblical archaeological findings.

Isaac La Peyrère and the Death of Adam

From earliest times, Jews and Christians knew of pagan accounts that traced the beginning of human history to an age antedating the Genesis narrative. However, they reasoned that the writings of Moses and other biblical prophets were more ancient than the pagan chronicles. After all, as the axiom goes, truth is more ancient than error. In the second century, Theophilus of Antioch began his chronology with Adam and defended it against the pagan narratives of Apollonius the Egyptian and Plato. Theophilus rejected Apollonius's claim that the world was 153,075 years old, as well as Plato's suggestion in *The Republic* that twenty-thousand years had passed since Noah's flood.[8] The third-century historian Sextus Julius Africanus, who dated Christ's birth to 5,500 years after Adam, ridiculed "the 30,000 years of the Phoenicians" and "the absurdity of the Chaldaeans, with their 480,000 years."[9] (From what we can tell, some ancient non-Jewish cultures, like the Chaldeans and Egyptians, calculated their chronologies by summing up the reigns of previous kings and combining them with astronomical records.)[10] Eusebius, the bishop of Caesarea, hewed closely to the conventional chronology, dating the birth of Christ 5,198 years from Adam.[11]

Although the chronologists all accepted the Genesis 5 and 11 genealogies as historically reliable and without any gaps,[12] they differed on which textual tradition preserved the original numbers and chronology: the Masoretic Text (MT), the Septuagint (LXX), or the Samaritan Pentateuch (SP). Scribes revised some of the numbers to accomplish certain chronological

8. Theophilus, *Ad Autolycus* 3.16. Theophilus confuses Plato's *The Republic* with his longer work *The Laws*—Plato's remark about twenty-thousand years appears in Plato, *Laws*, Book 3, 677d.

9. Sextus Iulius Africanus, *Iulius Africanus Chronographiae: The Extant Fragments*, ed. Martin Wallraff, trans. William Adler (Berlin: de Gruyter, 2007), 25.

10. McCalla, *Creationist Debate*, 29.

11. Ernst Breisach, *Historiography: Ancient, Medieval, and Modern*, 3rd ed. (Chicago: University of Chicago Press, 2007), 82.

12. As Davis Young and Ralph Stearley remark, "To arrive at the conclusion that the world was approximately 5,500 years old at the time of Christ, the fathers were compelled to hold to a strictly literal interpretation of the genealogies of Gen. 5 and 11. It did not occur to any of the early Christians that there could be gaps or omissions in those genealogies." Davis Young and Ralph Stearley, *The Bible, Rocks and Time: Geological Evidence for the Age of the Earth* (Downers Grove, IL: InterVarsity, 2008), 40.

objectives. While the text-critical issues are somewhat complex, rather than nullifying the viability of a biblical chronology per se, these textual differences point to a deeper consensus that creation began between 6500 and 3600 BCE.[13]

Even Augustine entered the lists when he endorsed Scripture's chronology against the histories of the Egyptians and the Chaldeans. He pilloried people who "babble away in their unfounded presumption, claiming to have calculated that it was more than a hundred thousand years ago that Egypt came to understand the system of the stars."[14] Rooting his position in divine revelation, he declaimed that opposing views were "completely false, no matter what may otherwise be the case in secular writings."[15] Augustine's position would dominate the field among Jewish and Christian thinkers for the next millennium.[16] Medieval churchmen who wrote on creation, including the likes of Robert Grosseteste and Thomas Aquinas, accepted the patristic consensus on prioritizing the chronology of Scripture.[17]

Such moves were losing force by the sixteenth and seventeenth centuries. Times were changing. As new evidence from non-Christian chronologies and previously unknown peoples on other continents became widely available, pious thinkers tried to reconcile these data with the creation narrative. They never doubted the reliability of the Hebrew chronology, yet they struggled "to synchronize the events reported in the various Gentile . . . chronicles with sacred history."[18] The immensely learned Joseph Justus Scaliger (1540–1609) epitomizes this growing discipline of chronology as it sought to correlate events in world history with the sacred history of Scripture.[19]

13. According to Nicolaas Rupke, "No fewer than 140 different estimates were put forward, ranging from 3616 to 6484 years B.C." Nicolaas Rupke, "Geology and Paleontology from 1700 to 1900," in *The History of Science and Religion in the Western Tradition: An Encyclopedia*, ed. Gary Ferngren (New York: Garland, 2000), 458.

14. Augustine, *The City of God* 18.40, in *The Works of Saint Augustine: The City of God XI–XXII*, trans. William Babcock (Hyde Park, NY: New City, 2013), 322. He makes similar judgments throughout the volume.

15. Augustine, *City of God*, 323.

16. Richard H. Popkin, "The Development of Religious Scepticism and the Influence of Isaac La Peyrère's Pre-Adamism and Bible Criticism," in *Classical Influences on European Culture, AD 1500–1700*, ed. Robert Ralf Bolgar (Cambridge: Cambridge University Press, 1976), 272.

17. Young and Stearley, *Bible, Rocks and Time*, 44: "Medieval works on creation strongly followed the thinking of the church fathers, and little new material of significance regarding the question of the age of the Earth appeared."

18. McCalla, *Creationist Debate*, 29.

19. On Scaliger's chronology, see Anthony Grafton, *Joseph Scaliger: A Study in the History of Classical Scholarship*, vol. 2, *Historical Chronology* (Oxford: Clarendon, 1993); and Anthony Grafton, *Defenders*

Scaliger's historiography is traditional by modern standards, but he came to understand that the Old Testament was inadequate on its own to decipher the chronology of ancient world history. He needed secular historical and astronomical data to supplement the timeline in Scripture. As David Livingstone explains, "[Scaliger's] belief that the temporal indications of the Hebrew Bible should be interpreted in tandem with Egyptian, Persian, and Babylonian evidence was revolutionary."[20] Other Christian Hebraists similarly tried to sleuth out dates for such episodes as the original creation, the flood, and the exodus, and then correlate them to known secular events. Their goal was to vindicate the eternal truth of Holy Writ.[21] Bishop James Ussher (1581–1656) contended that God began creating at 6:00 p.m. on Saturday, October 22, 4004 BCE, and that Noah's flood happened in 2350 BCE, and his was only one of countless similar chronologies in that era.[22]

The tradition of biblical chronology eventually collapsed but not before exposing a wealth of secular data that seemed to contradict the testimony of Moses. As Anthony Grafton remarks, "The very confusion they created helped to break the hold of the Bible on chronology," inviting the conclusion that Scripture was insufficient as a reliable history of the world.[23] Adam's fate was inseparable from Genesis as sacred history, yet by the seventeenth century that sacred history was under assault, not just from pagan chronologies but seemingly from every direction.

For example, ancient thinkers had long speculated about other beings, monstrous races, like humans but with different anatomies.[24] Such speculations ranged from Pliny the Elder's account of one-eyed races (cyclopes) to beings with faces on their chests (blemmyae). Other disorienting creatures filled the pages of encyclopedic texts and fascinated medieval readers. These monsters were mythical creatures or exaggerated depictions of foreign peoples by patristic and medieval thinkers as they imagined the extremities of the known world (e.g., the southern tip of Africa). Augustine, once again, weighs in with typical finality: "Either the written accounts

of the Text: The Traditions of Scholarship in an Age of Science, 1450–1800 (Cambridge, MA: Harvard University Press, 1994), 104–44.

20. David Livingstone, *Adam's Ancestors: Race, Religion, and the Politics of Human Origins* (Baltimore: Johns Hopkins University Press, 2009), 9.

21. Suzanne Marchand, "Where Does History Begin? J. G. Herder and the Problem of Near Eastern Chronology in the Age of Enlightenment," *Eighteenth-Century Studies* 47, no. 2 (2014): 159.

22. On the intricacies of the early modern chronology debate, see Anthony Grafton, *Joseph Scaliger: A Study in the History of Classical Scholarship*, vol. 2, *Historical Chronology* (Oxford: Clarendon, 1993).

23. Anthony Grafton, "Joseph Scaliger and Historical Chronology: The Rise and Fall of a Discipline," *History and Theory* 14, no. 2 (1975): 181.

24. My account on the monstrous races is indebted to Livingstone, *Adam's Ancestors*, 11–16.

of certain races are completely unfounded or, if such races do exist, they are not human; or, if they are human, they are descended from Adam."[25] Nevertheless, the supposed existence of these races and their absence from Scripture put further strain on the Adamic genealogy of humanity.

The forces arrayed against Adam coalesced around Isaac La Peyrère (1596–1676), born in Bordeaux to a Calvinist family.[26] He was an amateur scholar who knew minimal Greek and no Hebrew but read widely and was familiar with non-Christian chronologies. He read extensively in those ancient texts and struggled to grasp the full import of their discrepant timelines. Like other thinkers in the seventeenth century, he wrestled with emerging data from geography. The discovery of the New World sent shock waves in learned circles. As one eighteenth-century journalist declared, the discovery of America "changed the face of the universe."[27] The French cleric Corneille de Pauw agreed: "No event is more memorable for the human race than the discovery of America. Looking back from the present to the most remote ages, we see no event that can be compared with it; and indeed it is an impressive and terrible spectacle to see one-half of this globe so ill favoured by nature that all it contains is either degenerate or monstrous."[28]

The discovery of peoples so far removed from Europe, so strange in their customs, so "uncivilized" in behavior, invited endless speculations about their origins: "Were the inhabitants of America the descendants of Adam and Noah after all? If so, how did they find their way to the other side of the world? Did they experience a separate fall from grace?"[29] As a leading authority on Iceland and Greenland, La Peyrère knew that the New World challenged the geography of Scripture as it was commonly understood.[30] Ever since his youth, he had been haunted by the inconsistencies he saw in the Bible, especially in Genesis. These misgivings came to a head in 1642–43 when he dropped a theological bombshell, a two-part epic defending the

25. Augustine, *City of God* 16.8, quoted in Livingstone, *Adam's Ancestors*, 15–16.

26. See Richard H. Popkin, *Isaac La Peyrère (1596–1676): His Life, Work and Influence* (Leiden: Brill, 1987), 5–25.

27. Abbé Pierre Joseph André Roubaud's answer to the question "Was America a mistake?," from his *Histoire générale de l'Asie, de l'Afrique, et de L'Amérique*, 5 vols. (Paris, 1775), was translated and reproduced in *Was America a Mistake? An Eighteenth-Century Controversy*, ed. Henry Steele Commager and Elmo Giordanetti (New York: Harper & Row, 1967), 160.

28. Corneille de Pauw, *Recherches philosophiques sur les Américains, ou Mémoires intéressants pour servir à l'Histoire de l'Espèce humaine*, vol. 1 (London, 1774), 1, in Commager and Giordanetti, *Was America a Mistake?*, 76–77. I am grateful to Peter Harrison for this source and the one by Abbé Roubaud. Peter Harrison, *"Religions" and the Religions in the English Enlightenment* (Cambridge: Cambridge University Press, 1990), 222n155.

29. Livingstone, *Adam's Ancestors*, 19.

30. Livingstone, *Adam's Ancestors*, 27.

idea that Adam was not the first human but that people lived long before Adam and Eve.[31] That thesis, one authority writes, "was considered La Peyrère's greatest heresy in his day."[32] La Peyrère's startling claim would transform the shape and direction of the nascent modern world.

As remarkable as the interpretation was, it had little exegetical merit.[33] La Peyrère argued from Romans 5:12–14 that sin and death originated with pre-Adamites, *not* with Adam. In the 1656 English translation, Romans 5:13 reads, "For till the time of the Law sin was in the world, but sin was not imputed, when the Law was not." He reasoned that even though sin existed before the law, it was only imputed when the law was given to Adam. La Peyrère theorized that Genesis is only focused on the portion of humanity descended from Adam and Eve—biblical history is *Jewish* history. Genesis relays a partial history and thus leaves out the pre-Adamites—those human beings alive before Adam.[34]

The pre-Adamite doctrine made brief appearances in antiquity up to the Renaissance, often in relation to debates over non-Christian chronologies.[35] Jewish midrashic and kabbalistic literature in the twelfth century promoted the idea of prior worlds, which implied the existence of pre-Adamites, none of whom would have been alive when Adam was created. In the wake of the voyages of discovery, sixteenth-century thinkers like Paracelsus and Giordano Bruno speculated that God created humans throughout the world who were unrelated to Adam.[36] La Peyrère, however, was the match that ignited the public frenzy. He was eventually arrested, forced to recant his heresy, and received into the Catholic faith. Nonetheless, his ideas became

31. For the English translation, see Isaac La Peyrère, *Men before Adam, or, a Discourse upon the Twelfth, Thirteenth, and Fourteenth Verses of the Fifth Chapter of the Epistle of the Apostle Paul to the Romans: By Which Are Prov'd That the First Men Were Created before Adam* (London: n.p., 1656).

32. Popkin, *Isaac La Peyrère*, 2.

33. In his *Defenders of the Text*, 206, Grafton notes nineteen refutations printed in 1656. According to Popkin, *Isaac La Peyrère*, 80, there were "probably hundreds of answers in print" from Jews, Catholics, and Protestants—all united against the blaspheming French heretic.

34. This aspect of La Peyrère's thesis is a commonplace in Christian scholarship today. For example, see Carol A. Hill, "Original Sin with Respect to Science, Origins, Historicity of Genesis, and Traditional Church Views," *Perspectives on Science and Christian Faith* 73, no. 3 (2021): 136–37: "The intent of the Old Testament was *not* to cover the entire human race as it existed throughout the planet Earth at that time . . . but was *primarily* concerned with the genealogical line from Adam to Christ, and only marginally concerned with non-Adamite people groups or the non-Israelite (Gentile) line of Adam. In other words, it is *Jewish covenantal history*, not human history" (emphasis original).

35. See J. S. Slotkin, *Readings in Early Anthropology* (Chicago: Aldine, 1965), esp. x, 42–43; Richard H. Popkin, "The Pre-Adamite Theory in the Renaissance," in *Philosophy and Humanism: Renaissance Essays in Honor of Paul Oskar Kristeller*, ed. Edward P. Mahoney (Leiden: Brill, 1976), 50–69.

36. Stephen D. Snobelen, "Of Stones, Men and Angels: The Competing Myth of Isabelle Duncan's *Pre-Adamite Man* (1860)," *Studies in the History and Philosophy of Biology and the Biomedical Sciences* 31, no. 1 (2001): 61.

a mixture "potent enough to stimulate, to split, and eventually to transform the world of learning to which he never really belonged."[37]

La Peyrère's thesis was an attempt to integrate faith (Scripture) and reason (natural philosophy).[38] He had critical questions about the biblical text: Why did God mark Cain if Adam and Eve were the only humans alive? And where did Cain find his wife, given that there were no other adults besides his parents? Also, who inhabited the city that Cain built? These familiar questions, he thought, were irresolvable on the traditional interpretation of Scripture.[39] Premodern theologians addressed these textual ambiguities by appealing to Genesis as a highly selective narrative that leaves out other descendants of Adam and Eve (Gen. 5:4); thus John Calvin, commenting on Genesis 4:17, writes that it "is without controversy, that many persons, as well males and females, are omitted in this narrative."[40] La Peyrère dismissed that older reasoning and argued instead that Genesis 1 and 2 were independent accounts, claiming that Genesis 1 focuses on the origins of gentile humanity as such, whereas Genesis 2 zooms in on the origins of the Jewish people. Adam was father of the Jews, not gentiles. The genius of the pre-Adamite thesis was that it resolved the apparent textual contradictions.[41]

La Peyrère also drew on the extrabiblical history of ancient chronological records from "profane" nations, and scientific data from the voyages of discovery.[42] He suggested that Moses did not write the Pentateuch and that we lack an accurate text of Scripture because of copyist errors. Like others before him, he could not reconcile Mosaic authorship with the death of Moses in Deuteronomy 34. As he put it, "For how could Moses write after his death? They say, that Joshua added the death of Moses to Deuteronomie.

37. Grafton, *Defenders of the Text*, 212. See also G. Blair Nelson, "'Men before Adam!': American Debates over the Unity and Antiquity of Humanity," in *When Science and Christianity Meet*, ed. David Lindberg and Ronald Numbers (Chicago: University of Chicago Press, 2003), 161–81.
38. See the remarks in Klaus Scholder, *The Birth of Modern Critical Theology: Origins and Problems of Biblical Criticism in the Seventeenth Century*, trans. John Bowden (Philadelphia: Trinity Press International, 1990), 84–87.
39. La Peyrère's main work, titled *Prae-Adamitae*, divides into two parts: the first is *Men before Adam, or a Discourse upon the Twelfth, Thirteenth and Fourteenth Verses of the Fifth Chapter of the Epistle of the Apostle Paul to the Romans* (published in 1656); the second is *A Theological Systeme upon That Presupposition That Men Were before Adam* (published in 1655). The two parts were usually bound together as a single volume, titled *Prae-Adamitae*. La Peyrère describes his doubts about the Cain narrative in the preface of *A Theological Systeme*.
40. John Calvin, *Commentaries on the First Book of Moses Called Genesis*, trans. John King, 2 vols. (Grand Rapids: Eerdmans, 1948), 1:215.
41. La Peyrère, *A Theological Systeme* 3.4 (pp. 146–53). For a recent argument reminiscent of La Peyrère, see Richard James Fischer, *Historical Genesis: From Adam to Abraham* (Lanham, MD: University Press of America, 2008).
42. La Peyrère, *A Theological Systeme* 3.6–11 (pp. 164–99).

But, who added the death of Joshua to that book which is so call'd?"[43] La Peyrère's denial of Mosaic authorship, along with other alleged mistakes that he identified throughout Scripture, would become the basis for historical criticism of the Bible.[44]

The Frenchman's critical approach to the Bible influenced a wide range of European thinkers who continued to radicalize his original ideas.[45] Some of the most notable include the Dutch philosopher Baruch Spinoza (1632–77), the Quaker Samuel Fisher (1605–65), the French critic Father Richard Simon (1638–1712), and the Dutch theologian Isaac Vossius (1616–89). La Peyrère's ideas were also taken up by English deists and later Enlightenment polemicists like Charles Blount (1654–93), Matthew Tindal (1657–1733), and Voltaire (1694–1778). In Anthony Grafton's memorable summary: "'Strong wits' across Europe gossiped enjoyably about the origins of Cain's wife and the authorship of the report of Moses' death in Deuteronomy. The most powerful of texts had tumbled down."[46] Adam had to be dethroned and die in order for the modern world to rise from the ashes of Eden.

Reclaiming Sacred History and the Historical Adam

The debate over biblical chronology is instructive on two counts. First, early chronologists were overconfident in what they believed the Bible taught, or implied, about the world and its history. Scripture did not always support the inferences Christians were drawing from it. For example, the voyages of discovery demolished common assumptions about the geographical scope of humanity. But it is noteworthy that Genesis 1–11 never claims or even implies that Adam's descendants only lived in the world as it was known to sixteenth-century Europeans (i.e., Europe, North Africa, and parts of Asia). The presence of indigenous peoples in the New World did not as such falsify monogenism, the belief that every human being descends from Adam.

43. La Peyrère, *A Theological Systeme*, 4.1 (p. 205).

44. For documentation, see Richard H. Popkin, "Spinoza and La Peyrère," *Southwestern Journal of Philosophy* 8 (1977): 177–95; and Jeffrey Morrow, "Pre-Adamites, Politics and Criticism: Isaac La Peyrère's Contribution to Modern Biblical Studies," *Journal of the Orthodox Center for the Advancement of Biblical Studies* 4, no. 1 (2011): 1–23.

45. Popkin, *Isaac La Peyrère*, 80–93, 115–45; Eric Jorink, "'Horrible and Blasphemous': Isaac La Peyrère, Isaac Vossius and the Emergence of Radical Biblical Criticism in the Dutch Republic," in *Nature and Scripture in the Abrahamic Religions: Up to 1700*, ed. Jitse M. van der Meer and Scott Mandelbrote (Leiden: Brill, 2008), 429–50; David McKee, "Isaac de la Peyrère, a Precursor of the Eighteenth Century Critical Deists," *Publications of the Modern Language Association* 59 (1944): 456–85.

46. Anthony Grafton, *New Worlds, Ancient Texts: The Power of Tradition and the Shock of Discovery* (Cambridge, MA: Harvard University Press, 1992), 242.

Second, early modern Christians interpreted extrabiblical sources of knowledge optimistically, even naively. La Peyrère was right to engage the emerging data on geography and anthropology, but he should not have privileged extrabiblical claims over the internal witness of Scripture itself. Granted, extrabiblical knowledge can certainly correct faulty—even if established—readings of Scripture, but this theoretical possibility became the default position for La Peyrère and his intellectual heirs. That modus operandi led to the eclipse of Scripture for understanding God's action in history and creation.

After the demise of biblical chronology, people were more disposed to question the historical value of Genesis 1–11. By the eighteenth century, data from astronomy, geology, geography, archaeology, and other fields were driving Christians to reinterpret Genesis. And yet, despite these forces, and even after La Peyrère and his pre-Adamite thesis, most Christians by the turn of the nineteenth century still believed Adam and Eve were recent creations. Geologists had convinced them of earth's antiquity but not *human* antiquity; geological history, they thought, was God's patient mode of preparing earth for the late arrival of human life.[47] Christian geologists repeatedly questioned the antiquity of the fossil remains they were discovering—until the excavation of Brixham Cave in 1858–59.[48] In southwestern England, geologists excavated human flint tools in the same stratum as long-extinct mammals, and this finding became the tipping point for wide acceptance of human antiquity.[49] All of these factors undercut the classical understanding of Adam and Genesis 1–11.

Biblical realism resists these developments. The debate over non-Christian chronologies, embodied in Isaac La Peyrère, underscores the importance of sacred history for Adam's historicity. Setting aside the chronology of the text soon diminishes the plausibility of the Bible's primeval history. Alexander Ross, a Scottish clergyman, offers a verdict typical in the seventeenth century: "History, indeed is the Body, but Chronologie the Soul of Historical Knowledge; for History without Chronologie, or a Relation of

---

47. Nelson, "Men before Adam!," 163. As Snobelen remarks, "Until 1859, even most secular natural historians believed man was a recent arrival." Snobelen, "Of Stones, Men and Angels," 82.

48. Jacob W. Gruber, "Brixham Cave and the Antiquity of Man," in *Context and Meaning in Cultural Anthropology*, ed. Melford E. Spiro (New York: Free Press, 1965), 373–402; Glyn Daniel, *A Hundred and Fifty Years of Archaeology* (Cambridge, MA: Harvard University Press, 1976), 57–62.

49. David J. Meltzer, "The Antiquity of Man and the Development of American Archaeology," *Advances in Archaeological Method and Theory* 6 (1983): 4: "It was not until the late 1850s, following excavations organized by a committee of the Geological Society (London) at Brixham Cave in southwestern England, that evidence for the intermingling of man with the bones of extinct Pleistocene fauna was widely accepted."

things past, without mentioning the Times in which they were Acted, is like a Lump or Embryo without articulation, or a Carcass without Life."[50] According to an eighteenth-century polemicist, "Chronology has been justly called the *Soul of History*; for without Chronology History is lifeless, and no better than a dead Body without Sense or Understanding."[51] As Eugene Merrill put it more recently, "Chronology is to history what the skeleton is to the human body."[52] These aphorisms, anatomy and all, emphasize how the characters and events in Genesis 1–11 are enmeshed within our space-time, historical context. Stripped of Scripture's chronology, Adam becomes untethered and at the mercy of extrabiblical historical claims. To be sure, many Christians who have abandoned Genesis 1–11 as sacred history still hew closely to belief in the historical Adam, but since they deny most of the historical implications of early Genesis while accepting mainstream science's view on origins, the *logic* of their position is to dehistoricize Adam.

For eighteen hundred years of church history, Christians interpreted the genealogies of Genesis 5 and 11 as yielding an *absolute* chronology. They calculated the total number of years from Adam to Noah (Gen. 5:3–32) and from Noah to Abraham (11:10–32), which yielded a date for the creation of Adam. If the six days of Genesis 1 were twenty-four-hour days, one could then calculate the creation of the world.[53] To avoid the tensions with science, many liberal scholars reinterpreted the genealogies in light of ANE documents.[54] Others, like W. Robertson Smith, argued that ancient genealogies merely reflected the cultural milieu at the time of writing.[55] Historical critics dismissed the genealogies as late compositions in Israelite history and useless as historical sources.[56]

50. Alexander Ross, preface to *The History of the World: The Second Part, in Six Books, Being a Continuation of the Famous History of Sir Walter Raleigh* (London: John Saywell, 1652), cited in Daniel Rosenberg and Anthony Grafton, *Cartographies of Time: A History of the Timeline* (New York: Princeton Architectural, 2010), 253n49.

51. John Jackson, *Chronological Antiquities: Or, the Antiquities and Chronology of the Most Ancient Kingdoms, from the Creation of the World, for the Space of Five Thousand Years*, 3 vols. (London: J. Noon, 1752), 1:xxv, emphasis original.

52. Eugene Merrill, "Chronology," in *Dictionary of the Old Testament: Pentateuch*, ed. T. Desmond Alexander and David Baker (Downers Grove, IL: IVP Academic, 2003), 114.

53. Ussher's 4004 BCE derives from the MT; the LXX yields a creation date closer to 5500 BC. To avoid dating creation itself, Old Testament exegetes appealed to the "day-age" and "gap" theories, among other exegetical devices, to resolve tensions between geology and the days of creation in Gen. 1. Their liberal counterparts abandoned any historical sense to early Genesis (see chap. 2).

54. Ignác Goldziher, *Mythology among the Hebrews and Its Historical Development* (London: Longmans, Green, 1877), 278.

55. W. Robertson Smith, *Kinship and Marriage in Early Arabia*, 2nd ed. (London: Black, 1903), 1–39.

56. E.g., see Julius Wellhausen, *Prolegomena to the History of Ancient Israel* (Edinburgh: Black, 1885), 215, 308–33. My summary of the early liberal response draws from Robert R. Wilson, "Old Testament Genealogies in Recent Research," *Journal of Biblical Literature* 94, no. 2 (1975): 169–70.

Conservative biblical scholars who were motivated by hard concordism agreed that the genealogies had no historical value. In 1890, William Green gave what would become the standard concordist reading of the Genesis genealogies.[57] He argued that there were gaps in the genealogies which rendered them useless for generating a reliable chronology. Later, B. B. Warfield endorsed Green's thesis as the decisive response to the conflict between science and biblical chronology.[58] Since Green and Warfield accepted the scientific evidence for human antiquity, and since belief in inerrancy prevented them from conceding any errors in Scripture, they adopted a nonliteral reading of the genealogies.[59] They categorized the genealogies as theological rather than chronological, a position that would be dominant among later North American evangelicals.[60]

Green recognized that biblical genealogies often include gaps (e.g., 1 Chron. 26:24; Ezra 7:1–5; and Matt. 1:1–17). He assumed that genealogical gaps were present in Genesis 5 and 11 and that genealogical gaps imply chronological gaps. Thus, when Genesis 5:9 says "Enosh lived ninety years and begat Kenan," Kenan could have been "an immediate *or remote* descendant of Enosh."[61] According to Green and generations of exegetes after him, the Genesis genealogies were never meant for calculating a chronology. On closer inspection, however, this reasoning falls apart. Green's exegesis is motivated solely by extrabiblical considerations; nothing in the biblical canon gives reason to invoke *chronological* gaps in Genesis 5 and 11.[62] As Jeremy Sexton notes, even if there are gaps in the genealogies, "an unbroken

57. William Henry Green, "Primeval Chronology," *Bibliotheca Sacra* 47, no. 186 (1890): 285–303.
58. Warfield, "On the Antiquity and the Unity of the Human Race."
59. As Green remarks, the classical biblical chronology "is based upon the *prima facie* impression of these genealogies. But if these recently discovered indications of the antiquity of man, over which scientific circles are now so excited, shall, when carefully inspected and thoroughly weighed, demonstrate all that any have imagined they might demonstrate, what then? They will simply show that the popular chronology is based upon a wrong interpretation, and that, a select and partial register of ante-Abrahamic names has been mistaken for a complete one" (Green, "Primeval Chronology," 285–86). For a trenchant critique of this style of concordism, see James Barr, *Fundamentalism* (Philadelphia: Westminster, 1978), 40–45.
60. For evangelicals operating in the Green-Warfield tradition, see, inter alia, Ronald Youngblood, *The Book of Genesis: An Introductory Commentary* (Grand Rapids: Baker, 1991), 75–76; Victor P. Hamilton, *The Book of Genesis, Chapters 1–17* (Grand Rapids: Eerdmans, 1990), 254; Kenneth A. Mathews, *Genesis 1–11:26* (Nashville: Broadman & Holman, 1996), 295–305. For historical background, see Ronald Numbers, "'The Most Important Biblical Discovery of Our Time': William Henry Green and the Demise of Ussher's Chronology," *Church History* 69, no. 2 (2000): 257–76.
61. Green, "Primeval Chronology," 297, my emphasis.
62. As Gordon Wenham remarks, "The Hebrew gives no hint that there were large gaps between father and son in this genealogy. . . . It therefore requires special pleading to postulate long gaps elsewhere in the genealogy." Gordon Wenham, *Genesis 1–15*, Word Biblical Commentary 1 (Waco: Word, 1987), 133.

chronology does not logically or semantically require an unbroken *genealogy.*" The formula repeated throughout Genesis 5 and 11—"When A had lived X years, he brought forth B"—indicates the age of the ancestor A when his descendant B was born. Sexton continues: "As long as Seth was born when Adam was 130, and Enosh was born when Seth was 105, and Kenan was born when Enosh was 90 (whether Kenan was Enosh's son, grandson, great-grandson, or great-great-grandson), and so on, the chronology would remain intact."[63] Although Andrew Steinmann and others have tried to argue differently on linguistic grounds, their revisionist proposals clash with how the formula is typically rendered by classical Hebraists.[64] In short, the idea of chronological gaps has no intratextual merit.[65]

The modern rejection of Scripture's chronology relies on questionable exegesis.[66] Recent scholarship raises standard objections against a classical understanding of the biblical genealogies, but none of them is decisive. For example, the primeval life spans are dismissed as mythical or symbolic, since such long life spans are inconceivable today. Such ages, taken literally, imply that most of the patriarchs were contemporaries; as Francis Schaeffer complains, "It would mean that Adam, Enoch and Methuselah were contemporaries" and that after the flood, "all of the postdiluvians, including Noah, would have still been living when Abraham was 50 years of

---

63. Jeremy Sexton, "Who Was Born When Enosh Was 90? A Semantic Reevaluation of William Henry Green's Chronological Gaps," *Westminster Theological Journal* 77, no. 2 (2015): 197, emphasis original. For the same verdict, see Bernard White, "Revisiting Genesis 5 and 11: A Closer Look at the Chronogenealogies," *Andrews University Seminary Studies* 53, no. 2 (2015): 262–63.

64. Sexton's essay prompted a rejoinder in Andrew Steinmann, "Gaps in the Genealogies in Genesis 5 and 11?," *Bibliotheca Sacra* 174, no. 694 (2017): 141–58. For the subsequent exchange between Sexton and Steinmann, see Jeremy Sexton, "Evangelicalism's Search for Chronological Gaps in Genesis 5 and 11: A Historical, Hermeneutical, and Linguistic Critique," *Journal of the Evangelical Theological Society* 61, no. 1 (2018): 5–25; Andrew Steinmann, "A Reply to Jeremy Sexton Regarding the Genealogies in Genesis," *Journal of the Evangelical Theological Society* 61, no. 1 (2018): 27–37; and Jeremy Sexton, "Andrew E. Steinmann's Search for Chronological Gaps in Genesis 5 and 11: A Rejoinder," *Journal of the Evangelical Theological Society* 61, no. 1 (2018): 39–45.

65. Kenneth Kitchen's version of the genealogical gaps theory possibly avoids this conclusion. On Gen. 5 and 11, Kitchen argues that "'A begat B' may often mean simply that 'A begat (the line culminating in) B'" (Kenneth Kitchen, *Ancient Orient and Old Testament* [Downers Grove, IL: InterVarsity, 1966], 39). That is, the genealogical lists indicate family dynasties, *not* immediate descendants. Kitchen's proposal, however, oversimplifies the genealogies in Gen. 5 and 11 and is thus exegetically unconvincing—e.g., see Gerhard Hasel, "The Meaning of the Chronogenealogies of Genesis 5 and 11," *Origins* 7, no. 2 (1980): 54–55. As far as I can tell, there is no precedent for Kitchen's thesis anywhere in Scripture or in church history prior to the nineteenth century.

66. Gordon Wenham reflects the dominant opinion among scholars when he dismisses traditional chronology as "an extreme literalistic view." Gordon Wenham, "Response to James Hoffmeier," in *Genesis: History, Fiction, or Neither? Three Views on the Bible's Earliest Chapters*, ed. Charles Halton (Grand Rapids: Zondervan, 2015), 59.

age."[67] Such implications may indeed surprise us, but the biblical narrative itself has no qualms with overlapping patriarchal lives.[68]

These textual phenomena did not provoke incredulity in earlier theologians. Calvin, for one, reflects on the antediluvian life spans in his commentary on Genesis 5:4: "For through six successive ages, when the family of Seth had grown into a great people, the voice of Adam might daily resound, in order to renew the memory of the creation, the fall, and the punishment of man; to testify of the hope of salvation which remained after chastisement, and to recite the judgments of God, by which all might be instructed."[69] Martin Luther, too, accepts those ages at face value: "But Noah saw his descendants up to the tenth generation. He died when Abraham was about fifty-eight years old. Shem lived with Isaac about 110 years and with Esau and Jacob about fifty years. It must have been a very blessed church that was directed for so long a time by so many pious patriarchs who lived together for so many years."[70] Were these Reformers foolish readers of Scripture, or should we rather reassess our own post-Enlightenment assumptions?[71]

---

67. Francis Schaeffer, *Genesis in Space and Time: The Flow of Biblical History* (Downers Grove, IL: InterVarsity, 1972), 124. Similarly, see the incredulity reflected in William Lane Craig, *In Quest of the Historical Adam: A Biblical and Scientific Exploration* (Grand Rapids: Eerdmans, 2021), 146. Admittedly, several times Scripture itself describes Abraham and Sarah as being *old* people (Gen. 17:17; 18:11–12; 21:2, 7; 24:36; Rom. 4:19; Heb. 11:11), which might seem odd if they were also contemporaries of Noah, Shem, and others, who were far older. If we take the life spans literally, then the inhabited world would have been populated by persons at least two to six times *older* than Abraham and Sarah when they died. My response is that the Scriptures often describe individuals' ages with reference to others *within the same generation*, even though people from earlier generations lived much longer. Abraham and Sarah seem to know that life spans are dropping, and thus that their own life spans will be nowhere near those of the older patriarchs who came before them (or even those still living who were contemporary to their own time).

68. See chap. 6 for the possibility that sin instigated the gradual lowering of the human life span. One should note, too, that overlapping patriarchal ages in Gen. 5 occurs more often with the MT and SP genealogies than with the LXX.

69. Calvin, *Genesis*, 1:229.

70. Martin Luther, *Commentary on Genesis*, trans. J. Theodore Mueller (Grand Rapids: Zondervan, 1958), 199, cited in Travis Freeman, "A New Look at the Genesis 5 and 11 Fluidity Problem," *Andrews University Seminary Studies* 42, no. 2 (2004): 280. Interestingly, post-70 AD Jewish interpreters accepted the long primeval life spans—e.g., the rabbinic midrash identifies Shem with Melchizedek (Genesis Rabbah 44:7) and claims that Isaac studied the Torah with Shem (Genesis Rabbah 56:11). See the same perspective in Josephus, *Jewish Antiquities* 1.104–8, in *Jewish Antiquities, Books I–IV*, trans. H. St. J. Thackeray (Cambridge, MA: Harvard University Press, 1961), 51–53.

71. Would premodern theologians have read the Bible differently had they had access to modern science? Perhaps . . . but perhaps not. Interestingly, many post-Enlightenment theologians happily accepted the primeval life spans, including someone of Abraham Kuyper's extraordinary erudition:

In every social circle there are always things that must be regulated, judged, and punished, and no one will call into question that the authority for this rested first with Adam as father over his children and then as patriarch over his descendants. He would have exercised this authority for the first nine centuries, after which it transferred to Seth when Adam died. After

Others contend that the symmetry of the genealogies reflects ANE literary schematization. According to John Walton, Victor Matthews, and Mark Chavalas, "The genealogies between Adam and Noah, and Noah and Abraham, are each set up to contain ten members, with the last having three sons."[72] The literary artifice signals a nonhistorical intent. This argument fails on two counts. First, the genealogies in Genesis 5 and 11 are *not* symmetrical in the ten-ten pattern.[73] The Genesis 5 genealogy has ten names from Adam to Noah, with the last member (Noah) having three sons (Shem, Ham, and Japheth). The Genesis 11 genealogy has nine names from Shem to Terah, with the last member (Terah) having three sons (Abram, Nahor, and Haran).[74] Second, although the ten-ten pattern schematization thesis is a red herring, the two genealogies do seem to exhibit genuine patterning. For example, Noah and Abram are tenth in their respective lines and both of them play a central role in salvation history. Such patterning is often a sign of divine providence and need not entail artificial schematization. As Bernard White points out, "If we admit the direct hand of God in the creation of living creatures, we are drawn to the conclusion that God is a lover of symmetry and balance."[75] God's Son became incarnate in the fullness of time (Gal. 4:4), an event foretold in a prophecy based on numbers (Dan. 9:24–25).[76] Recurring patterns in Scripture often reflect the

---

having thus been transmitted, it must ultimately have devolved to Lamech, Noah's father. Lamech died five years before the flood, and during those last five years Noah himself must have been invested with patriarchal authority, which is also likely because otherwise that evil generation might have prevented the building of the ark. (Abraham Kuyper, *Common Grace: God's Gifts for a Fallen World*, 3 vols. [Bellingham, WA: Lexham, 2015], 1:349)

72. John H. Walton, Victor H. Matthews, and Mark W. Chavalas, *The IVP Bible Background Commentary: Genesis-Deuteronomy* (Downers Grove, IL: InterVarsity, 2000), 25. Craig Olson argues that the biblical authors used literary schematization to bestow honor on the patriarchs (see Craig Olson, *A Proposal for a Symbolic Interpretation of Patriarchal Lifespans* [PhD diss., Dallas Theological Seminary, 2017], esp. 171–97). Among his arguments against a face-value reading of the life spans are the textual difficulties it generates. For example, Abraham is said to have died "full of years" in Gen. 25:8, even though "Eber and Shem (Abraham's great x4, and his great x7 grandfathers) were still alive," Noah was still living right up to Abraham's birth, and so on (48–49). Based on such observations, Henry B. Smith Jr. has argued that the LXX chronology is more accurate than the MT (see his "The Case for the Septuagint's Chronology in Genesis 5 and 11," in *Proceedings of the Eighth International Conference on Creationism*, ed. John H. Whitmore [Pittsburgh: Creation Science Fellowship, 2018], 117–32). I defer to text-critical experts on the merits of his proposal.

73. This critique applies only to the MT and the SP but not to the LXX, since it includes Kainan.

74. Hasel, "Meaning of the Chronogenealogies," 59–60. As Hasel notes, "If Abraham is to be counted as the tenth patriarch in Genesis 11, then consistency requires that Shem is counted as the eleventh patriarch in Genesis 5, because each genealogy concludes with a patriarch for whom three sons are mentioned" (60).

75. Bernard White, "Schematized or Non-Schematized: The Genealogies of Genesis 5 and 11," *Andrews University Seminary Studies* 54, no. 2 (2016): 233.

76. White, "Schematized or Non-Schematized," 229.

providential hand of God. Granted, artificial schematization in and of itself
does not necessarily count against the work of providence (e.g., the genealogy in Matt. 1:1–17 with its fourteen-fourteen-fourteen pattern seems to
be a throne-succession list rather than a traditional family tree), but it is a
mistake to think that symmetry *always* implies artificial schematization.[77]

Carol Hill's proposal is more nuanced. She argues that the patriarchal
ages have numerological rather than historical significance, specifically
that the numbers in Genesis reflect a sexagesimal (base sixty) system common in the Mesopotamian world.[78] The two key ideas are *sacred* and *preferred* numbers: "sacred" numbers in Mesopotamia derived from numbers
like sixty and ten. Echoes of the Mesopotamian sexagesimal system live
on today "in the form of the 360-degree circle, with 60-minute degrees
and 60-second minutes, and with respect to time, the 60-minute hour and
60-second minute."[79] Hill also claims that "preferred" numbers like three,
seven, twelve, and forty were "consistent with the Hebrews' changing nu-
merical world view."[80] After listing the patriarchs from Adam to Abraham,
including their ages when the first son was born, the remaining years until
death, and life span, she writes that the ages in the Genesis 5 and 11 genealogies are all

> based on the sexagesimal (60) system and can be placed into one of two
> groups: (1) multiples of *five*; that is, numbers exactly divisible by five, whose
> last digit is 5 or 0; and (2) multiples of *five* with the addition of *seven* (or two
> sevens). . . . Note that for the 30 numbers listed for the antediluvian patriarchs
> up the Flood (from Adam to Noah), *all* of the ages end in 0, 5, 7, 2 (5 + 7 = 12),
> or 9 (5 +7 + 7 = 19)—*a chance probability of one in a billion!*[81]

She concludes that the numbers are contrived and we should therefore
interpret them symbolically, not literally. However, Hill's thesis is suspect

77. If one accepts the LXX genealogy (which includes Kainan), and if one accepts that Gen. 5 and
11 yield a chronology regardless of whether there are any genealogical gaps, then it is possible that
Moses omitted some names to create a ten-ten symmetrical structure (similar to Matt. 1). Perhaps
Enoch is not the direct son of Jared but a descendent born in Jared's 162nd year—although this
reasoning cannot apply to Adam-Seth-Enosh, Lamech-Noah, Noah-Shem, or Terah-Abram (since
Scripture elsewhere reveals that these are direct father-son relations). Moses may have deliberately
created a ten-ten symmetrical, chronological genealogy as a literary device and mnemonic aid.

78. Carol A. Hill, "Making Sense of the Numbers of Genesis," *Perspectives on Science and Christian
Faith* 55, no. 4 (2003): 239–51. Agreeing with Hill, see Paul Copan and Douglas Jacoby, *Origins: The
Ancient Impact and Modern Implications of Genesis 1–11* (New York: Morgan James, 2019), 129–44. The
sexagesimal hypothesis originated with Umberto Cassuto's Genesis commentary.

79. Hill, "Making Sense of the Numbers," 241.

80. Hill, "Making Sense of the Numbers," 243.

81. Hill, "Making Sense of the Numbers," 244, emphasis original.

since the ages in Genesis 5 and 11 are equally compatible with other *non-sexagesimal* number schemes. If one uses, say, the numbers three, seven, twelve, and forty—with the option of doubling or multiplying by ten—the same patriarchal ages are easily derivable.[82] As White rightly concludes, "the fact that all the numbers can be fitted into a sexagesimal system does not prove that they are *the product* of that system."[83]

Kenton Sparks develops a similar numerological argument, making much of the fact that the chronological figures end in zero, two, five, or seven. He calculates the probability of such ages as 0.00000006 percent and concludes, "These are certainly symbolic rather than literal."[84] This kind of argument, however, proves too much. In Richard Peachey's *reductio ad absurdum* argument, he lists ten historical British monarchs according to their ages at death (beginning with George I) and compares that list to the first ten patriarchs in biblical history. Among other observations, he discovers that: (a) the final digits of the patriarchs' ages are all elements of the set {0, 2, 5, 7, and 9}, while the final digits of the monarchs' ages are all elements of the set {0, 1, 6, 7, 8}; (b) the nonzero numbers in the patriarchs' set of final digits are related to each other by simple addition (2 + 5 = 7; 2 + 7 = 9), while the nonzero numbers in the monarchs' set of final digits are also related to each other by simple addition (1 + 6 = 7; 1 + 7 = 8); (c) two of the patriarchal ages have a final digit that is only used once (nine for Methuselah; seven for Lamech), while two of the monarchal ages also have a final digit that is only used once (eight for Edward VII; zero for George V)—and both sets of men were father and son! Hill and Sparks have inferred from such "coincidences" that the biblical chronologies are not real, even though the British monarchy, which displays precisely the same coincidences, was as real as any history could possibly be; their reasoning, ironically, leads to the absurd conclusion that the history of the British monarchy was contrived.[85] Numerological claims about early Genesis therefore have no textual basis and only seem plausible if one has already set aside the biblical chronology.

There are other concerns with the primeval genealogies, including text-critical worries.[86] But they tend to be *ex post facto* justifications for

---

82. For the calculation, see White, "Schematized or Non-Schematized," 220.

83. White, "Schematized or Non-Schematized," 220, my emphasis. White's entire critique of Hill's thesis is devastating. For a similarly unsparing critique of Hill, see Craig, *In Quest of the Historical Adam*, 148.

84. Kenton Sparks, "Genesis 1–11 as Ancient Historiography," in *Genesis: History, Fiction, or Neither? Three Views on the Bible's Earliest Chapters*, ed. Charles Halton (Grand Rapids: Zondervan, 2015), 120.

85. For this delightful *reductio*, see Richard Peachey, "The British Monarchy: Contrived History?," Creation BC, January 16, 2017, https://creationbc.org/index.php/the-british-monarchy-contrived-history.

86. For example, what should we make of the second Cainan between Shelah and Arphaxad in Luke's genealogy (Luke 3:35–36)—absent from the Gen. 11 list in the MT and SP, yet present in the

reinterpreting the text, and none of them count decisively against the scriptural chronology. The primary motivation for reinterpreting these genealogies is the evidence from archaeology and the natural sciences. Standard archaeology dates ANE civilization as far older than anything sanctioned by a biblical chronology.[87] A range of well-developed dating methods establish an absolute chronology vastly longer than the short biblical timeframe, including radiometric, tree-ring (dendrochronology), thermoluminescence, paleomagnetism, and obsidian hydration dating.[88] However, dating methodologies are not theologically neutral arbiters of the past; they carry embedded assumptions that adhere to uniformitarianism—the concept that natural laws and processes have remained consistent throughout earth's history. While uniformitarianism is the core principle in modern geology, the fact that it ignores the role of the global flood undermines the reliability of mainstream geological conclusions. Beyond archaeology, scientific methods corroborate the conventional dates, among them nucleocosmochronology, the cosmic microwave background radiation, the age of white dwarf stars, and coral growth layers.[89] Christians have tried to mount alternative young-earth models to explain these data points, but the results have been mixed.[90] In my opinion, much of that literature to date has been unable to compete scientifically with the mainstream consensus.[91]

LXX? How does one explain the significant chronological differences between the MT and the LXX (the MT Adam was created around 4000 BCE, the LXX Adam around 5500 BCE)? Addressing these questions would take us too far afield, but see a possible solution on the second Cainan in Henry B. Smith Jr., with Kris J. Udd, "On the Authenticity of Kainan, Son of Arpachshad," *Detroit Baptist Seminary Journal* 24 (2019): 119–54. On the case for the reliability of the LXX over the MT on Gen. 5 and 11, see Sexton, "Who Was Born When Enosh Was 90?," 212–18; and three essays by Henry B. Smith Jr.: "Methuselah's Begetting Age in Genesis 5:25 and the Primeval Chronology of the Septuagint," *Answers Research Journal* 10 (2017): 169–79; "MT, SP, or LXX? Deciphering a Chronological and Textual Conundrum in Genesis 5," *Bible and Spade* 31 (2018): 18–27; and "Case for the Septuagint's Chronology."

87. For example, see Margreet Steiner and Ann Killebrew, eds., *The Oxford Handbook of the Archaeology of the Levant, c. 8000–332 BCE* (Oxford: Oxford University Press, 2018).

88. For discussion, see Donald Brothwell and A. M. Pollard, eds., *Handbook of Archaeological Sciences* (Chichester: Wiley, 2001); and James H. Speer, *Fundamentals of Tree-Ring Research* (Tucson: University of Arizona Press, 2010).

89. E.g., see Michael Strauss, "Age of the Universe and Earth (Billions-of-Years View)," in *Dictionary of Christianity and Science*, ed. Paul Copan, Tremper Longman, Christopher Reese, and Michael Strauss (Grand Rapids: Zondervan Academic, 2017), 28–32.

90. For notable entries, see Larry Vardiman, Andrew Snelling, and Eugene Chaffin, eds., *Radioisotopes and the Age of the Earth: A Young-Earth Creationist Research Initiative* (El Cajon, CA: Institute for Creation Research, 2000); Larry Vardiman, Andrew Snelling, and Eugene Chaffin, eds., *Radioisotopes and the Age of the Earth: Results of a Young-Earth Creationist Research Initiative* (El Cajon, CA: Institute for Creation Research, 2005); and Andrew Snelling, *Earth's Catastrophic Past*, 2 vols. (Green Forest, AR: Master Books, 2014).

91. See the telling critique in Timothy Heaton, "Recent Developments in Young-Earth Creationist Geology," *Science & Education* 18, no. 10 (2009): 1341–58.

A Theological Account of ANE Religion

Even going back to antiquity, the debate over Adam and Eve and their significance for the biblical story has always been a debate over the discrepancies
between sacred and secular history. That clash entered a new phase with the
nineteenth-century discoveries of ANE culture.[92] In 1849, the archaeologist
Austen Henry Layard unearthed thousands of Akkadian cuneiform fragments, many of the tablets originally from Ashurbanipal's library (seventh
century BCE). By 1872, George Smith's analysis of those fragments had identified a portion of a flood story in the Gilgamesh epic. When he presented his
findings to the Society of Biblical Archaeology, he compared the Gilgamesh
story to the flood account in Genesis 6–9.[93] Similar discoveries from the ANE,
thought to be older than Genesis, challenged the uniqueness of the sacred
narrative (e.g., the Babylonian creation myth *Enuma Elish* and the Atrahasis
flood narrative). In a fervor of "parallelomania," scholars heralded countless
ancient parallels to Genesis, while detractors denied any parallels between
Genesis and ANE mythology ("parallelophobia").[94]

Since those early days, academic theorizing about ANE culture has
charted a middle ground that distinguishes similarities and differences
between broader ANE culture and the culture depicted in the Old Testament.[95] John Walton, for example, compares ANE civilization to a cultural
river, one "that flows through the societies and thoughts of the peoples
and nations of the ancient Near East. Israel was immersed in that cultural
river, embedded in that conceptual world."[96] Since our twenty-first century

92. For this paragraph, I am indebted to Richard Hess, "One Hundred Fifty Years of Comparative
Studies on Genesis 1–11: An Overview," in *I Studied Inscriptions from before the Flood: Ancient Near
Eastern, Literary, and Linguistic Approaches to Genesis 1–11*, ed. Richard Hess and David T. Tsumura
(Winona Lake, IN: Eisenbrauns, 1994), 3–26.

93. David T. Tsumura, "Rediscovery of the Ancient Near East and Its Implications for Genesis
1–2," in *Since the Beginning: Interpreting Genesis 1 and 2 through the Ages*, ed. Kyle Greenwood (Grand
Rapids: Baker Academic, 2018), 215–16.

94. Tsumura, "Rediscovery of the Ancient Near East," 216. For a penetrating discussion and
critique of parallelomania in Old Testament scholarship, see Craig, *In Quest of the Historical Adam*,
65–87. See also Murray Adamthwaite, "Paradise and the Antediluvian World: Genesis and ANE
Literature Compared," *Reformed Theological Review* 78, no. 2 (2019): 89–116.

95. For example, see W. W. Hallo, "Biblical History in Its Near Eastern Setting: The Contextual
Approach," in *Scripture in Context: Essays on the Comparative Method*, ed. C. D. Evans, W. W. Hallo,
and J. B. White (Pittsburgh: Pickwick, 1980), 1–26; John Walton, *Ancient Israelite Literature in Its
Cultural Context: A Survey of Parallels between Biblical and Ancient Near Eastern Texts* (Grand Rapids:
Zondervan, 1994); John Currid, *Against the Gods: The Polemical Theology of the Old Testament* (Whea-
ton: Crossway, 2013).

96. John Walton, "Interactions in the Ancient Cognitive Environment," in *Behind the Scenes of the
Old Testament: Cultural, Social, and Historical Contexts*, ed. Jonathan Greer, John Hilber, and John
Walton (Grand Rapids: Baker Academic, 2018), 335.

cultural river is very different from theirs, other ANE texts help us dip into their cultural river and come out better readers of the Old Testament.

In Walton's synopsis of how Old Testament authors interacted with their ANE cognitive environment, he lays out five main models in the literature:[97]

1. *Borrowing.* Israel's theologians had access to other ANE texts, some of which they incorporated into their own Old Testament traditions.
2. *Polemics.* Many Old Testament passages engage polemically with the content of specific ANE texts or traditions.
3. *Countertexts.* This term, coined by Yale professor Eckhart Frahm, describes how Old Testament passages are reacting—though not polemically—to earlier ANE texts; the biblical authors are simply offering their alternate position.
4. *Echoes.* The biblical authors are broadly aware of other ANE literature and allude to different themes and motifs within that cultural world.
5. *Diffusion.* Regardless whether Israel's theologians actually had access to other ANE literature, those traditions likely circulated in the broader culture in less formal ways, especially in oral traditions.

The borrowing, echoes, and diffusion models raise the most questions for understanding the biblical narrative on its own terms—but despite the fragmentary nature of the archaeological understanding of the ANE, they all use archaeological research as an evidential guide to exegesis. Some scholars even write as if there was indeed a uniform ANE world and that archaeological excavation reliably recovers it. Yet such assumptions are questionable. Even if the archaeological data *were* complete, the data underdetermine our explanatory constructs; we know little about how the data relate to Scripture or to the biblical authors.[98]

ANE studies can help us see cultural similarities between Israel and the surrounding nations. These conceptual and linguistic parallels can illuminate otherwise obscure passages of Scripture; the biblical authors swim in the same cultural river as their non-Israelite neighbors (to use Walton's apt image). However, John Oswalt rightly cautions that when ANE historical reconstructions feature too prominently, "they obscure the much more

---

97. Walton, "Interactions in the Ancient Cognitive Environment," 333–35. For a later account, see John Walton, "Genesis and the Conceptual World of the Ancient Near East," in *The Cambridge Companion to Genesis*, ed. Bill Arnold (Cambridge: Cambridge University Press, 2022), 148–67.

98. Noel Weeks, "The Ambiguity of Biblical 'Background,'" *Westminster Theological Journal* 72, no. 2 (2010): 219–36. See also his critique of Walton in "The Bible and the 'Universal' Ancient World: A Critique of John Walton," *Westminster Theological Journal* 78, no. 1 (2016): 1–28.

significant differences that affect every interpretation of the similarities."[99] When they do so, the resulting exegesis runs the risk of assuming a historical or cultural determinism, as if Scripture and the ANE necessarily share the same cognitive habits and worldview. Since ANE myths are ahistorical, that assumption naturally invites skepticism about Genesis 1–11 as a divine account of historical events. As Peter Enns notes, "If the foundational stories of Genesis seem to fit so well among other—clearly ahistorical—stories of the ancient world, in what sense can we really say that Israel's stories refer to fundamentally unique, revealed, historical events?"[100] This comparative approach has the advantage of removing conflict between early Genesis and the natural sciences; however, Enns and exegetes like him acquiesce too easily to archaeological judgments. One should recall that "archaeological remains are neither self-interpreting nor more objective than other kinds of evidence. The minute we begin to talk about material evidence, we are interpreting it. So we dare not forget what we ourselves, or the archaeologists we read, bring to the task of assessment."[101]

ANE background studies have had the overall effect of undercutting the uniqueness of the biblical narrative and the historical integrity of the events surrounding Adam and Eve. A theological account of ANE culture can offer a needed corrective. Such an account recognizes that Christian knowledge of primeval history is justified chiefly by Holy Writ, not archaeological reconstruction. In this way of thinking, inerrancy is a dogmatic rather than evidential position.[102] As a start, consider general revelation. According to Romans 1:19–20, "What can be known about God is plain to them, because God has shown it to them. For his invisible attributes, namely, his eternal power and divine nature, have been clearly perceived, ever since the creation of the world, in the things that have been made. So they are without excuse." In the words of Psalm 19:1, "The heavens declare the glory of God." The triune God reveals himself throughout creation, in nature, history, and human conscience.[103] However, the noetic effects of the fall distort our interpretation of general revelation; we are "dead in [our] trespasses and sins" (Eph. 2:1), and our minds are darkened by the foolishness of unbelief (Rom. 1:21; Eph. 4:17–19). Unbelievers can

---

99. John Oswalt, *The Bible among the Myths: Unique Revelation or Just Ancient Literature?* (Grand Rapids: Zondervan, 2009), 18.

100. Peter Enns, *The Evolution of Adam: What the Bible Does and Doesn't Say about Human Origins* (Grand Rapids: Baker Academic, 2012), 37.

101. V. Philips Long, *The Art of Biblical History* (Grand Rapids: Zondervan, 1994), 190.

102. For a methodological defense, see my earlier remarks on dogmatic inerrancy (chap. 2).

103. See Bruce A. Demarest, *General Revelation: Historical Views and Contemporary Issues* (Grand Rapids: Zondervan, 1982).

understand much about history and how the universe works—often better than Christians can—but they cannot rightly perceive God revealing himself through creation without cognitive regeneration by the extraordinary power of the Holy Spirit.

General revelation can also be seen metaphorically as divine speech (e.g., Pss. 19:1–6; 33:6; 147:15–18). The holiness, righteousness, and truth of God's character apply to his words in creation and providence just as they do to the divine words preserved in Scripture.[104] ANE religions were, at best, human interpretations of general revelation, and its practitioners were sinful, unregenerate people without the illumination of the Spirit. Their religious concepts and categories discerned the ways of the Lord imperfectly, though common grace allowed them to know nonsalvific truths about God and his claims on humanity.[105] Comparative studies are theological allies when they illuminate the historical milieu of the biblical authors and thus aid the interpretive task, but they are unreliable when they undermine the historicity of the events in Genesis 1–11. Only the triune discourse, as we have it in the inspired Genesis account, is authoritative; historical reconstructions of Scripture based on its extrabiblical milieu play an important hermeneutical role but should always be subordinate to the canonical self-witness.[106] If there are genuine ANE parallels, we should be cautious when drawing conclusions about their relationship to the revealed truth of the Old Testament.[107]

To begin with, the historical artifacts are fragmentary, and conclusions derived from them are largely speculative.[108] Having said that, we should not rule out any connections between the sacred text and its ANE environment, nor should we deny the possibility of genuine parallels. After all, the full humanity of Scripture implies social and historical conditioning throughout the canon. However, my concern with standard models for relating Scripture to its ANE context is a naturalistic tendency (especially with the models of borrowing, echoes, and diffusion). Such models limit their explanatory frameworks to human, nonspiritual, this-worldly horizons, and then theorize about Scripture's compositional history as if it were

104. Vern Poythress, *Redeeming Science* (Wheaton: Crossway, 2006), 127.

105. Gerald McDermott and Harold Netland, *A Trinitarian Theology of Religions: An Evangelical Proposal* (Oxford: Oxford University Press, 2014), 88.

106. For insightful analysis, see Don Collett, "Hermeneutics in Context: Comparative Method and Contemporary Evangelical Scholarship" (unpublished manuscript, n.d.).

107. Jeffrey J. Niehaus, *Ancient Near Eastern Themes in Biblical Theology* (Grand Rapids: Kregel, 2008), 177–78.

108. For example, see Noel Weeks, "Problems with the Comparative Method in Old Testament Studies," *Journal of the Evangelical Theological Society* 62, no. 2 (2019): 287–306.

like that of any other ancient body of texts, seemingly forgetting that these words are fundamentally divine—not merely human—discourse.

Keep in mind that religious and cultural similarities between Scripture and the ANE world are difficult to unravel and almost always lack a single explanation.[109] On one level, such parallels are the result of God's providence and his common grace, familiarizing his people with key concepts so that "his [revelatory] acts would be recognizable against their cultural background."[110] On another level, the religious distortions within ANE thought may also signal the wrath of God giving people over to their sinful suppression of truth that God has plainly revealed (Rom. 1:24). Some ANE distortions of—and alleged parallels to—the biblical material may even reflect demonic influence.[111] According to the apostle Paul, pagan religious sacrifices are oblations to demons (1 Cor. 10:20); indeed, the work of Satan often manifests itself as religious idolatry (e.g., 2 Cor. 11:13–15): "The Bible indicates that Satan and his angelic hordes *initiated* the beliefs and practices of the non-Christian religions. In the case of some faith systems, demonic angels assume the roles of various so-called deities for the purpose of receiving worship for themselves and keeping people from the knowledge of the One True God. In exchange for this adoration, they dispense certain kinds of 'power' and provide so-called 'revelations.' The Bible indicates that these foundational deceptions are received by human beings and expanded further because of the sinful, rebellious nature of humankind."[112] One can speculate, as Jeffrey Niehaus does, "that demonic spirits can distort common grace natural revelation and thus produce

109. Daniel Strange identifies four sources of idolatrous religion—i.e., imaginal, remnantal, influential, and demonic—which are "mixed together in a myriad of combinations and variations over time, meaning that untangling them will be very difficult" (Daniel Strange, *Their Rock Is Not Like Our Rock: A Theology of Religions* [Grand Rapids: Zondervan, 2014], 259). In addition, Vern Poythress suggests that ANE polytheism "distorted and confused the understanding of both providence and creation" and that "because of cross-cultural communication in the ancient Near East, distinct cultures and subcultures may have shared some stock images, analogies, and themes, such as analogies between the cosmos and a house or between the cosmos and a tent, or the thematic contrast between chaos and order or between darkness and light." Vern Poythress, "Correlations with Providence in Genesis 1," *Westminster Theological Journal* 77, no. 1 (2015): 91.

110. Niehaus, *Ancient Near Eastern Themes in Biblical Theology*, 30. I do not mean to endorse all the ANE parallels that Niehaus alleges—one can demur from some of his specific examples (e.g., see Stephen Dempster, "A Member of the Family or a Stranger? A Review Article of Jeffrey J. Niehaus, *Ancient Near Eastern Themes in Biblical Theology*," *Themelios* 35, no. 2 [2010]: 235–36; and Charles Halton's review of Niehaus's book in *Journal of the Evangelical Theological Society* 52, no. 1 [2009]: 132–33)—rather, it is his spiritual and theological interpretation of the parallels that I find salutary.

111. Niehaus, *Ancient Near Eastern Themes in Biblical Theology*, 179.

112. Larry Poston, "The Bible and the Religions," in *The Narrow Gate* (unpublished manuscript, n.d.), 78, cited in Strange, *Their Rock Is Not Like Our Rock*, 265–66, emphasis original.

darkened parallels."[113] He also suggests that the Spirit of God "provides some inspirations or guidance in the realm of common grace, *even in the cultural context of demonic religion*."[114] In light of all these factors, Christians should be circumspect about ANE discoveries that relativize or invalidate the biblical picture of Adam and Eve.

Old Testament scholarship that relies on ANE-inspired historical reconstruction can lead us astray when it departs from the analogy of Scripture—the idea that specific parts of Scripture should be interpreted in light of the clear witness of the whole Bible. Readers of Scripture know far more about the genre of the primeval narrative from the broader context of the biblical canon than we do from our limited and often ambiguous understanding of ANE cultures and texts. In particular, we know that Genesis 1–11 presents prose narrative attesting to real historical events, as those first eleven chapters are an integral part of a seamless narrative continuing from Genesis 12–50 through 2 Kings.[115] The narrative doubtless exhibits literary features throughout, but the mere presence of stylized prose is no strike against historical authenticity. In short, while I agree that our interpretation of the Old Testament can—and indeed should—benefit from the best available insights into the extratextual ANE world, the epistemic priority of special revelation underscores that the analogy of Scripture should remain the primary guide in exegesis.

Let me probe this last point further. Old Testament comparative work misses the potential significance of *unwritten* special revelation. In the prelapsarian world, God regularly conversed with Adam and Eve. He commanded them to procreate and gave them the cultural mandate (Gen. 1:28–30). He instructed Adam not to eat from the tree of the knowledge of good and evil (2:16; 3:2–3). Yahweh would walk in the garden of Eden, language that is redolent of intimacy and communion (3:8), and even after the fall, God still spoke to Adam and Eve (3:9–19). Scripture preserves very few of these conversations, including those involving the early descendants of Adam and Eve who likely experienced direct revelation from God.[116]

---

113. Jeffrey J. Niehaus, "How to Write—and How Not to Write—a Review: An Appreciative Response to Reviews of *Ancient Near Eastern Themes in Biblical Theology* by Dempster and Edgar," *Themelios* 35, no. 2 (2010): 248.

114. Niehaus, "How to Write," 248, my emphasis.

115. For an excellent defense of this claim, see Peter J. Williams, "Scripture, History, and Literary Genre," in *Young-Age Creationism: Restoring the Biblical Metanarrative*, ed. Hans Madueme and Stephen Lloyd (Phillipsburg, NJ: P&R, forthcoming).

116. See Herman Bavinck, *Reformed Dogmatics*, ed. John Bolt, trans. John Vriend, 4 vols. (Grand Rapids: Baker Academic, 2003–8), 1:311–12. My discussion in this and the following paragraph is indebted to William D. Barrick, "Conscience, Oral Tradition, Natural Religion, or Later Insertion?:

There is so much unwritten revelation that we know nothing about. How did Cain and Abel know to offer sacrifices to God (Gen. 4:2–4)? The text does not say, but since we already know that Adam and Eve regularly conversed with God (e.g., 1:28–30; 2:16–17; 3:3, 9, 11, 13, 16–19), Cain and Abel likely received direct revelation that was never written down.[117] Mart-Jan Paul asks rhetorically, "Would the God who gave Noah detailed instructions for building the ark (6:14–16) have neglected to give Adam, Cain, and Abel any verbal instructions regarding sacrifice?"[118] One thinks not. In addition, Abel is designated a prophet in Luke 11:50–51, which implies that he received revelations from God, none of which are recorded anywhere in Scripture. Noah knew the difference between "clean" and "unclean" animals (Gen. 7:2). "How is it possible," asks Umberto Cassuto, "to speak of animals that are clean and not clean at a time when the Torah laws distinguishing between these categories had not yet been formulated?"[119] Bruce Waltke offers an intriguing possibility: "Noah may have known of the distinction between pure and impure *through his walks with God*"[120]—that is, perhaps Noah received unwritten revelation.

At the start of history, Adam and Eve and their descendants had access to oral revelation that was never enshrined in canonical texts.[121] Cain passed down that oral revelation to his descendants in Nod (Gen. 4), as did Seth and the other antediluvian patriarchs (Gen. 5). At this stage of human history,

---

Unwritten Revelation in Genesis 1–11" (lecture at the Evangelical Theological Society annual meeting, San Francisco, CA, November 18, 2011, https://tinyurl.com/qrv2qas).

117. For a survey of the discussion, see Barrick, "Conscience, Oral Tradition, Natural Religion," 2–4.

118. Mart-Jan Paul, "Oral Tradition in the Old Testament and Judaism," in *Sola Scriptura: Biblical and Theological Perspectives on Scripture, Authority, and Hermeneutics*, ed. Hans Burger, Arnold Huijgen, and Eric Peels (Leiden: Brill, 2018), 124.

119. Umberto Cassuto, *A Commentary on the Book of Genesis*, trans. Israel Abrahams, 2 vols. (Jerusalem: Magnes Press, 1992), 2:75.

120. Bruce Waltke, with Cathi Fredricks, *Genesis: A Commentary* (Grand Rapids: Zondervan, 2001), 138, my emphasis.

121. The distinction between oral *revelation* and oral *tradition* was key to sixteenth- and seventeenth-century debates between Protestants and Catholics. According to the Catholic position, the faith of patriarchs like Noah and Abraham undermines the Protestant doctrine of biblical sufficiency. Since the patriarchs had no written revelation, Catholics argued, they must have had an unwritten tradition. Protestants responded "that before the OT was committed to writing, the 'church' at that time, which had existed long before the writing of Scripture, already had 'biblical' revelation in its prewritten form. Before and during the days of the patriarchs, the Bible existed in unwritten form and, as such, was a necessary part of the patriarchs' religious faith. . . . The OT church did not preserve a *tradition* of scriptural interpretation; rather, it possessed an unwritten record of divine *revelation*." John H. Sailhamer, *The Meaning of the Pentateuch: Revelation, Composition and Interpretation* (Downers Grove, IL: IVP Academic, 2009), 137, my emphasis.

all the descendants of Adam and Eve were likely familiar with this oral—
i.e., supernatural—revelation. As Bavinck remarks,

> Special revelation was then not yet given to a few individuals, nor limited
> to a single people, but was distributed among all who were then alive. The
> creation of the world, the forming of man, the history of paradise and of
> the fall, the punishment for sin, and the first announcement of God's grace
> (Gen. 3:15), as well as public worship (Gen. 4:26), the beginnings of culture
> (Gen. 4:17), the flood, and the building of the tower of Babel—these all are
> treasures which mankind has carried along as part of its equipment in its
> journey through the world.[122]

If Bavinck is right, then at the tower of Babel everyone living recalled a
time when God walked with men. They shared memories of sinless Eden,
the atoning sacrifices, the Nephilim, Noah's flood, and more. As God's judgment at Babel scattered the people, memory of that unwritten revelation
fractured and devolved in a hundred different ways. But it was also incorporated into the progressively unreliable human understanding of general revelation represented by national myths and pagan religions. Thus,
the universal memory of primeval history was largely gone, lingering in
confusing hints and traces scattered throughout the world's religions and
cultures. Yet God was merciful to leave humanity with the inspired account
in Genesis 1–11.[123]

Is there any extrabiblical evidence to support this theological speculation? The immediate difficulty is that we have no "neutral" facts regarding
primeval history. Peter Enns, for example, is not convinced by the argument
for an older unwritten revelation:

> If pressed, one could attempt to mount the argument that the Israelite stories
> were actually older than all the ancient Near Eastern stories but were only
> *recorded* later in Hebrew. Such a theory—for that is what it is, a theory—*assumes*
> that the biblical stories are the pristine originals and that all the other stories
> are parodies and perversions of the Israelite original, even though the avail-
> able evidence would be very difficult to square with such a conclusion. But
> could it have happened this way? Yes, I suppose one could insist on such a

---

122. Herman Bavinck, *Our Reasonable Faith* (Grand Rapids: Eerdmans, 1956), 45–46.
123. I am arguing for a primitive monotheism: ANE religions are a devolution from the original
monotheism of Yahweh worship. David Peterson describes three general approaches as "devolution,"
"evolution," and "revolution." David Peterson, "Israel and Monotheism: The Unfinished Agenda,"
in *Canon, Theology, and Old Testament Interpretation: Essays in Honor of Brevard S. Childs*, ed. G. M.
Tucker, D. L. Petersen, and R. R. Wilson (Philadelphia: Fortress, 1988), 93–95.

thing, but it would be very difficult for someone holding to such a view to have a meaningful conversation with linguists and historians of the ancient world. To argue in such hypothetical terms can sometimes become an excuse for maintaining a way of thinking that is otherwise unsupportable. It is just such explanations that some readers might find problematic, for these explanations seem motivated by a desire to protect dogmatic commitments rather than to engage the available evidence.[124]

Enns makes a fair point that I take seriously, but the case for unwritten special revelation is not so dire as he thinks. First, if we set aside the question of extrabiblical evidence, we do have the *internal* evidence of Scripture itself: as one reads the early chapters of Genesis in light of God's personal interaction with humanity elsewhere in Scripture, the concept of an unwritten verbal revelation is a plausible theory that helps us understand *the text*. I would argue that an oral primeval revelation is implied in the biblical narrative but seems foreign to people in Western contexts who no longer live in an oral culture. Second, while "the available evidence" (as Enns puts it) *is* often limited, a skeptical mind will likely remain unpersuaded by whatever evidence there is because interpreting the relevant historical data will always involve larger ideological commitments.

A case in point is Noah's flood, one of the "most remarkable parallels between the Old Testament and the entire corpus of cuneiform inscriptions from Mesopotamia."[125] In addition to the Gilgamesh epic, there are older Mesopotamian flood stories, including the Babylonian Atrahasis epic and the Sumerian flood account. The Sumerian King List also mentions a flood story, and several cuneiform texts allude to a global flood.[126] Beyond the ANE, countless deluge stories are preserved throughout the world—for example, in ancient Greece, Iceland, Wales, Lithuania, India, China, Mongolia, Australia, New Guinea, Melanesia, Central and South America, and Africa.[127]

Opinions vary on how to account for these flood traditions. As James Frazer notes, "The old answer to the question was that such a catastrophe actually occurred, that we have a full and authentic record of it in the

124. Peter Enns, *Inspiration and Incarnation: Evangelicals and the Problem of the Old Testament*, 2nd ed. (Grand Rapids: Baker Academic, 2015), 41, emphasis original.

125. Alexander Heidel, *The Gilgamesh Epic and Old Testament Parallels* (Chicago: University of Chicago Press, 1946), 244, cited in David T. Tsumura, "Genesis and Ancient Near Eastern Stories of Creation and Flood," in Hess and Tsumura, *I Studied Inscriptions from before the Flood*, 52.

126. Tsumura, "Genesis and Ancient Near Eastern Stories," 53.

127. James George Frazer, *Folk-Lore in the Old Testament: Studies in Comparative Religion, Legend and Law*, 3 vols. (London: Macmillan, 1918), 1:104–361.

Book of Genesis, and that the many legends of a great flood which we find scattered so widely among mankind embody the more or less imperfect, confused and distorted reminiscences of that tremendous cataclysm."[128] But Frazer thinks that geology renders this traditional view impossible for modern people, and most evangelical academics today share this perspective.[129] Tremper Longman and John Walton suggest that the reason for the countless flood legends "is that a catastrophic but local flood so impressed people that it was handed down and across cultures as a worldwide flood story."[130] They also doubt that the non-ANE flood stories were inspired by the biblical deluge.

But given the biblical testimony, such arguments lack credibility.[131] Noah's flood is consistently framed as a historical and global judgment: a de-creation followed by re-creation. The sequence of destruction in Genesis 7:21 mirrors the sequence of creation in Genesis 1:20–31 (days five and six). God then re-creates the world with dry land reemerging (8:1–5) and plants growing again (8:11). Noah is the new beginning of humanity, a second Adam, to whom God reiterates the creation mandate (compare 9:1 with 1:28). The notion that this was a local flood negates many details in the biblical account—the fact that *all* the mountains were covered (7:19–20), that the flood lasted 375 days (see 7:11 and 8:13), that God explicitly states that he will destroy *all* humans, land animals, and birds (6:7; 6:17; 7:4)— and, of course, had the flood been local, people and animals could simply have migrated to another region to escape the judgment (as Lot did with Sodom). In Genesis 9:11–16, God promises never again to send a flood to destroy the earth, but if Noah's flood was local then God is a liar who has frequently broken his promise. Furthermore, a global flood plays a central role in the Bible's storyline. A universal flood is assumed in 2 Peter 3:3–7, where creation, the flood, and the final judgment sit side by side, the thread of universality running through each episode.[132] It is noteworthy here that

128. Frazer, *Folk-Lore in the Old Testament*, 338. See also Alan Dundes, "The Flood as Male Myth of Creation," in *The Flood Myth*, ed. Alan Dundes (Berkeley: University of California Press, 1988), 168–69.

129. See Young and Stearley, *Bible, Rocks and Time*; Carol Hill, Gregg Davidson, Tim Helble, and Wayne Ranney, eds., *The Grand Canyon, Monument to an Ancient Earth: Can Noah's Flood Explain the Grand Canyon?* (Grand Rapids: Kregel, 2016).

130. Tremper Longman III and John H. Walton, *The Lost World of the Flood: Mythology, Theology, and the Deluge Debate* (Downers Grove, IL: IVP Academic, 2017), 163–64.

131. In this paragraph I have drawn from Kurt Wise, *Faith, Form, and Time: What the Bible Teaches and Science Confirms about Creation and the Age of the Universe* (Nashville: Broadman & Holman, 2002), 179–81; and Stephen Lloyd, "Flood Theology: Why Does Noah's Flood Matter?," *Origins* 59 (2014): 4–8.

132. That 2 Peter teaches a global flood is argued, inter alia, in Thomas Schreiner, *1, 2 Peter, Jude*, New American Commentary (Nashville: Broadman & Holman, 2003), 338; and Richard Bauckham, *Jude, 2 Peter*, Word Biblical Commentary (Waco: Word, 1983), 250, 298–99.

Jesus speaks about Noah's flood in the context of universal (eschatological) judgment, which also signals the universal scope of the flood (Matt. 24:38–39; Luke 17:27). For all these reasons, it is far more likely that orally transmitted memories of Noah's flood lie behind the flood myths.[133]

Extrabiblical corroboration also appears in the monumental work of Wilhelm Schmidt (1868–1954), an anthropologist and Catholic priest.[134] In the nineteenth century, E. B. Tylor (1832–1917) and other anthropologists relied on naturalistic, evolutionary models for the origins of religion; few of them "questioned the fundamental idea that religion must have matured from primitive, even childish, beginnings to the supposedly highly advanced religions such as those espousing monotheism."[135] One exception was Andrew Lang (1844–1912), who disputed this evolutionism; after his encounter with Australian aboriginal tribes, he became convinced that they and other primitive tribes believed in a supreme Creator God—an original monotheism (or *Urmonotheismus*). Schmidt developed Lang's work using his own unique method of cultural history.

In Schmidt's study of multiple cultures across the world, he demonstrated that the people considered the most primitive in world history were monotheists. His ethnological research is consistent with a primordial memory of God's supernatural activity in creation and world history. As the missiologist Johan Bavinck wrote,

> all peoples have kept some recognizable memory of what happened in Paradise, be it ever so distorted. In particular those peoples, that we usually call primitive, have numerous myths telling of the glorious primeval age in which gods and men had free intercourse. And according to the myths this blessed period was finished by some blunder or accident. It is plain that human guilt is reasoned away, or at least smoothed over in all those myths. But it is equally plain that something of the common memory of the things that are related in the first few chapters of Genesis is kept alive by all peoples. So, considering

133. Assessments vary depending on how one judges the likelihood that geology is accurate against the likelihood that Scripture describes a global flood; one may resolve the tension by rejecting key aspects of the geological consensus (as I do) or by reinterpreting the relevant biblical texts (as Longman and Walton do)—neither option is without cost.

134. See Wilhelm Schmidt, *The Origin and Growth of Religion: Facts and Theories*, trans. H. J. Rose, 2nd ed. (New York: Humanities Press, 1936), given its definitive defense in his *Der Ursprung der Gottesidee*, 12 vols. (Münster: Aschendorff, 1912–55). The best English-language defense of original monotheism, making Schmidt accessible to a wider audience, is Winfried Corduan, *In the Beginning God: A Fresh Look at the Case for Original Monotheism* (Nashville: Broadman & Holman, 2013).

135. Winfried Corduan, *A Tapestry of Faiths: The Common Threads between Christianity and World Religions* (Downers Grove, IL: InterVarsity, 2002), 32.

non-Christian religions, we are not only confronted with general revelation, but also with memories of God's revelation in the remotest history of man.[136]

Schmidt was criticized by fellow anthropologists, but the published objections to his work were often ideologically driven and based on a superficial understanding of his research methods and his substantive claims.[137] Critics often grudgingly conceded Schmidt's academic expertise but claimed nonetheless that his Catholic faith predetermined his conclusions, prompting this quip from Winfried Corduan directed at Schmidt's detractors: "This is not really a criticism; it is bigotry."[138] After reviewing the general reception of Schmidt's work and analyzing the most significant critiques, Corduan concludes that the core argument for original monotheism remains secure.[139]

Nevertheless, skeptical complaints about insufficient extrabiblical evidence will likely never be satisfied since they tend to be red herrings. The only sure knowledge of primeval history comes from faith, the internal testimony of the Holy Spirit, and the self-witness of Scripture. The omniscient God is the only reliable witness to the primeval events. As Cornelis Van Dam notes, "Since Genesis 1 and 2 give a record of events that cannot be verified as having actually happened as recorded, that fact alone will mean that critical scholars cannot accept these chapters as a reliable historical account."[140] These texts are special revelation, which is epistemologically decisive. "This material did not arise from the human mind and the surrounding culture," Van Dam clarifies, "but it ultimately came from God Himself who ensured that what has been written is true."[141]

Even inerrantists, however, who seek to engage critical scholars on shared evidential grounds will sometimes accept the alleged lack of extrabiblical evidence as indication that the flood passages must be reinterpreted. But such moves expose the weakness of evidential inerrancy because it privileges the testimony of science over core doctrinal concepts as more reliable than the clear biblical witness. True enough, one must always separate the *interpretation* of Scripture from its inerrancy—equating the two invites all kinds of mischief—and yet, that otherwise helpful distinction confuses the

---

136. Johan H. Bavinck, "General Revelation and the Non-Christian Religions," *Free University Quarterly* 4, no. 1 (1955): 51.

137. For assessment of the debate, see Corduan, *In the Beginning God*, 225–66.

138. Corduan, *In the Beginning God*, 142, 272.

139. Corduan, *In the Beginning God*, 225–66.

140. Cornelis Van Dam, *In the Beginning: Listening to Genesis 1 and 2* (Grand Rapids: Reformation Heritage, 2021), 15.

141. Van Dam, *In the Beginning*, 21. Van Dam's remarks about Gen. 1–2 apply equally to Gen. 3–11.

real issue here. Those who already believe that science has falsified the classical interpretation of Noah's flood are usually the ones accentuating the hermeneutical subtleties of the flood narrative; they need an exegetical justification for their position. In my judgment, however, for reasons I have already given, the universality of Noah's flood is not hermeneutically ambiguous or uncertain. The issue is not hermeneutics but that inerrancy is fundamentally a dogmatic rather than an evidential concept. Science cannot compete epistemically with a special revelation from God.

Conclusion

The historical picture of our first parents depicted in the early chapters of Genesis has often been held hostage to a wide range of conflicting extrabiblical information. Ever since the seventeenth century, emerging disciplines of geography, archaeology, geology, biology, and other natural sciences have painted a very different picture of human origins. Often driven by a burden to reconcile Christianity with the conclusions of science or by a desire to render the faith more palatable to unbelievers, Isaac La Peyrère and his critical heirs transformed core aspects of the received tradition. Since all truth is God's truth, they preferred to resolve the tensions between faith and reason rather than live with contradiction.

Once the biblical chronology was laid to rest, Adam and Eve as historical people and the broader primeval events of Genesis 1–11 became more vulnerable to the shifting counterclaims of extrabiblical disciplines. God's query in the wake of the fall—*Adam, where art thou?*—was now the incredulous cry of orphaned moderns fashioning new identities in a post-Darwinian world. This should not be.

The prima facie exegesis of Genesis 5 and 11 points to historically referential genealogies, and the attempts to reinterpret them are textually unconvincing. Sacred history prevails against the extrabiblical challenges and breathes life into Adam and Eve as historical persons. Even the efforts in ANE studies by George Smith and his legatees to relativize the revelational truths of Genesis fall short.

Comparative methodology is misguided when it uses extrabiblical research magisterially, instead of ministerially, in reading Holy Scripture. The ANE parallels arise from God's wise providence, his common grace, and the deceptive powers of darkness. They also reflect cultural memories, traces of ancient oral revelation that go back to the original monotheism of Yahweh, the God of Adam and Eve. Reframing ANE religions theologically avoids the dangers of relativizing Scripture to contested extrabiblical sources and preserves the dogmatic integrity of the infallible Word of God.

Grasping the full measure of Adam and his significance for hamartiology demands an unfettered reading of Genesis. The origin of sin is difficult to understand at the best of times, but nigh impossible if Scripture's revelational authority is diminished or sidelined altogether. This chapter has been an exercise in ground clearing: "The grass withers and the flower fades, but the word of our God will stand forever" (Isa. 40:8). The path now lies wide open, and we can turn our attention to the unity of the human race.

4

The Unity of the Human Race

Nothing can be plainer than the testimony of [Gen. 1–3], that Adam and Eve were the only human dwellers on this earth until the birth of their children.

—Donald Macdonald[1]

The writings of Moses offered no shadow of evidence in favor of the unity of the human family. Nor are they intended for any such purpose, because that is a purely physical subject; whereas, the whole Mosaic record, when duly understood, pertains only to morality and religion.

—Charles Caldwell[2]

The fact that Paul considered Adam to be the progenitor of the human race does not mean that we need to find some way to maintain his view within an evolutionary scheme. Rather, we should gladly acknowledge his ancient view of cosmic and human origins and see in that very scenario the face of a God who seems far less reluctant to accommodate to ancient points of view than we are sometimes comfortable with.

—Peter Enns[3]

1. Donald Macdonald, *Creation and the Fall: A Defence and Exposition of the First Three Chapters of Genesis* (Edinburgh: Thomas Constable, 1856), 372.
2. Charles Caldwell, *Thoughts on the Original Unity of the Human Race*, 2nd ed. (Cincinnati: J. A. & U. P. James, 1852), viii.
3. Peter Enns, *The Evolution of Adam: What the Bible Does and Doesn't Say about Human Origins* (Grand Rapids: Baker Academic, 2012), 139.

olygenism and monogenism were fiercely debated in the eighteenth and nineteenth centuries. Polygenists inherited Isaac La
Peyrère's pre-Adamism and believed that different "races" of
human beings had separate creations, while monogenists held that the one
human race descended from Adam and Eve through Noah and his extended
family.[4] The growing awareness of new people groups and physical diversity
at the extremities of the known world challenged classical monogenism.
Some scientists, like Samuel Morton (1799–1851), Josiah Nott (1804–73),
and Louis Agassiz (1807–73), used polygenism as a racialized argument
that each race had separate, geographical origins. More recently, paleoanthropology and population genetics have eclipsed this nineteenth-century
monogenism-polygenism debate and purport to rule out any possibility
that all human beings descended from Adam and Eve.

The standard paleoanthropological account of human origins runs like
this.[5] Every organism that has ever lived shares a common ancestry going
back roughly 3.5 billion years. Our closest living relatives are chimpanzees,
and our lineages split off from our last common ancestor some 5–8 million
years ago. The fossil record also reveals several extinct species that are
closer to us than chimps on the evolutionary tree—taxonomically allied
with humans, they are collectively named "hominins."[6] One of the earliest
of these hominin species lived about 3–4 million years ago (*Australopithecus
afarensis*). Within our own genus, *Homo*,[7] *Homo habilis* lived 1.4–2.4 million

4. G. Blair Nelson, "'Men before Adam!': American Debates over the Unity and Antiquity of Humanity," in *When Science and Christianity Meet*, ed. David Lindberg and Ronald Numbers (Chicago:
University of Chicago Press, 2003), 161–81.

5. My summary of the science draws on Bernard Wood, *Human Evolution: A Very Short Introduction* (Oxford: Oxford University Press, 2005); and Ian Tattersall, *Masters of the Planet: The Search for
Our Human Origins* (New York: Palgrave Macmillan, 2012). Since the field of paleoanthropology is
constantly evolving due to new findings and interpretations, some of the details will likely change
in the future.

6. Prior to the 1980s, humans and their evolutionary ancestors were classified as "hominids"
(i.e., part of the family Hominidae) to distinguish them from the great apes and their family
lineage (Pongidae). However, more recent studies influenced by new molecular research clas-
sify humans and chimps within the family Hominidae, specifically in the subfamily Homininae.
The tribe Hominini within subfamily Homininae contains humans and their closest relatives
excluding chimpanzees; the term "hominin" derives from this revised classification. Although
nonspecialists still use the older taxonomy (hominid instead of hominin), I will use the term
"hominin" when referring to human evolutionary ancestors unless I am citing primary sources.
E.g., see Alan Barnard, *Social Anthropology and Human Origins* (Cambridge: Cambridge University
Press, 2011), 19–20.

7. Modern biological classification (or taxonomy) has four main levels in a hierarchy: (1) order,
(2) family, (3) genus, and (4) species. Thus, humans are in the order Primates, the family Hominidae, the genus *Homo*, and the species *sapiens*. This system builds on the hierarchy first developed
by Carolus Linnaeus (1707–78), who classified organisms by kingdom, class, order, and genus.

years ago, *Homo ergaster* 1.8 million years ago, and *Homo heidelbergensis* 600,000–700,000 years ago. Over time, *Homo heidelbergensis* may have given rise to *Homo sapiens*, *Homo neanderthalensis* (Neanderthal), and the Denisovans. *Homo sapiens* are anatomically modern humans who appeared about 200,000–300,000 years ago in Africa. Recent genetic research stirred things up when scientists discovered evidence of interbreeding between *Homo sapiens* and both Neanderthals and Denisovans.[8] While such findings remind us that the classification of hominin species and subspecies keeps evolving and being contested in equal measure, the standard scientific picture of human origins is difficult to reconcile with the monogenist reading of early Genesis.[9]

After a thirteen-year international effort, the Human Genome Project (1990–2003) identified the roughly twenty-three thousand human genes and sequenced most of the three billion chemical base pairs in human DNA.[10] Then, in 2005, scientists were able to compare the complete genomes of humans and chimpanzees after sequencing the chimpanzee genome.[11] Genomic analysis suggests that humans have evolutionary ancestors who passed down unique genetic elements and patterns that are now "fossilized" in the human genome.[12] The genetic data also suggest that humans evolved as a population rather than from a single pair and that this ancestral population never fell below some thousands of individuals. As Dennis Venema concludes, "Every genetic analysis estimating ancestral

8. See Richard E. Green et al., "A Draft Sequence of the Neandertal Genome," *Science* 328, no. 5979 (May 2010): 710–22; Federico Sánchez-Quinto et al., "North African Populations Carry the Signature of Admixture with Neandertals," *PLoS One* 7, no. 10 (October 2012): e47765; Sharon R. Browning et al., "Analysis of Human Sequence Data Reveals Two Pulses of Archaic Denisovan Admixture," *Cell* 173, no. 1 (2018): 53–61.

9. For a discussion of recent paleoanthropology and some theological implications, see Ronald Cole-Turner, "New Perspectives on Human Origins: Three Challenges for Christian Theology," *Theology and Science* 18, no. 4 (2020): 524–36. See also Ronald Cole-Turner, *The End of Adam and Eve: Theology and the Science of Human Origins* (Pittsburgh: TheologyPlus, 2016).

10. See Victor K. McElheny, *Drawing the Map of Life: Inside the Human Genome Project* (New York: Basic Books, 2010). See International Human Genome Sequencing Consortium, "Finishing the Euchromatic Sequence of the Human Genome," *Nature* 431, no. 7011 (2004): 931–45. The full human genome sequence of 3.055 billion nucleotides was eventually published in 2022: Sergey Nurk et al., "The Complete Sequence of a Human Genome," *Science* 376, no. 6588 (2022): 44–53.

11. The Chimpanzee Sequencing and Analysis Consortium, "Initial Sequence of the Chimpanzee Genome and Comparison with the Human Genome," *Nature* 437, no. 7055 (2005): 69–87.

12. See Dennis Venema, "Genesis and the Genome: Genomics Evidence for Human-Ape Common Ancestry and Ancestral Hominid Population Sizes," *Perspectives on Science and Christian Faith* 62, no. 3 (2010): 166–78. In the words of Nicholas Lombardo, "The genetic evidence now at our disposal . . . definitively settles the question. It demonstrates that we could not have descended exclusively from a single human couple." Nicholas Lombardo, "Evolutionary Genetics and Theological Narratives of Human Origins," *Heythrop Journal* 59, no. 3 (2018): 523.

population sizes has agreed that [living *Homo sapiens*] descend from a population of thousands, not a single ancestral couple."[13] In short, the scientific consensus indicates that prior to some three hundred thousand years ago, the first *Homo sapiens* evolved from a population of another hominin species.[14]

None of this bodes well for Adam and Eve. Can we reconcile Scripture with this post-Darwinian picture of human origins? Does it force Christians to choose polygenism over monogenism?[15] And what are the implications for original sin and salvation, among other doctrines? In this chapter, I will address these and other questions. First, I review recent debates among Christians over the monogenism-polygenism question and argue that monogenism is essential to the unity of the human race. Second, I critique the common strategy of accepting the scientific story as fixed and then inserting Adam into that narrative frame. Third, I defend the authority of the apostolic interpretation of early Genesis and respond to several objections.

Christians Debating Polygenism and Monogenism

Christians who locate Adam and Eve within an evolutionary framework usually adopt one of two strategies: evolutionary monogenism or punctiliar polygenism.[16] In evolutionary monogenism, God chose two individuals from a population of hominins and directly raised their status to morally accountable humans. At some point they sinned, the other pre-humans became extinct, and Adam and Eve became progenitors of the entire

13. Dennis Venema and Scot McKnight, *Adam and the Genome: Reading Scripture after Genetic Science* (Grand Rapids: Brazos, 2017), 55. See also Karl Giberson and Francis Collins (*The Language of Science and Faith: Straight Answers to Genuine Questions* [Downers Grove, IL: InterVarsity, 2011]), who write, "Recently acquired genetic evidence also points to a population of several thousand people from whom all humans have descended, not just two" (209). For a helpful analysis of population genetics arguments against a founding pair, see William Lane Craig, *In Quest of the Historical Adam: A Biblical and Scientific Exploration* (Grand Rapids: Eerdmans, 2021), 338–55.

14. Current taxonomies implicitly equate humans with *Homo sapiens*; however, for reasons we will address below, the "human" category may be broader and encompass other species of the genus *Homo*.

15. From the Roman Catholic tradition, Lombardo's reasoning is common: "To identify the enduring doctrinal content of earlier magisterial interventions on human origins, we must interpret them in ways other than their authors understood them. *Otherwise we will end up with results contradicting the scientific evidence.* This point is worth bearing in mind. We can certainly argue for some version of monogenism, but the possibility of arguing for the kind of monogenism once held universally by Christians no longer exists." Lombardo, "Evolutionary Genetics," 530, my emphasis.

16. For this terminology, see Denis Lamoureux, *Evolutionary Creation: A Christian Approach to Evolution* (Eugene, OR: Wipf & Stock, 2008), 290–91.

human race. In punctiliar polygenism, at a particular point in history God raised the moral status of *all* the hominins (or, perhaps, a select number of them), who then became morally responsible for the first time. In this view, hundreds or thousands of Adams and Eves (not just two individuals) soon fell into sin. Ever since Darwin's *On the Origin of Species*, Roman Catholic and Protestant thinkers have developed various permutations of these two proposals.[17]

On the Roman Catholic side, Karl Rahner exemplifies the shift from historic monogenism to polygenism. In 1954, Rahner defended the view that all human beings are descendants of Adam and Eve and inherit their sin. Citing Pope Pius XII's encyclical *Humani Generis*, he argued from Scripture, metaphysics, and Catholic tradition that monogenism was theologically certain.[18] However, with mounting pressure from the natural sciences, Rahner had changed his mind by 1967 and subsequently viewed polygenism as consistent with original sin. He entertained two possible scenarios, one in which Adam was a single man among other hominins whose fall then affected the entire group, and the other where Adam refers to a community of hominins who sinned as a group—and as a result of the first transgression all their descendants enter a world already fraught with sin.[19]

More recently, the Catholic philosopher Kenneth Kemp imagines an initial population of five thousand hominins, and then God ensouls two of them who become truly human. The other 4,998 hominins are merely

17. Some Christian thinkers evade easy labels; for example, B. B. Warfield would have allowed for evolutionary monogenism, though he likely would have resisted the "evolutionary" label (preferring instead the notion of *mediate creation*) and would have insisted that God created Eve supernaturally apart from evolution (Gen. 2:21–22). See Bradley Gundlach, "B. B. Warfield (1851–1921): Evolution, Human Origins, and the Development of Theology," in *Science and the Doctrine of Creation: The Approaches of Ten Modern Theologians*, ed. Geoffrey Fulkerson and Joel Chopp (Downers Grove, IL: IVP Academic, 2021), 59–83.

18. Karl Rahner, "Theological Reflexions on Monogenism," in *Theological Investigations*, trans. Cornelius Ernst, 23 vols. (Baltimore: Helicon, 1961), 1:229–96. The monogenism-polygenism debate was lively in Roman Catholic circles at the time (see the long bibliography in "Theological Reflexions on Monogenism," 1:229–30). In Roman Catholic theology, "theological certainty" is not the highest epistemic accolade—doctrines that are *de fide* (i.e., immediately revealed truths) and teachings proximate to the faith (i.e., truths of revelation) enjoy a higher order of certainty. See Arthur Carl Piepkorn, *Profiles in Belief: The Religious Bodies of the United States and Canada*, vol. 1 (New York: Harper & Row, 1977), 212–13.

19. Karl Rahner, "Evolution and Original Sin," trans. Theodore L. Westow, in *The Evolving World and Theology*, ed. Johannes Metz (New York: Paulist Press, 1967), 61–73; Karl Rahner, "Erbsünde und Monogenismus," in *Theologie der Erbsünde*, ed. Karl-Heinz Weger (Freiburg: Herder, 1970), 176–223. Many Catholic theologians side with the later Rahner. See Zachary Hayes, *A Window to the Divine: Creation Theology* (Winona, MN: St. Mary's Press, 2007), 56: "If we assess these two areas of biblical interpretation with reference to the question of monogenism or polygenism, we can conclude that monogenism is not directly taught nor necessarily implied by Scripture."

"biologically" human, while Adam and Eve have the added value of being "theologically" human. The theological humans interbreed with biological humans and then over time take over the population: "These first true human beings also have descendants, which continue, to some extent, to interbreed with the non-intellectual hominids among whom they live. If God endows each individual that has even a single human ancestor with an intellect of its own, a reasonable rate of reproductive success and a reasonable selective advantage would easily replace a non-intellectual hominid population of 5,000 individuals with a . . . human population within three centuries."[20] Theological human beings would have Adam and Eve among their ancestors, even though the original human population never dipped as low as two individuals. As Kemp summarizes, "This theory is monogenetic with respect to theologically human beings but polygenetic with respect to the biological species."[21]

In a similar proposal, Antoine Suarez speculates that after modern human beings evolved, God transformed a single couple (or group) of those *Homo sapiens* and gifted them with moral responsibility and personhood.[22] In dialogue with Thomas Aquinas, Suarez suggests that when those responsible humans eventually sinned, God granted personhood to all the other coexisting *Homo sapiens*; they transitioned from "non-personal human (an animal)" to "personal modern human."[23] However, since God rendered them personal and responsible after the fall, he withheld original grace so that they began their responsible existence in a state of original sin. Meanwhile, all the descendants of the original sinners inherited sin by biological generation; thus, *all* human beings—whether part of the original human population or physical descendants—became sinners. Suarez's proposal avoids Kemp's interbreeding scenario because, after the first sin, God transforms all the remaining *Homo sapiens*. Nevertheless, both models count as punctiliar polygenism.

Although Protestants were facing similar dilemmas, young-earth creationists consistently defended classical monogenism.[24] Many old-earth creationists also resisted the consensus of paleoanthropology in favor of

20. Kenneth Kemp, "Science, Theology, and Monogenesis," *American Catholic Philosophical Quarterly* 85, no. 2 (2011): 232.

21. Kemp, "Science, Theology, and Monogenesis," 232.

22. Antoine Suarez, "Can We Give Up the Origin of Humanity from a Primal Couple without Giving Up the Teaching of Original Sin and Atonement?," *Science and Christian Belief* 27, no. 1 (2015): 59–83; Antoine Suarez, "'Transmission at Generation': Could Original Sin Have Happened at the Time When *Homo sapiens* Already Had a Large Population Size?," *Scientia et Fides* 4, no. 1 (2016): 253–94.

23. Suarez, "Can We Give Up the Origin of Humanity?," 76.

24. See Nigel Cameron, *Evolution and the Authority of the Bible* (Exeter, UK: Paternoster, 1983), 86.

monogenism. For example, in 1995 John Bloom argued from Genesis 2:7 that God created Adam and Eve supernaturally without any evolutionary relationship to preexisting hominins.[25] He claimed that "little or no interbreeding" had taken place and speculated "that this preadamic hominid population formed a cultural 'safety net' for Adam and Eve, so that after they were expelled from the Garden they could survive in the wild by adapting the skills of the hominids around them."[26] Hugh Ross and his colleagues at Reasons to Believe, also old-earth creationists, championed the special creation of Adam and Eve as sole progenitors of the human race who lived in Eden "somewhere near the juncture of Africa, Asia, and Europe in the relatively recent past (less than 100,000 years ago)."[27] They categorized preexisting hominins as animals that are qualitatively different from human beings. However, since making that judgment in 2006, Ross and Fazale Rana now accept the evidence of human interbreeding between Neanderthals and Denisovans, which they categorize as bestiality. Human-Neanderthal bestiality, they say, is consistent with the early human depravity of Genesis 6 and the divine condemnation in Leviticus 18:23. But they still interpret the data as evidence of common design rather than common descent. "Just because humans and Neanderthals interbred," they write, "does not mean they must be the same species. Mammals in the same family have been known to interbreed to produce viable hybrids."[28] They give the example of lions and tigers producing "ligers" and dolphins and whales producing "wholphins."[29]

Forty years earlier Derek Kidner, an evangelical Old Testament scholar, speculated that Adam lived in the Neolithic period, eight to ten thousand years ago. Adam evolved from an evolutionary ancestor when God supernaturally conferred his image on him, but Adam's first sin affected not only his descendants but all the other coexisting hominins. Kidner explains, "Adam's 'federal' headship of humanity extended . . . outwards to his contemporaries as well as onwards to his offspring, and his disobedience

25. John A. Bloom, "On Human Origins: A Survey," *Christian Scholar's Review* 27, no. 2 (1997): 198.
26. Bloom, "On Human Origins," 200. Of course, when Bloom's article came out there was no evidence of Neanderthal and Denisovan hybridization with modern humans.
27. Hugh Ross, *Creation as Science: A Testable Model Approach to End the Creation/Evolution Wars* (Colorado Springs: NavPress, 2006), 151.
28. Fazale Rana, with Hugh Ross, *Who Was Adam? A Creation Model Approach to the Origin of Humanity*, 2nd ed. (Covina, CA: RTB Press, 2015), 310–11. However, eleven years previously, when scientists lacked evidence of hybridization, Rana had insisted, "If Neanderthals interbred with modern humans, then by definition, they must be human." Fazale Rana, "Did Neanderthals and Humans Interbreed?," *Connections*, April 1, 2004, https://reasons.org/explore/publications/connections /read/connections/2004/04/01/did-neanderthals-and-humans-interbreed.
29. Rana, with Ross, *Who Was Adam?*, 311.

disinherited both alike."[30] Building on Kidner's polygenic federal headship model, John Stott rooted human uniqueness in the image of God and thought it was of no consequence whether God created Adam directly or using a preexisting hominin. The other hominin species were "pre-Adamic hominids, still *Homo sapiens* and not yet *Homo divinus*."[31]

Kidner's punctiliar polygenism inspired a cottage industry of views trying to locate Adam within a population of hominins.[32] Joshua Swamidass is a case in point. He fully embraces mainstream evolutionary biology but argues that every person alive today could be descended from a single couple as recently as six thousand years ago. His main thesis centers on the distinction between "genealogical" and "genetic" ancestry. Genetic ancestry is a recent method of tracing the history of DNA in our genome; by contrast, genealogical ancestry is an ordinary, nontechnical way of recording our ancestors. As Swamidass explains, "Our fathers, mothers, and grandparents are our ancestors. Going back into our history, all their grandparents are our ancestors too. In this sense, genealogical ancestry matches an ordinary understanding of ancestry."[33] Human beings are reproducing creatures, which means that each of us have parents, grandparents, great-grandparents, great-great-grandparents, and so on. Our genealogical records are not complete and are sometimes mistaken due to recording errors, adoption, or infidelity. Such problems reflect the limits of our knowledge, but they do not change the identity of our genealogical ancestors.

The problem is that human DNA does not capture most of our genealogical relationships. According to Swamidass, genetic ancestry is only one facet of a wider genealogy: "Consider a child's father and grandfather. They both are fully the child's genealogical ancestors. However, they are only

30. Derek Kidner, *Genesis*, Tyndale Old Testament Commentaries 1 (Downers Grove, IL: Inter-Varsity, 1967), 29.

31. John Stott, *Romans: God's Good News for the World* (Leicester, UK: Inter-Varsity, 1994), 164. Stott first used the expression *"homo divinus"* in the *Church of England Newspaper* (June 17, 1968). See Denis Alexander, *Creation or Evolution: Do We Have to Choose?*, 2nd ed. (Oxford: Monarch, 2014), 483n248.

32. For example, see Alexander, *Creation or Evolution*, 252–304, 316–65; E. K. Victor Pearce, *Who Was Adam?*, 2nd ed. (Exeter, UK: Paternoster, 1976) (originally published 1969); R. J. Berry, *God's Book of Works: The Nature and Theology of Nature* (London: T&T Clark, 2003), 227–30; R. J. Berry, "Did Darwin Dethrone Humankind?," in *Darwin, Creation and the Fall: Theological Challenges*, ed. R. J. Berry and T. A. Noble (Nottingham, UK: Apollos, 2009), 55–63; Tim Keller, "Creation, Evolution, and Christian Laypeople," BioLogos, February 23, 2012, http://biologos.org/uploads/projects/Keller_white _paper.pdf; Dick Fischer, *The Origins Solution: An Answer in the Creation-Evolution Debate* (Lima, OH: Fairway, 1996), who often cites the earlier work by Dominick M'Causland, *Adam and the Adamite: Or the Harmony of Scripture and Ethnology* (London: Richard Bentley, 1864).

33. S. Joshua Swamidass, *The Genealogical Adam and Eve: The Surprising Science of Universal Ancestry* (Downers Grove, IL: IVP Academic, 2019), 32.

partially the child's genetic ancestors, approximately 1/2 and 1/4, respectively. The same is true of the child's mother and grandmothers. Genetic ancestry continues to dilute each generation: 1/8, 1/16, 1/32 . . . to a number so small it is unlikely a descendant has any genetic material from most of their ancestors. The many genealogical ancestors that pass us no DNA are not our genetic ancestors."[34] This difference between genealogical and genetic ancestry leads to surprising results. For example, Swamidass argues, mainstream evolution is entirely consistent with the claim that God directly created Adam and Eve about six thousand years ago as the ancestors of all human beings alive today. In fact, genealogical ancestry suggests that *multiple* couples in our distant past are ancestors of every living person today. However, Swamidass's hypothesis assumes that Adam and Eve were not the first human beings.[35] Other "biological" humans made in God's image lived outside Eden: "They are not yet affected by Adam's fall. They have a sense of right and wrong, written on their hearts (Rom 2:15), but they are not morally perfect. They do wrong at times. They are subject to physical death, which prevents their wrongdoing from growing into true evil (Gen 6:3)."[36] As with Kenneth Kemp's proposal, Swamidass's genealogical Adam and Eve interbred with people outside Eden and, after multiple generations, became ancestors of every living human.[37]

The Resilience of Biblical Monogenism

As these new proposals keep proliferating, it is clear that the evolutionary picture has held us captive. Against these trends, my counterthesis is *biblical monogenism*: God supernaturally created Adam and Eve as the sole progenitors—genealogical *and* genetic—of the entire human race without a coexisting interbreeding population or preexisting ancestors. God creates the first human beings on the sixth day (Gen. 1:27), and the broader context

---

34. Swamidass, *Genealogical Adam and Eve*, 35–36.

35. Swamidass is engaging in a thought experiment and does not necessarily believe that his genealogical hypothesis is true (Swamidass, *Genealogical Adam and Eve*, 8, 24–25). Some of my comments here draw from my review: Hans Madueme, "Evolution *and* Historical Adam? A Provocative but Unconvincing Attempt," Gospel Coalition, March 2, 2020, https://www.thegospelcoalition.org/reviews/genealogical-adam-eve-swamidass/.

36. Swamidass, *Genealogical Adam and Eve*, 175.

37. For a similar genealogical account that has Adam and Eve living a few thousand years ago, interbreeding with other hominins, and eventually becoming common ancestors of all humanity, see Jon Garvey, *The Generations of Heaven and Earth: Adam, the Ancient World, and Biblical Theology* (Eugene, OR: Cascade Books, 2020); and Andrew Loke, *The Origins of Humanity and Evolution: Science and Scripture in Conversation* (London: T&T Clark, 2022).

of Genesis 1–5 informs us that their names are Adam and Eve. The human race does not begin with a population but with two people.

However, this form of monogenism is increasingly challenged exegetically. John Walton, for example, thinks that God created a large population of human beings in Genesis 1 before creating Adam and Eve in Genesis 2.[38] Walton notes that Genesis uses the word *adam* in various ways, sometimes with or without a definite article. He says we should normally take *adam* as generic, archetypal, or representative, implying that "the representational role is more important than the individual."[39] Even so, Walton's distinction between archetypal Adam and historical Adam is needlessly disjunctive and contradicts Scripture. The apostle Paul, citing Genesis 2:7 and 2:22, straightforwardly assumes Adam is a historical individual (1 Tim. 2:13); furthermore, Genesis 5:1–2 reiterates Genesis 1:27 and explicitly identifies the first human being *as* Adam ("This is the written account of Adam's family line" [Gen. 5:1]). The idea of an original population is foreign to Scripture.

The fact that God forms Adam from the dust of the earth, where he will return in death (Gen. 3:19), reflects a continuity between Adam and the soil (*adamah*). But there is stark discontinuity too. Adam becomes a living being when God breathes into his nostrils (2:7), with no hint of an evolutionary process.[40] Some interpret the "dust" in 2:7 as symbolic of evolutionary ancestors, but details in the narrative militate against this move.[41] First, the divine verdict in 3:19 that "you are dust, and to dust you shall return" implies that the dust is the soil that awaits Adam upon death, not an ancestral hominin; for consistency, we should interpret dust in 2:7 similarly. Second, any evolutionary ancestor of Adam would have been a *nephesh* creature: "Now out of the ground the LORD God had formed every beast of the field and every bird of the heavens and brought them to the man to see what he would call them. And whatever the man called every living creature [*nephesh*], that was its name" (2:19). In 2:7, however, when God breathed into Adam's nostrils, he *became* a living being, which of course implies that he was *not* a living being beforehand. The inspired account of Adam's creation contradicts human evolution.[42]

38. John Walton, *The Lost World of Adam and Eve: Genesis 2–3 and the Human Origins Debate* (Downers Grove, IL: IVP Academic, 2015), 58–69, and passim. He writes that "Adam and Eve should be considered as having been included in that [larger population]" (183).

39. Walton, *Lost World of Adam and Eve*, 61.

40. John Murray, "Origin of Man," in *Collected Writings of John Murray*, 4 vols. (Edinburgh: Banner of Truth Trust, 1977), 2:7.

41. Millard Erickson, *Christian Theology*, 3rd ed. (Grand Rapids: Baker Academic, 2013), 447–48.

42. This conflict between Adam's creation and evolution heightens if we consider Eve's creation in Gen. 2:21–22. Here, too, we see a supernatural creation far removed from any plausible evolutionary

Other details in Genesis 1–4 support biblical monogenism. The description of Eve as the "mother of all living" (3:20) confirms Adam and Eve as genealogical ancestors of the human race.[43] Walton resists this conclusion because of "similar statements in Genesis 4:20–21, where Jabal is 'the father of those who live in tents and raise livestock' and Jubal is 'the father of all who play stringed instruments.'"[44] Walton is correct that Jabal and Jubal are only "fathers" in a metaphorical sense, but the context of Genesis 3:20 invites the literal reading for several reasons: there was no man to till the ground (2:5), Adam was alone (2:18), and when he named the animals he found no one else like him (2:19–20). After Adam names the animals, God forms Eve from his rib. Adam calls her "woman," in contrast to "man," implying that she is the first woman and that he is naming a being that hadn't existed before (unlike the animals). Furthermore, "Adam" often signifies the generic term for humanity ("sons of mankind"); men and women are "sons of Adam" (Pss. 11:4; 49:1; 62:8; 1 Kings 8:39). This linguistic nuance—the same Hebrew word for both Adam and humanity—reflects the canonical mindset that the human race derives from Adam the first man. The Genesis flood narrative corroborates this position, typologically, when it presents the post-flood world as a new creation and Noah as a new Adam and father of post-flood humanity.[45]

---

scenario. C. John Collins notes that Gen. 2:7 may not rule out a developmental process: "There is the way that Psalm 103:14 sings (with words from Gen. 2:7), 'for he [God] knows how we are *formed*; he remembers that we are *dust*' (using ESV margin). Each of us is, ultimately, 'formed of dust,' even if the dust has gone through a few intermediate (genetic) steps!" (C. John Collins, "A Historical Adam: Old-Earth Creation View," in *Four Views on the Historical Adam*, ed. Matthew Barrett and Ardel Caneday [Grand Rapids: Zondervan, 2013], 170). Collins makes a fair point, and we might also add Job 10:9. However, the broader contexts of Job 10:9 and Ps. 103:14 allude metaphorically to human growth. Nothing in the immediate context of Gen. 2:7 even hints at the evolutionary creation of Adam.

43. Michael LeFebvre disagrees with my reading of Gen. 3:20 and argues instead that "[Gen. 3:20] is about 'all living' human beings—in the *soteriological* sense of the term in light of Gen. 3:15—being those found among 'the seed of the woman.' She is the mother of all who have the hope of life, not the mother of all humans" (Michael LeFebvre, "Adam Reigns in Eden: Genesis and the Origins of Kingship," *Bulletin of Ecclesial Theology* 5, no. 2 [2018]: 52, my emphasis). While Adam may be hinting proleptically to Eve as the mother of those whom God will make spiritually alive, that richer meaning need not contradict the complementary truth that she is the physical mother of all humanity as such.

44. John Walton, "A Historical Adam: Archetypal Creation View," in Barrett and Caneday, *Four Views on the Historical Adam*, 97. Walton also argues that the word "living" in Gen. 3:20 "can refer to all creatures, yet all animals are not biological descendants of Eve" (Walton, *Lost World of Adam and Eve*, 187). These arguments are not compelling and are guilty of the fallacy of illegitimate totality transfer: "One instance of a word will not bear all the meanings possible for that word." Moisés Silva, *Biblical Words and Their Meaning: An Introduction to Lexical Semantics* (Grand Rapids: Zondervan, 1983), 25.

45. Daniel Streett, "As It Was in the Days of Noah: The Prophets' Typological Interpretation of Noah's Flood," *Criswell Theological Review* 5, no. 1 (2007): 33–51, esp. 37–38.

The New Testament shares this monogenism. Luke's genealogy extends all the way back to Adam because he was the first human being (Luke 3:23–38).[46] Paul likewise assumes a biblical monogenism when he writes, "For Adam was formed first, then Eve; and Adam was not deceived, but the woman was deceived and became a transgressor" (1 Tim. 2:13–14). Paul simply takes it for granted that Adam was the first human based on reading Genesis 2–3 historically.[47] He does the same in 1 Corinthians 11:8–9, where he gives instructions about worship and assumes that Adam and Eve were the first human beings (and that Adam came first). These canonical witnesses are not mere proof texts; rather, they undergird the apostolic conception of a single couple as biological progenitors—not merely representatives—of the entire human race.

The monogenist Adam shows up in Acts 17:26 during Paul's Areopagite address: "From one man he made all nations, that they should inhabit the earth" (NIV). The oldest manuscripts have no noun after "one" (*enos*). This textual ambiguity gives theologians like Gijsbert van den Brink wiggle room to argue that Acts 17:26 "cannot serve as a proof text for the belief that all humans stem from a single couple."[48] In van den Brink's summary of the science of human origins, the "Out of Africa" hypothesis posits that modern humans share a common origin in Africa (monophyletism), while the rival "Multiregional" hypothesis claims that they evolved in different parts of the world (polyphyletism).[49] He takes Acts 17:26 to be teaching monophyletism without monogenism: humans derive from one stock, not from a single

46. I return to Luke's genealogy below.

47. Commenting on 1 Tim. 2:13–14 and other Pauline passages, Walton writes, "No claims are made in the New Testament that all humans are biologically descended from Adam and Eve and therefore genetically derived from them" (Walton, "Historical Adam," 107). Walton may be right that Paul says nothing *explicitly* about material origins, but Paul doesn't have to. The implicit meaning is obvious to readers.

48. Gijsbert van den Brink, *Reformed Theology and Evolutionary Theory* (Grand Rapids: Eerdmans, 2020), 163n8. For a detailed argument with the same conclusion, see William Horst, "From One Person? Exegetical Alternatives to a Monogenetic Reading of Acts 17:26," *Perspectives on Science and Christian Faith* 74, no. 2 (2022): 77–91. Similarly, see Kemp, "Science, Theology, and Monogenesis," 218.

49. However, van den Brink's proposal is based on outdated science. The consensus today is that different parts of the human genome have different ancestries and that interbreeding has been a dominant factor in shaping the modern human genome. Thus there is continued support for *both* an African and a multiregional origin—*Homo sapiens sapiens* spread from Africa and interbred with existing populations they encountered in Eurasia. In addition, they also interbred with a ghost population while they were still in Africa. See Alan R. Templeton, "The Importance of Gene Flow in Human Evolution," *Human Population Genetics and Genomics* 3, no. 3 (2023). For a contrasting position, see Chris Stringer, "Why We Are Not All Multiregionalists Now," *Trends in Ecology and Evolution* 29, no. 5 (2014): 248–51.

couple. However, while monophyletism is preferable to polyphyletism, it still falls short. The unity of the human race is not a post-Darwinian metaphysical unity but an Adamic ancestral bond.[50] In addition, Adamic ancestry fits seamlessly with the broader context of Paul's Areopagite address in Acts 17, including his mention of the Lord who made heaven and earth (v. 24), and who gives life and breath to everyone (v. 25), both of which echo Adam's creation in Genesis 1 and 2. The monogenist reading also recalls Paul's frequent use of the word *enos* in Romans in association with Adam (see Rom. 5:15, 16, 17, 18, and 19) and fits with how Luke ends his genealogy with Adam (Luke 3:38). No wonder commentators today, and in the past, overwhelmingly identify the "one" in Acts 17:26 with Adam.[51]

Biblical monogenism is central to Romans 5:12–21 and 1 Corinthians 15:21–22, where Paul's argument relies on the fact that Adam is the first human and everyone else a descendant. In Romans 5:12, Paul draws on Genesis 3 to reiterate the first man's disobedience and then, two verses later, explains that death reigned from the time of Adam to the time of Moses (Rom. 5:14). *All* human beings after the dawn of humanity until the Mosaic era died because of Adam's sin, even though none disobeyed an explicit command as Adam had done.[52] The logic of Paul's argument requires Adam to be the first human and progenitor of humanity, building on Paul's earlier insistence that no one is righteous: both Jews and gentiles are sinners (Rom. 2:1–3:20). Every descendant is doomed to sin because Adam is the first human and the first sinner.

My monogenist reading of 1 Corinthians 15:21–22 is informed by Paul's statement later in verses 45 and 47 where he explicitly identifies Adam as the first man. Walton is skeptical: "Here Adam is called the 'first' man, but in the context of the contrast with Christ as the 'last' Adam, it cannot be seen as a claim that Adam was the first biological specimen. Since

50. Walton suggests that Paul is referring to Noah, not Adam: "If this is true, this verse could be removed from the discussion about Adam as the genetic/biological forebear of all humanity" (Walton, "Historical Adam," 105). Walton's interpretation is possible but unlikely.

51. The NIV translation (one *man*) reflects the majority opinion among commentators that Paul is alluding to Adam. See Flavien Pardigon, *Paul against the Idols: A Contextual Reading of the Areopagus Speech* (Eugene, OR: Wipf & Stock, 2019), 166–67; Craig Keener, *Acts: An Exegetical Commentary*, 4 vols. (Grand Rapids: Baker Academic, 2012–15), 3:2645–47. Several later manuscripts read "from one blood," but that rendering is still an allusion to Adam. See Darrell Bock, *Acts* (Grand Rapids: Baker Academic, 2007), 574; Bruce Metzger, *A Textual Commentary on the Greek New Testament: A Companion Volume to the United Bible Societies' Greek New Testament*, 4th ed. (New York: United Bible Societies, 1994), 404–5.

52. Paul highlights Adam's sin instead of Eve's *prior* sin because it was Adam who received the direct command and God appointed him humanity's representative. On Rom. 5:14, see Thomas Schreiner, *Romans*, 2nd ed. (Grand Rapids: Baker Academic, 2018), 283–86.

Christ was not the last biological specimen, we must instead conclude that this text is talking about the first archetype and the last archetype."[53] But Walton's reasoning is not convincing. While it is true that Adam plays an archetypal role, Paul also presupposes Adam as the first man *biologically*. He is the "first" of all that bear his image, which implies that Adam was the prototype. Genesis 5:3 states that Seth is born in the image of Adam through ordinary generation; hence when Paul speaks about the image of the "man of dust" in 1 Corinthians 15:49, he is assuming the same process of physical descent. In the biblical context, Adam must have been the first human being in order to pass on his own image to all his descendants. Remarking on this verse, Richard Gaffin writes, *"Image bearers of Adam* is hardly an apt, much less valid or even intelligible, description of human beings who are held either to have existed before Adam or subsequently not have descended from him. . . . There is no hope of salvation for sinners who do not bear the image of Adam by ordinary generation."[54] Adam's archetypal function is worthless unless he is also the first human being.

Paul is unambiguous when he parses the biological implications of the future resurrection. In 1 Corinthians 15:39 he writes, "For not all flesh is the same, but there is one kind for humans, another for animals, another for birds, and another for fish." That there is *one* kind of "flesh" for humanity already suggests an underlying unity rather than plurality. As Paul goes on to explain, our human flesh is a "natural body" with physical frailties that will ultimately lead to death; but God will raise the dead into a new kind of physical existence that Paul calls a "spiritual body" (1 Cor. 15:42–44). Paul even traces the attributes of the natural body all the way back to Adam's condition when he was created in Genesis 2:7 (cited in 1 Cor. 15:45).[55] In other words, the one kind of flesh that all human beings share is rooted in our physical descent from the first man Adam. Reading 1 Corinthians 15:45 in light of the rest of the chapter, we see that in Paul's inspired mind the resurrection *implies* biblical monogenism.

Admittedly, readers of Genesis 1–4 ever since Isaac La Peyrère have noticed textual details that raise the possibility that Adam and Eve were not alone. For instance, the Cain and Abel narrative in Genesis 4 covers

53. Walton, "Historical Adam," 107.

54. Richard Gaffin Jr., *No Adam, No Gospel: Adam and the History of Redemption* (Phillipsburg, NJ: P&R, 2015), 12, emphasis original. "Ordinary generation" should be interpreted expansively to mean not "ordinary birth" alone but also cases like C-section, IVF, and the like—individuals born in such cases are still genealogical and genetic descendants of Adam.

55. Paul's remarks in 1 Cor. 15:42–45, especially his citation of Gen. 2:7, raise intriguing questions about the prelapsarian condition (see chap. 6).

the early stages of humanity when only a handful of people were alive—
Adam, Eve, Cain, Abel—yet, according to Walter Moberly, the text itself
assumes a larger population.[56] Consider the old puzzle of Cain's wife: Who
was she? Where did she come from? Did Cain commit incest by marrying
his sister, or did he marry someone else biologically unrelated to Adam?
In Genesis 4:2, we notice that Abel is a keeper of sheep and Cain a tiller
of the ground, which suggests to Moberly an already existing population
with those tasks already well-delineated. Cain later murders Abel in an
open field (Gen. 4:8), presumably to avoid any populated settlements and
to do the dark deed in secret. Again, Genesis itself seems to assume an
already populated planet.

There is more. After slaying his brother, Cain bemoans his fate as a "wan-
derer on the earth," on the run from those who would kill him (Gen. 4:14).
If only a few people were living on the planet, Moberly surmises, "the more
Cain wandered, the farther away [he would be] from these other people."[57]
However, Cain's fear assumes quite the opposite: a *populated* world. Without clan protection, he's a sitting duck for outside marauders. Let us not
forget, too, that Cain famously builds a city in verse 17; while we are not to
think of a sprawling metropolis, Moberly likens it to a sizable settlement,
which of course still contradicts the idea that only a few people were alive
at the time. From all this he infers that "if the story in itself presupposes
a regularly populated earth, while its context requires an almost entirely
unpopulated earth, there is a hypothesis that readily commends itself. This
is that the story itself has a history, and in the course of that history, it
has changed locations, moved from an original context within the regular
parameters of human history—presumably, the world of ancient Israel,
which would have been familiar to the narrator—to its present context at
the very outset of human history."[58]

Moberly alleges similar discrepancies in Genesis 4:17–24, a passage listing Cain's descendants. To his mind, the narrative implies that these descendants are "known in the time of the narrator."[59] Tentmakers, flute play-
ers, and the rest are all familiar to the Genesis narrator, else why take the
time to mention those ancestors? Yet *all of Cain's descendants were destroyed
by the flood*; only Noah and his family survived (descendants of Seth, not

56. I am following Walter Moberly, "How Should One Read the Early Chapters of Genesis?," in
Reading Genesis after Darwin, ed. Stephen C. Barton and David Wilkinson (Oxford: Oxford University
Press, 2009), 5–21.

57. Moberly, "How Should One Read?," 8.

58. Moberly, "How Should One Read?," 9.

59. Moberly, "How Should One Read?," 13.

Cain). Moberly explains this apparent discrepancy by invoking his earlier hypothesis—namely, that these individual narratives have their own unique histories: "They have been transposed from their original context and relocated in their present context. In that way, one can both do justice to the implications of the particular units in their own right and still appreciate the use to which they have been put in their narrative context."[60] In short, Moberly views the early chapters of Genesis as a quasi-fictional narrative constructed with disparate pieces that originate from much later, disconnected historical periods.

Moberly resolves the textual ambiguities of early Genesis by using historical criticism, while Walton appeals to a larger population of hominins: "It would mean that there may be other people (in the image of God) in Genesis 2–4, not just Adam and Eve and their family."[61] Against such speculative claims, biblical monogenism accepts the explicit monogenist texts reviewed earlier and thus preserves Scripture's historical and divine integrity. The mysteries of Nod's residents and Cain's fear after murdering Abel resolve once we recognize that Genesis 1–11 is a highly compressed and selective narrative that covers *centuries* of history stripped down to a few high points. The text does not narrate any details in the lives of many of the descendants of Adam and Eve (e.g., Gen. 5:4, "After Seth was born, Adam lived 800 years *and had other sons and daughters*" [NIV]).[62]

This recognition that Adam and Eve had many children whose lives are not recorded in Genesis answers the puzzle that haunted La Peyrère (and others). The people living in Nod were descendants of Adam and Eve. Cain's mark and his fear make sense because many younger relatives were alive at the time, all of them passed over in early Genesis. As for the mystery of Cain's wife, he almost certainly married one of his sisters, which is the dominant view in both Jewish and Christian tradition.[63] Admittedly, the idea that Cain married his sister and was thus involved in an incestuous relationship raises a different set of challenges, but I am assuming that, at this early stage of redemptive history, incest by necessity did not yet have

---

60. Moberly, "How Should One Read?," 13.

61. Walton, *Lost World of Adam and Eve*, 64. For my misgivings about Moberly's theology of revelation, see Hans Madueme, "Adam Revisited: First Man or One of Many?," *Books at a Glance*, May 2, 2016, https://www.booksataglance.com/blog/adam-revisited-first-man-one-many/.

62. See John Calvin, *Commentaries on the First Book of Moses Called Genesis*, trans. John King, 2 vols. (Grand Rapids: Eerdmans, 1948), 1:215: "This, however, is without controversy, that many persons, as well males and females, are omitted in this narrative."

63. On the fascinating Jewish discussion, beginning with Jubilees 4:1–11, see John Byron, *Cain and Abel in Text and Tradition: Jewish and Christian Traditions of the First Sibling Rivalry* (Leiden: Brill, 2011), 24–29.

any ethical or moral connotations (on later prohibitions, see Lev. 18:1–18; 20:11–20).[64]

Adam as the original man grounds the unity of the human race. In Genesis 5:3, we learn that being in someone's image and likeness is tied to sonship. Seth, as the image of Adam, "has been born from Adam, reflects Adam's nature, and is Adam's son."[65] So, too, Adam; he is the son of God because he is made in God's image and likeness (Gen. 1:26). Luke's genealogy lists thirty-seven names documenting each father and culminating in Luke 3:38—"the son of Enos, the son of Seth, the son of Adam, the son of God." Adam is God's "earthly son," and human procreation then enlarges the divine family by incorporating Adam's posterity.[66] Similarly, Acts 17:29 identifies human beings as God's offspring, part of God's family; to be human is to be related to Adam genealogically and thereby share a divine origin.[67] Given the biblical association between God *creating* Adam and fathers *begetting* children, the basis for all humans bearing God's image is that Adam and Eve are "the mother and father of all peoples."[68]

Physical descent from Adam implies that all human beings—for example, Africans, Asians, South Americans, and Europeans—have the same ontological status. Biblical monogenism thus rejects the racism of nineteenth-century polygenism and also undermines the logic of modern racism. Nevertheless, we should clarify that while monogenism served as a necessary bulwark against racism, it proved insufficient in isolation. For instance, North American Christians throughout history often maintained racist views while adhering to monogenism; they believed humanity originated

64. Incest produces harmful traits and reduces the offspring's chances of survival—that is, "inbreeding depression." However, "at this early date, harmful mutations had not yet occurred, and there would have been no bad results from inbreeding. Furthermore, the cultural taboo against incest would also not have existed." Todd Wood and Joseph Francis, "Genetics of Adam," in *What Happened in the Garden? The Reality and Ramifications of the Creation and Fall of Man*, ed. Abner Chou (Grand Rapids: Kregel, 2016), 91.

65. G. K. Beale, *A New Testament Biblical Theology: The Unfolding of the Old Testament in the New* (Grand Rapids: Baker Academic, 2011), 402.

66. Henri Blocher, *In the Beginning: The Opening Chapters of Genesis*, trans. David G. Preston (Downers Grove, IL: InterVarsity, 1984), 89.

67. See Gavin Ortlund, "Image of Adam, Son of God: Genesis 5:3 and Luke 3:38 in Intercanonical Dialogue," *Journal of the Evangelical Theological Society* 57, no. 4 (2014): 673–88. According to Brian Rosner (*Known by God: A Biblical Theology of Personal Identity* [Grand Rapids: Zondervan, 2017]), "Our very identity as human beings is tied up with being children of God made in the image of God. And the story of redemption is one of God choosing to bless Abraham and the children of Abraham as the restored children of God" (84).

68. J. Daniel Hays, *From Every People and Nation: A Biblical Theology of Race* (Downers Grove, IL: InterVarsity, 2003), 48.

from Adam and Eve, later diversifying into distinct races.[69] Notwithstanding those complexities, monogenism's enduring legacy is in establishing the profound unity that binds all humans together.

This unity of the human race is the very basis of the atonement and the forgiveness of sins, the foundation for the entire structure of sin and salvation.[70] Sin and death entered the world through Adam the biological head of the human race (Rom. 5:12; 1 Cor. 15:22). Since humanity belongs to one biological family, the Son of God entered into that same family, taking on the very same nature in the incarnation (John 1:14). As Gregory of Nazianzus said, "For that which He has not assumed He has not healed."[71] Jesus is therefore the savior of all people (1 Tim. 4:10; 1 John 4:14), and the possibility of atonement extends to all who hail from the same family as Adam and Eve. As the nineteenth-century churchman and naturalist Thomas Smyth avowed, "The unity of the human race is absolutely necessary, therefore, to account for the present condition of human nature in consistency with the wisdom and justice of God, and also to render salvation possible to ANY human being."[72]

There may be an even deeper logic to biblical monogenism. Scripture is relatively silent here, but we can speculate in one or two directions. Since the triune God is a unity-in-diversity, his image bearers (Adam and his offspring) necessarily reflect that triune shape. The divine image is not merely a loose collection of individuals but an organic unity of every man and woman.[73] Obeying the command to be fruitful and multiply manifests the divine image throughout creation (Gen. 1:25–27; 9:1, 7). As Bavinck describes in soaring prose,

> Not the man alone, nor the man and woman together, but only the whole of humanity is the fully developed image of God, his children, his offspring. The

69. See Colin Kidd, *The Forging of Races: Race and Scripture in the Protestant Atlantic World, 1600–2000* (Cambridge: Cambridge University Press, 2006), esp. 121–67.

70. For a typical patristic example of how the unity of the human race in Adam is assumed in soteriology, see Ellen Scully, "The Soteriology of Hilary of Poitiers: A Latin Mystical Model of Redemption," *Augustinianum* 52, no. 1 (2012): 159–95, esp. 188–93.

71. This idea goes back to Origen and was famously deployed by Gregory of Nazianzus against the Apollinarian heresy. Gregory of Nazianzus, "To Cledonius the Priest against Apollinarius" (Letter 101), in *Nicene and Post-Nicene Fathers*, 2nd series, vol. 7, ed. Philip Schaff and Henry Wace (New York: Christian Literature, 1894), 440.

72. Thomas Smyth, *The Unity of the Human Races Proved to Be the Doctrine of Scripture, Reason and Science* (New York: Putnam, 1850), 48, emphasis original.

73. My thinking here is indebted to Nathaniel Sutanto, "Herman Bavinck on the Image of God and Original Sin," *International Journal of Systematic Theology* 18 (2016): 174–90. Sutanto's analysis builds on James Eglinton, *Trinity and Organism: Towards a New Reading of Herman Bavinck's Organic Motif* (New York: T&T Clark, 2012).

image of God is much too rich for it to be fully realized in a single human being, however richly gifted that human being may be. It can only be somewhat unfolded in its depth and riches in a humanity counting billions of members. Just as the traces of God . . . are spread over many, many works, in both space and time, so also the image of God can only be displayed in all its dimensions and characteristic features in a humanity whose members exist both successively one after the other and contemporaneously side by side. . . . Not as a heap of souls on a tract of land, not as a loose aggregate of individuals, but as having been created out of one blood; as one household and one family, humanity is the image and likeness of God.[74]

On this model, biological descent from Adam is integral to displaying the divine image.

Monogenism may also clarify important distinctions between human beings and other creatures. In the biblical hierarchy, human beings have greater value than other creatures, as when Jesus says that we have greater worth than sparrows (Matt. 10:31; see also 12:12). Although animals are part of the groaning creation, they experience no sin, much less Christ making personal atonement for them.[75] They share a biological unity but without the intelligence, creativity, wisdom, relationality, or ability to exercise dominion associated with the *imago Dei* (Gen. 1:25–27). In the case of angelic beings, Scripture suggests that some of their number sinned and that Satan is a fallen angel.[76] The first angelic sin corrupted a host of angels who became demonic spirits, while the rest remained holy. Since God is omnipotent, presumably he could have redeemed all the fallen angels; Scripture does not tell us why he chooses to reserve his mercy for sinful humans. However, given what God reveals about monogenism, it is possible that the devil's sin, unlike Adam's, did not spread to *every* angel because angels cannot procreate and thus exist as independent, atomistic entities (Matt. 22:30). One might speculate further that the absence of a genealogical unity among angels explains why fallen angels are unredeemable—the

74. Herman Bavinck, *Reformed Dogmatics*, ed. John Bolt, trans. John Vriend, 4 vols. (Grand Rapids: Baker Academic, 2003–8), 2:577. See also Brian Mattson, *Restored to Our Destiny: Eschatology and the Image of God in Herman Bavinck's Reformed Dogmatics* (Leiden: Brill, 2011), 145–48. Bavinck's notion of the image of God has both a corporate and an individual component; thus, the image of God as most fully realized in humanity *corporately* should not be set against the biblical teaching that each human *individually* is made in God's image. Also, Bavinck's remark above that the image of God is not "fully realized in a single human being" does not negate the fact that Jesus Christ—the God-man—*does* fully realize the image of God (cf. 2 Cor. 4:4; Col. 1:15; Heb. 1:3).

75. The question of whether animals are capable of sinning is debated, especially among ethologists (see my discussion in chaps. 5 and 7).

76. On the angelic fall, see Graham Cole, *Against the Darkness: The Doctrine of Angels, Satan, and Demons* (Wheaton: Crossway, 2019), 81–82, 90–94.

Son of God could not assume an angelic substance with the capacity to incorporate multiple angels. Angels lack the image of God and the generative ability (or begetting) that mirrors and thereby manifests the tri-personal God. These differences, between human beings on the one hand and angels and animals on the other, suggest that biblical monogenism is integral to the redemptive story.[77]

Adam between Science and Dogma

The monogenism debate has implications for the fall of Adam and Eve. Non-lapsarian theologians have long made peace with the relevant sciences and deny that sin had a beginning in history.[78] Other theologians, however, have tried to reconcile a historical Adam with the evolutionary and genomic evidence, believing that some kind of "fall" is essential to the biblical story. Some proposals have an event-like character to the fall, while others opt for a more gradualist picture.[79] This kind of research will often demand interdisciplinary dialogue and the space for theologians to float hypothetical theories. In those instances when scientific theories conflict with the traditional interpretation of Scripture, it can help to speculate about what theological implications follow if the theories were actually true.[80] But such hypothetical proposals should never be binding on the church.

The Adam-of-the-Gaps Fallacy

Nevertheless, a weakness of many evolutionary lapsarian proposals is that they often succumb to the "Adam-of-the-gaps" fallacy. Paleoanthropology, genomic science, and associated disciplines are taken as the most reliable sources of truth that provide the main story; the theologian's task then becomes to locate the historical Adam *within* that story. Much like nineteenth-century hard concordism, Adam is held hostage to the fortunes of science. Rahner's shift from monogenism to polygenism exemplifies this

77. Admittedly, evolutionary monogenism and related positions can affirm much of what I have laid out here (B. B. Warfield comes to mind). I am grateful for the agreement but wonder whether such positions rely on borrowed capital that retains dogmatic implications of biblical monogenism—e.g., the unity of the human race—while wrongly dropping some of its essential commitments.

78. I interact with non-lapsarian theologies in chap. 6.

79. See the discussion in Alexander, *Creation or Evolution*, 287–94, 316–19, 355–65; and Thomas McCall, *Against God and Nature: The Doctrine of Sin* (Wheaton: Crossway, 2019), 383–403.

80. I take that to be C. John Collins's intent in his "mere historical Adam-and-Eve-ism" and the speculative scenarios in *Did Adam and Eve Really Exist? Who They Were and Why You Should Care* (Wheaton: Crossway, 2011), 105–31.

dynamic (see above).[81] The same holds for Henri Blocher, who originally dated Adam around 40,000 BCE but retreated to 100,000 BCE as new data came in.[82] Rahner and Blocher are searching for Adam within the gaps of the paleoanthropological record.

The Adam-of-the-gaps fallacy reflects a deeper problem of scientific developments curtailing the available theological options. Each new batch of scientific models with some theory about Adam is hailed as a sign of progress only to be replaced by the next generation of proposals, every iteration further removed from the biblical narrative. Along these lines, James K. A. Smith's fall account is temporal rather than punctiliar, positing a large population that gradually falls away from its original mandate: "Since we're dealing with a larger population in this 'garden,' so to speak, there is not one discrete event at time T_1 where 'the transgression' occurs. However, there is still a temporal, episodic nature of a Fall. We might imagine a Fall-in-process, a sort of probationary period in which God is watching. . . . So the Fall might take place over time T_1-T_3. But there is some significant sense of before and after in this scenario."[83]

One strength of Smith's proposal is his recognition that a historical fall functions as a theodicy in Christian theology. However, his proposal suffers from several weaknesses, not least a very minimal notion of original goodness; that is, since the hominins gradually began to disobey God, there must have been a prior phase of "innocence" (in chap. 5, I argue that Scripture presents a far more radical picture of original goodness). Furthermore, Smith's polygenism clashes with explicit biblical texts and is vulnerable to the problems I laid out earlier. Such tensions are inevitable because the dialogue between Adam and science is a trade-off between biblical and scientific plausibility. To the degree that our doctrines of creation and fall hew closely to the biblical story, they will strain against the standard evolutionary story. Smith's proposal shares the same strengths and weaknesses of nineteenth-century hard concordism: as the science inevitably moves on, his proposal will also likely need revision.[84]

81. For background, see Kevin A. McMahon, "Karl Rahner and the Theology of Human Origins," *Thomist* 66, no. 4 (2002): 499–517.

82. See Henri Blocher, "The Theology of the Fall and the Origins of Evil," in Berry and Noble, *Darwin, Creation and the Fall*, 171–72.

83. James K. A. Smith, "What Stands on the Fall? A Philosophical Exploration," in *Evolution and the Fall*, ed. William Cavanaugh and James K. A. Smith (Grand Rapids: Eerdmans, 2017), 62.

84. Having said that, I recognize that Smith's essay is a speculative exercise, not a dogmatic proposal; as he says, "My project is more a thought project meant to stretch and prompt our theological imagination" (Smith, "What Stands on the Fall?," 56). Celia Deane-Drummond's attempt to integrate niche construction theory (NCT) with human origins shares some of the same problems (NCT is a

The Adam-of-the-gaps strategy gives science too much power and over-looks the possibility that the current science of human origins is unreliable despite our best efforts. This dynamic is reminiscent of ANE comparative studies. Regarding the latter, Don Collett writes, "the sense relations created by Scripture's own literary form are either marginalized or subordinated to a historically reconstructed referent, the latter of which allegedly has a better chance than Scripture's own literary form of providing modern readers with access to the Bible's 'real' meaning."[85] Adam-of-the-gaps pro-posals deploy evolutionary and genetic science in the same way and thus undermine the apostolic testimony. In the Protestant principle of Scripture, however, the apostolic reading of Genesis is epistemically binding and supersedes any conflicting scientific understanding of human origins—call this the *New Testament dogmatic rule*. This dogmatic rule assumes that apostolic interpretation of the Old Testament is infallible and therefore nonnegotiable. Christians should agree with the apostles that Adam was historical, the first man, and (alongside Eve) sole ancestor of the human race. However, for many of the lapsarian proposals engaging evolutionary biology, epistemic authority no longer lies in the canonical text but has been ceded to extratextual sources of knowledge (e.g., natural science). But if Christians can reject the historical judgments of the apostles, then the very idea of special revelation collapses.

Apostolic Authority and the New Testament Dogmatic Rule

Objections to this New Testament dogmatic rule lie thick on the ground. First, some will rejoin that God speaks with a lisp, accommodating his Word to the lowly capacities of human beings. Biblical monogenism is scientifi-cally mistaken, the charge goes, and reflects the fact that God inspired the biblical authors to speak in categories appropriate to their limited capaci-ties. Kenton Sparks defends this idea when he explains that errors in the Bible "stem, not from the character of our perfect God, but from his adoption in revelation of the finite and fallen perspectives of his human audience."[86]

---

concept in evolutionary biology emphasizing the role of organisms in actively shaping their environ-ments and ecological niches). Her argument for reading Genesis in light of NCT is an unconvincing concordism (see Celia Deane-Drummond, "In Adam All Die? Questions at the Boundary of Niche Construction, Community Evolution and Original Sin," in Cavanaugh and Smith, *Evolution and the Fall*, 23–47). She evidently recognizes the challenge facing this brand of concordism, but her essay seems to exemplify, rather than overcome, the difficulty.

85. Don Collett, "Hermeneutics in Context: Comparative Method and Contemporary Evangelical Scholarship" (unpublished manuscript, n.d.), 19.

86. Kenton Sparks, *God's Word in Human Words: An Evangelical Appropriation of Critical Biblical Scholarship* (Grand Rapids: Baker Academic, 2008), 256.

Granted, accommodation was a common idea among theologians in the patristic era through the Reformation (and beyond), but they understood it differently from Sparks. The classical doctrine "had been used to eliminate apparent errors in the text, in essence arguing that the text is true because it was accommodated to the people's needs."[87] Sparks, by contrast, adopts a radical accommodation thesis—one that Faustus Socinus popularized in the sixteenth century—which holds that the text contains factual error that is irrelevant to its gospel message.[88] Many theistic evolutionists argue similarly that the ancient (i.e., mistaken) science of Genesis 1–2 is one of many instances where God accommodates his Word to the prescientific worldview of ancient people. Old Testament believers, presumably, were too ignorant to comprehend evolutionary ideas.[89] This argument is flawed, however, for it ignores the fact that evolutionary concepts were present in antiquity[90]—for example, the Babylonian Atrahasis epic depicts the first humans emerging, in progressive stages, from an original seven pairs of humans.[91] In the Sumerian *Hymn to E'engura*, human beings sprout from the ground instead of being created de novo.[92] According to one Egyptian creation myth, the primeval waters (Nun) existed before creation; after a very long time (perhaps millions of years), Atum—the creator god—emerged out of those waters "and from him evolved the other gods and goddesses who represent the various parts and forces of nature."[93] Other such evolutionary motifs from the ancient Near East could be cited.[94] Therefore, even by the logic of the radical accommodation thesis, God had no reason to

87. Glenn Sunshine, "Accommodation Historically Considered," in *The Enduring Authority of the Christian Scriptures*, ed. D. A. Carson (Grand Rapids: Eerdmans, 2016), 258.

88. In Sparks's own words, "Accommodation is God's adoption in inscripturation of the human audience's finite and fallen perspective. Its underlying conceptual assumption is that in many cases God does not correct our mistaken human viewpoints but merely assumes them in order to communicate with us." Sparks, *God's Word in Human Words*, 230–31.

89. For this kind of argument, see Denis Lamoureux, *Evolution: Scripture and Nature Say Yes!* (Grand Rapids: Zondervan, 2016), esp. 85–112.

90. My discussion here, including the sources cited, is indebted to Vern Poythress, *Interpreting Eden: A Guide to Faithfully Reading and Understanding Genesis 1–3* (Wheaton: Crossway, 2019), 195. See also Ken Coulson, *Creation Unfolding: A New Perspective on Ex Nihilo* (n.p.: Phaneros, 2020), 150–54.

91. W. G. Lambert and A. R. Millard, *Atra-ḥasis: The Babylonian Story of the Flood* (Winona Lake, IN: Eisenbrauns, 1999), 60–63; tablet I.255–260; S iii 5–14.

92. Richard J. Clifford, *Creation Accounts in the Ancient Near East and in the Bible* (Washington, DC: Catholic Biblical Association of America, 1994), 31, from line 3 of the Sumerian hymn.

93. Tremper Longman, *Genesis*, The Story of God Bible Commentary (Grand Rapids, Zondervan, 2016), 31. For the primary source, see "From Coffin Texts Spell 714," trans. James P. Allen, in *The Context of Scripture: Canonical Compositions from the Biblical World*, ed. William Hallo, 3 vols. (Leiden: Brill, 2003), 1.2: 6–7.

94. For further discussion and examples, see Ángel M. Rodríguez, "Biblical Creationism and Ancient Near Eastern Evolutionary Ideas," in *The Genesis Creation Account and Its Reverberations in the Old Testament*, ed. Gerald Klingbeil (Berrien Springs, MI: Andrews University Press, 2015), 293–328.

"accommodate" to the ancient Hebrew mindset, since basic evolutionary notions were already circulating in the cultural milieu.

This revisionist style of accommodation is attractive because it diminishes any conflicts between science and theology. However, readers are left to rely on their own extrabiblical assumptions to adjudicate which parts of Scripture are dispensable. As Arnold Huijgen puts it,

> The idea of accommodation does not seem helpful in the question of the relation between theology and science. As it functioned in the 17th century discussions, it has shown to be an ever regressive principle, which opened the way for a thoroughly rationalist understanding of Scripture. For once applied, there seems no limit to the application of the accommodation principle. . . . So, when the accommodation principle was used in a defensive way against the natural sciences, it showed an ever regressive nature to retract to safer grounds once natural science claimed another area of reality.[95]

Appealing to accommodation as a way to circumvent monogenism creates a canon within a canon and leaves Scripture oscillating haphazardly between "accommodated" and "non-accommodated" language. In my view, the creator-creature distinction implies rather that *all* divine revelation is *necessarily* accommodated; the infinite creator must communicate with his creatures in a manner they can understand.[96]

In a similar vein, some argue that the biblical authors necessarily reflect the frailties and imperfections of their fallenness and that the apostles shared opinions and assumptions with other first-century people that we now know today to be false.[97] According to this objection, just because the apostles believed that Adam and Eve existed and that they were the first human beings doesn't mean we today are bound by such ancient beliefs.[98]

95. Arnold Huijgen, *Divine Accommodation in John Calvin's Theology: Analysis and Assessment* (Göttingen: Vandenhoeck & Ruprecht, 2011), 375. For background, see Hoon Lee, "Accommodation—Orthodox, Socinian, and Contemporary," *Westminster Theological Journal* 75, no. 2 (2013): 335–48; and Martin Klauber and Glenn Sunshine, "Jean-Alphonse Turrettini on Biblical Accommodation: Calvinist or Socinian?," *Calvin Theological Journal* 25, no. 1 (1990): 7–27.

96. See the discussion in Vern Poythress, "Rethinking Accommodation in Revelation," *Westminster Theological Journal* 76, no. 1 (2014): 143–56.

97. For example, see Christopher Hays and Stephen Lane Herring, "Adam and the Fall," in *Evangelical Faith and the Challenge of Historical Criticism*, ed. Christopher Hays and Christopher Ansberry (Grand Rapids: Baker Academic, 2013), 24–54, esp. 41–45; Kenton Sparks, "The Sun Also Rises: Accommodation in Inscripturation and Interpretation," in *Evangelicals and Scripture: Tradition, Authority, and Hermeneutics*, ed. Vincent Bacote, Laura Miguélez, and Dennis Okholm (Downers Grove, IL: InterVarsity, 2004), 112–32; and Sparks, *God's Word in Human Words*.

98. Such moves were common in nineteenth-century British debates over historical criticism. See Nigel Cameron, *Biblical Higher Criticism and the Defense of Infallibilism in 19th Century Britain* (Lewiston, ME: Edwin Mellen, 1987), 157–78.

Peter Enns adopts this stance when he denies the Mosaic authorship of the Pentateuch and takes issue with Jesus's belief that Moses wrote the Pentateuch: "I do not think that Jesus's status as the incarnate Son of God requires that statements such as John 5:46–47 be understood as binding historical judgments of authorship. Rather, Jesus here reflects the tradition that he himself inherited as a first-century Jew and that his hearers assumed to be the case."[99] Enns goes on to say that Paul was wrong to believe in a historical Adam even though he was right about the gospel.[100]

But on what basis does Enns accept Paul's soteriology and reject his protology (and hamartiology for that matter)? Enns offers this reply: "For Paul, the resurrection of Christ is the central and climactic *present-day event* in the Jewish drama—and of the world. One could say that Paul was wrong, deluded, stupid, creative, whatever; nevertheless, the resurrection is something that Paul believed to have happened in his time, *not primordial time*."[101] In other words, we should not accept apostolic beliefs at face value when they merely reflect inherited traditions, but the apostles *are* reliable when they communicate events they themselves experienced. By this logic, however, readers should not readily accept *any* of the Old Testament redemptive-historical events ratified by the New Testament—since none of the apostles experienced them. Enns assumes that readers can adjudicate truth from error in the apostolic witness, a move that wrecks the very idea of special revelation.[102]

One might still object that Scripture accepts monogenism without explicitly *asserting* it. This distinction between what the biblical authors believed and what the text itself affirms allows readers to reject monogenism since only biblical assertions are epistemically binding. This objection relies on a principle defended in article 11 of the Chicago Statement on Biblical Inerrancy: "We affirm that Scripture, having been given by divine inspiration, is infallible, so that, far from misleading us, it is true and reliable *in all the matters it addresses*."[103] As Kevin Vanhoozer puts it, "the authors speak the truth in all things they affirm (when they make affirmations), and will eventually be seen to have spoken truly (when right readers read

99. Enns, *Evolution of Adam*, 153n19.

100. Enns, *Evolution of Adam*, 119–35.

101. Enns, *Evolution of Adam*, 125, my emphasis.

102. Scot McKnight has made similar arguments in Venema and McKnight, *Adam and the Genome*, esp. 147–92. I reviewed the book in Hans Madueme, "Rumors of Adam's Demise: One More and Counting," The Gospel Coalition, March 17, 2017, https://www.thegospelcoalition.org/article /book-review-adams-genome.

103. International Council on Biblical Inerrancy, "The Chicago Statement on Biblical Inerrancy," art. 11, 1978, my emphasis, https://www.etsjets.org/files/documents/Chicago_Statement.pdf.

rightly)."[104] While I happily endorse this principle, as far as it goes, it does not undercut biblical monogenism.

This is clear when we consider the genealogy of Luke 3:23–38. Luke is not directly *asserting* the historicity of Adam or that Adam was the first human being. "The point of the genealogy," I. Howard Marshall writes, "is rather to show that Jesus has his place in the human race created by God."[105] However, even if Luke is not directly asserting monogenism, he clearly *assumes* the historicity of Adam as the first human being. The illocutionary force of Luke 3:23–38 may have nothing to do with monogenism, yet as David Clark notes, "the nondescriptive functions of language are, in very complex ways, completely dependent on background realities. Propositions that describe these background realities speak about the metaphysical context in which the nondescriptive utterances occur. Nondescriptive utterances are parasitic on this metaphysical context. Without these background realities, described accurately by true propositions, the nondescriptive utterances lose their force."[106] The genealogy is dependent on Adam's historicity. Biblical monogenism *must* be true, otherwise Luke's genealogy misfires and fails as divine discourse. The same insight applies to other New Testament monogenist passages; either the texts affirm historical truths about Adam and, since Scripture is infallible, must therefore be true (e.g., Rom. 5:12–21; 1 Cor. 15:21–22), or texts that do not assert anything historical about Adam have background historical assumptions about him that *must* be true if the text has the force God intended (e.g., Matt. 19:4–5; 1 Tim. 2:13–14; 1 Cor. 11:8–9).[107]

James K. A. Smith criticizes biblical monogenism as literalistic and missing the stylistic nuances of early Genesis: "Our options are not *either* ahistorical 'theological' claims or literalist 'historical' claims. We shouldn't

104. Kevin Vanhoozer, "Augustinian Inerrancy: Literary Meaning, Literal Truth, and Literate Interpretation in the Economy of Biblical Discourse," in *Five Views on Biblical Inerrancy*, ed. James Merrick and Stephen Garrett (Grand Rapids: Zondervan Academic, 2013), 207, italics removed.

105. I. Howard Marshall, *The Gospel of Luke: A Commentary on the Greek Text*, New International Greek Testament Commentary (Grand Rapids: Eerdmans, 1978), 161.

106. David Clark, "Beyond Inerrancy: Speech Acts and an Evangelical View of Scripture," in *For Faith and Clarity: Philosophical Contributions to Christian Theology*, ed. James Beilby (Grand Rapids: Baker Academic, 2006), 124.

107. William Lane Craig contests this point in his book *In Quest of the Historical Adam*, esp. 204–44, where he emphasizes the difference between apostles citing Old Testament texts "assertorically" (and therefore historically) and apostles citing them in a merely illustrative or literary—and thus nonhistorical—way. For my critique, see Hans Madueme, "Literality, Incredulity, and Hermeneutical Schizophrenia," Carl F. H. Henry Center for Theological Understanding, January 6, 2022, https://henrycenter.tiu.edu/2022/01/literality-incredulity-and-hermeneutical-schizophrenia/.

confuse or reduce 'historical' to mean something like a blow-by-blow chronology recorded by CNN. We need to develop more nuanced accounts of history in order to do justice to the theological."[108] As much as I resonate with this sentiment, the term "literalism" is the shibboleth you reserve for interpretations more literal than your own—like beauty, literalism is in the eye of the beholder. Instead of casting aspersions on the literalism bogeyman, it is more useful if all sides would marshal specific exegetical and theological arguments to support their preferred reading. We can then judge the readings on their substantive merits.

My thesis is that the apostolic hermeneutic is decisive. The New Testament depicts Adam as the first human being and progenitor of the entire human race—and we should believe the same. Scripture *authorizes* monogenism. That raises one last objection—namely, that biblical monogenism conflicts with our best sciences and therefore *should* prompt me to revise my exegesis of the relevant texts. I agree that science should sometimes lead believers to revise traditional interpretations, but I cannot accept the scientific verdict against monogenism because it violates the New Testament dogmatic rule. The intratextual warrant for biblical monogenism—rooted in clear exegesis, deep catholic support, and high dogmatic rank—surpasses the warrant for the relevant judgments in evolutionary biology, paleoanthropology, and population genetics.

Associated with the scientific question, Smith's argument states that biblical monogenism faces a significant theological objection:

> In light of accumulating archeological and genetic evidence, it is difficult today to *simply* affirm the existence of an original human couple, Adam and Eve. Indeed, such an affirmation entails a unique *theological* challenge: If all humans are descended from a single pair, why would the Creator of the universe seem to indicate in his creation (i.e., via general revelation) that humanity has a long, evolutionary origin and is descended from many more individuals? Any assertion of this received account of one historical couple will have to grapple not only with the scientific evidence to the contrary, but also with the theological problem that is generated when the "book of nature" seems to say something very different.[109]

---

108. Smith, "What Stands on the Fall?," 69. Smith's reasoning is inseparable from nineteenth- and twentieth-century debates over the interpretation of Gen. 1–2, especially in the wake of geological and evolutionary science. Douglas F. Kelly, *Creation and Change: Genesis 1.1–2.4 in the Light of Changing Scientific Paradigms*, rev. ed. (Fearn, Ross-shire, UK: Mentor, 2017), 155–65. See also chap. 1 of the present monograph.

109. Smith, "What Stands on the Fall?," 55, emphasis original.

Smith is right that a mere assertion of monogenism fails in our post-Darwinian setting. But what he terms the "accumulating archeological and genetic evidence" is our best scientific effort at understanding the inner workings of creation; it is not infallible. Like many others, Smith identifies science as the interpretation of *general revelation*, but that move is questionable and tends to legitimize science as an epistemologically autonomous activity (see my discussion in chap. 2).[110]

Furthermore, Smith downplays the theological function of monogenism within the structure of Christian theology. On the one hand, I concede that my argument for biblical monogenism would be stronger if I had a compelling scientific explanation of the physical data. Multidisciplinary research is imperative in order to address the substantial empirical questions facing monogenism, but that task is beyond my brief here.[111] On the other hand, polygenism itself entails a unique theological challenge (to borrow Smith's own words). Given the decisive canonical and theological arguments for biblical monogenism, it is premature and reckless to reinterpret Scripture in light of science. In addition, the current scientific consensus makes assumptions that invite critical scrutiny, such as the idea that hominin species like *Australopithecus afarensis* diverged from the lineage that led to humans (and that they did so after chimpanzees diverged from the same lineage). Such judgments already presuppose an evolutionary framework that I reject. On the contrary, as I reflect on the current thinking about fossil morphology in light of biblical monogenism, my present view is that some hominin species are descendants of Adam and Eve, while others are nonhuman animals.[112]

---

110. For example, see the helpful remarks in Nicolaas H. Gootjes, "General Revelation and Science: Reflections on a Remark in Report 28," *Calvin Theological Journal* 30 (1995): 94–107.

111. Scientists who work in this mode are young-earth creationists, but their human origins research is still in its infancy. For example, see Todd Wood, "The Chimpanzee Genome and the Problem of Biological Similarity," *Occasional Papers of the BSG* 7 (2006): 1–18; and Marcus Ross, P. S. Brummel, and Todd Wood, "Human History from Adam to Abraham: Integrating Paleoanthropology with a Young-Age Creation Perspective," in *Proceedings of the Ninth International Conference on Creationism*, ed. John H. Whitmore (Cedarville, OH: Cedarville University International Conference on Creationism, 2023), 66-87.

112. For analysis along these lines, see Marcus Ross, "The Recent Adam and Eve View: A Modern Young-Earth Approach," in *Perspectives on the Historical Adam and Eve: Four Views*, ed. Kenneth Keathley (Nashville: Broadman & Holman, 2024); Todd Wood, "Baraminological Analysis Places *Homo habilis, Homo rudolfensis*, and *Australopithecus sediba* in the Human Holobaramin," *Answers Research Journal* 3 (2010): 71–90; and Todd Wood, "Baraminology, the Image of God, and *Australopithecus Sediba*," *Journal of Creation Theology and Science Series B: Life Sciences* 1 (2011): 6–14. One should note that classification systems are debated among paleoanthropologists—e.g., see Jeffrey Schwartz and Ian Tattersall, "Defining the Genus *Homo*," *Science* 349, no. 6251 (August 28, 2015): 931–32.

Conclusion

I am keenly aware that monogenism faces stiff challenges in a post-Darwinian context; the ongoing tensions between scientific and theological accounts of human origins are disturbing. Nevertheless, arguments against monogenism violate the apostolic reading of Genesis. The epistemic priority of the canonical witness reminds us that current science is not infallible on the matters in question. Rather than trying to relieve the conflict between a historical Adam and natural science by dropping monogenism, we should live with the tension.

The direct creation of Adam and Eve as the sole genealogical ancestors of the human race is not an isolated doctrinal claim but is at the root of what unites every member of the human race. Biblical monogenism is a strong critique of racism as a violation of human beings as sons and daughters of Adam and Eve, a multitude from every nation, tribe, people, and language (Rev. 7:9)—indeed, images of God. Sin and redemption depend on monogenism. Since every sinner belongs to one biological family, the Father sent his Son in the incarnation to bind himself with that human family and atone for our sins. Jesus can save us because we are children of Adam and thus children of God. This need for salvation points to our current state of sin and, as we shall see in the next chapter, our former state of innocence.

5

The Doctrine of Original Goodness

Evolutionary science . . . has rendered the assumption of an original cosmic perfection, one allegedly debauched by a temporally "original sin," obsolete and unbelievable.

—John Haught[1]

There never was a golden age. There is no point in looking back to one. The first man was immediately the first sinner.

—Karl Barth[2]

God made man in His image and likeness. A soul was given him which is a spirit like God Himself and also immortal, although it has a beginning. The soul He adorned with every endowment of His goodness, power, wisdom, holiness, righteousness and all the virtues, just because in man you might as with the eye see God Himself.

—Confession of the Reformed Congregation at Frankfurt (1554)[3]

Sin entered the world through Adam, but it was not always so. Since God is good—the substance and sum of all goodness—original goodness is the norm, and sin a vile aberration that ruined the

1. John Haught, *God after Darwin: A Theology of Evolution* (Boulder, CO: Westview, 2000), 149.
2. Karl Barth, *Church Dogmatics*, IV/1, *The Doctrine of Reconciliation*, trans. Geoffrey Bromiley (Edinburgh: T&T Clark, 1956), 509.
3. In Heinrich Heppe, *Reformed Dogmatics: Set Out and Illustrated from the Sources*, trans. G. T. Thomson (London: George Allen & Unwin, 1950), 237.

state of innocence and precipitated the great things of the gospel (Gen. 3:15). However, this doctrine of original goodness has largely been abandoned today. As Arthur Peacocke remarks, "There is no evidence for a past paradisal, fully integrated, harmonious virtuous existence of *Homo sapiens*."[4] In this chapter, I explain why I think Peacocke is mistaken.

First, I explore recent proposals by Christian evolutionists to justify the violence and the suffering in prehuman evolutionary history, and I show why such strategies face severe theological challenges. Second, I argue that the doctrines of original goodness and a cosmic fall resolve these challenges; animal suffering, violence, and death are all postlapsarian realities that signify the brokenness of creation. Third, I offer concluding reflections on the doctrine of original goodness in light of biblical realism.

Evolution and the Problem of Evil

The goodness of God is difficult to reconcile with animal pain and the gruesome levels of suffering and death in the evolutionary past—the anguish of it all, so much, and so relentless.[5] Evolution is impossible without the death of organisms. According to John Schneider, "We now know that 99.5 percent of all species that ever walked the earth are gone, most often in a violently horrific, cataclysmic fashion, many of them without leaving so much as a genetic legacy to generations yet to come."[6] He goes on to say that "if the God of theism did create species, it was by an extraordinarily inefficient, wasteful, and brutal means. Is it not rather the best part of rationality to see the thesis of natural selection as almost inherently atheistic?"[7] Darwin himself wrote, "What a book a devil's chaplain might write on the clumsy, wasteful, blundering, low and horridly cruel works of nature!"[8]

---

4. Arthur Peacocke, "Science and the Future of Theology: Critical Issues," in *Evolution: The Disguised Friend of Faith? Selected Essays* (Philadelphia: Templeton Foundation, 2004), 179.

5. This section is a significant revision and expansion of some of the material in my article "The Theological Problem with Evolution," *Zygon* 56, no. 2 (2021): 481–99 (used with permission).

6. John R. Schneider, *Animal Suffering and the Darwinian Problem of Evil* (Cambridge: Cambridge University Press, 2020), 3. This high percentage of extinct species is often stated as a fact, but it is a mathematical inference that depends on the truth of deep time. The actual fossil record indicates about three hundred thousand species compared to roughly nine million living species (cf. John Alroy, "How Many Named Species Are Valid?," *Proceedings of the National Academy of Sciences USA* 99, no. 6 [2002]: 3706–11). If one does not assume deep time, the number of extinct species may only be a fraction of the total number of species that have ever lived. I am grateful to Kurt Wise for his insights on this question.

7. Schneider, *Animal Suffering*, 4.

8. Charles Darwin, "Letter to J. D. Hooker (July 13, 1856)," in *More Letters of Charles Darwin: A Record of His Work in a Series of Hitherto Unpublished Letters*, vol. 1, ed. Francis Darwin and A. C. Seward (London: John Murray, 1903), 94.

These difficulties predate Darwin. Anyone who accepts animal death before the fall swims in the same pond, yet the problem looms large with an evolutionary creation that by divine design includes animal suffering and death over millions of years.[9] Schneider draws on Job, among other sources, to develop an *aesthetic* theodicy. God can defeat evolutionary evil, Schneider writes, "when it is integrated as a constitutive part of a valuable composite whole that not only outweighs the evil, but could not be as valuable as it is *without* the evil. In that instance, the evil remains evil in its own right, but it is defeated, since it is made to be a good-making, non-regrettable part of the whole."[10] On this model, God is morally justified to authorize the evil that animals suffer so long as he defeats it in the end. Schneider envisions an eschatology in which God will resurrect all animals to everlasting life.

The problem with Schneider's evolutionary theodicy—a problem that haunts all non-lapsarian theodicies—is that it renders God the author of evil, which he then uses for the greater good.[11] God forbid! The Lord is the thrice-holy God of Isaiah 6:3: "Holy, holy, holy is the LORD of Hosts; the whole earth is full of his glory." Scripture never impugns God's character by depicting him as the direct cause of evil. To be sure, the biblical narrative often presents him as directly causing illness, pestilence, plagues, and death, but such cases are instances of divine punishment for personal sin or for the transgression of Adam. Therefore, given the holiness and omnibenevolence of God, I take it as an axiom that from the beginning nothing he created could contain the presence of sin, evil, or the consequence of either.[12] In a world that is *already* fallen, God can and does use evil to bring about good (Gen. 50:20; Rom. 8:28)—as he did preeminently in Christ's atonement—but in such cases, it is always the creature, never God, who is morally culpable for evil. In evolutionary accounts without a historical fall, however, natural evil is part of the warp and woof of creation and not a divine judgment. God is blameworthy.

9. Evolutionary biologists clarify that natural selection is not driven by differences in organismal mortality as such, but, rather, differential *reproductive* success is the main engine of natural selection.

10. Schneider, *Animal Suffering*, 7.

11. For a similarly flawed evolutionary theodicy, see Denis Lamoureux, "Toward an Evangelical Evolutionary Theodicy," *Theology and Science* 18, no. 1 (2020): 12–30.

12. This axiom holds despite the presence of Satan in the garden before the fall. Divine holiness and omnibenevolence also entail that any angels and other celestial creatures he created *in heaven* could not have been sinful, evil, or the consequence of sin or evil. Rather, sin entered heaven with the fall of Lucifer (see chap. 6). Adam and Eve were fully able to resist the temptation of the serpent; had they done so, the fall with all its repercussions throughout the (nonheavenly) cosmos would have been avoided.

Against my lapsarian worries, some will say that the punishment does not fit the crime. It seems monumentally unfair that Adam's one misstep unleashed all the misery of natural (and moral) evil.[13] This reaction is understandable, but our intuitions are likely skewed. Adam's sin and its aftermath disclose the deep solidarity that unites God's creatures; the fate of humanity and the cosmos is inseparable from the first man's destiny. The tragedy of a fallen creation, itself a divine judgment, signals the enormity of sin and its cosmic dimensions (Gen. 3:17; Rom. 8:18–22).[14]

Others challenge the very idea of natural evil and would question whether earthquakes and other natural disasters should be considered evil in *any* sense. For example, scientists remind us that life as we know it would be impossible without physical death, animal predation, and other so-called natural evils. Ecologists report that predation and other kinds of organismal death are essential for population control in ecosystems; as one Christian biologist remarks, "Nothing in ecology makes sense apart from the operations of physical death."[15] Nevertheless, if Adam's fall had cosmic repercussions, then it is possible that the ecological and population dynamics in the prelapsarian world were significantly different from our own postlapsarian situation, and that our planet currently lies in the shadow of sin and the curse. I acknowledge that my position is open to debate and lacks any empirical confirmation (especially if one excludes special revelation from the category of "empirical"). However, as I will argue later in this chapter, Scripture supports the idea of an unfallen creation. If I am right, then we simply do not know how the prelapsarian world would have functioned or what kind of providential role God would have played in sustaining the shalom of his good creation.

But we do know that evolution drives a wedge between creation and redemption.[16] On the one hand, God the creator uses suffering, pain, and death

13. A striking statement of this objection is in Marilyn McCord Adams, "Theodicy without Blame," *Philosophical Topics* 16 (1988): 215–45. For one response to Adams's objections, see Katherin Rogers, "The Abolition of Sin: A Response to Adams in the Augustinian Tradition," *Faith and Philosophy* 19, no. 1 (2002): 69–84.

14. In light of the geological conclusion that most natural evil preceded human evolution, William Dembski has argued that pre-Adamic predation and death *were* caused by Adam's fall but only *retroactively*, much like Christ's atonement was "retroactively" effective for Old Testament believers (William Dembski, *The End of Christianity: Finding a Good God in an Evil World* [Downers Grove, IL: InterVarsity, 2009]). Horace Bushnell defended this thesis a century and a half earlier in *Nature and the Supernatural* (New York: Charles Scribner, 1858), 194–219. Despite its ingenuity, this solution nullifies the redemptive-historical and temporal sequence of Adam's fall and its effects as they are revealed in Scripture.

15. John Wood, "An Ecological Perspective on the Role of Death in Creation," *Perspectives on Science and Christian Faith* 68, no. 2 (2016): 78.

16. Michael Lloyd, "Are Animals Fallen?," in *Animals on the Agenda: Questions about Animals for Theology and Ethics*, ed. Andrew Linzey and Dorothy Yamamoto (London: SCM, 1998), 156.

to advance the evolutionary process and bring his creatures into being.[17] On the other hand, God the redeemer vanquishes sin and death, restores nature, and eradicates animal suffering. The theological incoherence is stark: God's work of creation contradicts his work of redemption. This position gives the impression that grace is radically opposed to being human. Michael Lloyd writes perceptively, "If, theologically, we see creation and redemption pulling in different directions, then, pastorally, we shall ourselves be pulled in different directions. If, however, we see redemption as precisely *re*demption of the created order, then we shall see, and experience, redemption as becoming ourselves."[18] This wedge between creation and redemption is not the human inability to grasp the full picture that stems from the creator-creature divide or divine incomprehensibility. Rather, nonlapsarian evolutionary accounts create an *ontological* problem: the God of creation is fundamentally different from God as revealed in redemption.

Theologians have tried to escape this tangled mess by redefining the divine attributes. Evolutionary evil is a nonissue if God cannot prevent all suffering and evil. Process thinkers thus claim that every level of creation has a degree of freedom to resist God. Earthquakes, tornadoes, violence, and death result from creaturely freedom, not divine sovereignty. As Jerry Korsmeyer puts it, "There is no detailed pre-ordained plan for our existence, because our response, and that of all God's creatures, cannot be coerced or exactly predicted. . . . Since all creatures really have some measure of self-creativity, they have responded only imperfectly. They partially share with God the directions evolution has taken. God can only suggest the way evolution should go, and then must experience with creatures the results of the decisions that they make."[19] According to process theologians, God cannot prevent evil in the world.[20] While these moves resolve the riddle of theodicy, it is a pyrrhic victory; by rejecting divine omnipotence, these theologians cut themselves loose from the God of orthodoxy.

Less controversially, one might deny that animals are morally innocent and argue instead that millions of creatures suffer and die because they

---

17. Some reject natural selection as the driving force for evolution, replacing it instead with mutuality, cooperation, and altruism as the more dominant factors; evolution is no longer solely about competition and nature red in tooth and claw. E.g., see Martin Nowak and Sarah Coakley, eds., *Evolution, Games and God: The Principle of Cooperation* (Cambridge, MA: Harvard University Press, 2013).

18. Lloyd, "Are Animals Fallen?," 153, emphasis original.

19. Jerry Korsmeyer, *Evolution and Eden: Balancing Original Sin and Contemporary Science* (New York: Paulist Press, 1998), 104.

20. For a typical expression, see Charles Hartshorne, *Omnipotence and Other Theological Mistakes* (Albany: State University of New York Press, 1984).

are being punished for their sins. Cognitive ethologists and evolutionary biologists suggest that animals experience some degree of consciousness, choice, and intention.[21] They can resist God's will. If that is true, then (non-angelic) moral evil already existed before humans came on the scene. Joshua Moritz defends this view as a *"free creatures defense* to the problem of evolutionary evil."[22] Nonhuman animals were morally culpable for their free choices and are responsible for evolutionary suffering.

However, this position is based on very slender scientific evidence, and Scripture gives no support to the idea that sin arises from animal misdemeanors. Moritz appeals to the serpent in Genesis 3 as evidence of animals behaving badly, but he reads too much into that episode; the canonical significance of the serpent is diabolical, not ethological. He also argues that animals are blameworthy because they died in the flood (Gen. 6) and were named in the Noahic covenant (9:8–17); God even called them to repentance (Jon. 3:7–9; 4:11) and held them accountable for killing humans (Exod. 21:28–32).[23] None of these texts, however, support the idea that animals can sin. The biblical witness consistently affirms that only humans can sin because we are uniquely God's image bearers; sin entered the world *through Adam,* not through animal misdeeds (Rom. 5:12).

Others have appealed to a *free-process defense,* a variant of the free-will defense. In John Polkinghorne's view, "God allows the physical world to be itself, not in Manichaean opposition to him, but in that independence that is Love's gift of freedom to the one beloved."[24] He thinks God allows the universe to be autonomous, so that natural evil is the product of chance and necessity. Natural evil is the price the universe pays for freedom. Polkinghorne explains, "[God] is not the puppetmaster of either men *or matter.*"[25]

21. For example, see Marc Bekoff, Colin Allen, and Gordon Burghardt, eds., *The Cognitive Animal: Empirical and Theoretical Perspectives on Animal Cognition* (Cambridge, MA: MIT Press, 2002).

22. Joshua Moritz, "Animal Suffering, Evolution, and the Origins of Evil: Toward a 'Free Creatures' Defense," *Zygon* 49, no. 2 (2014): 373, emphasis original. For a similar defense that animals experience their version of virtue and vice, see Celia Deane-Drummond's "Are Animals Moral? A Theological Appraisal of the Evolution of Vice and Virtue," *Zygon* 44, no. 4 (2009): 932–50, and her "Shadow Sophia in Christological Perspective: The Evolution of Sin and the Redemption of Nature," *Theology and Science* 6, no. 1 (2008): 13–32. Nicola Creegan has suggested that "if sinfulness at least in latent form begins with animals, then the traditional story of creation, fall, and redemption can no longer hold." Nicola Creegan, *Animal Suffering and the Problem of Evil* (Oxford: Oxford University Press, 2013), 23.

23. Joshua Moritz, "Animals and the Image of God in the Bible and Beyond," *Dialog* 48, no. 2 (2009): 134–46.

24. John Polkinghorne, *Science and Providence: God's Interaction with the World* (Philadelphia: Templeton Foundation, 2005), 77. Polkinghorne's position is a *kenotic* theology of creation. See John Polkinghorne, "Kenotic Creation and Divine Action," in *The Work of Love: Creation as Kenosis,* ed. John Polkinghorne (Grand Rapids: Eerdmans, 2001), 90–106.

25. Polkinghorne, *Science and Providence,* 78, my emphasis.

The free-process defense is close kin to the "only way" theodicy, the view that evolutionary evil was the *only way* for God to create our rich cosmos. The goods of evolution outweigh the necessary harms.[26] Christopher Southgate writes, "I acknowledge the pain, suffering, death, and extinction that are intrinsic to a creation evolving according to Darwinian principles. Moreover, I hold to the (unprovable) assumption that an evolving creation was the only way in which God could give rise to the sort of beauty, diversity, sentience, and sophistication of creatures that the biosphere now contains. As shorthand I call this the 'only way' argument."[27] This argument is perplexing. Why can an omnipotent God not create a world without evolutionary evil?[28] If God were unable to secure such a world at the beginning, why think suffering and death will cease in the new heaven and new earth (Rev. 21:4)? Only-way theodicies leave creation and eschatology at cross-purposes; and, worse yet, since evil is intrinsic to creation, they implicate God in evil.[29]

If evolutionary evil is necessary for God to create the kind of world we live in, then he must have had morally sufficient reasons to do so, otherwise he would not have created in the first place. One possibility for a morally sufficient reason is that regular laws of nature are a necessary antecedent condition for the evolution of human free will, even while those same laws inevitably give rise to evil.[30] Another possibility is Friedrich Schleiermacher's notion that evil is the inevitable byproduct of a good creation.[31] However,

---

26. According to Nathan O'Halloran, the "only way" argument recalls earlier premodern positions adopted by theologians like Augustine and Aquinas, both of whom argued that *createdness* necessarily leads to corruption and evil (Nathan O'Halloran, "Cosmic Alienation and the Origin of Evil: Rejecting the 'Only Way' Option," *Theology and Science* 13, no. 1 [2015]: 49–51). Such ancient views were shaped by Greek philosophy (specifically, Neoplatonism), whereas "only way" evolutionary theodicies are shaped by natural philosophy (specifically, modern science). I engage patristic views of corruptibility in chap. 6.

27. Christopher Southgate, *The Groaning of Creation: God, Evolution, and the Problem of Evil* (Louisville: Westminster John Knox, 2008), 16. Similarly, Niels Henrik Gregersen writes that "it seems that death, pain and mental suffering are the price to be paid for living in a developing world with highly complex and intense forms of sentient life" (Niels Henrik Gregersen, "The Cross of Christ in an Evolutionary World," *Dialog* 40, no. 3 [2001]: 200). For an anthropocentric version of this argument, see John Hick's soul-making theodicy in *Evil and the God of Love*, rev. ed. (New York: Harper & Row, 1978), 243–386.

28. See the salient remarks in Robert Francescotti, "The Problem of Animal Pain and Suffering," in *The Blackwell Companion to the Problem of Evil*, ed. Justin McBrayer and Daniel Howard-Snyder (Malden, MA: Wiley-Blackwell, 2013), 121–25.

29. For Southgate's response to these concerns, see Christopher Southgate, "'Free Process' and 'Only Way' Arguments," in *Finding Ourselves after Darwin: Conversations about the Image of God, Original Sin, and the Problem of Evil*, ed. Stanley Rosenberg (Grand Rapids: Baker Academic, 2018), 293–305.

30. Michael Murray, *Nature Red in Tooth and Claw: Theism and the Problem of Animal Suffering* (New York: Oxford University Press, 2008), 130–92.

31. According to Schleiermacher—and somewhat paradoxical—the human inability to do good "was present in human nature before the first sin, and . . . accordingly what is now innate sinfulness

such instrumentalist proposals clash with deep canonical motifs; in rendering evil *necessary* (or, less strongly, inevitable) in order to establish the contingency of creation, they vitiate God's holy character.[32] The problem is not that evil in God's initial creation could result from the *free action* of creatures—after all, the classical Christian theodicy roots the first sin in the direct agency of creatures rather than God—but that God structured material creation so that its contingency necessarily or inevitably moves toward evil.[33]

Given the difficulty of the problem, several thinkers have abandoned finding the answer in mundane history and appeal instead to a primordial angelic fall as the origin of evolutionary evil. Natural evils like animal predation, disease, and death are symptoms of angelic rebellion in heaven.[34] The fall of Satan and his minions sparked disaster for the material world. Thomas Chalmers (1780–1847) and C. I. Scofield (1843–1921) speculated that an angelic fall ruined an earlier creation by instigating millions of years of pre-Adamic animal suffering and death. These events happened, so they claim, in the timeframe (the "gap") between Genesis 1:1 and 1:2.[35]

The angelic fall theodicy preserves the historical origin of evil but pushes it further back, with the payoff that it absolves God without falling afoul of science.[36] In reply, I affirm that demonic powers are God's enemies and that Scripture frequently ascribes physical disease to demons (e.g., Matt.

was something native also to the first pair. . . . A timeless original sinfulness always and everywhere inher[ed] in human nature and co-exist[ed] with the original perfection given along with it" (Friedrich Schleiermacher, *The Christian Faith*, ed. H. R. Mackintosh and J. S. Stewart [Edinburgh: T&T Clark, 1928], 301–3). For background and analysis, see Daniel J. Pedersen, *Schleiermacher's Theology of Sin and Nature: Agency, Value, and Modern Theology* (New York: Routledge, 2020).

32. After the fall, God certainly uses evil instrumentally for good (e.g., Gen. 50:20; Rom. 8:28); the problem with non-lapsarian evolutionary accounts is that evil is coextensive with original creation in Gen. 1–2.

33. For a fascinating analysis of young-earth creationism in light of theodicy, see Richard A. Peters, "Theodicic Creationism: Its Membership and Motivations," in *Geology and Religion: A History of Harmony and Hostility*, ed. Martina Kölbl-Ebert (London: The Geological Society, 2009), 317–28.

34. For a recent defense, see Michael Lloyd, "The Fallenness of Nature: Three Non-Human Suspects," in Rosenberg, *Finding Ourselves after Darwin*, 262–79. See also Gregory Boyd, *Satan and the Problem of Evil* (Downers Grove, IL: InterVarsity, 2001), 242–318; and Paul Griffiths, *Decreation: The Last Things of All Creatures* (Waco: Baylor University Press, 2014), 134. Advocates for a cosmic fall instigated by fallen angels include C. S. Lewis, Hans Urs von Balthasar, Alvin Plantinga, T. F. Torrance, and Stephen Webb.

35. Thomas Chalmers, "Remarks on Cuvier's Theory of the Earth," in *The Select Works of Thomas Chalmers*, 4 vols. (New York: Robert Carter, 1848), 1:180–93 (originally published 1814); C. I. Scofield, ed., *The Scofield Reference Bible* (New York: Oxford University Press, 1909), 3. For the wide impact of Scofield's annotation, see R. Todd Mangum and Mark Sweetnam, *The Scofield Bible: Its History and Impact on the Evangelical Church* (Colorado Springs: Paternoster, 2009), 151–58.

36. Nicola Creegan similarly argues for a "modified dualism" wherein evolutionary evil is a symptom of a cosmic fall caused mysteriously by Satan and his cohorts. Creegan, *Animal Suffering*, 127–37.

9:32; 12:22; Mark 9:17–29; Luke 4:39; 13:11–13). Nevertheless, the premise of fallen angel theodicy—that sometime in the distant past, after God's initial creation and before Adam's fall, demons transformed the material creation into a disordered realm in which animals would experience suffering and death over millions of years—is speculative and lacks compelling exegetical support. Moreover, it is odd that Scripture calls creation "good" in Genesis 1 (vv. 10, 12, 18, 21, 25, and 31) when demonic powers had by then supposedly corrupted the creaturely order.[37]

Perhaps animal suffering and death are not evil after all. Some scholars argue that prehuman animal suffering is *morally neutral* and results from "the natural working out of life's creative processes."[38] In the light of Calvary, suffering and death through natural selection are seen as consonant with the suffering and death of Christ on the cross; evolutionary suffering follows a christological pattern.[39] In conservative evangelicalism, one often finds an emphasis on animal predation as not only morally neutral but worthy of God's praise (e.g., Pss. 104; 147; Job 38–41). Such scholars insist that only *human*, not animal, death was a consequence of Adam's fall (Rom. 5:12 and 1 Cor. 15:21–22).[40] In their view, Western attitudes toward animal death and predation reflect a modern sentimentalism and a tendency to anthropomorphize animal experience.

The "neo-Cartesian" position gives a philosophical rationale for this belief that animal suffering and death are not morally significant.[41] Neo-Cartesianism represents a family of views, with some denying that animals are conscious and others affirming that animals are sentient but lack higher-order access to the experience of suffering. According to this latter position, animals cannot think about their thoughts because they are

37. Thomas Oord has recently tried to explain natural evil by appealing to the presence of chaos (*tehom*) in Gen. 1 (Thomas Oord, "An Open Theology Doctrine of Creation," in *Creation Made Free: Open Theology Engaging Science*, ed. Thomas Oord [Eugene, OR: Wipf & Stock, 2009], 28–49). For critical discussion of Oord's proposal, see Bethany Sollereder, *God, Evolution, and Animal Suffering: Theodicy without a Fall* (New York: Routledge, 2018), 16–17.

38. That position is defended in Elizabeth Johnson, *Ask the Beasts: Darwin and the God of Love* (London: Bloomsbury, 2014), 185.

39. George Murphy, *The Cosmos in the Light of the Cross* (Harrisburg, PA: Trinity Press International, 2003). See also Johnson, *Ask the Beasts*, 181–210.

40. See Henri Blocher, "The Theology of the Fall and the Origins of Evil," in *Darwin, Creation and the Fall: Theological Challenges*, ed. R. J. Berry and T. A. Noble (Nottingham, UK: Apollos, 2009), 165–68; and C. John Collins, *Genesis 1–4: A Linguistic, Literary, and Theological Commentary* (Phillipsburg, NJ: P&R, 2006), 162–66.

41. For defenses of the neo-Cartesian position, see Peter Harrison, "Theodicy and Animal Pain," *Philosophy* 64 (1989): 79–92. For critical responses, see Donna Yarri, *The Ethics of Animal Experimentation: A Critical Analysis and Constructive Christian Proposal* (Oxford: Oxford University Press, 2005), 57–84; and Robert Wennberg, "Animal Suffering and the Problem of Evil," *Christian Scholar's Review* 21, no. 2 (1991): 121–22.

not persons.[42] In his analysis of neo-Cartesianism, Gijsbert van den Brink explains that "animals can at best go through momentary sentient states of pain, but they cannot realize that they do so since there is no 'I,' no self-conscious subject, to realize anything at all."[43] Most neo-Cartesians accept that animals can experience pain but without "any higher-order states of being aware of themselves as being in first-order states."[44]

Neo-Cartesianism is difficult to disprove, not least because we have no direct epistemic access to the internal experience of animals. Our best scientific evidence, however, while by no means definitive, suggests that animals indeed experience pain and suffering.[45] Research in primatology and ethology indicates that many animals experience emotions like joy, fear, and grief; these emotions are analogous to human emotions and suggest that attributing pain and suffering to animal experiences is not a crude anthropomorphism. As van den Brink remarks, "It is reasonable to suppose that there is a continuum here, with animals having increased capacities of experiencing conscious pain to the extent that their neuro-anatomy and neuro-physiology more closely resemble ours."[46] This correspondence is also consistent with the widespread intuition that people who torture animals for fun are morally disordered.

From a biblical perspective, the reality that animals can and do suffer is never taught explicitly, but it resonates with the frequent appeal in Scripture to care for animals (e.g., Deut. 25:4; Prov. 12:10; Luke 14:5). I shall also argue shortly from an eschatological framework that animal suffering detracts from creation's goodness: animal predation and violence are consistently portrayed as absent from the new heavens and new earth (e.g., Ezek. 34:25, 28; Isa. 11:6–9). In the end, the theological difficulties proliferating around evolutionary theodicies and other perspectives that normalize animal suffering reflect the absence of original goodness.

42. On these distinctions, see Murray, *Nature Red in Tooth and Claw*, 41–72. For a Thomistic defense that animals do not suffer because they are not persons, see B. Kyle Keltz, *Thomism and the Problem of Animal Suffering* (Eugene, OR: Wipf & Stock, 2020).

43. Gijsbert van den Brink, "God and the Suffering of Animals," in *Playing with Leviathan: Interpretation and Reception of Monsters from the Biblical World*, ed. Koert van Bekkum, Jaap Dekker, Henk van de Kamp, and Eric Peels (Leiden: Brill, 2017), 184. Van den Brink does not advocate neo-Cartesianism.

44. Murray, *Nature Red in Tooth and Claw*, 55. Murray also mentions another neo-Cartesian proposal: "Most nonhuman animals lack the cognitive faculties required to be in a higher-order state of recognizing themselves to be in a first-order state of pain. Those that can on occasion achieve a second-order access to their first-order states of pain nonetheless do not have the capacity to regard that second-order state as undesirable" (57).

45. For example, see Hope Ferdowsian and Debra Merskin, "Parallels in Sources of Trauma, Pain, Distress, and Suffering in Humans and Nonhuman Animals," *Journal of Trauma & Dissociation* 13, no. 4 (2012): 448–68; Lynne Sneddon, Robert Elwood, Shelley Adamo, and Matthew Leach, "Defining and Assessing Animal Pain," *Animal Behaviour* 97 (2014): 201–12.

46. Van den Brink, "God and the Suffering of Animals," 186.

Retrieving Original Goodness

"Original goodness" is the idea that God's initial creation was free from sin as well as the biological decay and physical corruption resulting from sin. Adam and Eve in the state of innocence possessed original righteousness and were morally untainted. Original goodness, I shall argue, extends to the entire created order as it came fresh from the hands of God.[47] Adam's sin not only had wide-ranging effects on the human condition, but by provoking divine judgment it instigated the fall of material creation. Let us call this latter doctrine *the cosmic fall.*[48]

On Cosmic Fall and Restoration

In the New Testament, Paul alludes to Genesis 3:17–19 when he says God subjected the whole creation to frustration and the bondage of decay (Rom. 8:19–22). God subjected creation "to corruption, decay, and death . . . a state of futility with hope."[49] Paul uses the word creation (*ktisis*) to mean the whole cosmos, without humans and angels, the entirety of "subhuman nature both animate and inanimate."[50] He interprets the cursed ground as a synecdoche for the entire cosmos and is likely reading Genesis 3:17 canonically in light of Old Testament prophetic texts about the new creation (e.g., Isa. 41:17–20; 42:9; 43:18–21; 65:17; 66:22).[51] Such texts often picture the end as a new beginning; the expectation that all of nature will be redeemed implies that all of nature was fallen.[52] The consequences of the fall extend wider than humanity to all creation.[53]

47. I will address Adam's original righteousness and fall in later chapters.

48. The "cosmic fall," as I define it, has no relation to Origen's *pre*-cosmic (or precorporeal) fall of human souls. On the latter, see Peter W. Martens, "Origen's Doctrine of Pre-existence and the Opening Chapters of Genesis," *Zeitschrift für Antikes Christentum* 16, no. 3 (2013): 516–49; and Mark S. M. Scott, *Journey Back to God: Origen on the Problem of Evil* (Oxford: Oxford University Press, 2012), 49–73.

49. Joseph Fitzmyer, *Romans*, Anchor Bible 33 (New York: Doubleday, 1993), 505.

50. C. E. B. Cranfield, *A Critical and Exegetical Commentary on the Epistle to the Romans*, 2 vols., International Critical Commentary (Edinburgh: T&T Clark, 1975), 1:411–12.

51. Synecdoche is a frequent device in Scripture when "the whole could stand for the part, or a part for the whole." Walter Kaiser and Moisés Silva, *Introduction to Biblical Hermeneutics: The Search for Meaning*, rev. ed. (Grand Rapids: Zondervan, 2007), 148.

52. As Bernhard Anderson observes regarding Old Testament eschatology, "The goal of history will be a return to the beginning, not in the sense of a historical cycle that repeats itself, but in the sense that the original intention of the Creator, frustrated by creaturely rebellion . . . will be realized." Bernhard Anderson, *From Creation to New Creation: Old Testament Perspectives* (Minneapolis: Fortress, 1994), 38.

53. A cosmic fall is the dominant interpretation of Rom. 8:19–22 among New Testament scholars. See James D. G. Dunn, *Romans 1–8*, Word Biblical Commentary 38A (Dallas: Word, 1988), 469–71; Richard Longenecker, *The Epistle to the Romans*, New International Greek Testament Commentary (Grand Rapids: Eerdmans, 2016), 719–21; Douglas Moo, *The Letter to the Romans*, 2nd ed., New

The eschatological reality that God will renew the created order and forever remove the ravages of sin is consistent with a prior cosmic fall.[54] The cosmic fall depicts a creation that has been cursed by God and is now "groaning as in the pains of childbirth right up to the present time" (Rom. 8:22 NIV). The world is bent out of shape, but God will make things right through the blood of Christ (Col. 1:19–20). Christ's atonement brings shalom (v. 20), not merely for sinners but for the broader creation.[55] Paul, writes Scot McKnight, "believes all of creation is out of sorts with its Creator, and all of creation is in need of reconciliation."[56] The promise of cosmic renewal pervades the New Testament. From the beginning, it was God's plan "to unite all things in [Christ], things in heaven and things on earth" (Eph. 1:10). Here "all things" (*ta panta*) refers to "God's creation, animate and inanimate, which are going to be united under Christ,"[57] which is necessary because Adam's sin had ruptured the whole cosmos.[58]

In Matthew's Gospel, the language of restoration and renewal implies the original goodness of all creation: the Son of Man sits on his glorious throne "at the renewal of all things" (Matt. 19:28 NIV). At the eschaton, God will be "restoring all the things about which [he] spoke by the mouth of his holy prophets long ago" (Acts 3:21). Commenting on this verse, Darrell Bock writes that the "anticipated end was seen as establishing again the original creation's pristine character."[59] In the arc of redemption, the end of the story will naturally mirror the opening scenes of creation: "The end will renew the beginning; eschatology restores protology."[60]

Ezekiel's vision shares this eschatology with its promise that the future covenant of peace will banish animal predation and violence (Ezek. 34:25,

---

International Commentary on the New Testament (Grand Rapids: Eerdmans, 2018), 529–41; and Harry A. Hahne, *The Corruption and Redemption of Creation: Nature in Romans 8:19–22 and Jewish Apocalyptic Literature* (London: T&T Clark, 2006), 171–209.

54. One might instead argue that future cosmic renewal only requires a human—not cosmic—fall; the idea here is that the selfish exploitation of sinful humans is sufficient to negatively affect creation. However, the cosmic fall interpretation is more exegetically compelling.

55. Douglas Moo, *The Letters to the Colossians and Philemon*, Pillar New Testament Commentaries (Grand Rapids: Eerdmans, 2008), 136–37.

56. Scot McKnight, *The Letter to the Colossians*, New International Commentary on the New Testament (Grand Rapids: Eerdmans, 2018), 162.

57. Harold W. Hoehner, *Ephesians: An Exegetical Commentary* (Grand Rapids: Baker Academic, 2002), 223.

58. Andrew T. Lincoln, *Ephesians*, Word Biblical Commentary (Dallas: Word, 1990), 33.

59. Darrell Bock, *Acts*, Baker Exegetical Commentary on the New Testament (Grand Rapids: Baker Academic, 2007), 177. See also David G. Peterson, *The Acts of the Apostles*, Pillar New Testament Commentaries (Grand Rapids: Eerdmans, 2009), 182.

60. David Turner, *Matthew*, Baker Exegetical Commentary on the New Testament (Grand Rapids: Baker Academic, 2008), 475. As I argue below, however, eschatology will also far surpass protology.

28). One commentator describes the prophecy as a "dream of a return to paradise, an abjuration of violence among peoples, and, beyond that, *a total harmony within nature*."[61] Hosea similarly describes how God will make a covenant with "the beasts of the field, the birds of the heavens, and the creeping things of the ground" (Hosea 2:18). The three animal groupings originate in the creation week of Genesis 1:1–31, and the effects of the covenant "are cosmic, bringing in security, peace, and prosperity for all."[62] Commentators often interpret these animal references as merely metaphorical descriptions of God's covenant with Israel, but this view overlooks other relevant considerations: God does care about animals (Jon. 4:11), human sin is sometimes the cause of animal death (e.g., Gen. 7:21–23), the judgment and salvation of the Passover included animals (Exod. 12:12, 29), and other eschatological passages make pointed claims about the absence of animal suffering in the future.

Isaiah's picture of the new heaven and new earth, in particular, describes the absence of animal predation, when the cosmic fall will be undone:

> The wolf will live with the lamb,
>   the leopard will lie down with the goat,
> the calf and the lion and the yearling together;
>   and a little child will lead them.
> The cow will feed with the bear,
>   their young will lie down together,
>   and the lion will eat straw like the ox.
> The infant will play near the cobra's den,
>   and the young child will put its hand into the viper's nest.
> They will neither harm nor destroy
>   on all my holy mountain,
> for the earth will be filled with the knowledge of the LORD
>   as the waters cover the sea. (Isa. 11:6–9 NIV)

To be sure, even this familiar passage is often interpreted figuratively so that the animals represent Israel's enemies; allegedly, the prophet is not telling us anything about the nature of animals in the new heavens and

---

61. Joseph Blenkinsopp, *Ezekiel*, Interpretation: A Bible Commentary for Teaching and Preaching (Louisville: Westminster John Knox, 1990), 161, my emphasis.

62. J. Andrew Dearman, *The Book of Hosea*, New International Commentary on the Old Testament (Grand Rapids: Eerdmans, 2010), 126. As David Allan Hubbard (*Hosea*, Tyndale Old Testament Commentaries [Downers Grove, IL: InterVarsity, 1989], 86) notes, "The picture of total harmony in creation recalls Genesis 1:30 and its Edenic setting before the symphony turned discordant at the initial act of human disobedience (Gen. 3:15, 17–19; cf. Isa. 11:6–9; 35:9)."

new earth. The metaphorical language encourages the reader that when the messiah comes, Israel will no longer have any enemies and all the nations will flourish in the kingdom of God.[63] While I do not disagree that the coming of the messiah will include these and many other blessings, Isaiah's vivid images seem to picture something more, a peaceable future reminiscent of Eden with the absence of any interspecies animosity or violence: "The lion shall eat straw like the ox" (Isa. 65:25).

If eschatology restores protology, I think we may infer that animal predation and death were absent in the pre-fallen world—but for which animals specifically? Here we must tread carefully, as Scripture is exegetically silent on many of our specific questions. The biblical authors, for example, are not concerned with microbial or insect death, nor do they say much about the life of sea creatures. The vegetarianism of Eden is directed at "every beast of the earth and to every bird of the heavens and to everything that creeps on the earth" (Gen. 1:30). At a minimum, therefore, I claim that the suffering and death of *higher-order animals* (e.g., primates and mammals) that can experience pain was absent before the fall and will be absent in the eschaton when all creatures will dwell together in harmony.[64]

Some object to my core thesis that Adam's moral integrity and the integrity of the created order are mutually implicated because, so the worry goes, it implies that God created a defective world in which the fate of

63. For this metaphorical reading, see, inter alia, Gary Smith, *Isaiah 1–39*, Christian Standard Commentary (Nashville: Broadman & Holman, 2007), 268–69; John Oswalt, *The Book of Isaiah, Chapters 1–39*, New International Commentary on the Old Testament (Grand Rapids: Eerdmans, 1986), 284.

64. Some scholars argue that Scripture depicts the garden of Eden as a local paradise, an idyllic place without suffering and death, which means that the rest of the world outside Eden was chaotic and disorderly. Bernard Ramm, for example, writes that "ideal conditions existed only in the Garden. There was disease and death and bloodshed in Nature long before man sinned" (Bernard Ramm, *The Christian View of Science and Scripture* [Grand Rapids: Eerdmans, 1954], 334). He goes on to say that "outside of the Garden of Eden were death, disease, weeds, thistles, thorns, carnivores, deadly serpents, and intemperate weather. To think otherwise is to run counter to an immense avalanche of fact" (335). Similarly, fellow evangelical Arthur Lewis ("The Localization of the Garden of Eden," *Bulletin of the Evangelical Theological Society* 11 [1968]: 172) writes, "Many distinctive qualities of the garden emphasize its superiority to the rest of nature outside: the abundance of water, the edible plants and fruit-trees, the non-violent behavior of the animals, the absence of thorns and thistles, the stewardship apart from toilsome labor." This local-paradise position is relatively common among evangelical scholars. I agree that Scripture depicts Eden in a more pristine state than the rest of creation, hence God commanding Adam to "subdue" the earth (Gen. 1:28). But the mere fact of a local paradise implies nothing about the presence of sin, suffering, and death in the rest of creation. Besides, the biblical testimony to animal herbivory—with God's command that animals should eat "every green plant for food"—appears in Gen. 1:30 and is therefore not localized to Eden but is part of the whole creation that God deems "very good" (v. 31). And the divine curse of Gen. 3:17 and Rom. 8:20–22 implies that the whole earth—not just Eden—was unfallen.

nature depends on the moral choices of humans. Michael Murray gives voice to this concern:

> In order for moral wrongdoing to leave such catastrophic consequences in its wake it must be the case that God created things so that the integrity of the natural order was, in some important sense, initially *dependent upon* the integrity of the moral order. And this fact itself stands in need of some sort of explanation. If God were omniscient, he would surely know that the natural order was fragile in this way. Unless there is some reason why the fragility of nature is necessary, or why making it fragile in this way makes possible certain outweighing goods, the fragility of nature itself seems to be a puzzling defect in creation.[65]

However, God's original creation had no intrinsic "fragility." Adam's sin by itself had no intrinsic power to change the structure of nature. It was God's response to the broken commandment—the divine curse of Genesis 3:17—that unleashed the cosmic fall. The fallen order of creation is ontologically continuous with the original creation and yet is at key points different (e.g., the presence of physical death). Creation was thus "subjected to futility" (Rom. 8:20). Far from signaling a "defect" or "fragility" in the initial creation of Genesis 1 and 2, the cosmic fall is one of many clues to the gravity of sin and our need for a redeemer.

The ancient Jewish pseudepigrapha may also attest to original creational goodness and the hermeneutical assumptions of early readers of Scripture.[66] The book of Jubilees (second century BCE) assumes that animals once spoke Hebrew. On the day Adam sinned, "the mouth of all the beasts and cattle and birds and whatever walked or moved was stopped from speaking because all of them used to speak with one another with one speech and one language" (Jubilees 3:28). This teaching shows up in the Apocalypse of Moses (ca. first century CE) when Eve witnesses a wild animal attacking her son Seth. She implores the animal:

> "O you evil beast, do you not fear to attack the image of God? How was your mouth opened? How did your teeth grow strong? How did you not remember your subjection, for you were once subjected to the image of God?" Then

---

65. Murray, *Nature Red in Tooth and Claw*, 83. See also John Schneider, "The Fall of 'Augustinian Adam': Original Fragility and Supralapsarian Purpose," *Zygon* 47, no. 4 (2012): 949–69, emphasis original.

66. English translations of Jubilees and the Apocalypse of Moses are from James Charlesworth, ed., *The Old Testament Pseudepigrapha*, vol. 2 (Garden City, NY: Doubleday, 1985); and for 4 Ezra, see James Charlesworth, ed., *The Old Testament Pseudepigrapha*, vol. 1 (Garden City, NY: Doubleday, 1983).

the beast cried out, saying, "O Eve, neither your greed nor your weeping are due to us, but to you, since the rule of the beasts has happened because of you. How is it that your mouth was opened to eat from the tree concerning which God commanded you not to eat from it? Through this also our nature was changed. Therefore now you would not bear it if I begin to reprove you." (Apocalypse of Moses 10:3–11:3)

This quote is noteworthy because the animal blames Eve's disobedience for directly causing the change in the *nature* of the beasts. In the same text, God tells Adam, "And the animals over which you ruled will rise up against you in disorder, because you did not keep my commandment" (24:4). In *Jewish Antiquities*, penned by Josephus (early second century CE), the animal kingdom in Eden was not only peaceful but "at that epoch all the creatures spoke a common tongue" (1.41).[67] While no one today should believe that animals could once talk like humans—Scripture supports no such "Narnian" past—these noncanonical texts hint of an earlier day of intimacy between humans and animals (and perhaps between animals) and thus add further evidence of a widespread Jewish belief in the cosmic fall (see *Jewish Antiquities* 1.49; 4 Ezra 7:10–13).[68]

The ancient provenance of a cosmic fall should not be surprising since eschatology and protology are closely linked in Scripture. Yet some complain that the inference from eschatology to protology is illegitimate because eschatology is bigger, better, and brighter than protology. Our resurrected bodies will be more glorious than Adam's ever was (1 Cor. 15:42–49). Augustine and Irenaeus both believed Adam and Eve had the capacity to sin in Eden, but we know that sinning will be impossible in the new Jerusalem when God's people will be impeccable like Jesus (*non posse peccare*). Since eschatology is not merely a return to Eden, can we even infer *anything* about protology from Isaiah and other eschatological passages?

Yes, we can! In making inferences about the state of creation before Adam fell, we are not shooting in the dark. Scripture allows us to infer the nature of original goodness from eschatological passages that echo themes from the original creation in Genesis 1–2. The main acts of the

67. Josephus, *Jewish Antiquities* 1.41, in *Jewish Antiquities, Books I–IV*, trans. H. St. J. Thackeray (Cambridge, MA: Harvard University Press, 1961), 21.
68. Matthew Warnez challenges the idea that Jewish apocalyptic literature supports a fallen creation. Most of these pseudepigraphal sources, he argues, defend the idea that creation retains its original integrity, while a small number affirm a corruption of creation caused by the sins of the Watchers (Gen. 6:1–4); only the book of Jubilees and the Apocalypse of Moses allude to Adam's sin causing a fallen creation (see Matthew T. Warnez, "The Apocryphal Backdrop to Rom 8,19–22," *Biblica* 102, no. 4 [2021]: 585–92). In light of Warnez's careful analysis, I consider the pseudepigraphal evidence for a fallen creation to be suggestive, not decisive.

biblical drama give us light to see with: in act 1, we glimpse the world as it was before Adam's fall (Gen. 1–2); in act 2, we see the fallout of his disobedience and what God has done for our salvation (Gen. 3–Rev. 20); in act 3, God will finally put all wrongs to rights and usher us into an even better place than we enjoyed at the beginning (Rev. 21–22).[69] Thus, while some passages do promise greater glories that far exceed protology and therefore cannot tell us anything meaningful about the original creation (cf. 1 Cor. 2:9), other eschatological texts echo specific features of Genesis 1–2 that were lost in Genesis 3 (e.g., immortality, the absence of violence, peace between humans and animals). In these latter instances, we are right to infer particular features of the prelapsarian creation from these eschatological promises. Similarly, since the curse will be abolished (Rev. 22:3) and sin will vanish forever (22:15), and since the curse and sin both result from Adam's disobedience, we can infer—and the canonical narrative itself assumes (Rom. 5:12)—human sinlessness at the beginning.

At the parousia, suffering and death will pass away: "Death shall be no more, neither shall there be mourning, nor crying, nor pain anymore, for the former things have passed away" (Rev. 21:4). Jesus himself as the Alpha and Omega will restore the created order (Col. 1:15–20; Eph. 1:8–10). In the wisdom of God, eschatology restores protology, not by mere repristination but by turning it toward Christ—not only healing what had been corrupted by sin, not only redirecting what had been misdirected, and not only re-storing what God himself had cursed but also heightening, enhancing, and glorifying it forever.[70]

Fallen Nature and Recent Critics

The doctrine of a cosmic fall has many detractors. In an influential essay published in 2006, John Bimson concludes that the concept of a fallen creation has no biblical basis.[71] In his analysis of Romans 8:19–22, he rightly interprets *ktisis* in verse 21 as "the entire material universe . . . including sun, moon, planets and stars."[72] But then he says that Paul was

69. I am only using the three-act schema heuristically (otherwise it grossly oversimplifies; for one thing, the eschatological dimension of act 3 is interwoven throughout Scripture, not merely isolated to the last two chapters).

70. I borrow the wording from Bruce Ashford and Craig Bartholomew's excellent monograph, *The Doctrine of Creation: A Constructive Kuyperian Approach* (Downers Grove, IL: IVP Academic, 2020), 334, but I have added the missing element of the divine curse.

71. John J. Bimson, "Reconsidering a 'Cosmic Fall,'" *Science and Christian Belief* 18, no. 1 (2006): 63–81.

72. Bimson, "Reconsidering a 'Cosmic Fall,'" 74.

not interpreting Genesis 3:17–19, because Paul's perspective in Romans 8 "seems to go far beyond God's cursing of the ground."[73] As I have argued already, however, we should be reading the Genesis curse in the context of the broader Old Testament witness to a new creation. Bimson also denies that Colossians 1:20 teaches a cosmic fall: "In view of the uncertainties involved in the interpretation of this verse," he writes, "it would be exceedingly precarious to use it to support the doctrine of a cosmic fall."[74] I disagree, especially since he ignores other New Testament passages that echo Colossians 1:20's allusion to a cosmic fall (e.g., Matt. 19:28; Acts 3:21; Eph. 1:9–10, as discussed above).

Bimson's strongest argument comes in his analysis of Old Testament nature poetry. He argues against traditional interpretations of Genesis 3:17–19 and Isaiah 11:6–10 because "the rest of the Old Testament *implies nothing at all about the natural world being fallen or distorted in any way.*"[75] Instead, he insists that those texts portray nature "as 'good'/'very good' as God pronounced it to be in Genesis 1:25 and 1:31."[76] He cites Psalms 104 and 145, and Job 38:29–39:30, in each case highlighting how "the Hebrew poets had no problem with the natural world's being the way it is. They were fully aware of nature's redness in tooth and claw, and its apparent wastefulness, but did not find this incompatible with belief in a wise and loving Creator; they thus saw no need to invoke a 'cosmic fall' to excuse those aspects that we find offensive."[77] Bimson has a point. However, these wisdom texts are not addressing the fallenness or unfallenness of creation but are foregrounding God's providence and the glory of creation. Bimson's conclusion that creation is unfallen infers too much from such passages.

Part of the confusion is that Scripture affirms the goodness of creation while insisting that it is now fallen; that in turn prompts the question: After the fall, is God's creation *still* good, or has it lost its goodness?[78] God cannot negate the essential goodness of his own work. The cosmic fall describes God's judgment of Adam's sin and how it inflicted disease, disorder, and death *without undoing the underlying goodness of creation.* As Albert Wolters notes, "The central point to make is that, biblically speaking, sin neither

---

73. Bimson, "Reconsidering a 'Cosmic Fall,'" 74.
74. Bimson, "Reconsidering a 'Cosmic Fall,'" 76.
75. Bimson, "Reconsidering a 'Cosmic Fall,'" 71, emphasis original.
76. Bimson, "Reconsidering a 'Cosmic Fall,'" 71.
77. Bimson, "Reconsidering a 'Cosmic Fall,'" 73.
78. For an illuminating discussion of the problem, see Ted Peters, *Playing God? Genetic Determinism and Human Freedom*, 2nd ed. (New York: Routledge, 2003), 88–90.

abolishes nor becomes identified with creation."[79] Every creaturely entity comes from the hand of God and is therefore good. Irenaeus's second-century dispute with Gnosticism, and Augustine's later break with Manichaeism, turned on precisely this question.

Nevertheless, after Adam's fall we must qualify creational goodness. Sin entered the world (Rom. 5:12). God cursed the ground (Gen. 3:17). Nature groans while longing for final renewal and redemption (Rom. 8:19–22). Having lost the aboriginal goodness of Genesis 1 and 2, creation's post-lapsarian goodness is relative, not absolute. Wolters distinguishes between structure and direction: "*Structure* denotes the 'essence' of a creaturely thing, the kind of creature it is by virtue of God's creational law. *Direction*, by contrast, refers to a sinful deviation from that structural ordinance and renewed conformity to it in Christ."[80] Since the essence of creation necessarily reflects its creator, we rightly expect Scripture to praise the natural world as "valuable in its own right" (to use Bimson's words).[81] Creation's fallenness or misdirection are at best only tacit in such passages, but as readers we must still keep the broader canonical and redemptive-historical context in mind.

Consider how Jael killed Sisera in Judges 4, yet the Song of Deborah praises her in the next chapter: "Most blessed of women be Jael, the wife of Heber the Kenite, most blessed of tent-dwelling women. . . . 'So may all your enemies perish, LORD! But may all who love you be like the sun when it rises in its strength'" (Judg. 5:24, 31 NIV). Does it follow from the mere fact that Scripture calls Jael "most blessed" that what she did was unqualifiedly good? Surely not; goodness is qualified by the context. Here is another example: Israel's practice of consigning its enemies to destruction was known as *herem*. "In the cities of these peoples that the LORD your God is giving you for an inheritance, you shall save alive nothing that breathes, but you shall devote them to complete destruction, the Hittites and the Amorites, the Canaanites and the Perizzites, the Hivites and the Jebusites, as the LORD your God has commanded" (Deut. 20:16–17). Does it follow from the mere fact that God commanded his people to destroy those nations that what they did reflected the original goodness of Genesis 1–2? Surely not; goodness is qualified by the fallen context.

God enabled his judges to defeat Israel's enemies, including Samson's routine thrashing of the Philistines (Judg. 13–16); and while blessing Abram,

---

79. Albert Wolters, *Creation Regained: Biblical Basics for a Reformational Worldview*, 2nd ed. (Grand Rapids: Eerdmans, 2005), 57.
80. Wolters, *Creation Regained*, 88, emphasis original.
81. Bimson, "Reconsidering a 'Cosmic Fall,'" 72.

God told him that he would go to his "ancestors in peace and be buried at a good old age" (Gen. 15:15 NIV)—is killing our enemies, or dying of old age, an unqualified good? Surely not, and that's the point. Although these examples only involve human death, we can discern the same pattern with animal death. After all, God commanded Jews to kill, exsanguinate, and eat nonhuman animals as a regular part of the Levitical priestly duties. We are not to conclude that animal death is good just because God instituted the sacrificial system; rather, the context of a fallen world indicates only a qualified goodness in the death of animals. The original vegetarianism of Genesis 1–2 and the eschatological texts pointing to the end of animal suffering in the new heaven and new earth (e.g., Isa. 11:6–9; 65:17, 25) suggest that God's institution of animal sacrifices is qualified by the fall.[82]

Furthermore, if I am right that animal suffering and death are part of the fallenness of our world and therefore *not* good, we should not infer from God instituting the sacrificial system that he condones animal death, but rather that the sacrificial system—including all the attendant death and suffering—was a daily reminder of the *gravity of sin*. As Hebrews 9:22 states, "Under the law almost everything is purified with blood, and without the shedding of blood there is no forgiveness of sins" (cf. Lev. 17:11)—and, of course, the animal sacrifices foreshadowed Christ's atonement. Bimson is, therefore, right that the Old Testament psalms and other wisdom texts speak positively about nature's wild side, but it does not follow that such realities were part of God's original design or that they will persist into the eschaton. Such passages merely reflect the present ambiguity of God's world, the creation that is inherently good because of the creator but fallen because of sin and judgment.[83]

This goodness of creation has been almost eclipsed by the modern environmental crisis. These environmental concerns lead some biblical scholars to challenge the cosmic fall doctrine because a fallen creation seems less worthy of our protection.[84] Laurie Braaten is a noteworthy ex-

---

82. For the exegetical case for original vegetarianism and the eschatological end to animal suffering and death, see my analysis in the previous section.

83. Denis Lamoureux, who agrees with Bimson on the science, argues that Scripture *does* teach a cosmic fall. However, Lamoureux thinks modern Bible readers should sift the wheat of spiritual truth from the chaff of ancient biology: "Incidental ancient scientific concepts such as *de novo* creation, cosmic fall, and cosmic redemption were inadvertently conflated with inerrant spiritual truths of the Bible. To move beyond concordism and conflation, it is necessary to separate the incidental ancient science from the Holy Spirit's life-changing messages of faith." Denis Lamoureux, "Beyond the Cosmic Fall and Natural Evil," *Perspectives on Science and Christian Faith* 68, no. 1 (2016): 55.

84. But why not the other way around? A fallen creation may need *more* environmental care, not less.

ample.[85] He questions whether God's curse of the ground extends to the whole creation: "Those who interpret the curse on the ground as a fall of creation also have to reckon with Gen 8:21, where a (the?) curse on the ground is reversed, or alleviated."[86] This claim is not original to Braaten but goes back to a 1961 essay by the German Old Testament scholar Rolf Rendtorff arguing that the curse of Genesis 3:17 was rescinded in Genesis 8:21.[87] Others followed suit.[88] However, the curse of Genesis 3:17–19 gave rise to painful labor and recalcitrant soil with thorns and thistles—yet those punishments all persisted *after* the flood. Based on the Hebrew wording of Genesis 8:21, Gordon Wenham explains that "God is not lifting the curse on the ground pronounced in 3:17 for man's disobedience, but promising not to add to it. The flood was a punishment over and above that decreed in 3:17."[89] Since the curse remains part of our present experience, Rendtorff's thesis falls apart.[90]

Braaten's central idea is "that the curse is primarily on human labor in connection with the ground, not on God's creation per se."[91] He draws on the Bible's language of the earth mourning over human sin; throughout the prophetic literature, creation frequently mourns human sinfulness and God's ensuing punishment. "There is no faithfulness or steadfast love, and no knowledge of God in the land; there is swearing, lying, murder, stealing, and committing adultery; they break all bounds, and bloodshed follows bloodshed. *Therefore the land mourns*" (Hosea 4:1–3). According

85. Others have endorsed Braaten's thesis, including Richard Bauckham's *Bible and Ecology: Rediscovering the Community of Creation* (London: Darton, Longman & Todd, 2010), 92–101, and his "The Story of the Earth according to Paul: Romans 8:18–23," *Review and Expositor* 108, no. 1 (2011): 91–97; William Horst, "Creation's Slavery to (Human) Corruption: A Moral Interpretation of Romans 8:20–22," *Perspectives on Science and Christian Faith* 73, no. 2 (2021): 79–90; and Sollereder, *God, Evolution, and Animal Suffering*, 31–36.

86. Laurie J. Braaten, "The Groaning Creation: The Biblical Background for Romans 8:22," *Biblical Research* 50 (2005): 23n10. Sollereder endorses this interpretation (Sollereder, *God, Evolution, and Animal Suffering*, 23–30).

87. Rolf Rendtorff, "Gen 8,21 und die Urgeschichte des Jahwisten," *Kerygma und Dogma* 7 (1961): 69–78.

88. For example, see Gerhard von Rad, *Genesis: A Commentary*, rev. ed. (Philadelphia: Westminster, 1972), 122; Terence E. Fretheim, "The Book of Genesis," in *The New Interpreter's Bible Commentary*, ed. Leander E. Keck et al. (Nashville: Abingdon, 1994), 393; and Brian Curry, "Christ, Creation and the Powers: Elements in a Christian Doctrine of Creation," in *Christ and the Created Order: Perspectives from Theology, Philosophy, and Science*, ed. Andrew Torrance and Thomas McCall (Grand Rapids: Zondervan, 2018), 89n39.

89. Gordon Wenham, *Genesis 1–15*, Word Biblical Commentary 1 (Waco: Word, 1987), 190. See also Kenneth A. Mathews, *Genesis 1–11:26* (Nashville: Broadman & Holman, 1996), 394; and Bruce Waltke, with Cathi Fredricks, *Genesis: A Commentary* (Grand Rapids: Zondervan, 2001), 142.

90. Laurence Turner, *Announcements of Plot in Genesis* (Sheffield, UK: JSOT Press, 1990), 40.

91. Braaten, "Groaning Creation," 23.

to Jeremiah, the weeping prophet, God's judgment of Israel's sin left the land ruined. "Therefore *the earth will mourn* and the heavens above grow dark, because I have spoken and will not relent, I have decided and will not turn back" (Jer. 4:28).[92] Regarding Romans 8, Braaten interprets Paul as alluding to the mourning motif in Isaiah 24, where ongoing human sins have led creation to suffer under divine judgment (Rom. 8:21 and the Septuagint translation of Isa. 24:3 use the same word for "decay"). Braaten also discusses Isaiah 33:7–9 and Joel 1:5–20 as "earth mourns" passages that may be in the background of Paul's reasoning in Romans 8.[93] "The notion that creation groans due to ongoing human sin," Braaten avers, "is sufficiently documented in the scriptures, and is satisfactory for explaining Paul's reference to a groaning creation."[94] Appeal to a primeval fall of nature is therefore moot.

Braaten's mourning earth motif is insightful and illuminates the biblical narrative. But I fear he has created a false dichotomy between Adam's primal sin and the reality of sin and divine punishment in Israel's history—Scripture witnesses to both realities. In Romans 8:19–22, Paul's allusion to Genesis 3:17–19 is more textually evident than any alleged echoes of Isaiah's lament over creation mourning. Even Jonathan Moo, who agrees with Braaten's reading of Isaiah 24–27, concedes that "it seems nearly certain that Genesis 3 has influenced Paul's thinking in Romans 8."[95] Braaten's environmental worries are justified, but Scripture itself regularly urges us to be good stewards of the earth and the animals,[96] so we need not sacrifice the cosmic fall on the altar of creation care. We can have both.

Aside from environmental issues, others have raised exegetical and historical objections to the cosmic fall. In his book *God's Good Earth: The Case for an Unfallen Creation*, Jon Garvey claims that the idea of a fallen creation is antithetical to the biblical witness and most of pre-Reformation church history. He argues that the Genesis 3:17 curse was limited to the soil (not the cosmos) and was abrogated in Genesis 8:21 after Noah's flood. He notes that "agricultural imagery is not used in the flood narrative at all.

92. Braaten also discusses mourning texts in Jer. 12:1–4, 7–13; and 23:9–12 (Braaten, "Groaning Creation," 30–31).

93. See also Laurie J. Braaten, "All Creation Groans: Romans 8:22 in Light of the Biblical Sources," *Horizons in Biblical Theology* 28, no. 2 (2006): 131–59.

94. Braaten, "All Creation Groans," 152.

95. Jonathan Moo, "Romans 8.19–22 and Isaiah's Cosmic Covenant," *New Testament Studies* 54 (2008): 84. See also Nicholas Meyer, *Adam's Dust and Adam's Glory in the Hodayot and the Letters of Paul: Rethinking Anthropogony and Theology* (Leiden: Brill, 2016), 216–17n124.

96. See Douglas Moo and Jonathan Moo, *Creation Care: A Biblical Theology of the Natural World* (Grand Rapids: Zondervan, 2018).

. . . Neither is the word 'curse' mentioned within the narrative about the flood, but the word instead harks directly back to what God says to Adam in chapter 3."[97] In his analysis, the Septuagint's translation of Genesis 8:21, and most English translations, all use language recalling Genesis 3:17–19. However, Garvey's exegesis is mistaken: first, the word for "curse" in 8:21 is different and milder than the word used in 3:17 and suggests that the flood is the right referent in 8:21 (note, too, "the intention of man's heart" in v. 21 recalls Gen. 6:5).[98] Second, as we have already established, the punishments of Genesis 3:17 continued after the flood and were therefore not rescinded in Genesis 8. God was referring back to the flood, not the fall.

Garvey faults original vegetarianism for being "scientifically unrealistic"[99] and for committing us to absurd scenarios like immortal insects and plankton taking over the planet. Given what we know biologically, "it is quite impossible that any ecosystem could survive with just green plants as its food source, or that anteaters, chameleons, or swifts could even begin to survive on them."[100] Garvey endorses Derek Kidner's judgment on Genesis 1:30: "The assigning of every green plant for food (RSV) to all creatures must not be pressed to mean that all were once herbivorous, any more than to mean that all plants were equally edible to all. It is a generalization, that directly or indirectly all life depends on vegetation, and the concern of the verse is to show that we are all fed from God's hand."[101]

Kidner is right that Genesis 1:29–30 does not explicitly prohibit the eating of meat, but it is reasonable to draw the inference from the text. God only permitted meat eating after the judgment of Noah's flood (9:1–3), although the new dominion mandate was now under the conditions of animals being in constant rebellion against humanity: "So severe would the imposition of that dominion be," writes Eugene Merrill, "that man would from thenceforth be allowed to slay animals for food (9:3), a concession to the altered conditions brought about by sin, conditions that fostered antipathy where there had been harmony and death where there had been nothing but life."[102] Although original vegetarianism strikes me as the most plausible reading, the ambiguity of these texts is reflected in the varying opinions in

97. Jon Garvey, *God's Good Earth: The Case for an Unfallen Creation* (Eugene, OR: Cascade Books, 2019), 28.

98. Wenham, *Genesis 1–15*, 190.

99. Garvey, *God's Good Earth*, 31.

100. Garvey, *God's Good Earth*, 32.

101. Derek Kidner, *Genesis* (Downers Grove, IL: InterVarsity, 1967), 52. For a similar perspective, see Collins, *Genesis 1–4*, 165.

102. Eugene Merrill, *Everlasting Dominion: A Theology of the Old Testament* (Nashville: Broadman & Holman, 2006), 151–52. Also defending original vegetarianism, see Richard Hess, *The Old Testament: A*

the history of interpretation. Therefore, while I affirm original goodness dogmatically, I am less dogmatic about the more narrow claim of original vegetarianism.[103]

In defense of original vegetarianism, many young-earth creationists often argue that only animals and humans are "living" creatures or have "life" (*nephesh*), whereas plants do not. Since humans and animals are *nephesh chayyah* (Gen. 1:30), "man did not eat animals and animals did not eat each other."[104] Henry Morris, the doyen of modern creationism, explains: "The word 'life' occurs for the first time in [1:20] (Hebrew *nephesh*). Actually, this is the word also for 'soul,' and is frequently used to refer to both the soul of man and the life of animals. In the Biblical sense, plants do not have real life, or soul (or consciousness); but both animals and men do."[105] Then again, this linguistic argument is questionable. Scripture not only attributes the term *nephesh* to dead bodies (Lev. 19:28; 21:1, 11; Num. 5:2; 6:6, 11), but it sometimes draws an analogy between plant and human death that blunts the linguistic argument by some creationists that plant death is uniquely different from human death (Job 14:7–12; John 12:20–33).[106] I am therefore doubtful that the word *nephesh* can bear the philological weight my fellow creationists are placing on it.[107] Scripture never tells us whether prelapsarian plants, microbes, or insects were subject to death; that we take it as obvious is a function of postlapsarian norms. Prior to

Historical, Theological, and Critical Introduction (Grand Rapids: Baker Academic, 2016), 41; and John Currid, *A Study Commentary on Genesis*, 2 vols. (Darlington, UK: Evangelical Press, 2003), 1:88.

103. On the range of exegesis of Gen. 9:3, see Thomas Whitelaw, *Genesis*, ed. H. D. M. Spence and Joseph Exell, 5th ed., Pulpit Commentary (London: C. Kegan Paul, 1881), 139.

104. James Stambaugh, "Whence Cometh Death? A Biblical Theology of Physical Death and Natural Evil," in *Coming to Grips with Genesis: Biblical Authority and the Age of the Earth*, ed. Terry Mortenson and Thane H. Ury (Green Forest, AR: New Leaf, 2008), 383.

105. Henry Morris, *The Genesis Record: A Scientific & Devotional Commentary on the Book of Beginnings* (Grand Rapids: Baker, 1976), 69. See also Jonathan Sarfati, *The Genesis Account: A Theological, Historical, and Scientific Commentary on Genesis 1–11* (Powder Springs, GA: Creation Book Publishers, 2015), 247–48, 267–70.

106. According to Stambaugh, "Biblically speaking, there is a sharp and significant difference between, on the one hand, humans and animals (which live and die in the same physical sense), and on the other hand, plants (which do not live and die in that same sense). The NT words for death reflect the OT usage in that the words describing death are used of humans and animals" (Stambaugh, "Whence Cometh Death," 380). Stambaugh does engage with Job 14:7–12 and John 12:20–33 but does not think they undermine his overall thesis.

107. Robert R. Gonzales Jr., "Predation and Creation: Animal Death before the Fall?" (paper presented at the annual meeting of the Evangelical Theological Society, Worcester, MA, November 13, 2013), 2n4. Henri Blocher (*In the Beginning: The Opening Chapters of Genesis*, trans. David G. Preston [Downers Grove, IL: InterVarsity, 1984], 185n31) argues similarly that this use of *nephesh* "is philologically unacceptable, for the smallest marine organisms and terrestrial animals, insects, etc., are explicitly classified as *nepeš* in [Gen.] 1:20f., 24."

the fall, when Genesis 1 describes the human diet as "every plant yielding seed" and "every tree with seed in its fruit" (v. 29), and the animal diet as "every green plant" (v. 30), it is conceivable that fruit, seed, and vegetation were eaten without destroying individual plants. I simply do not know; Scripture does not serve my every curiosity and is largely silent on these questions. Thus, I defend original vegetarianism as the claim that in the prelapsarian world humans and higher-order animals were vegetarians that only experienced suffering and death after Adam's fall.

Garvey also evaluates other biblical texts, including Romans 8:18–22 and the Isaiah passages. He denies that Paul teaches a fallen creation in Romans 8 and insists that none of the church fathers—except Chrysostom—believed that Paul taught a cosmic fall (specifically, Irenaeus, Methodius, Archelaus, Origen, and Augustine).[108] In his analysis, Romans 8:18–22 is about our new creation in Christ with an eye to the new heaven and new earth, *not* a pre-fall beginning: "The natural creation . . . has been, from its original foundation, tied to mortality but longing for immortality, to corruption but awaiting incorruption, to the naturally empowered . . . but destined for the spiritually empowered."[109] As for Isaiah 11 and 65, Garvey cautions against a literal interpretation. In light of Isaiah 65:20 and its reference to dying in old age, Garvey concludes: "Isaiah's vision of the future age still contains human death, giving no support at all for the fictional time of deathlessness for animals claimed for the beginning."[110] Garvey takes Isaiah to be speaking metaphorically about the longevity of animals (and humans), unlike the case of New Testament eschatology, where the language of "new earth" is "clearly on the understanding of eternal life and the defeat of death in the light of the Resurrection."[111] In Garvey's defense, the Isaiah 65:20 reference to people experiencing death in the new heaven and new earth has long puzzled readers of Scripture. Some commentators (usually amillennial) argue that this text is figurative for eternal life; others (premillennial) discern *two* separate timeframes in Isaiah 65:17–25 (vv. 17–19 are limited to the final state and vv. 20–25 to a prior millennial kingdom, a time when people will have unusual longevity but still experience death).[112] Since these verses are opaque, I concede that Garvey's interpretation is no less plausible than the others.

108. Garvey, *God's Good Earth*, 45–47. As we shall see, Garvey has misread Irenaeus and others.
109. Garvey, *God's Good Earth*, 49.
110. Garvey, *God's Good Earth*, 51.
111. Garvey, *God's Good Earth*, 51.
112. On the amillennial view, see G. K. Beale, "An Amillennial Response to a Premillennial View of Isaiah 65:20," *Journal of the Evangelical Theological Society* 61, no. 3 (2018): 461–92; and Richard

Nevertheless, the fallenness of creation still makes the best sense canonically, redemptive-historically, and dogmatically. Despite some helpful insights in Garvey's book, he seems overconfident in the scientific assumptions of our age informed by geology and shaped by evolutionary thought. As a result, his argument betrays a post-Enlightenment naivete, especially in chapter 6 of his book where he argues that virtually all patristic and medieval theologians adopted an unfallen creation (save for the lone Chrysostom). He also claims that the Reformers invented the doctrine of a fallen creation, sometime after 1517.[113] Garvey could not be more wrong.

A History of a Contested Doctrine

Long before the Reformation, large segments of the early church affirmed original vegetarianism and a cosmic fall. Since Garvey and other Christian scholars often miss this point, I will allow the primary sources to speak for themselves.[114] The second-century writer Theophilus of Antioch believed that the animal world changed as a result of Adam's sin. The animal kingdom sinned with Adam, writes Theophilus, "not as if they had been made evil or venomous from the first—for nothing was made evil by God, but all things good, yea, very good,—but the sin in which man was concerned brought evil upon them. For when man transgressed, they also transgressed with him."[115] Animals will recover their "original gentleness" when Christ returns.

In *Against Heresies*, Irenaeus of Lyons (ca. 130–ca. 200) clearly rejects the pessimistic view of creation held by his Gnostic opponents.[116] Yet his reading of Genesis 3 implies that creation is fallen. God, he writes,

---

Schultz, "Intertextuality, Canon, and 'Undecidability': Understanding Isaiah's 'New Heavens and New Earth' (Isaiah 65:17–25)," *Bulletin for Biblical Research* 20, no. 1 (2010): 19–38; on the premillennial view, see Craig Blaising, "Premillennialism," in *Three Views on the Millennium and Beyond*, ed. Stanley Gundry and Darrell Bock (Grand Rapids: Zondervan, 1999), 202; and Walter Kaiser, *Preaching and Teaching the Last Things: Old Testament Eschatology for the Life of the Church* (Grand Rapids: Baker Academic, 2011), 160–61.

113. Garvey, *God's Good Earth*, 91.

114. For other critics of original vegetarianism, see Ronald E. Osborn, *Death before the Fall: Biblical Literalism and the Problem of Animal Suffering* (Downers Grove, IL: InterVarsity, 2014); Iain Provan, *Discovering Genesis: Content, Interpretation, Reception* (Grand Rapids: Eerdmans, 2016), 120–24; Iain Provan, *Seriously Dangerous Religion: What the Old Testament Really Says and Why It Matters* (Waco: Baylor University Press, 2014), 221–50.

115. Theophilus of Antioch, *Letter of Autolycus* 2.17, in *Ante-Nicene Christian Library: Translations of the Writings of the Fathers*, vol. 3, ed. Alexander Roberts and James Donaldson (Edinburgh: T&T Clark, 1880), 84. Garvey tries to argue, unconvincingly, that Theophilus only addresses the origins of carnivory, *not* a cosmic fall (Garvey, *God's Good Earth*, 74). However, as most interpreters of Theophilus recognize, the former implies the latter.

116. For background, see Peter Bouteneff, *Beginnings: Ancient Christian Readings of the Biblical Creation Narratives* (Grand Rapids: Baker Academic, 2008), 73–85.

"pronounced no curse against Adam personally, but against the ground, in reference to his works, as a certain person among the ancients has observed: 'God did indeed transfer the curse to the earth, that it might not remain in man.'"[117] At the final consummation, creation will be "renovated and set free"; it will "fructify with an abundance of all kinds of food, from the dew of heaven, and from the fertility of the earth."[118] Irenaeus's language bespeaks a cosmic fall. The animals, he continues, will "become peaceful and harmonious among each other, and be in perfect subjection to man."[119] Later in the same work, while discussing Isaiah 11:6–9 and 65:25, Irenaeus describes animals at the resurrection reverting "to the food originally given by God (for they had been originally subjected in obedience to Adam), that is, the productions of the earth." In other words, they will revert to vegetarianism and become peaceful again. Commenting on Isaiah's picture of the lion feeding on straw, Irenaeus writes: "And this indicates the large size and rich quality of the fruits. For if that animal, the lion, feeds upon straw [at that period], of what a quality must the wheat itself be whose straw shall serve as suitable food for lions?"[120]

In his polemic against the second-century heretic Hermogenes, Tertullian (ca. 160–ca. 220) reasons that if evil will expire one day, it must have had a beginning. After Adam's fall, "immediately spring up briers and thorns, where once had grown grass, and herbs, and fruitful trees. Immediately arise sweat and labour for bread, where previously on every tree was yielded spontaneous food and untilled nourishment."[121] Elsewhere, he says that original goodness will be regained at the parousia, "when the cattle restored in the innocence and integrity of their nature shall be at peace with the beasts of the field, when also little children shall play with serpents."[122] Tertullian never explicitly defends a fallen creation, but his few comments are consistent with it.

---

117. Irenaeus, *Against Heresies* 3.23.3, in *Ante-Nicene Fathers*, vol. 1A, ed. Alexander Roberts and James Donaldson (Grand Rapids: Eerdmans, 1996), 456.

118. Irenaeus, *Against Heresies* 5.33.3 (*ANF* 1A:562–63).

119. Irenaeus, *Against Heresies* 5.33.3 (*ANF* 1A:563).

120. Irenaeus, *Against Heresies* 5.33.4 (*ANF* 1A:563). Ashford and Bartholomew (*Doctrine of Creation*, 51) claim that "Irenaeus acknowledges the curse of the earth following humankind's fall but rejects the notion of a cosmic fall." Since "the notion of a cosmic fall" is precisely the idea that the earth is cursed by dint of Adam's fall, I find this statement confusing. I suspect they mean to underscore the point that Irenaeus affirms the *goodness* of creation in spite of its fallenness. I agree, but the ontological goodness of creation—as distinct from its fallenness—is a doctrinal claim that is entirely compatible with a post-creation cosmic fall.

121. Tertullian, *Against Marcion* 2.11, in *Ante-Nicene Fathers*, vol. 3, ed. Alexander Roberts and James Donaldson (Grand Rapids: Eerdmans, 1986), 306.

122. Tertullian, *Against Hermogenes* 11 (*ANF* 3:483).

The doctrine of original goodness is even more prevalent in Eastern Christianity. Based on his reading of Genesis 3:17, Origen (ca. 185–ca. 254) thinks that the earth "was originally cursed for the transgression of Adam."[123] The curse was not limited to a small section of creation, but "it is plain that *all parts of the earth* share in the curse."[124] Origen, the first systematic theologian, clearly endorsed the doctrine of a cosmic fall—as did the writings attributed to Macarius of Egypt (300–91), the Coptic monk, in his description of Adam's temptation: "When he was thus seized, *creation, which served him and ministered to him, was seized with him.*"[125] The first sin corrupted the rest of creation.

Ephrem the Syrian (306–73), a preeminent theologian in the Syrian church and a poet, sees the fallen creation as integral to the Christian story. Peace reigned between Adam and the animals until his transgression: "The animals came to Adam as to a loving shepherd. Without fear they passed before him in orderly fashion, by kinds and by species. They were neither afraid of him nor were they afraid of each other. A species of predatory animals would pass by with a species of animal that is preyed upon following safely right behind."[126] Ephrem captures this drama in one of his hymns—the eschatological restoration of the fallen cosmos will satisfy our hearts' longing for all things to be right again:

> In the world there is struggle,
> in Eden, a crown of glory.
> At our resurrection
> both earth and heaven will God renew,
> liberating all creatures,
> granting them paschal joy, along with us.
> Upon our mother Earth, along with us,
> did He lay disgrace
> when He placed on her, with the sinner, the curse;
> so, together with the just, will He bless her too;
> this nursing mother, along with her children,
> shall He who is Good renew.[127]

123. Origen, *Against Celsus* 7.28, in *Ante-Nicene Fathers*, vol. 4, ed. Alexander Roberts and James Donaldson (Grand Rapids: Eerdmans, 1979), 622.

124. Origen, *Against Celsus* 7.29 (*ANF* 4:622), my emphasis. Garvey overlooks Origen's fallen creation doctrine and only mentions Origen's exegesis of Rom. 8. Garvey, *God's Good Earth*, 46.

125. Macarius of Egypt, *Homilies* 11.5, in *Fifty Spiritual Homilies of St. Macarius the Great*, trans. A. J. Mason (London: SPCK, 1921), 81, my emphasis.

126. Ephrem the Syrian, *Commentary on Genesis* 2.9.3, in *St. Ephrem the Syrian: Selected Prose Works*, ed. K. McVey, trans. Edward G. Mathews and Joseph P. Amar (Washington, DC: Catholic University of America Press, 1994), 103.

127. Ephrem the Syrian, *Hymns on Paradise* 9.1, trans. Sebastian Brock (Crestwood, NY: St. Vladimir's Seminary Press, 1990), 136 (used with permission).

As a contemporary of Ephrem, Basil of Caesarea (330–79)—a.k.a. Basil the Great—seems to have rejected original vegetarianism and the fall of creation. He mentions how God made "venomous animals, destroyers and enemies of our life" as a means of disciplining humanity. God gave bears, lions, and tigers short necks because they "have no need to bend down to the earth; they are carnivorous and eat the animals upon whom they prey."[128] Carnivorous beasts, with their "pointed teeth," were part of God's originally good creation. Even poisons like hemlock, hellebore, monkshood, and mandrake were among the newly created vegetation of Genesis 1:11. God made everything for a reason, Basil remarks, including many poisons that have turned out to be useful to humanity. "With mandrake doctors give us sleep; with opium they lull violent pain."[129]

On the witness of such statements, scholars usually take Basil as an advocate of an unfallen creation, a judgment that resonates with evidence that Gregory of Nazianzus (ca. 329–90), Ambrose of Milan (339–97), and Basil's younger brother Gregory of Nyssa (ca. 335–ca. 395) all interpreted creation as unfallen.[130] However, one of Basil's homilies paints a remarkably different picture. In his homily on Genesis 2, Basil imagines that "the restoration after the present age will be such as was the first creation." In that paradise, Adam and Eve only ate divine fruits and vegetables: "As life was, it was without want of more. How little human beings needed to lead their life; the cause of our variety in diet was the introduction of sin. For since we fell away from the true delight that was in paradise, we invented adulterated delicacies for ourselves. And since we no longer see the tree of life, nor do we pride ourselves in that beauty, there have been given to us for our enjoyment cooks and bakers, and various pastries and aromas, and such things console us in our banishment from there."[131] Before the fall, carnivores were strict vegetarians. The laws of nature in Eden were sufficiently different that fruits could sustain the leopard and the lion.[132] The wild beasts of Genesis 1 did not originally "claw prey, for they were not carnivores. . . . But all followed the diet of swans and all grazed the meadows."[133] This homily presents such a strikingly different perspective

128. Basil, *Hexaemeron* 9.5, in *Basil: Letters and Selected Works*, in *Nicene and Post-Nicene Fathers*, 2nd series, vol. 8, ed. Philip Schaff, trans. Blomfield Jackson (New York: Christian Literature, 1895), 105.

129. Basil, *Hexaemeron* 5.4 (*NPNF*² 8:78).

130. For documentation, see Matthew Warnez, "*De Natura*: The Church Fathers on Creation's Fallenness," *Nova et Vetera* 19, no. 3 (2021): 956–63.

131. Basil the Great, *On the Human Condition*, trans. Nonna Verna Harrison (Crestwood, NY: St. Vladimir's Seminary Press, 2005), 54.

132. Basil, *On the Human Condition*, 53.

133. Basil, *On the Human Condition*, 53.

on the fallenness of creation in comparison to the nine homilies of the *Hexaemeron* that some have questioned its authenticity.[134] If the Genesis 2 homily was written near the end of Basil's life, as some scholars have suggested, the discrepancy may signal a change in his thinking about a fallen creation. However, given the ongoing debate among experts about the authenticity of this homily and an accompanying one on Genesis 1, it is more prudent to consider him an equivocal witness for that tradition.[135]

In his commentary on Romans 8, John Chrysostom (ca. 349–407) offers a striking account of creation as fallen. Adam is at fault for creation being "made subject to vanity" not only because he became "mortal and liable to suffering" but because "the earth too hath received a curse, and brought forth thorns and thistles."[136] At the resurrection, "this body of the heaven, the earth, and the whole creation, shall be incorruptible, and free from injury."[137] Original vegetarianism was the state in Eden. Peace reigned between Adam and the animals: "Lions, panthers, snakes, scorpions, serpents, and . . . all the other animals fiercer than those, came in complete subjection to him as to a master and accepted the names, while Adam had no fear of these wild beasts."[138] In a different homily, Chrysostom reiterates that "none of the wild beasts then existing caused fear either to the man or to the woman; on the contrary, they recognized human direction and dominion, and as with tame animals these days, so then even the wild and savage ones proved

---

134. For arguments against the authenticity of the Gen. 1 and 2 homilies, see Markos A. Orphanos, *Creation and Salvation according to St. Basil of Caesarea* (Athens: Gregorios Parisianos, 1975), 70–71. However, most Basil specialists see them as a continuation of his *Hexaemeron*. For example, see Bouteneff, *Beginnings*, 136–37; Stephen M. Hildebrand, *Basil of Caesarea* (Grand Rapids: Baker Academic, 2014), 171n3; Andrew Louth, "The Fathers on Genesis," in *The Book of Genesis: Composition, Reception, and Interpretation*, ed. Craig A. Evans, Joel N. Lohr, and David L. Petersen (Leiden: Brill, 2012), 569; and Nonna Verna Harrison's introduction to St. Basil the Great, *On the Human Condition*, trans. Nonna Verna Harrison (Crestwood, NY: St. Vladimir's Seminary Press, 2005), 14, which notes that "Alexis Smets and Michel van Esbroeck, the editors of the *Sources chrétiennes* edition translated here, consider [the two homilies] to be Basil's homilies ten and eleven *On the Six Days of Creation*."

135. On this tension in Basil, see Piet Slootweg, *Teeth and Talons Whetted for Slaughter: Divine Attributes and Suffering Animals in Historical Perspective (1600–1961)* (Kampen, Netherlands: Summum, 2022), 39–41. Garvey's analysis of Basil ignores the evidence from his two extra homilies (Garvey, *God's Good Earth*, 78–80). In his illuminating study of patristic views on creation's fallenness, Warnez's assessment of Basil also ignores his homily on Gen. 2. Warnez, "*De Natura*," 955–56.

136. John Chrysostom, *The Homilies of S. John Chrysostom, Archbishop of Constantinople, on the Epistle of S. Paul the Apostle to the Romans*, trans. J. B. Morris, 3rd ed. (Oxford: James Parker, 1877), 244.

137. John Chrysostom, *The Homilies of S. John Chrysostom, Archbishop of Constantinople, on the Statues, or to the People of Antioch*, trans. Edward Budge (Oxford: John Henry Parker, 1842), 185.

138. John Chrysostom, *Homilies on Genesis 1–17*, trans. Robert C. Hill (Washington, DC: Catholic University of America Press, 1986), 191.

to be subdued."[139] Since they had not yet fallen with Adam, animals were naturally tame.[140]

One finds similar notes in Nemesius, a late fourth-century bishop, who thought Adam and the animals were originally vegetarian. Meat eating is a postlapsarian accommodation. After the fall, Adam lost "immortality" and "was permitted also the enjoyment of meats."[141] In short, the cosmic fall and prelapsarian vegetarianism were mainstream patristic beliefs that were rooted firmly in Scripture and held by many church fathers.[142] Nevertheless, other interpretations were also prevalent, sometimes even in the same thinker. As did others under the sway of Platonic and Neoplatonic ideas, Origen often expressed negative views of the material world. Origen argued for two stages of creation: God first created spiritual beings who were in communion with him, then—after falling—those souls became embodied. But it was Augustine's position that would prove significant in the West.[143]

On the one hand, Augustine agrees with other fathers that Adam's first sin affected the rest of creation. Animals and humans lived in peaceful harmony before the transgression.[144] Commenting on Genesis 3:18, Augustine acknowledges that thorns were present in God's original creation but only as a harmless part of the animal diet. Yet he also believes that the human relationship with thorns—indeed with agriculture as a whole—changed after Adam's sin, work becoming laborious and punitive.[145]

On the other hand, Augustine sees animal violence and predation as part of the original goodness of creation and a reflection of God's glory.[146] He insists that God's curse in Genesis 3:17 was a punishment of man, not the earth, saying, "It was through the man's sin that the earth was cursed,

139. Chrysostom, *Homilies on Genesis 1–17*, 209.

140. For a nuanced analysis of Chrysostom's position, see Warnez, *"De Natura,"* 944–48.

141. Nemesius, *On the Nature of Man*, trans. R. W. Sharples and P. J. van der Eijk (Liverpool: Liverpool University Press, 2008), 42.

142. We can assume that these beliefs were more widespread than what the written artifacts preserve.

143. My remarks in this paragraph are indebted to Thomas E. Clarke, "St. Augustine and Cosmic Redemption," *Theological Studies* 19 (1958): 133–64.

144. While sparring with Julian, Augustine agrees with Chrysostom that the human fear of animals arose after the fall. See Augustine, *Answer to Julian* 1.6.25, in *The Works of Saint Augustine: Answer to the Pelagians*, ed. John Rotelle, trans. Roland J. Teske, 4 vols. (Hyde Park, NY: New City, 1998), 2:284–85.

145. Augustine, *The Literal Meaning of Genesis* 3.18.27, in *The Works of Saint Augustine: On Genesis*, trans. Edmund Hill (Hyde Park, NY: New City, 2002), 232–33.

146. For documentation, see Gavin Ortlund, "Augustine on Animal Death," in *Evil and Creation: Historical and Constructive Essays in Christian Dogmatics*, ed. David Luy, Matthew Levering, and George Kalantzis (Bellingham, WA: Lexham, 2020), 84–110.

so as to bring forth thorns, not so that the earth itself should feel the punishment, since it lacks sensation, but that it might always be setting the criminal nature of human sin before people's very eyes, and thus admonishing them to turn away at some time or other from their sins and turn back to God's commandments."[147] Given his earlier association with the Manichaean sect, this interpretation likely reflects his desire to avoid any hint of their doctrine that the cosmos is evil.

This "anthropocentric" exegesis shows up again in Augustine's reading of Romans 8:19–23.[148] In the history of interpretation, Augustine's interpretation of *ktisis* as limited to humanity is relatively unusual. As Thomas Clarke notes, "No one among the Greeks or Latins seems to have restricted the extension of the phrase to man alone."[149] Augustine intended to *affirm* the world by denying any solidarity between Adam's sin and creation—he was rejecting any appearance of evil in God's good creation. Harry Hahne's comment is insightful: "Unfortunately, however, [Augustine] missed the equally biblical theme of the dysteleology present in nature because of the Fall. Rom. 8:19–22 and much of the OT affirm that things are presently not right with the natural world due to the effects of human sin, and so there is a need and hope for the redemption of all of creation. While Augustine anticipated an eschatological renewal of creation, this was not to correct the damage caused by sin but simply to enhance the clarity with which God's glory is displayed in creation."[150]

147. Augustine, *A Refutation of the Manichees* 1.13.19, in Hill, *Works of Saint Augustine: On Genesis*, 51. See also Augustine, *Unfinished Work in Answer to Julian* 6.27.25, in Rotelle, *Works of Saint Augustine: Answer to the Pelagians*, 3:683.

148. C. John Collins is Augustinian—that is, anthropocentric—in his exegesis of Gen. 3:17–19 (see Collins, *Science & Faith: Friends or Foes?* [Wheaton: Crossway, 2003], 147–60; and Collins, *Genesis 1–4*, 162–66). He also denies that Rom. 8:19–22 is alluding to Gen. 3:17 or teaching a cosmic fall; instead he thinks that Paul is alluding to the flood narrative (Collins, *Genesis 1–4*, 183–84). See also C. John Collins, *Reading Genesis Well: Navigating History, Poetry, Science, and Truth in Genesis 1–11* (Grand Rapids: Zondervan Academic, 2018), 235–38; and C. John Collins, "The Place of the 'Fall' in the Overall Vision of the Hebrew Bible," *Trinity Journal* 40, no. 2 (2019): 165–84, esp. 171–80.

149. Clarke, "St. Augustine and Cosmic Redemption," 139. According to Harry Hahne, "Augustine . . . was the first to consistently and explicitly limit κτίσις to humanity" (Harry Hahne, "The Corruption and Redemption of Creation: An Exegetical Study of Romans 8:19–22 in Light of Jewish Apocalyptic Literature" [PhD diss., University of Toronto, 1997], 20). The first chapter of Hahne's dissertation was left out of the published version.

150. Hahne, "Corruption and Redemption of Creation," 23. Stanley Rosenberg documents the Platonic elements in Augustine's concept of creaturely contingency. For Augustine, decay and death are necessary features of creaturely reality; creatures are not absolute and thus tend—by nature—toward nonbeing. See Stanley P. Rosenberg, "Can Nature Be 'Red in Tooth and Claw' in the Thought of Augustine?," in Rosenberg, *Finding Ourselves after Darwin*, 226–43.

In the medieval period, the Eastern and Western traditions part ways on the cosmic significance of Adam's disobedience: "Where Western Christianity focused more on personal and social salvation, Eastern Christianity saw salvation as both personal and cosmic."[151] Eastern theologians for their part eagerly took up the cosmic fall. Maximus the Confessor (ca. 580–662) believed that Adam's sin presses "the nature of (all) created beings toward mortal extinction."[152] In one of his letters, he maintains that the fall of man corrupts the entire world.[153]

John of Damascus (675–ca. 749) is ambiguous in his remarks on original creation. On the one hand, he describes the pristine planet yielding fruit "of its own accord" while "there was neither rain nor tempest on the earth." When Adam fell, "the thorn sprung out of the earth in accordance with the Lord's express declaration and was conjoined with the pleasures of the rose, that it might lead us to remember the transgression on account of which the earth was condemned to bring forth for us thorns and prickles."[154] Taken at face value, the Damascene seems to be endorsing a fallen creation and possibly original vegetarianism.

But the latter possibility is uncertain, given what he says in the following words:

> Moreover, at the bidding of the Creator it produced also all manner of kinds of living creatures, creeping things, and wild beasts, and cattle. All, indeed, are for the seasonable use of man: but of them *some are for food, such as stags, sheep, deer, and such like*: others for service such as camels, oxen, horses, asses, and such like: and others for enjoyment, such as apes, and among birds, jays and parrots, and such like. Again, amongst plants and herbs some are fruit bearing, others edible, others fragrant and flowery, given to us for our enjoyment, for example, the rose and such like, and others for the healing of disease.[155]

John's remarks here include carnivory in the prelapsarian setting, which flies in the face of original vegetarianism. Yet if we continue reading to the end of that paragraph, the fuller context resolves some of the tension: "For

151. Hahne, "Corruption and Redemption of Creation," 31.

152. Maximus the Confessor, *On the Cosmic Mystery of Jesus Christ*, trans. Paul Blowers and Robert Louis Wilken (Crestwood, NY: St. Vladimir's Seminary Press, 2003), 137.

153. Maximus, *Letter 10, to John Cubicularius*, in Patrologia Graeca 91, ed. Jacques Paul Migne (Paris: Migne, 1865), col. 449–50.

154. John of Damascus, *Exposition of the Orthodox Faith* 10, in *The Nicene and Post-Nicene Fathers*, 2nd series, vol. 9, ed. Philip Schaff and Henry Wace, trans. S. D. F. Salmond (New York: Charles Scribner's Sons, 1908), 28.

155. John of Damascus, *Exposition of the Orthodox Faith* 10 (NPNF²9:28), my emphasis.

He Who knew all things before they were, saw that in the future man would go forward in the strength of his own will, and would be subject to corruption, and, therefore, He created all things for his seasonable use, alike those in the firmament, and those on the earth, and those in the waters."[156] How should we reconcile John's statements? I agree with Matthew Warnez's suggestion that, for John, "there was no need for animals to change their nature at the fall—they were proleptically constituted for postlapsarian life."[157] Had Adam and Eve not sinned, it is not clear to me from what John says whether carnivory would ever have expressed itself in a prelapsarian world. John's account strikes me as standing halfway between the unfallen and fallen creation positions.[158]

Two more Eastern theologians deserve mention: Symeon the New Theologian (949–1022) and Gregory of Sinai (ca. 1265–1346). Symeon was in no doubt that Adam's sin corrupted the entire creation. Although God spared Eden, he cursed "the whole rest of the earth, which also was incorrupt and brought forth everything by itself; and this was in order that Adam might not have any longer a life free from exhausting labors and sweat." Creation's fall meant that it was "deprived of its original productivity by which fruits were produced from it by themselves without labor."[159] Like others before him, Symeon cites Romans 8:20 for support: "Do you see that this whole creation in the beginning was incorrupt and was created by God in the manner of Paradise? But later it was subjected by God to corruption, and submitted to the vanity of men."[160] Unlike Augustine, Symeon recognizes that the curse extended down the length and breadth of creation:

> Then also all creatures, when they saw that Adam had been banished from Paradise, no longer wished to submit to him, the criminal: the sun did not wish to shine for him, nor did the moon and the other stars wish to show themselves to him; the springs did not wish to gush forth water, and the rivers to continue their course; the air thought no longer to blow so as not to allow Adam, the sinner, to breathe; the beasts and all the other animals of the earth, when they saw that he had been stripped of his first glory, began to despise him, and all immediately were ready to fall upon him. The heaven,

---

156. John of Damascus, *Exposition of the Orthodox Faith* 10 (NPNF²9:28).

157. Warnez, "*De Natura*," 974.

158. Given some of the ambiguity of John's views, I can understand why others interpret him as endorsing an unfallen creation (e.g., see Warnez, "*De Natura*," 973–76).

159. Symeon the New Theologian, *The Sin of Adam and Our Redemption: Seven Homilies*, trans. Seraphim Rose (Platina, CA: St. Herman of Alaska Brotherhood, 1979), 68.

160. Symeon, *Sin of Adam*, 75.

in a certain fashion, was about to strive to fall upon him, and the earth did not wish to bear him any longer.[161]

According to Gregory of Sinai, original creation "was not subject to flux and corruption." Reflecting on Romans 8:20–21, he speculates about the final redemption: "This deliverance from corruption is said by some to be a translation to a better state, by others to require a complete transmutation of everything sensory. Scripture generally makes simple and straightforward statements about matters that are still obscure."[162] These notes are all familiar, for Gregory is humming a popular patristic and medieval tune.

As a rule, medieval theologians in the West rejected the doctrine of the cosmic fall, though it is difficult to explain why. Paul Santmire lays the blame on their view of the universe as a hierarchy of being. Through the influence of John Scotus Eriugena (815–77) and Pseudo-Dionysius (fifth to sixth century), Latin theologians inherited the hierarchy of being as key to understanding nature: "The imagination of the twelfth century readily approached the world in terms of a spiritual emanation from the One, to the spiritual, and finally to the material, many."[163] Santmire argues that this hierarchy of being was typically associated with Plato's *Timaeus*—at the top of the chain of being was the One, an overflowing goodness that reaches all the way down the chain into the material creation. In this kind of intellectual milieu, the "notion of the biophysical world as an essentially fallen or evil world faded from sight."[164] Any notion of a cosmic fall, in the West, was doomed.

Santmire's thesis, however, is hard to square with what we know about medieval Eastern theology. Pseudo-Dionysius's chain of being ontology was just as common—if not more so—among medieval Eastern theologians. Neoplatonic assumptions were widely embraced by Eastern thinkers. If the chain of being hierarchy led Western thinkers to reject the corruption of creation, why did such assumptions not have the same effect on the medieval East? I am thus unpersuaded by Santmire's historiography. Perhaps the difference between medieval East and West lies in the fact that the two

161. Symeon, *Sin of Adam*, 68.
162. Gregory of Sinai, "On Commandments and Doctrines, Warnings and Promises; on Thoughts, Passions and Virtues, and Also on Stillness and Prayer: One Hundred and Thirty-Seven Texts," in *Philokalia*, ed. and trans. G. E. H. Palmer, Philip Sherrard, and Kallistos Ware, 5 vols. (London: Faber and Faber, 1979–2023), 4:214.
163. H. Paul Santmire, *The Travail of Nature: The Ambiguous Ecological Promise of Christian Theology* (Philadelphia: Fortress, 1985), 80.
164. Santmire, *Travail of Nature*, 81.

sides were trying to guard against opposing errors.[165] As with Augustine, fears of Manichaean dualism compelled Western medieval theologians to defend creation as unfallen. Meanwhile, for their Eastern counterparts a fallen creation readily resonated with the doctrine of *theosis* and the idea of salvation as a gradual movement from lower to higher states of spiritual development. Affirming a cosmic fall allowed them to resist the error that salvation concerns only human beings—or, even worse, only human souls—and not the universe as a whole.[166] In sum, the opposing medieval reactions to the idea of a fallen creation may reflect the distinctive concerns of the Eastern and Western traditions.

In any event, medieval optimism about nature shows up in Western theologians like Alain of Lille (ca. 1128–1202), Euthymius Zigabenus (eleventh to twelfth century), Francis of Assisi (1182–1226), Bonaventure (1221–74), and Thomas Aquinas (1224–74).[167] According to the Thomistic account, God never causes physical suffering in the world; rather, "indirect physical consequences are the inevitable results of the fact of there being a material world such as the one we inhabit, with its particular natural processes."[168] Even in a sinless world—a prelapsarian world—physical suffering is inevitable whenever material processes compete with each other. Aquinas therefore denies the fallenness of creation.

Speaking of Eden before the fall, he writes: "In the opinion of some, those animals which now are fierce and kill others, would, in that state, have been tame, not only in regard to man, but also in regard to other animals. But this is quite unreasonable. *For the nature of animals was not changed by man's sin, as if those whose nature now it is to devour the flesh of others, would then have lived on herbs, as the lion and falcon.*"[169] According to Aquinas, animal violence and predation were always part of God's good creation. Although Aquinas describes a change in the relationship between humanity and creation after Adam's sin, the change is only from the human side (following Augustine, whom he cites). For example, since Adam "would have used the things of this world conformably to the order designed, poisonous

165. This dynamic recurs throughout church history—e.g., in the debate over whether Christ assumed a fallen or an unfallen nature. See Kelly Kapic, "The Son's Assumption of a Human Nature: A Call for Clarity," *International Journal of Systematic Theology* 3, no. 2 (2001): 154–66.

166. I am indebted to Donald Fairbairn, in correspondence, for his insights regarding this difference between the medieval East and West.

167. Hahne, "Corruption and Redemption of Creation," 32–36.

168. Joel Daniels, *Theology, Tragedy, and Suffering in Nature: Toward a Realist Doctrine of Creation* (New York: Peter Lang, 2016), 21.

169. Thomas Aquinas, *Summa Theologica* I.96.1, trans. Fathers of the English Dominican Province, 2nd ed., 22 vols. (London: Burns, Oates & Washbourne, 1911–25), 4:328, my emphasis.

animals would not have injured him."[170] Aquinas's Augustinian theology of creation had a lasting impact on Western theology.[171]

Our survey confirms that patristic and medieval theologians held conflicting opinions about the cosmic fall and original vegetarianism; yet scholars tend to downplay the number of church fathers who held the fallen creation view.[172] The doctrine of a fallen creation is not a Reformation innovation but has earlier roots in the patristic and (especially Eastern) medieval traditions. Nevertheless, throughout the first millennium the church fathers generally favored the unfallen creation position. In this regard, the history of the doctrine of original goodness may be in the same boat as the Augustinian (or Western) doctrine of original sin. In the latter case, Augustine's notion of inherited guilt was not embraced by the Greek fathers who tended to emphasize free will and personal responsibility in reaction to the deterministic Gnostic heresies. But even in that intellectual environment, Augustinian or proto-Augustinian motifs were not entirely absent from the East but prevailed as a minority report.[173] "Though falling short of Augustinianism," J. N. D. Kelly writes about the patristic position, "there was here the outline of a real theory of original sin. The fathers might well have filled it in and given it greater sharpness of definition had the subject been directly canvassed in their day."[174]

In much the same way, I suspect that the notion of a fallen cosmos did not become part of the doctrinal consensus of the early church for two main reasons: First, given the prevalent Gnosticism in their context, the fathers usually defended the goodness of creation (and matter)—Augustine's anti-Manichaean interpretation of Genesis 8:19–23 is symptomatic of this outlook. Second, the premodern perspective on creation reflected a relatively anthropocentric perspective. Their knowledge of the variety and biology of the countless animal species on the planet was primitive compared

170. Thomas Aquinas, *Summa Theologica* I.72 (3:256).

171. On the significance of the Thomistic tradition on animals, see Ryan McLaughlin, *Christian Theology and the Status of Animals: The Dominant Tradition and Its Alternatives* (New York: Palgrave Macmillan, 2014), 8–20.

172. In my judgment, Garvey's central historical thesis in *God's Good Earth* is unreliable; his analysis throughout chaps. 6–8 is too often superficial, mistaken, or question-begging. Sollereder, though far more reliable, also misleadingly suggests that the cosmic fall was a Johnny-come-lately in church history (see Sollereder, *God, Evolution, and Animal Suffering*, 14–15). Even Slootweg's massive study misses some of the premodern witness for an unfallen creation (Slootweg, *Teeth and Talons*, esp. 373–76).

173. For an interesting argument that Irenaeus actually paved the way for Augustine's doctrine of original sin, see Manfred Hauke, *Heilsverlust in Adam: Stationen griechischer Erbsündenlehre: Irenäus-Origenes-Kappadozier* (Paderborn, Germany: Bonifatius, 1993).

174. J. N. D. Kelly, *Early Christian Doctrines*, 4th ed. (London: Adam and Charles Black, 1968), 351.

to what we know today. "Though many of the Fathers held a remarkably high view of lower creation," writes Warnez, "they, unlike moderns, were unabashedly anthropocentric, never equating the dignity of man with that of animals, nor even daring to study animals (let alone love them) for their own sake."[175] They were inclined to consider humanity in relation to God, not animals: "The ancient theologians' view of the human place in creation is based on, not anthropocentrism, not biocentrism, but theocentrism."[176]

Furthermore, the patristic (and medieval) understanding of animal species, their rates of extinction, mechanisms of disease, and so on, was comparatively undeveloped if not nonexistent. Premodern theology had not yet encountered the kinds of historical and scientific questions that could help develop a deeper understanding of Adam's fall. In our day, by contrast, we have witnessed a growing awareness of new empirical data over the past two or three centuries, including rock strata, layers of coral growth, the fossil record, and modern genetics (to name a few). Such physical data have not only given rise to the modern disciplines of geology and evolution but have raised concrete questions that have elicited the kind of dogmatic development that would not have been possible for premodern Christianity.[177]

Revisiting Biblical Realism

Protology is not for the fainthearted. Most of what I have defended so far does not measure up to modern science.[178] Given the world as we know it today, how does one make sense of original vegetarianism and my thesis that higher-order animal suffering is a postlapsarian reality? Not easily. I think there is enough ambiguity in the biblical witness itself that it would be unwise to be unduly dogmatic. As a rule, a biblical realist is dogmatically committed to particular doctrines when Scripture is clear—or clear

175. Warnez, "De Natura," 978.
176. H. F. Stander, "Ecology and the Church Fathers," Acta Patristica et Byzantina 11, no. 1 (2000): 172.
177. Needless to say, what counts as genuine dogmatic development is deeply contested. One of the main arguments of this chapter is that the cosmic fall doctrine counts as such, while mainstream geological and evolutionary positions do not.
178. So Christopher Southgate, "Cosmic Evolution and Evil," in The Cambridge Companion to the Problem of Evil, ed. Chad Meister and Paul Moser (Cambridge: Cambridge University Press, 2017), 153: "The notion of a 'cosmic fall' is . . . deeply problematic in the light of the scientific record. There is not the slightest evidence that humans ever lived harmoniously with all other creatures in a vegetarian paradise as depicted in Genesis 2. Moreover, predation and disease preceded human life by hundreds of millions of years."

enough—but is far less dogmatic when Scripture is less forthcoming. Some aspects of original vegetarianism fall into this latter category.

The least controversial position holds that mammals and other higher-order animals did not experience any suffering before Adam's fall. In this view, the carnivorous natures of lions and tigers are part of the original goodness of creation; they experienced no change of nature as a result of the fall. In the prelapsarian setting, carnivores presumably had a fundamentally different relationship with humanity and the rest of the animal kingdom; their dietary needs did not require killing and consuming prey. To be sure, even this modest prelapsarian scenario is inconceivable given the scientific consensus in evolutionary biology and allied fields. Then again, Christian theological positions must sometimes live in tension with widely held scientific theories. Theistic evolution, however, faces its own distinctive problem given that it posits evolutionary continuity between higher-order animals and humanity; if the former group experienced millions of years of suffering and death before the emergence of *Homo sapiens*, then it is difficult not to conclude that suffering and death are *essential* features of humans as created by God. On balance, this modest version of original vegetarianism seems preferable to the evolutionary alternative, though it remains vaguely defined since God has not revealed many details about primeval history. Agnosticism may be the better part of wisdom here. But some will want us to say more.

Three further proposals deserve attention, though they are more controversial—and more speculative. The first may be one way of fleshing out the undeveloped views of John of Damascus. The idea here is that God created animals with the genetic capacities for predatory behavior and left them in the "off" position, knowing by divine foreknowledge (the Arminian view) or foreordination (the Reformed one) that he would activate those genes the moment Adam sinned. The nineteenth-century Hebraist Franz Delitzsch proposed this model in his commentary on Genesis.[179] Contemporary young-earth creationists regularly endorse this argument.[180] However, does the idea of God designing such capacities *from the beginning*—even if only potentially—threaten divine holiness and the original goodness of creation? After all, carnivorous behaviors that inflict intense suffering on mammals are symptoms of a *fallen* creation. This dilemma may be alleviated by drawing an analogy between pre-fall Adam and pre-fall creation:

179. Franz Delitzsch, *A New Commentary on Genesis*, vol. 1 (Edinburgh: T&T Clark, 1899), 102–3.

180. For example, see Paul Garner, *The New Creationism: Building Scientific Theories on a Biblical Foundation* (Darlington, England: Evangelical Press, 2009), 162; and Sarfati, *Genesis Account*, 399–400.

just as Adam was originally righteous and able to sin or refrain from sinning (*posse peccare et posse non peccare*), so, too, prelapsarian animals were originally vegetarian and had the capacity to become carnivorous if Adam sinned *or* to remain peaceful if Adam had not sinned. The genetic capacities that could give rise to carnivorous behavior were present from the beginning but were kept inactive by divine providence—until Adam sinned.[181]

In a second scenario, carnivorous behavior originated in the divine curse (Gen. 3:17). Against C. S. Lewis and others who root these harmful biological structures in diabolical activity, this proposal traces the origin of predatory mechanisms to God's judicial action. Adam's sin prompted the Lord to bring about the instant transformation of herbivorous animals (and other erstwhile benign features of creation). At the second advent, God will restore the creation to what it once was and will even surpass it. Here, too, young-earth creationists have trademarked such arguments.[182]

In the third scenario, the effects of Adam's fall and the divine curse take effect *over time*, perhaps culminating in Noah's flood. The curse led to the gradual, post-fall perversion of organisms. As Herman Bavinck puts it, "Left to itself, emancipated from the dominion and care of humans, and burdened by a divine curse, nature *gradually* became degraded and adulterated and brought forth thorns and thistles, all sorts of vermin, and carnivorous animals."[183] Thorns and thistles are symptomatic of the deformation of God's creation. Bavinck clarifies that though "the form of things was changed by sin, the essence remained the same."[184] This lapsarian timescale of deformation may be relatively short for some aspects of creation but drawn out for others.

All well and good, yet none of these speculations are plausible given prevalent scientific perspectives. Academia has crowned young-earth creationism the inglorious antithesis of knowledge. Creationist scientists are valiantly (some would say misguidedly) developing alternative models to explain the physical data, but their work remains undeveloped.[185] But even if extrabiblical scientific judgments clash with my arguments in part 2 of this

181. I first encountered this solution in Robert Gonzales Jr., *Where Sin Abounds: The Spread of Sin and the Curse in Genesis with Special Focus on the Patriarchal Narratives* (Eugene, OR: Wipf & Stock, 2009), 49n115.

182. See Andrew Kulikovsky, *Creation, Fall, Restoration: A Biblical Theology of Creation* (Fearn, UK: Mentor, 2009), 209.

183. Herman Bavinck, *Reformed Dogmatics*, ed. John Bolt, trans. John Vriend, 4 vols. (Grand Rapids: Baker Academic, 2003–8), 3:181, my emphasis.

184. Bavinck, *Reformed Dogmatics*, 3:180.

185. Some of the best examples include Kurt Wise, *Faith, Form, and Time: What the Bible Teaches and Science Confirms about Creation and the Age of the Universe* (Nashville: Broadman & Holman, 2002); Todd Wood, *The Quest: Exploring Creation's Hardest Problems* (Nashville: Compass Classroom,

book, those judgments are not decisive. They cannot be decisive because of the role of the Holy Spirit speaking through Scripture as we come to know doctrinal truth. For many believers, their knowledge of creation, the fall, redemption, resurrection, consummation, and the other great things of the gospel comes to them intuitively, or immediately, by the supernatural work of the Spirit in the reading of Scripture. Defending this view, Alvin Plantinga writes that

> I needn't be able to find a good argument, historical or otherwise, for the resurrection of Jesus Christ, or for his being the divine Son of God, or for the Christian claim that his suffering and death constitute an atoning sacrifice whereby we can be restored to the right relationship with God. On the [extended Aquinas/Calvin] model, the warrant for Christian belief doesn't require that I or anyone else have this kind of historical information; the warrant floats free of such questions. It doesn't require to be validated or proved by some source of belief *other* than faith, such as historical investigation.[186]

But believers are not all the same and come in different shapes and sizes. Unlike Plantinga's paradigm case, the theological beliefs of many Christians are "a complex mixture of personal, social, and evidential factors in addition to pneumatological factors such as the internal instigation of the Holy Spirit."[187] Many of those beliefs are not received immediately by the internal witness of the Spirit but include evidential sources as well. Some begin their faith pilgrimage holding most of their beliefs noninferentially on the basis of divine revelation, but then over time, as they become increasingly aware of scholarly debate and controversy, they switch over to holding the same beliefs on the basis of extratextual evidence—while others experience the reverse.[188] Biblical realism recognizes these personal differences in how believers arrive at their convictions; yet when there is direct conflict between central doctrines known from Scripture by faith and extrabiblical claims from science or archaeology, dogmatic inerrancy in conjunction with scientific fallibilism requires that the knowledge of faith should be decisive.

The epistemic status of scientific and historical arguments is probabilistic. According to Elliott Sober, "The evidence that scientists have for

2018); Garner, *New Creationism*; Andrew A. Snelling, *Earth's Catastrophic Past: Geology, Creation and the Flood*, 2 vols. (Green Forest, AR: Master Books, 2014).

186. Alvin Plantinga, *Warranted Christian Belief* (Oxford: Oxford University Press, 2000), 259.

187. James Beilby, *Epistemology as Theology: An Evaluation of Alvin Plantinga's Religious Epistemology* (Burlington, VT: Ashgate, 2005), 192–93.

188. Beilby, *Epistemology as Theology*, 196.

their theories does not render those theories certain. . . . Science uses the evidence at hand to say which theories are *probably* true."[189] Natural science is an abductive discipline, an inference to the best explanation. Given the fallibility of scientists and the underdetermination of the physical data, scientific conclusions cannot attain epistemic certainty. As van den Brink and his colleagues write, "Even established theories that have withstood severe scrutiny remain tentative, if only slightly so. Since theories are supposed to *account for* the observations by ordering and explaining them, they are at some remove from those observations themselves and this introduces error possibilities and room for alternative theoretical accounts."[190] Similarly, ordinary historical investigation usually employs arguments to the best explanation and arguments from statistical inference. In Michael Licona's estimation, such theorizing yields historical certainty that ranges from "certainly not historical, very doubtful, quite doubtful, somewhat doubtful, indeterminate (neither improbable nor probable, possible, plausible)," on the one hand, to "somewhat certain (more probable than not), quite certain, very certain (very probably true), certainly historical," on the other.[191] That is to say, historical investigation using human resources alone will rarely attain historical certainty given our finitude and fallibility.

Christian theologians, however, are not limited to human resources alone. God has given us Holy Scripture, and his Spirit testifies in our hearts that its teaching comes with God's authority. As the Belgic Confession puts it, "We believe without a doubt all things contained in [the Scriptures]— not so much because the church receives them and approves them as such, but above all because the Holy Spirit testifies in our hearts that they are from God, and also because they prove themselves to be from God."[192] Our conviction of the Bible's authority, John Calvin notes, comes from "a higher place than human reasons, judgments, or conjectures, that is, in the secret testimony of the Spirit."[193] Christians by faith are confident in the authority of Scripture: "The testimony of the Spirit," Calvin says, "is

189. Elliott Sober, *Evidence and Evolution: The Logic behind the Science* (New York: Cambridge University Press, 2008), 1, emphasis original. See my earlier discussion of Sober's analysis in chap. 2.

190. Gijsbert van den Brink, Jeroen de Ridder, and René van Woudenberg, "The Epistemic Status of Evolutionary Theory," *Theology and Science* 15 (2017): 458, emphasis original.

191. Michael R. Licona, *The Resurrection of Jesus: A New Historiographical Approach* (Downers Grove, IL: InterVarsity, 2010), 122.

192. Belgic Confession, art. 5, cited in Alvin Plantinga, "Two (or More) Kinds of Scripture Scholarship," *Modern Theology* 14, no. 2 (1998): 246.

193. John Calvin, *Institutes of the Christian Religion*, 1.7.4 (see also 3.1.3; 3.2.15; 3.2.33–36). My citations are from *Institutes of the Christian Religion*, ed. John McNeill, trans. Ford Lewis Battles (Philadelphia: Westminster, 1960).

more excellent than all reason."[194] Since God is the surest witness to his own authority, he seals his Word in our hearts by the instigation of the Spirit. In cases of conflict between the clear deliverances of Scripture and the claims of scientific investigation, the knowledge of faith is decisive. Extrabiblical archaeological and scientific data that support the biblical witness can increase the justification for our beliefs; and when they conflict with central doctrines they can threaten to defeat what we know by faith. Christians are right to engage such objections apologetically, but our warrant for believing those central doctrines lies elsewhere. This methodological position signals a key difference between evidential and dogmatic inerrancy (see chap. 2).

Since the reliable basis of faith is God's Word received by the internal testimony of God's Spirit (Rom. 10:17; 1 John 5:6), then controversial truths taught in Scripture like the sacred chronology, biblical monogenism, and original goodness surpass any potential scientific defeaters. Although my knowledge of these doctrines is fallible, it is based on special revelation, which is more reliable than the attestation of the natural sciences. My confidence in sacred history and the cosmic fall is a function of special revelation and is not ultimately rooted in the presence (or absence) of archaeological or scientific evidence; it is rooted in God's trustworthiness mediated by the Holy Spirit—the text constrains. The findings of science are weighty, but other factors weigh more heavily.[195] Furthermore, the fact that Christians have not yet succeeded in developing scientific models that are objectively better than the current consensus does not mean such models do not exist.[196] I resist the consensus when it conflicts with Scripture and remain confident that there is convincing empirical support in favor of sacred history and original goodness. While I currently lack a full understanding of what that empirical support might be, I have no doubt *that* it exists. The truth will prevail, even if it still eludes us, and even if we must wait until the eschaton (1 Cor. 13:12).[197]

194. Calvin, *Institutes*, 1.7.4.
195. However, I have already conceded that scientific discoveries can sometimes prompt a believer to revise his or her interpretation of Scripture. If the doctrine ranks highly, the threshold for a *successful* scientific defeater would be very high—*impossibly* high for core doctrines.
196. For an earlier defense of this thesis, see my "All Truth Is God's Truth: A Defense of Dogmatic Creationism," in *Creation and Doxology*, ed. Gerald Hiestand and Todd Wilson (Downers Grove, IL: InterVarsity, 2018), 59–76.
197. Many young-earth creationists would insist that they have developed models with greater explanatory and predictive power than conventional theories. That may be, but my argument here takes a worst-case scenario—even if none of the current creationist models succeed, the viability of the thesis remains secure.

Perhaps I am wrong about biblical chronology or monogenism. Perhaps I have confused my interpretation with Scripture itself, ignoring the literary artifice of Genesis 1–11.[198] Christians of goodwill can take the genealogies as God's inerrant Word without interpreting them as literal, gap-free lineages. Other believers will naturally think differently from me on these matters. This chapter, too, you may say, might be wrong about original goodness. Perhaps I am illegitimately reading the eschatological promises of Scripture into the irretrievable primeval past. Surely good Christians can disagree.

Indeed, protology is not as vital as the resurrection. Yet it is inseparable from Adam, the fall, and other key threads of the gospel story.[199] In light of the canonical criteria—clarity, centrality, catholicity—denying Scripture's chronology and original goodness will have significant implications for core doctrines. In chapter 2, I insisted that conflict is not essential to the science-theology relationship, but the historical sciences in particular do overlap and sometimes conflict with the biblical narrative.[200] Since Holy Scripture is my warrant for holding to biblical chronology and original goodness and since potential historical or scientific defeaters compete with central elements of the canonical story, they will never be decisive.

Biblical realism resonates with the patristic and medieval witnesses, including the likes of Augustine and Aquinas, who warned against holding dogmatic positions that were falsifiable by future scientific proof: "The literal meaning of a text was always preferable, even where multiple interpretations were unavoidable, as with supracelestial waters. But wherever a scriptural passage conflicted with a scientifically demonstrated proposition—as happened in Psalm 103:2—the scientific interpretation must prevail to prevent any erosion of confidence in scriptural truth. Under such circumstances, an allegorical interpretation was required so that truth and Scripture would be in harmony."[201] Geological and evolutionary sciences fall short of demonstrable knowledge; historical sciences can never reach that

198. In my view, figurative (or poetic) language and historicity are not mutually exclusive. Scripture often depicts historical events with figurative language—e.g., Pss. 78; 105–6 (the history of Israel); Judg. 4–5 (Jael's defeat of Sisera during Deborah's reign); Isa. 5:1–2 (Yahweh's love for his people); and Rom. 11:17–24 (God's relationship with Jews and gentiles in salvation history). The presence of figurative language in Gen. 1–11 and other parts of the canon does not preclude imparting knowledge of historical events.

199. For example, Luke 3 traces the birth of Jesus (the incarnation) all the way back to Adam and the Gen. 5 and 11 genealogies.

200. Although young-earth creationists sometimes oversimplify the distinction between "operational" and "historical" science, the basic epistemic worry is legitimate. See my analysis in chap. 2.

201. Edward Grant, "Science and Theology in the Middle Ages," in *God and Nature: Historical Essays on the Encounter between Christianity and Science*, ed. David Lindberg and Ronald Numbers (Berkeley: University of California Press, 1986), 65.

threshold, in principle. I am not maximally certain about biblical chronology or original goodness in the same way that I am about, say, the resurrection of the dead, but I am confident of these things and I think Scripture warrants that confidence.

Am I then *anti*-science? Does my position hinder Christian witness by erecting roadblocks to the gospel? At one level, yes, people will draw the false inference. Many will dismiss these dogmatic commitments as a negligent counsel to sacrifice the intellect; they will use the strangeness of the biblical world as a pretext to reject the God of infinite wisdom. Yet Henri Blocher's remarks in a different setting ring true here: "On many points of criticism, the data actually available would tip the balance of probability *against* the Bible, if these were all that we had to consider—but in fact other considerations weigh more heavily with us."[202] Scripture constrains us. But this fact gives no license to the kind of anti-intellectual, anti-science rhetoric that makes a mockery of biblical Christianity throughout the world.[203]

Among Christians, it is tempting amid the diversity of opinions relating to hard questions at the interface of science and theology to domesticate our disagreements—to agree to disagree—so that we can all get along. This noble but flawed sentiment results in an ever-growing list of doctrinal questions placed under the adiaphora column. Before long, little within Christianity will really matter dogmatically. Instead, I say that Christians should have convictions drawn from Scripture and enter into dialogue and friendship when we disagree.[204] Fellow believers can disagree over strongly held convictions and still share fellowship around the essential dicta of faith.[205] Churches will adjudicate these issues in ways consistent with their own dogmatic and denominational priorities. Some academic or ecumenical settings will invite a minimalist, big-tent approach, while other ecclesial contexts will demand narrower confessional boundaries. That seems right to me.

Conclusion

The original goodness of creation gets short shrift in theological discourse. There is no room for paradise within the citadel of evolutionary science,

202. Henri Blocher, "Sacrificium Intellectus," *European Journal of Theology* 1, no. 2 (1992): 100.
203. For a history of the origins of anti-intellectualism in North American Christianity, see Nathan Hatch, *The Democratization of American Christianity* (New Haven: Yale University Press, 1989).
204. For one example, see Todd Wood and Darrel Falk, *The Fool and the Heretic: How Two Scientists Moved beyond Labels to a Christian Dialogue about Creation and Evolution* (Grand Rapids: Zondervan, 2019).
205. See my discussion in chap. 2 on the differences between doctrinal taxonomies that use "gospel" criteria and those that use "canonical" criteria.

and we have seen myriad theological attempts to abolish or alleviate the conflict between the scientific picture and the traditional notion of a fallen cosmos. Ironically, these strategies have only multiplied the difficulties—pitting creation against redemption, creation against eschatology, and worse. Slay one head, and two more arise! Evolutionary theodicies are in danger of dismantling the internal coherence of revealed doctrinal truth and, in some cases, risk detaching themselves from the world of the early creeds and confessions.

The twin doctrines of original goodness and a cosmic fall resolve these challenges dogmatically. Biblical realism interprets animal suffering, predation, and death as postlapsarian tragedies within a fallen creation. Not only does Paul read Genesis 3:17–19 as a divine judgment on creation, but the broader canonical witness to a cosmic renewal presupposes that creation is broken. Original goodness is not a sectarian innovation but is corroborated in the theological exegesis of church fathers and especially Eastern medieval saints. While it is true that Augustine and Aquinas's rejection of a cosmic fall would mark the Western medieval tradition, their anthropocentric position may have been biased by anti-Gnostic and (especially for Augustine) anti-Manichaean fears.

In part 2 of the book, I have tried to recover a theological interpretation of primeval history. This sketch of human origins opens up the possibility of a robust dogmatic account of sin with an eye to scientific questions. The remaining chapters will set out this hamartiology, beginning with the fall of Adam and Eve.

PART 3

HAMARTIOLOGY

We believe that by the disobedience of Adam original sin has been spread through the whole human race.

It is a corruption of the whole human nature—an inherited depravity which even infects small infants in their mother's womb, and the root which produces in humanity every sort of sin.

It is therefore so vile and enormous in God's sight that it is enough to condemn the human race, and it is not abolished or wholly uprooted even by baptism, seeing that sin constantly boils forth as though from a contaminated spring.

—Belgic Confession, article 15

6

The Fall of Adam and Eve

There is very little of importance in Christian theology, hence also in doxology and practice, that is not at stake in the question of whether or not we allow a historical dimension to the Fall.

—Douglas Farrow[1]

A historical Fall is a non-negotiable article of faith.

—Henri Blocher[2]

It does not seem too much to say that the theory of the Fall occupied a place as central and unquestioned in the anthropology of the Church up to the modern era as the theory of evolution occupies in any discussion of human nature at the present day.

—H. Wheeler Robinson[3]

Charles Darwin turned the world upside down when he published his *On the Origin of Species* (1859), a book that with its companion volume, *The Descent of Man* (1871), radically redefined the relationship between human beings and the animal kingdom. Those two books leveled the knockout blow against Adam and Eve as the first sinners. "Putting

1. Douglas Farrow, "Fall," in *Oxford Companion to Christian Thought*, ed. Adrian Hastings, Alistair Mason, and Hugh Pyper (Oxford: Oxford University Press, 2000), 234.
2. Henri Blocher, "The Theology of the Fall and the Origins of Evil," in *Darwin, Creation and the Fall: Theological Challenges*, ed. R. J. Berry and T. A. Noble (Nottingham, UK: Apollos, 2009), 169.
3. H. Wheeler Robinson, *The Christian Doctrine of Man*, 3rd ed. (Edinburgh: T&T Clark, 1926), 164 (originally published 1911).

it bluntly," one historian writes, "even if evolution was conceived as the unfolding of God's plan, the element of progress made nonsense out of the idea of original sin (since there could be no Fall from an earlier state of grace)."[4] Many Catholics and Protestants tried placing Adam within the evolutionary timeline (see chap. 4), but others rejected such "conservative" rescue efforts and instead began the difficult task of rewriting the biblical story without Adam and Eve.

One such example was Henry Drummond (1851–97), professor of natural science in the Free Church College in Glasgow (now known as Trinity College). He was also a celebrated evangelist who integrated Christian faith and evolution in response to Darwin's *Descent of Man*.[5] His book, *The Ascent of Man*, gives short shrift to Adam's fall, and the title's central idea of an "ascent" implicitly denies the received tradition.[6] More assertively, the longtime headmaster and then canon of Worcester, James Maurice Wilson (1836–1931), dismissed the fall as an obsolete account of sin's origin. Wilson pictures sin as "the survival, or misuse, of habits and tendencies that were incidental to an earlier stage in development, whether of the individual or the race, and were not originally sinful, but were actually useful."[7] As the first humans evolved a moral conscience, they were able to resist lower habits and tendencies: "This fall from innocence was in another sense a rise to a higher grade of being."[8]

These accounts—and there were others in the nineteenth century[9]— paved the way for Frederick Tennant's groundbreaking proposal in his 1901–2 Hulsean Lectures delivered at the University of Cambridge.[10] Tennant's rejection of the fall doctrine involves the usual suspects of biblical criticism, comparative religion, geology, and evolution.[11] Our post-Darwinian setting, he argues, renders meaningless the idea of Adam and

4. Peter Bowler, *Reconciling Religion and Science: The Debate in Early-Twentieth-Century Britain* (Chicago: University of Chicago Press, 2001), 211.

5. Henry Drummond, *The Ascent of Man* (New York: James Pott, 1894).

6. Other accounts of theistic evolution from that period struggled to integrate the origin of sin into the evolutionary story. See James McCosh, *The Religious Aspect of Evolution* (New York: Putnam, 1888), 78–80; and Joseph LeConte, *Evolution: Its Nature, Its Evidences, and Its Relation to Religious Thought*, 2nd ed. (New York: D. Appleton, 1894), 360–75.

7. James M. Wilson, "The Bearing of the Theory of Evolution on Christian Doctrine," in *The Official Report of the Church Congress Held at Shrewsbury, October, 1896*, ed. C. Dunkley (London: Bemrose & Sons, 1896), 132.

8. Wilson, "Bearing of the Theory of Evolution," 133.

9. For example, see Ebenezer Griffith-Jones, *The Ascent through Christ: A Study of the Doctrine of Redemption in the Light of the Theory of Evolution*, 4th ed. (London: James Bowen, 1900), esp. 73–238.

10. Frederick R. Tennant, *The Origin and Propagation of Sin: Being the Hulsean Lectures Delivered before the University of Cambridge, 1901–02*, 2nd ed. (Cambridge: Cambridge University Press, 1906).

11. Tennant, *Origin and Propagation of Sin*, 27.

Eve committing the first sin and forfeiting their innocence—"for us there has emerged an alternative view of man's original condition."[12] Sin does not trace back to Adam's fall but to our animal ancestry; sin arises as the human spirit battles the base impulses we have inherited from evolution.[13] Tennant's rejection of a historical fall allowed him to refashion the doctrine of original sin and cemented his status as the grandfather of later evolutionary hamartiologies.[14]

Given that Adam's fall and inherited sin are sacred dogmas, the Roman Catholic magisterium opposed any evolutionary concessions at the First Vatican Council (1869–70) and the Pontifical Biblical Commission (1909).[15] In 1950, however, Pope Pius XII's encyclical *Humani Generis* cracked the door open to the possibility that Adam's physical body evolved but insisted that his soul was supernaturally created. Polygenism remained off limits.[16] Nearly a half century later, on October 22, 1996, Pope John Paul II acknowledged that evolution was "more than a hypothesis."[17]

By the end of the century, Catholics and Protestants felt free to theologize without Adam. For example, within twentieth-century Roman Catholicism, a growing cadre of thinkers were less reluctant to abandon Adam's originating sin.[18] Piet Schoonenberg (1911–99), Dutch Jesuit professor of dogmatic theology, denies that Scripture or tradition has any bearing on biological or paleontological evidence.[19] He reinterprets the fall as "the whole history of sinful deeds."[20] Henri Rondet (1898–1979), a French Jesuit, does not

---

12. Tennant, *Origin and Propagation of Sin*, 11.

13. Tennant, *Origin and Propagation of Sin*, 11.

14. He recapitulated his argument eleven years later in *The Concept of Sin* (Cambridge: Cambridge University Press, 1912). For helpful background, see Jonathan Chappell, "Rethinking the Historical Fall in the Light of Evolution: F. R. Tennant and After," *Science and Christian Belief* 25, no. 2 (2013): 131–54.

15. Tatha Wiley, *Original Sin: Origins, Developments, Contemporary Meanings* (Mahwah, NJ: Paulist Press, 2002), 120–25.

16. Pope Pius XII, *The Encyclical "Humani Generis" with a Commentary*, trans. A. C. Cotter, 2nd ed. (Weston, MA: Weston College Press, 1952), 43.

17. John Paul II, "Address to the Pontifical Academy of Sciences (October 22, 1996)," in *Papal Addresses to the Pontifical Academy of Sciences 1917–2002* (Vatican City: Pontifical Academy of Sciences, 2003), 371n3. In using the phrase "more than a hypothesis," he meant that evolution had a significant empirical basis.

18. A note on terminology: "originating sin" refers to the fall of Adam and Eve, while "originated sin" is the inborn, moral corruption of their descendants (on which, see chap. 7).

19. Piet Schoonenberg, *Man and Sin: A Theological View*, trans. Joseph Donceel (Notre Dame, IN: University of Notre Dame Press, 1965), 187–88. See the similar judgments by fellow Dutch Jesuit Stephanus Trooster in his *Evolution and the Doctrine of Original Sin*, trans. John A. Ter Haar (New York: Newman, 1968), 43.

20. Piet Schoonenberg, "Original Sin and Man's Situation," in *The Mystery of Sin and Forgiveness*, ed. Michael J. Taylor (New York: Alba House, 1971), 249.

rule out a historical Adam but prefers to see him as "mankind taken as a whole" who in union with Christ becomes the object of God's redemptive love.[21] Writing in *First Things*, more recently, Edward Oakes insists that we unshackle original sin from "a 'literal' interpretation of the Garden of Eden in Genesis 2–3."[22]

On the Protestant side, similar judgments abound. Karl Barth, for example, reads early Genesis as "saga," not history, which means that Adam is a symbol for humanity. While Barth does not as such deny Adam's historicity, he (conveniently) ousts him to a suprahistorical realm insulated from historical investigation.[23] For Emil Brunner, the modern picture of time and space renders the fall impossible.[24] He praises historical science for eliminating "the historical element from the story of the Creation and of the Fall."[25] Similarly, Paul Tillich states, "Biblical literalism did a distinct disservice to Christianity in its identification of the Christian emphasis on the symbol of the Fall with the literalistic interpretation of the Genesis story."[26] Reinhold Niebuhr patronizingly labels anyone who thinks that Adam is historical as having "childlike answers" to "childlike questions."[27] Rounding out this crowd, David Kelsey describes the doctrine of the fall as "unintelligible" and "no longer believable."[28] We could keep piling on more witnesses, but let us take stock. This remarkable rise of non-lapsarian theology is a radical departure from Scripture and the catholic consensus.[29]

21. Henri Rondet, *Original Sin: The Patristic and Theological Background*, trans. Cajetan Finegan (New York: Alba House, 1972), 263–64.

22. Edward T. Oakes, "Original Sin: A Disputation," *First Things* 87 (November 1998): 21–22. For broader discussion on the Catholic side, see Don O'Leary, *Roman Catholicism and Modern Science: A History* (New York: Continuum, 2006).

23. Karl Barth, *Church Dogmatics*, IV/1, *The Doctrine of Reconciliation*, ed. Geoffrey Bromiley and T. F. Torrance (Edinburgh: T&T Clark, 1969), 507–8. Barth also contrasts saga with myth; in his view a saga, unlike a myth, has a historical substratum.

24. Emil Brunner, *Dogmatics*, vol. 2, *The Christian Doctrine of Creation and Redemption*, trans. Olive Wyon (Philadelphia: Westminster, 1952), 48–52.

25. Emil Brunner, *Man in Revolt: A Christian Anthropology*, trans. Olive Wyon (Philadelphia: Westminster, 1947), 144 (originally published 1939). In *Christian Doctrine of Creation and Redemption*, 89, Brunner reinterprets the fall on a "strictly christocentric basis." For Rudolf Bultmann, a historical fall and original sin could not survive demythologization. See his *New Testament and Mythology and Other Basic Writings*, ed. and trans. Schubert M. Ogden (Philadelphia: Fortress, 1984), 6–7.

26. Paul Tillich, *Systematic Theology*, 3 vols. (Chicago: University of Chicago Press, 1957), 2:29.

27. Reinhold Niebuhr, *Beyond Tragedy: Essays on the Christian Interpretation of History* (New York: Charles Scribner's Sons, 1937), 147–48. See also Søren Kierkegaard's negative judgments on the Augustinian doctrine of the fall in *The Concept of Anxiety*, ed. and trans. Reidar Thomte with Albert B. Anderson (Princeton: Princeton University Press, 1980), 25–26.

28. David Kelsey, *Eccentric Existence: A Theological Anthropology*, 2 vols. (Louisville: Westminster John Knox, 2009), 1:35.

29. The Eastern tradition (represented by Irenaeus) is part of that consensus, though it is often touted as the antithesis of the Western "Augustinian" fall tradition; such claims are overblown and

While these shifts reflect the power of science over doctrinal development, they also raise questions about how one justifies the presence of sin
in the human experience. If not from Adam, where then does sin ultimately
come from? According to some Christian evolutionists, sin emerges from
the amalgam of inherited genes and social conditioning. Daniel Harlow
writes, "We share a transtemporal and universal biological and cultural
heritage that predisposes us to sin."[30] The origin of sin lies in the merging of
nature and nurture. Others, like Gregory Peterson, think that the evolutionary origin of sinfulness is rooted in human freedom. "It is only because of
our considerable sophistication that we do it [falling] in the first place, and
it is because of our psychological sophistication that such falling seems to
be an inevitable consequence of human freedom."[31] Humanity experiences
sin as the price for evolutionary freedom. At a more fundamental level,
some see the fall as a symbol for physical entropy. Our moral capacities for
good and evil arise from analogous capacities within animal forebears, and
those capacities in turn originate from physical processes within nature.
Entropy, according to Robert Russell, is the "background, predisposition,
or precursor to what emerges in us as sin."[32] Russell's evolutionary hamartiology traces sin to the physical structure of creation itself.

In this chapter, I take exception to Tennant and his modern scions. Doctrines are not atomistic entities like marbles in a jar that we can rearrange
without consequence. Doctrines are more like threads in a tapestry: pulling
on the fall unravels other doctrines and disrupts the biblical story's inner
coherence. Whatever the logic of non-lapsarian arguments, they are fundamentally at odds with Scripture's account of history. I first argue from
Scripture that theology cannot avoid the historicity of Adam and his role
in originating sin.[33] I then show how the fall of Adam and Eve is integral to
the doctrine of original righteousness, the scriptural perspective on death,
and a theodicy that absolves God of direct blame for sin. Finally, I conclude
that the loss of Adam's fall warps the structure of the gospel narrative.

typically reflect scholars who are seeking patristic blessing for their evolutionary accounts of sin. See
the telling critique in Andrew McCoy, "Becoming Who We Are Supposed to Be: An Evaluation of
Schneider's Use of Christian Theology in Conversation with Recent Genetic Science," *Calvin Theological Journal* 49, no. 1 (2014): 63–84, esp. 66–74.

30. Daniel Harlow, "After Adam: Reading Genesis in an Age of Evolutionary Science," *Perspectives
on Science and Christian Faith* 62, no. 3 (2010): 191.

31. Gregory R. Peterson, *Minding God: Theology and the Cognitive Sciences* (Minneapolis: Fortress,
2003), 179.

32. Robert J. Russell, *Cosmology, Evolution, and Resurrection Hope* (Kitchener, ON: Pandora, 2006), 32.

33. Earlier chapters largely assumed these matters, but now I shall try to defend them more
explicitly. As we shall see, Adam's fall has ample biblical support (which supplements the exegetical
material I presented in chap. 4).

The Biblical Witness

The historicity of Adam is assumed throughout Scripture, not least in the biblical genealogies. Genesis 5 begins with the generations of Adam, linking the events in Genesis 1–4 to real people in antediluvian history—Shem, Ham, Japheth, Noah, Lamech, Methuselah, Enoch, and company. The genealogy in Genesis 11:10–32 is part of the same historical timeline, connecting Noah and his sons to Abraham and his descendants. Even if one accepts chronological gaps in the genealogies of Genesis 1–11, those genealogies "link Father Abraham, whom the people of Israel took to be historical, with Adam, who is otherwise hidden from the Israelites in the mists of antiquity."[34] Adam and Eve are no less historical than Noah and Abraham. Adam's and Israel's histories stand or fall together in both the Old (1 Chron. 1:1) and New Testaments (Luke 3:38; Jude 14).

Aside from the genealogies, later Old Testament passages are suggestive of the historicity of the Eden narratives (Eccles. 7:29; Ezek. 28:11–19; Hosea 6:7),[35] but in the New Testament these allusions are now unambiguous when Paul reflects on women in the church (1 Cor. 11:3–12; 1 Tim. 2:13–14), polemicizes against false apostles (2 Cor. 11:1–3), and contrasts the roles of Adam and Christ (Rom. 5:12–21; 1 Cor. 15:21–22). At every point, Paul draws *historically* on particular details in Genesis 1–3 (see also Matt. 19:4; John 8:44; Acts 17:26; Rev. 12:9; 20:2).[36] Scripture always presents Adam as a flesh-and-bones ancient individual. Skepticism about Adam is only conceivable for Christians who reinterpret the biblical chronology and demote Genesis 1–11 to nonhistorical ancient literature.

Adam's *fall* also has impeccable exegetical credentials. In Genesis 2:17, God commanded Adam not to eat of the tree of the knowledge of good and evil. While the text never describes Adam and Eve's disobedience as a "fall," the unfolding narrative chronicles the spread of sin in the wake of their rebellion culminating in the global flood.[37] Even after the flood, sin permeates the human experience, which prompts the Lord's mercy in the call of Abraham, the election of Israel, the era of the judges, priests, kings, and

---

34. C. John Collins, *Did Adam and Eve Really Exist? Who They Were and Why You Should Care* (Wheaton: Crossway, 2011), 57.

35. Admittedly, the meaning of Hosea 6:7 is contested, as is the referent of Ezek. 28:11–19. For discussion and further canonical allusions to Adam and Eve, see Collins, *Did Adam and Eve Really Exist?*, 51–92.

36. The same historical assumptions pervade Second Temple Jewish literature (Sirach 25:24; 2 Baruch 18:2; 23:4; 48:42–43; 54:15; 2 Esdras 7:118–26).

37. On the propriety of using the term "fall" despite its absence in Scripture, see C. John Collins, "May We Say That Adam and Eve 'Fell'?," *Presbyterion* 46, no. 1 (2020): 53–74.

prophets, all of it culminating in the incarnation of his Son (John 1:14). The story invites the reader to ask *why* all sin and die. Why are Jews and gentiles alike under sin (Rom. 3:9)? In Matthew 19:1-11 (// Mark 10:1-9), Jesus contrasts the Mosaic permission to divorce with the creation ordinance in Genesis 1:27 and 2:24. "But from the beginning it was not so" (Matt. 19:8)— by which the Lord not only endorses the historical force of Genesis 1-2 but also mourns the original righteousness from which Adam's descendants had fallen.[38] Guided by Paul in Romans 5:12-21 and 1 Corinthians 15:21-22, we rightly identify Genesis 3 as the origin of sin in the human experience. Sin entered the world through one man: Adam (Rom. 5:12).

Yet sin has a deeper origin. Based on Isaiah 14:12-15 and Ezekiel 28:12-19, many church fathers thought that the angel Lucifer degenerated into the shadowy figure of Satan when he revolted against Yahweh and was cast out of heaven.[39] Although both passages seem to have historical personages in mind—the king of Babylon in Isaiah 14 and the king of Tyre in Ezekiel 28—early interpreters see a deeper reference to Satan's revolt. The King James Version reflects that tradition in Isaiah 14:12: "How art thou fallen from heaven, O Lucifer, son of the morning!" Before Satan fell, he was a glorious angel named "Lucifer" (the Vulgate translation of "morning star"). The references to Eden in the Ezekiel passage were seen as further allusions to the fall of Satan.

Although such readings are out of fashion among academics, the idea that angels fell in times past is confirmed in 2 Peter 2:4 and Jude 6. Canonical testimony also invites us to identify the serpent in Genesis 3 as a surrogate for the devil (John 8:44; Rom. 16:20; Rev. 12:1-17; 13:1-3; 16:13; 20:2). Two things are emphatically true in the world of Scripture: the devil is one of God's creatures, and he could not have been evil from the beginning since God cannot be the author of sin. The ultimate origin of sin lies in the rebellion of an angel who was once holy but then fell—inexplicably and irredeemably—and is now the great antagonist and spoiler of God's people.[40] Since God did not give Lucifer dominion over creation, the rest

38. Henri Blocher, *In the Beginning: The Opening Chapters of Genesis*, trans. David G. Preston (Downers Grove, IL: InterVarsity, 1984), 163–64.

39. Early Jewish tradition interpreted Gen. 6:1-8 as a fall story in which the "watchers"—fallen angels—introduced wickedness on earth. See N. P. Williams, *The Ideas of the Fall and of Original Sin: A Historical and Critical Study* (London: Longmans, Green, 1927), 20–29; and Graham Cole, *Against the Darkness: The Doctrine of Angels, Satan, and Demons* (Wheaton: Crossway, 2019), 118–19.

40. Graham Cole, "The Great Antagonist," in *Hearing and Doing the Word: The Drama of Evangelical Hermeneutics*, ed. Daniel Treier and Douglas Sweeney (London: Bloomsbury T&T Clark, 2021), 79–91. Scholars debate how a sinless angel could ever be motivated to sin in the first place. For analysis, see William Wood, "Anselm of Canterbury on the Fall of the Devil: The Hard Problem,

of creation remained unfallen even after the first angelic sin. Creation was only cursed in response to the sin of the first man.

Original Righteousness

The reality of Adam's fall implies that he was once sinless and was created in a state of integrity (*status integritatis*) with original righteousness (*iustitia originalis*).[41] In the words of the Westminster Confession, "[Our first parents] fell from their original righteousness and communion with God."[42] Charles Hodge comments that Adam was made in God's moral image and resembled his maker in "knowledge, righteousness, and holiness."[43] William G. T. Shedd, fellow Presbyterian theologian, describes Adam at creation being inclined to a "positive holiness . . . enlightened in the spiritual knowledge of God and divine things."[44] This doctrine of original righteousness was debated among Roman Catholic, Reformed, and Lutheran theologians, but they all agreed that Adam was morally upright from the start.[45] As Herman Bavinck remarks, "Goodness, for a human being, consists in moral perfection, in complete harmony with the law of God, in holy and perfect being, like God himself. . . . If man was created good, he must have been created with original justice."[46] Protestant theologians appealed to Ephesians 4:24 and Colossians 3:10 as allusions to Genesis 1:26 and 5:1, concluding from such passages that righteousness and holiness were part of the original image (see Eccles. 7:29). Since Adam was the image of God, in Eden he was morally righteous like God.[47]

Such claims about Adam's original righteousness are generally absent from modern scholarship. James Barr, for example, accuses premodern

---

the Harder Problem, and a New Formal Model of the First Sin," *Religious Studies* 52, no. 2 (2016): 223–45.

41. Adam and Eve's original righteousness is the human component of the original goodness that I mapped out in chap. 5.

42. The Westminster Confession of Faith 6.2, in *The Book of Confessions* (Louisville: Office of the General Assembly, Presbyterian Church [USA], 2002), 128.

43. Charles Hodge, *Systematic Theology*, 3 vols. (Grand Rapids: Eerdmans, 1975), 2:99 (cf. Westminster Confession of Faith 4.2).

44. William G. T. Shedd, *Dogmatic Theology*, ed. Alan W. Gomes, 3rd ed. (Phillipsburg, NJ: P&R, 2003), 496.

45. Herman Bavinck, *Reformed Dogmatics*, ed. John Bolt, trans. John Vriend, 4 vols. (Grand Rapids: Baker Academic, 2003–8), 2:530–62.

46. Bavinck, *Reformed Dogmatics*, 2:558.

47. For disagreement with this classic interpretation of Eph. 4:24 and Col. 3:10, see John Murray, "Man in the Image of God," in *Collected Writings of John Murray*, 4 vols. (Edinburgh: Banner of Truth Trust, 1977), 2:40–41.

thinkers of inferring a prelapsarian perfection from Paul's teaching on sin and death even though Genesis 1 itself teaches nothing of the sort. Adam was imperfect from day one.[48] According to N. P. Williams, it was inevitable that past Christians would exaggerate the perfections of paradise in order to bring Adam's fall into the sharpest relief. He documents this tradition in several Old Testament pseudepigrapha (and even notes, from 2 Enoch 32, that Adam's holiness lasted almost six hours!).[49]

Williams holds up Augustine as the epitome of this tradition, especially his view of Adam as "exempted from all physical evils, and endowed with immortal youth and health which could not be touched by the taint of sickness or the creeping debility of old age. The gift of immortality lay within his reach. . . . His intellect was endowed with an 'infused knowledge' which, we are told, made his mental powers as far superior to those of the most brilliant modern philosophers as the flight of birds surpasses in swiftness the sluggish movement of the tortoise."[50] Williams pulls no punches when he accuses original righteousness of lacking "the slightest foundation in Scripture" and contrasts this tradition with Irenaeus's picture of an imperfect beginning. We cannot overestimate, he writes candidly, "how enormously the repudiation of 'original righteousness' as an alleged phase of human history eases the strain of the *prima facie* discordance between traditional theology and modern science as to the origins and primal condition of man."[51]

Wolfhart Pannenberg is another who dismisses Adam's original righteousness as lacking biblical support. He takes Paul to be teaching Adam's original corruptibility (1 Cor. 15:47) and faults the Reformers for inferring original holiness from Colossians 3:10 and Ephesians 4:24, "assuming without proof that we may see the NT sayings about the image of God as on the same plane as those in the original story."[52] Perfection was never realized in Genesis but is our future destination in Christ: "Christology can contribute positively to our understanding of man if his original state is seen as being one of openness to his future destiny and if he himself is regarded as possessing a fundamentally new aim, that of moving in history

48. James Barr, *The Garden of Eden and the Hope of Immortality* (Minneapolis: Fortress, 1993), 92–93. Similarly, D. Brent Laytham remarks, "Yet for all the power of the image of original perfection, it is not read out of the text but rather read in." D. Brent Laytham, "(Re)forming the Image: A Narrative Reading of Imago Dei" (PhD diss., Duke University, 1999), 224.

49. Williams, *Ideas of the Fall*, 57.

50. Williams, *Ideas of the Fall*, 361. The quote is from Augustine, *Unfinished Work in Answer to Julian* 5.1.

51. Williams, *Ideas of the Fall*, 453–54.

52. Wolfhart Pannenberg, *Systematic Theology*, 3 vols. (New York: T&T Clark, 2004), 2:212, 214.

towards the salvation that has appeared in Christ."[53] In short, Pannenberg redefines pre-fall Adam christologically and eschatologically.

These three witnesses—Barr, Williams, and Pannenberg—reflect the consensus of modern theology.[54] On one level, this consensus makes sense given that original righteousness defies current scientific dicta and can appeal to few direct biblical texts. Even John Murray, a proponent of the doctrine, observed that Colossians 3:10 and Ephesians 4:24 are at best allusions to Genesis 1:26–27. Paul's main emphasis in those passages is *re-creation*, not creation. As Murray argues, "In the context of Genesis 1:26 it is the nature and dignity of man in contradistinction from all other animate creatures (vv. 24, 25) that are being emphasized."[55] Adam's moral rectitude is not the focus of Genesis 1:26 and 5:1.

But we should not miss the forest for the trees; original righteousness is not merely an exegetical comment on isolated verses but rather a *doctrinal* synthesis making explicit what is only implicit across a range of biblical texts. The redemptive-historical arc of Scripture assumes that righteousness—or at least moral *innocence*—prevailed at the beginning. In Genesis 1, God made everything "good" (Gen. 1:10, 12, 18, 21, and 25), indeed "very good" (v. 31), an original creation free from sin. Thus, when Old Testament scholars object that the Hebrew word "good" (*tov*) is more functional than moral, the fact of divine holiness renders this exegetical debate largely moot.[56] The creator is the Holy One of Israel (Ezek. 29:7; Hab. 1:12), the light in whom there is no darkness (1 John 1:5). Original righteousness is a corollary of the doctrine of God, for God cannot create something unholy without denying his very own nature. As the psalmist says, "You are good, and what you do is good" (Ps. 119:68 NIV).

Modern scholars often claim that, aside from Genesis and a few Pauline epistles, the fall is barely mentioned in Scripture.[57] Even if Genesis 3

53. Wolfhart Pannenberg, "The Christological Foundation of Christian Anthropology," in *Humanism and Christianity*, ed. Claude Geffré (New York: Herder and Herder, 1973), 90. Pannenberg draws especially on the eighteenth-century philosopher Johann Gottfried Herder.

54. See the fascinating analysis in John Andrew Bernstein, "Ethics, Theology and the Original State of Man: An Historical Sketch," *Anglican Theological Review* 61, no. 2 (1979): 162–81. Reinhold Niebuhr represents another modern theologian who thought the human race had never experienced a historical period without sin. Reinhold Niebuhr, *The Nature and Destiny of Man: A Christian Interpretation*, 2 vols. (Louisville: Westminster John Knox, 1996), 1:265–300. See Braden Molhoek, "Reinhold Niebuhr's Theological Anthropology in Light of Evolutionary Biology: Science Shaping Anthropology Shaping Ethics" (PhD diss., Graduate Theological Union, 2016).

55. Murray, "Man in the Image of God," 41.

56. For a standard functional reading, see John Walton, *The Lost World of Genesis One: Ancient Cosmology and the Origins Debate* (Downers Grove, IL: IVP Academic, 2009), 51.

57. Some even deny *any* account of the fall in Scripture. E.g., see W. Sibley Towner, "Interpretations and Reinterpretations of the Fall," in *Modern Biblical Scholarship: Its Impact on Theology and*

were the sole mention of the primeval sin—a point that I dispute—Blocher reminds us that "frequency of occurrence could not be the sole measure of importance." He goes on to say, "Its place in the canon is significant. It is obvious that the Eden story is no peripheral anecdote or marginal addition; it belongs decisively to the structure of Genesis and to that of the Torah."[58] At any rate, the reality of a past fall and the memory of original righteousness are largely unstated assumptions running through the length of Scripture; they are also implicit in the biblical idea of sin (since sin is against God, it can hardly have been present at the beginning!). The picture of God "walking in the garden" in Genesis 3:8 hints at a level of intimacy between the couple and their maker—such communion is unthinkable unless they were at one point sinless.[59] Since original righteousness and the fall concern a unique time in the primordial past, it is not surprising that these originating events are rarely directly addressed in the rest of the biblical story, where the focus is on what has happened since; it would be like complaining when a history of the United States does not constantly refer back to the "discovery" of the New World by Christopher Columbus.[60]

Original righteousness is part of the logic of salvation. The current state of humanity is abnormal and the need for redemption implies that something was lost. The Old and New Testaments are the history of redemption as God extends forgiveness to wayward people. Israel came to know God as compassionate and gracious, slow to anger, and abounding in steadfast love (Exod. 34:6), and the entire Old Testament sacrificial system contained a logic of atonement and the forgiveness of sins (Leviticus). That system was the harbinger of the true Lamb of God whose name is Jesus (John 1:29; cf. Heb. 10), "for he will save his people from their sins" (Matt. 1:21). That same Jesus says, "Those who are well have no need of a physician, but those who are sick. I came not to call the righteous, but sinners" (Mark 2:17). And Paul agrees: "For all have sinned and fall short of the glory of God" (Rom. 3:23). Of course, no orthodox Christian disagrees that redemption is for sinners, but the twin truths that God is creator of humanity and the savior of sinners stand on the pillar of original righteousness (and the fall). Take away a sinless original humanity and Christianity becomes an odd message about God saving us from a problem he himself instigated—not

---

Proclamation, ed. Francis A. Eigo (Villanova, PA: Villanova University Press, 1984), 53–85. For a decisive rebuttal, see Collins, "May We Say That Adam and Eve 'Fell'?"

58. Henri Blocher, *Original Sin: Illuminating the Riddle* (Downers Grove, IL: InterVarsity, 1997), 32.

59. Augustus H. Strong, *Systematic Theology* (Philadelphia: American Baptist Publication Society, 1907), 517.

60. On the other possible alternatives, see Russell Freedman, *Who Was First? Discovering the Americas* (New York: Clarion, 2007).

just odd but *cruel*, like a biologist who intentionally introduces a deadly disease into the world only to turn around and offer the antidote. God the redeemer stands against God the creator.

Despite the rhetoric of some scholars, original righteousness is a catholic doctrine. At the end of his history of paradise, Jean Delumeau contrasts Augustine and Irenaeus. He laments Augustine's notion of perfection that gave "rise to a gloomy image of humanity and of God,"[61] unlike Irenaeus's picture of humanity rising from infancy to beatific vision. Like N. P. Williams before him, Delumeau latched on to Irenaeus for his potential to relieve tensions with evolutionary science. To be sure, the Augustinian tradition sometimes goes too far in its speculation about Adam's capacities before the fall, whereas Irenaeus's Adam was imperfect and infant-like: "It was necessary that he should grow, and so come to (his) perfection."[62] Augustine emphasizes perfection, while Irenaeus emphasizes immaturity.[63] Notwithstanding these notable differences, *both church fathers are as one in affirming a sinless prelapsarian state.* Irenaeus believes that sin came only after the serpent's deception:

> This commandment [not to eat of the tree of the knowledge of good and evil] the man kept not, but was disobedient to God, being led astray by the angel who, for the great gifts of God which He had given to man, was envious and jealous of him, and both brought himself to nought *and made man sinful*, persuading him to disobey the commandment of God. So the angel, becoming by his falsehood *the author and originator of sin*, himself was struck down, having offended against God, and man he caused to be cast out from Paradise.[64]

Irenaeus affirms original sinlessness without embellishing Adam's primeval condition. Let us also not forget that when Augustine distinguishes *posse peccare et posse non peccare* (in Eden) and *non posse peccare* (in glory), he implicitly recognizes that God had always intended prelapsarian Adam to experience growth and development: "Consequently, the paradisiacal state, though a holy and happy state, was not equal to the heavenly state.

61. Jean Delumeau, *History of Paradise: The Garden of Eden in Myth and Tradition*, trans. Matthew O'Connell (New York: Continuum, 1995), 233.

62. Irenaeus, *The Demonstration of the Apostolic Preaching*, trans. Armitage Robinson (London: SPCK, 1920), 81.

63. Gavin Ortlund explains that even though Augustine used the perfection language, "[he] apparently did not think of the pre-fallen state of humanity as permanent—rather, he seems to have thought of the existence of Adam and Eve in Eden as a kind of provisional test period." Gavin Ortlund, *Retrieving Augustine's Doctrine of Creation: Ancient Wisdom for Current Controversy* (Downers Grove, IL: InterVarsity, 2000), 210–11.

64. Irenaeus, *Demonstration*, 84, my emphasis.

It had not the safety and security of the latter. Eden differed from heaven as holiness differs from indefectibility of holiness, as a mutable perfection differs from an immutable. The perfection of holy Adam was relative, not absolute."[65] Augustine and Irenaeus both affirm Edenic sinlessness with the prospect of an even greater level of moral development, which is enough for a catholic doctrine of original righteousness.

Sin and Physical Death

Modern theologians often reject the concept of original righteousness because it suggests prelapsarian immortality and therefore contradicts standard biology. As Niels Henrik Gregersen writes, "Death is the price to be paid for living as highly complex creatures far beyond thermodynamical equilibrium. The more complex and improbable a creature is, the surer is the fate of death."[66] Human existence is inexplicable without death. Karl Barth concurs when he insists that death "belongs to human nature, and is determined and ordered by God's good creation and to that extent right and good, that man's being in time should be finite and man himself mortal."[67]

Situating Death Canonically

This concept of natural mortality, which modern society takes for granted, strains against the biblical point of view. On the sixth day, God miraculously fashioned the first man from the ground to live forever with his maker, to steward his creation, and to populate the world with many descendants (Gen. 1:26–28). Adam's sin, however, brought down God's judicial curse of death, "for you are dust, and to dust you shall return" (3:19).

---

65. Shedd, *Dogmatic Theology*, 536. Shedd is not expounding Augustine here, but these words encapsulate Augustine's position.

66. Niels Henrik Gregersen, "The Cross of Christ in an Evolutionary World," *Dialog* 40, no. 3 (2001): 198. According to Ernst Conradie (*Redeeming Sin? Social Diagnostics amid Ecological Destruction* [Lanham, MD: Lexington Books, 2017], 201), "Biological death should be regarded as part of God's good creation and is indeed implied in the notion of being a finite creature."

67. Karl Barth, *Church Dogmatics*, III/2, *The Doctrine of Creation*, ed. Geoffrey Bromiley and T. F. Torrance (Edinburgh: T&T Clark, 1960), 632. For reflections on Barth's position, see Robert Song, "Technological Immortalization and Original Mortality," in *Eternal God, Eternal Life: Theological Investigations into the Concept of Immortality*, ed. Philip G. Ziegler (New York: Bloomsbury T&T Clark, 2016), 187–209. For similar defenses of natural mortality, see, inter alia, David Fergusson, *Creation* (Grand Rapids: Eerdmans, 2014), 38; John D. Zizioulas, *The Eucharistic Communion and the World*, ed. Luke Ben Tallon (New York: Continuum, 2011), 173; J. Richard Middleton, "Reading Genesis 3 Attentive to Human Evolution: Beyond Concordism and Non-overlapping Magisteria," in *Evolution and the Fall*, ed. William Cavanaugh and James K. A. Smith (Grand Rapids: Eerdmans, 2017), 79.

Adam becoming a mortal being always tending toward death was not God's original design but the unnatural consequence of sin.[68]

Now the questions come fast and furious. Wouldn't unfallen Adam have died if he had run out of oxygen to breathe, or food to eat, or water to drink? Wouldn't he have died if he had fallen off a steep cliff? Or fallen into an active volcano? However, such hypothetical scenarios distract us from the real issue. Adam's prelapsarian immortality is not a thesis about human "indestructibility" as if he were some kind of Marvel or DC superhero; rather, Adam's world *externally* and his body *internally* were substantially different before his disobedience in Genesis 3. To begin with, any threats of accidental death or physical deprivation would have been impossible since there was no sin in the world and God's providence would therefore have preserved perfect shalom.[69] Additionally, pre-fall Adam had no *tendency* toward deterioration or death. He was constitutionally different from post-fall humanity in that senescence had no hold on him. Even after hundreds, thousands, or millions of years, he would not have experienced cataracts, presbyopia, sarcopenia, hearing loss, cardiovascular disease, arthritis, or any other symptoms of aging and sickness. Unlike every human creature east of Eden, prelapsarian Adam and Eve were not programmed to die.

Before we proceed any further, it will help to gain more clarity on what we mean by the contested terms "mortality" and "immortality."[70] First, immortality as an absolute category refers to something unending that cannot be destroyed. Only God is immortal in this sense (1 Tim. 1:17; 6:16).[71] God is eternal without beginning or end (Ps. 90:2; Isa. 57:5; John 8:58). He is

---

68. Gijsbert van den Brink ("Human Death in Theological Anthropology and Evolutionary Biology: (Im)mortality as Ecumenical Solution," *Zygon* 57, no. 4 [2022]: 869–88) thinks that created mortality follows from the fact that Adam was created from the dust. Adam's punishment of dying, he says, was *not* contrary to how God created him but its culmination. However, I find it difficult to see how this "punishment" rises to the level of a divine *curse* (since, on his view, dying is part of our created design). Instead, I suggest that God's punishment of Adam (and his descendants) in Gen. 3:19 is the programmed *undoing* of his created nature so that he will grow old and die, thus slipping back to his material origins ("for you are dust, and to dust you shall return").

69. Does the fact that angelic sin was already present in Eden undermine my point here? I don't think so. Adam and Eve could genuinely have resisted Satan's temptation—and had they done so, the fall would not have corrupted humanity or led to the broader corruption of the natural world. My remark about "perfect shalom" is limited to Adam's relationship to the visible world over which God had given him (not Satan) stewardship.

70. Here I am drawing from Geerhardus Vos, *Reformed Dogmatics: A System of Christian Theology*, ed. and trans. Richard Gaffin (Bellingham, WA: Lexham, 2020), 234–38 (originally published 1910).

71. Reflecting on 1 Tim. 6:16, Francis Turretin helpfully distinguishes between an "essential and absolute immortality," which only God possesses, and a "comparative and participative immortality," which Adam and Eve possessed in Eden. Francis Turretin, *Institutes of Elenctic Theology*, ed. James T. Dennison, trans. George Musgrave Giger, 3 vols. (Phillipsburg, NJ: P&R, 1992), 1:473.

self-existent and has life in himself (John 5:26); every portion of creation depends on him for its continued existence (John 1:3–4; Col. 1:16–17; Rev. 4:11).

Second, immortality can apply to any creature that God has created and will never abandon to destruction; they will persist in being forever. Such immortality belongs to Adam before the fall, humanity after the fall, indeed humanity in *all* phases of existence, extending all the way to heaven and hell; not merely human creatures but fallen and unfallen angels also possess this form of immortality.

Third, immortality can be an attribute of human *souls*. This doesn't mean souls have metaphysical indestructibility in the Platonic sense, which would exclude the New Testament teaching of bodily resurrection. Instead, it affirms the biblical truth that every soul survives physical death, while still upholding the centrality of bodily resurrection in Christian doctrine. The immortality of the soul reflects the doctrine of the intermediate state (the teaching that people continue to exist in a temporary disembodied state between death and the final resurrection).[72]

Fourth, one can attribute mortality to a creature for whom physical and spiritual death is a *theoretical possibility*. In that sense, prelapsarian Adam was mortal: God told him explicitly that he would die if he disobeyed the commandment (Gen. 2:17)—death was theoretically possible. Conversely, resurrected saints will be immortal, for death will no longer be possible; as Paul indicates, they will exchange the natural for a spiritual body that is "imperishable" forever (1 Cor. 15:35–57).

The remaining option is the view of mortality and immortality that I will be defending in what follows: immortality means that Adam and Eve had no *natural* disposition or tendency toward death. They did not have the seeds of death within their unfallen nature.[73] Adam and Eve before the fall were fundamentally different from post-fall humanity since they had none of the corruptions that come with disease and death. Let us call this position "original immortality"—namely, that Adam and Eve were naturally immortal. They possessed a created immortality derived from God

---

72. John W. Cooper, *Body, Soul and Life Everlasting: Biblical Anthropology and the Monism-Dualism Debate*, 2nd ed. (Grand Rapids: Eerdmans, 2001), esp. 196–98; Murray Harris, "A Comparison of Immortality in the New Testament with Immortality in Plato," in *Raised Immortal* (Grand Rapids: Eerdmans, 1985), 201–6.

73. Louis Berkhof uses similar language in his *Systematic Theology* (Grand Rapids: Eerdmans, 1996), 209: "Man, as he was created by God, did not bear within him the seeds of death and would not have died *necessarily* in virtue of the original constitution of his nature. Though the possibility of his becoming a victim of death was not excluded, he was not liable to death as long as he did not sin" (emphasis original).

that would have allowed them to live forever had they not eaten from the forbidden tree. Their immortality was, therefore, *conditional*, for they had the theoretical capacity to die *if they sinned*—they lacked the permanent immortality of glorified saints.[74]

In the history of theology, Pelagius was one of the first to reject this position when he defended the natural mortality of pre-fall Adam. Physical mortality had to be intrinsic to human nature as created, he argued, because infants experience death despite their being sinless. In the fifth century at the Council of Carthage, Pelagius and his cobelligerents were condemned for teaching original mortality.[75] Their position resurfaced in the sixteenth-century Radical Reformation theology of Socinianism (spearheaded by Lælius Socinus and his nephew Faustus Socinus).[76] And more recently, through the writings of Friedrich Schleiermacher and Karl Barth, original mortality has become the dominant position in modern theology.[77]

The thesis of original immortality contradicts everything we know about human biology and our current experience of the world. This tension has prompted readers to find other possible ways of interpreting Genesis 3:19. For example, some appeal to the sentiment expressed in 2 Baruch, that Adam's first sin "brought untimely death upon all" (2 Bar. 54:15).[78] Hence the divine curse in Genesis 3:19 is *premature* death rather than death itself. However, the immediate context of Genesis 3:17–19 pictures a long life of toilsome labor culminating in death. Adam dying at 930 years (5:5), much

74. For a similar account, see Bavinck, *Reformed Dogmatics*, 2:560. In the words of John Andrew Quenstedt, the sixteenth-century Lutheran theologian: "It is one thing not to be able to die, and another to be able not to die, and still another not to be able not to die. The last belongs to all sinners, the second to Adam in his state of integrity, and the first to the blessed" (John Andrew Quenstedt, *Theologia Didactico-Polemica*, 2 vols. [originally published 1685], 2:8, quoted in Heinrich Schmid, *The Doctrinal Theology of the Evangelical Lutheran Church*, trans. Charles A. Hay and Henry E. Jacobs, 5th ed. [Philadelphia: Lutheran Publication Society, 1876], 249). These distinctions go back to Augustine, who famously distinguishes humanity's (1) ability not to sin (*posse non peccare*) and thus not to die (*posse non mori*)—pre-fall; (2) inability not to sin (*non posse non peccare*) and not to die (*non posse non mori*)—post-fall; and (3) inability to sin (*non posse peccare*) and to die (*non posse mori*)—in eschatological glory. E.g., see Augustine, *On Rebuke and Grace* 12.33; Augustine, *City of God* 22.30.

75. Eugene TeSelle, "Rufinus the Syrian, Caelestius, Pelagius: Explorations in the Prehistory of the Pelagian Controversy," *Augustinian Studies* 3 (1972): 61–95.

76. George Huntston Williams, *The Radical Reformation*, 3rd ed. (Kirksville, MO: Sixteenth Century Journal, 1992), 978–90.

77. See the account in Ray S. Anderson, "Toward a Theology of Human Death," in *Theology, Death, and Dying* (New York: Basil Blackwell, 1986), 37–63, esp. 51–55.

78. "The Syriac Apocalypse of Baruch," trans. R. H. Charles, rev. L. H. Brockington, in *The Apocryphal Old Testament*, vol. 1, ed. H. F. D. Sparks (Oxford: Clarendon, 1984), 874 (2 Baruch is a Jewish pseudepigraphal account from the first or second century CE). For similar claims that Gen. 3:19 refers to premature death, see the sources listed in John Levison, *Portraits of Adam in Early Judaism: From Sirach to 2 Baruch* (New York: Bloomsbury Academic, 2015), 228n19.

like the lengthy antediluvian life spans that follow, seems to rule out the idea that the original curse was premature death.[79] Other scholars propose that Adam's disobedience introduced *spiritual*, not physical, death,[80] but this creative exegesis founders on Romans 5:12 and 1 Corinthians 15:21 where Paul's remarks on Genesis 3 reinforce the nexus between sin and physical death. Henri Blocher rightly says about both passages, "The primary point is the death of the body, since its antithesis is the resurrection of the body."[81] The first sin caused spiritual *and* physical death.

Some evangelicals argue that Adam and Eve were created mortal but were able to stave off death by eating from the tree of life. Once God expelled them from Eden, they lost access to the tree with its rejuvenating properties and succumbed to their innate mortality.[82] However, in assuming that the tree of life had magical properties that could impart longevity to humanity, this conclusion misunderstands the tree's function.[83] No one knows whether Adam and Eve ate from the tree of life. I suspect they ate regularly from the tree, since they were only forbidden to eat from the tree of the knowledge of good and evil. Yet it is equally possible, as Geerhardus Vos argues, based on what God says in Genesis 3:22 ("The man has now become like one of us, knowing good and evil. He must not be allowed to reach out his hand and take also from the tree of life and eat, and live

79. Geerhardus Vos, *Biblical Theology: Old and New Testaments* (Grand Rapids: Eerdmans, 1948), 48. Granted, one can imagine Adam being created mortal with a life span of ten thousand years; if so, dying at 930 years would technically be a "premature" death. However, not only is this reading weak exegetically, but such a life span would be inconceivable to theistic evolutionists.

80. E.g., see R. J. Berry, "This Cursed Earth: Is 'the Fall' Credible?," *Science and Christian Belief* 11, no. 1 (1999): 34: "When the bible—and particularly Paul—speak of 'death' they are concerned essentially with spiritual death." William Horst tries to bolster this argument for spiritual instead of physical death by reading Romans in light of Platonic and Hellenistic ideas that Paul might have been familiar with (William Horst, "Morality, Not Mortality: The Inception of Death in the Book of Romans," *Perspectives on Science and Christian Faith* 71, no. 1 [2019]: 24–36). Alas, Horst's thesis has little to commend it (especially with respect to Rom. 5:12); motivated by the conflict with evolution—as he concedes in the article (24, 33–34)—he reads Paul through a highly selective Platonic interpretive lens that is far inferior to the classical interpretation of the apostle's discourse. The latter prioritizes the intratextual and canonical contexts of Paul's own statements. For Horst's longer monograph, see *Morality, Not Mortality: Moral Psychology and the Language of Death in Romans 5–8* (Lanham, MD: Lexington Books, 2022), which I review critically in *Journal of the Evangelical Theological Society* (forthcoming).

81. Blocher, *In the Beginning*, 184.

82. John Walton defends this position in *The Lost World of Adam and Eve: Genesis 2–3 and the Human Origins Debate* (Downers Grove, IL: IVP Academic, 2015), 74, as does William Lane Craig, *In Quest of the Historical Adam: A Biblical and Scientific Exploration* (Grand Rapids: Eerdmans, 2021), 235–38.

83. Modern theological perspectives on the tree range widely from the literal to the highly symbolic. For a brief survey, see Daniel Treier, Dustyn Elizabeth Keepers, and Ty Kieser, "The Tree of Life in Modern Theological Thought," in *The Tree of Life*, ed. Douglas Estes (Leiden: Brill, 2020), 365–86.

forever" [NIV]), that they had not yet eaten of the tree.[84] Either way, the tree of life had a *sacramental* meaning—it was most likely a literal tree that sacramentally represented the richer life-giving presence of God, anticipating Christ and the eternal life we receive from eating his flesh and drinking his blood (John 6:47–58). Had the tree been merely physical, then it could only offer physical power, but because of its deeper sacramental role, God could impart *spiritual* life through what the fruit represented (much as the water for baptism and the bread and wine of the Lord's Supper impart spiritual life).[85] The tree of life ultimately foreshadows union with Christ and the eschatological tree of life in Revelation 22:2.[86] The Father gives life in his Son (1 John 5:11), and his Son gives life to whomever he pleases (John 5:21), *eternal* life welling up like an endless spring of water (4:14).

Our first parents were holy, and some have even argued that they were *indwelt* by God's Spirit (Gen. 2:7). Adam's nature, Bavinck writes, "was from the very beginning fit for the indwelling of the Holy Spirit."[87] We should nonetheless be careful when making such statements that we are not illicitly importing the language of redemption, our status in Christ, back into Genesis.[88] The Holy Spirit was certainly involved at some level in giving Adam life—there is no life independent of God! But the nature of the relationship was different from the Spirit-filled life of New Testament believers in union with Christ. In Genesis 1–2, the earth does not seem to be God's dwelling place but rather his "vacation home" or "second residence" that he visits regularly. Although the text does not specify, we presume that God's dwelling is in heaven. Adam enjoys close fellowship with God, but it is the relationship of a friend. In the new creation, God's main dwelling is

---

84. Vos, *Biblical Theology*, 38. I took the same view in my essay "An Augustinian-Reformed View," in *Original Sin and the Fall: Five Views*, ed. J. B. Stump and Chad Meister (Downers Grove, IL: IVP Academic, 2020), 20. However, I am no longer certain whether Adam and Eve had eaten from the tree of life.

85. Willem J. Ouweneel, *Adam, Where Are You?—and Why This Matters: A Theological Evaluation of the Evolutionist Hermeneutic* (Jordan Station, ON: Paideia, 2018), 210–11.

86. For this sacramental reading, see Turretin, *Institutes of Elenctic Theology*, 1:476, 580–82; Vos, *Biblical Theology*, 37–39; Robert Letham, *Systematic Theology* (Wheaton: Crossway, 2019), 352, 637–38; Toby Jennings, *Precious Enemy: A Biblical Portrait of Death* (Eugene, OR: Pickwick, 2017), 51–53. For a nonsacramental reading, see R. Gregory Jenks, "A Tale of Two Trees: Delinking Death from Sin by Viewing Genesis 2–3 Independently from Paul," *Bulletin for Biblical Research* 28, no. 4 (2018): 533–53. In my view, reading Gen. 2–3 independently of Paul is a losing proposition.

87. Bavinck, *Reformed Dogmatics*, 2:558. Donald Fairbairn writes, similarly, "Genesis 2:7 may mean that God breathed not the breath of life but the Spirit of life (that is, the Holy Spirit) into Adam, just as Jesus later breathes on the disciples as a way of communicating the Holy Spirit to them [John 20:21–22]." Donald Fairbairn, *Life in the Trinity: An Introduction to Theology with the Help of the Church Fathers* (Downers Grove, IL: InterVarsity Academic, 2009), 62.

88. I am especially indebted to Stephen Lloyd for the ideas in this paragraph and the next.

now a joining of a new heaven and a new earth (Rev. 21:1–3). Our fellowship with God is not entirely different from what Adam enjoyed, but it is a
relationship of marriage, not mere friendship. Even if the actual experience
of fellowship is similar, the basis of the relationship is different. We are
part of the divine family. There is a union of persons—joined to the Son,
by the Spirit—different from the situation Adam was in. At a minimum,
we can say that Adam and Eve were holy, while we sinner-saints are being
progressively sanctified and will be forever holy when the trumpet sounds;
they were conditionally immortal, while we are presently mortal but will
be immortal forever at the resurrection (1 Cor. 15:42–44).

Gijsbert van den Brink, in dialogue with Augustine, marshals a different
set of arguments on behalf of original mortality. He lays out four modal
options to clarify the possible states of the human condition: (1) *strong
immortality*, or the condition of not being able to die; (2) *weak immortality*,
or the condition of not having to die; (3) *weak mortality*, or the condition
of being able to die; (4) *strong mortality*, or the condition of having to die.[89]
"It seems that no Christian," van den Brink writes, "however traditional
she may want to be, is bound to the view that humans were created in
a state in which it was physically impossible to die, that is, in a state in
which our bodies were constituted in such a completely different way that
our physical lives could not come to an end."[90] God created us with weak
mortality and weak immortality, meaning that it was simultaneously possible for Adam to die and not to die (*posse mori et posse non mori*). Van den
Brink concludes that there is no constitutional difference between Adam
before and after the fall. In his view, Adam and Eve were mortal from the
beginning and would have died naturally without divine intervention. God
could keep Adam and Eve alive indefinitely by miraculously counteracting
the biological process of aging.

Several objections should be raised against van den Brink's proposal.
First, his argument for created mortality is difficult to reconcile with the
consistent biblical testimony to the causal nexus between sin and death.
As John Stott writes, "The Bible everywhere views human death not as a
natural but as a *penal* event. It is an alien intrusion into God's good world,
and not part of his original intention for humankind."[91] In the world of

---

89. Van den Brink, "Human Death in Theological Anthropology," 875.
90. Van den Brink, "Human Death in Theological Anthropology," 874.
91. John R. W. Stott, *The Cross of Christ* (Leicester, UK: Inter-Varsity, 1986), 65. In agreement,
Pannenberg believes that "sin in particular must have death for its natural consequence, inasmuch
as the opposition to God contained in sin reaches its logical term in a complete separation from
God that is sealed by death." Wolfhart Pannenberg, *Anthropology in Theological Perspective*, trans.

Scripture, physical death is never possible without the prior presence of *spiritual* death. Therefore, unfallen Adam and Eve did not—and indeed could not—have had the seeds of mortality in their created being. At this point, some might wonder whether Jesus is a counterexample—he is the God-man who had no inner moral corruption (i.e., spiritual death), yet he died physically. Jesus is the exception: as the eternal Son, he experienced death because he made atonement for our sins by coming in the likeness of sinful flesh (Rom. 8:3).

Second, if aging and death are natural features of prelapsarian Adam, then either God created them with inherent physical defects or he placed them in a harmful world (or both). The problem is clear when we consider the scientific theories of aging (biogerontology), which fall into two broad categories: *program* theories and *error* theories.[92] Program theories describe aging as a genetic process built into the human condition that leads to progressive deterioration over the individual's life (perhaps from hormonal, immunological, or other factors). By contrast, error theories portray aging as caused by factors outside the body, including environmental damage from the wear and tear of the organism (due to radiation, ultraviolet light, or toxins), the harmful accumulation of free radicals in the body, or the effect of genetic mutations over the life span of the individual. But regardless which theory of aging wins the day, van den Brink's notion of created mortality implies that in a prelapsarian world God would have been performing regular miracles to protect Adam and Eve from any biological or environmental damage. Such a scenario would undermine the creaturely integrity of the first humans.

In van den Brink's account, prelapsarian Adam and Eve would inevitably age and die apart from God's supernatural grace. The processes of aging and death, he writes, "were most probably ingrained in our physical structures from the beginning" and would have been held back by divine miraculous activity.[93] In this picture of Eden, Adam and Eve lack any *intrinsic* integrity as sinless creatures who can live forever in God's presence. However, van den Brink's insistence that God's supernatural grace is solely responsible for preventing senescence is analogous to the mistake of occasionalism. In the

Matthew J. O'Connell (Philadelphia: Westminster, 1985), 140. In dialogue with Paul Tillich, he goes on to speculate whether the biblical account of death can be reconciled with the modern biological conception (140–42).

92. I am drawing on Nancy Pachana, *Ageing: A Very Short Introduction* (Oxford: Oxford University Press, 2016). See also Allyson Palmer and James L. Kirkland, "The Biology of Aging," in *Reichel's Care of the Elderly: Clinical Aspects of Aging*, ed. Jan Busby-Whitehead et al., 7th ed. (Cambridge: Cambridge University Press, 2016), 17–27.

93. Van den Brink, "Human Death in Theological Anthropology," 884.

doctrine of providence, occasionalists deny that created things have their own genuine causal or natural power; for instance, Nicolas Malebranche (1638–1715) thought there was no necessary connection between my will to move my arm and the subsequent movement of my arm. "It is true that they are moved when we will it," Malebranche concedes, "and that thus we are the natural cause of the movement of our arms. But *natural* causes are not true causes; they are only *occasional* causes that act only through the force and efficacy of the will of God."[94] Conversely, Scripture everywhere assumes that created things have their own natures and causal powers.[95] Creatures are secondary causes, while God is the primary cause. Occasionalism rightly affirms the overwhelming biblical teaching on God's primary agency in creation, but it fails to recognize the genuine secondary agency of creaturely things. Likewise, van den Brink rightly affirms that dying and death were absent in Adam and Eve because of God's grace, but he fails to grant that this grace enables and sustains their own *natural* immortality.

Life is a gift from the Spirit of God (Gen. 2:7). Death is the antithesis of creation, the absence of life, separation from the living God. Death is punishment for breaking the law: "Whoever strikes a man so that he dies shall be put to death" (Exod. 21:12; see also Gen. 9:5–6; Lev. 20:2, 9–13, 15–16, 27; Deut. 22:21, 24, and passim). God himself orders the death of the wicked, as he did at Sodom and Gomorrah (Gen. 18–19) and among the Canaanites (Num. 21:2–3; Josh. 6:17, 21), the Amalekites (1 Sam. 15:1–9), the Hittites, the Hivites, the Amorites, the Perizzites, the Jebusites, and so on (e.g., Deut. 20:16–18). The common assumption that death was included in how God originally created humanity clashes with this canonical picture of death as divine *punishment*. The wages of sin, Scripture says, is death (Rom. 6:23). Paul's brutal indictment of humanity in Romans 1:18–32 consistently traces death back to wickedness and idolatry without any sense of death having its origin in finitude or creatureliness—"those who practice such things deserve to die" (Rom. 1:32).[96] Death is the last enemy (1 Cor. 15:26),

94. Nicolas Malebranche, *The Search after Truth*, trans. Thomas M. Lennon and Paul J. Olscamp (Columbus: Ohio State University Press, 1980), 449.
95. On the exegetical support, see C. John Collins, *The God of Miracles: An Exegetical Examination of God's Action in the World* (Wheaton: Crossway, 2000), 73–86. For helpful theological critique of occasionalism, see Alfred J. Freddoso, "God's General Concurrence with Secondary Causes: Why Conservation Is Not Enough," *Philosophical Perspectives* 5 (1991): 553–85.
96. On Rom. 1:32, James D. G. Dunn notes, "It is the Adam background which shines through most clearly once again. Adam/man knew God's warning ('In the day you eat of it you shall die' [Gen. 2:16]), and yet went ahead and ate. . . . Man generally (not just the Jew) knows what is right, knows it in fact (or in effect) to be the requirement of God, and knows that to flout it is to court death, a death justly deserved." James D. G. Dunn, *Romans 1–8*, Word Biblical Commentary 38A (Dallas: Word, 1988), 76.

and Isaiah prophesies a day when death will be no more (Isa. 25:8), when God will wipe away all tears forever (Rev. 21:4). The logic of redemption shatters if death is native to God's original creation.

Additionally, Christ's atonement is meaningless without the strong causal nexus between sin and death.[97] Consider the countless animals that were slaughtered in the Old Testament for the sake of Israelite sinners, animal death atoning for human sin. The sinner's guilt was transferred to the slain animal, its sprinkled blood a token of the victim's life (Lev. 17:11).[98] In the Passover, God commanded every Hebrew family to kill an innocent lamb and apply its blood to the doorframes of their houses (Exod. 12:1–30); the Lord struck down the firstborn of the Egyptian families whose sins were not covered. The sacrificial system typically assumes this causal connection between sin and death, and that pattern is exemplified by Isaiah's suffering servant who pours out his life unto death because he bears the sin of many (Isa. 53:12). Jesus Christ was that suffering servant who fulfilled the Old Testament administration as the perfect sacrifice (Heb. 10:1–18).

Death in the Bible can mean *spiritual* death, the terrifying reality of separation from God, or its apogee, *eternal* damnation in hell—but in either case death is never less than *physical* death. Christ died not only spiritually, forsaken by the Father, but also on the cross in brutal physical fashion. His death was part of his atoning work as he bore the penalty for sin. Jesus died for our sins according to the Scriptures (1 Cor. 15:3), and he reconciled us by his physical body through death (Col. 1:20–22). As Peter says, Jesus bore our sins on his body on the tree "that we might die to sin and live to righteousness. By his wounds you have been healed" (1 Pet. 2:24). Because death entered the world through the first Adam's sin (Rom. 5:12), it was in dying—being obedient to death on a cross (Phil. 2:8)—that the last Adam secured our justification, sanctification, and glorification. Thus, the very idea that human death is part of God's original creation renders the drama of redemption incoherent.

To be sure, Scripture sometimes speaks of death in neutral or even seemingly positive ways: Abraham died at a "good old age" and "full of years" (Gen. 25:8), as did his son Isaac (35:29). Old Testament texts routinely describe people living to an old age and then being gathered to their ancestors. In the New Testament, the suffering that leads to death can be a means of sanctification and a deepening of our communion with Christ. Since Jesus suffered for us, even unto death, he left us an example to imitate (1 Pet.

---

97. Stephen Lloyd, "Chronological Creationism," *Foundations* 72 (May 2017): 76–99.

98. Bruce A. Demarest, *The Cross and Salvation: The Doctrine of Salvation* (Wheaton: Crossway, 1997), 169; Jay Sklar, *Sin, Impurity, Sacrifice, Atonement: The Priestly Conceptions* (Sheffield, UK: Sheffield University Press, 2005), 168–73.

2:21). Paul describes death as gain (Phil. 1:21–23), and the risen Christ promises the crown of life to the church in Smyrna if they are faithful unto death (Rev. 2:10). As Stephen Lloyd remarks, however, "These are examples of those who have hope even in the face of death because its 'sting' has been removed (1 Cor. 15:56). Physical death itself is the inevitable end to a process that is not viewed so positively: the body is 'wasting away' (2 Cor. 4:16). The fact that death can be a source of rejoicing for a believer does not make it something good, any more than rejoicing in suffering makes suffering good."[99] Although death is a normal and universal experience in a fallen world, we should not read that normality into the prelapsarian world.

Sin also underlies the suffering and decay that presage death. The healing miracles of Jesus ostensibly reverse the effects of sin. The death of Christ, Isaiah prophesies, will atone for human suffering and disease (Isa. 53:4; Matt. 8:17). Losing the people that we love is tragic; watching them die is a constant reminder that our world is broken. We use doctors and medicine to stave off the inevitability of death. Death horrifies us. But the idea of original mortality turns all this on its head. The idea that death is intrinsic to the world or part of God's original creation resonates with post-Darwinian scientific sensibilities, but it clashes with the human experience. Our anger at death expressed when we mourn at funerals is wrongheaded if death is part of the goodness of creation. Normalizing death drives a wedge between Christ as creator and Christ as redeemer, forcing us to believe that death was part of the Son's original creation, only for him to defeat it at the cross (1 Cor. 15:55), that disease and death are natural processes, even though Jesus healed the sick and raised the dead throughout his earthly ministry.[100] Jesus's words to Mary and Martha—"Everyone who lives and believes in me shall never die" (John 11:26)—are baffling if indeed he originated death from the beginning.[101] Non-lapsarian theologies inevitably pit creation and redemption against each other.

99. Stephen Lloyd, "Christian Theology and Neo-Darwinism Are Incompatible: An Argument from the Resurrection," in *Debating Darwin: Two Debates; Is Darwinism True and Does It Matter?*, by Graeme Finlay, Stephen Lloyd, Stephen Pattemore, and David Swift (Milton Keynes, UK: Paternoster, 2009), 17.

100. Those who believe that death is natural at this point in redemptive history may still believe that it will be conquered in the future; they could draw on 1 Cor. 15:42–49 to point out that the Gospels portray these healings and resurrections as anticipations of the future kingdom of God, where there will be no sickness and death—death is normal now but will not be when Christ returns. However, while this position is correct about the anticipatory nature of Christ's healing miracles, it misses the equally important presumption that our *present* experience of the world is disordered. Sickness, disease, and death are not the way it's supposed to be; it was not so at the beginning and will not be so in the end. I will address 1 Cor. 15:42–49 later in this chapter.

101. See also Martin Williams, "The Gospel, Disease, and Theistic Evolution," *Reformed Theological Review* 81, no. 2 (2022): 120–38.

Some will raise questions at this point. Given that the Father in his Son has delivered us from the penalty of sin, why do Christians still experience death? If death is the last enemy, defeated by Christ's atonement, how can it possibly continue to play a role within God's redemptive purposes? It is true that those who are united with Christ will not be judged for the guilt of original sin, or for any individual sins—"he is faithful and just to forgive us our sins and to cleanse us from all unrighteousness" (1 John 1:9). Christ atoned for all the eternal consequences of sin, but as we wait for the eschaton God allows temporal consequences to remain in a fallen world (including physical death).[102] God in his wisdom has chosen to postpone the full implications of Christ's redemptive work until the Lord comes in glory.

The antediluvian patriarchs are stark reminders that senescence and death are effects of Adam's fall. Leading up to Noah, the life spans cluster around 900 years, with Adam living 930 years, Seth 912 years, Enosh 905 years, Lamech 777 years, and so on. Noah himself dies at 950, while Methuselah's 969 years takes the crown. The life spans then shorten dramatically from Noah to Abraham: Shem dies at 600 years, Arpachshad 438 years, Peleg and Reu die at the same age of 239, and Abraham is only 175 when he is gathered to his people "full of years" (Gen. 25:8).[103] Then from Abraham to Moses, the life spans shrink down further—Isaac lives to 180 years, Jacob 147 years, and Moses 120 years (6:3). Skeptical arguments against taking these life spans at face value tend to be rationalistic (see chap. 3), while those who accept them as historical have appealed to diet, climate, physiology, and other factors to justify the radical difference between the ancient world and today.[104] Carl Wieland, for example, speculates that our patriarchal ancestors lived longer because their genetics contributed to greater longevity.[105]

---

102. Millard Erickson, *Christian Theology*, 3rd ed. (Grand Rapids: Baker Academic, 2013), 1076–77. For an analytic theological perspective, see Christopher Woznicki, "Revisiting the Somatic Death Objection to Penal Substitution: Original Sin and the Nature of Consequences," *Irish Theological Quarterly* 87, no. 1 (2022): 50–65.

103. I recognize that the MT life spans for Arpachshad, Peleg, and Reu differ from those of the LXX, but that textual issue is incidental to my main point. For discussion, see Henry B. Smith Jr.: "Methuselah's Begetting Age in Genesis 5:25 and the Primeval Chronology of the Septuagint," *Answers Research Journal* 10 (2017): 169–79.

104. For example, see Josephus, *Jewish Antiquities* 1.105 (diet); Henry Morris, *The Genesis Record* (San Diego: Creation-Life, 1976), 155 (climate); James G. Murphy, *A Critical and Exegetical Commentary on the Book of Genesis* (Andover: Draper, 1866), 174 (human physiology). For the extensive seventeenth-century debate over these (and other) theories for explaining antediluvian longevity, see Philip C. Almond, *Adam and Eve in Seventeenth-Century Thought* (Cambridge: Cambridge University Press, 1999), 19–27. Over the past two centuries, all these theories have been widely criticized.

105. While his genetic thesis has promise, I defer to scientific experts to adjudicate its merits. See Carl Wieland, "Decreased Lifespans: Have We Been Looking in the Right Place?," *Creation ex nihilo Technical Journal* 8, no. 2 (1994): 138–41; Carl Wieland, "Living for 900 Years," *Creation* 20,

All the same, the decline in life spans from Genesis 5 to 25 is consistent with sin having devastating effects on the human condition. Adam's fall was the precipitating cause, and while God did say that disobedience would trigger death (Gen. 2:17), he graciously delayed the death sentence on humanity by hundreds of years.[106] The decrease in life spans is the progressive realization of that initial death sentence; sin, after all, is the sting of death (1 Cor. 15:56).[107] The common disbelief in antediluvian life spans is rooted in a naturalistic assumption that life expectancy is a fixed biological constant, immutable since the dawn of humanity. Quite the opposite, for Scripture indicates a progressive devolution unleashed by Adam's sin—devolution from the prelapsarian condition to the postlapsarian reign of death.

Paul on Resurrection and Immortality

Paul's intriguing remarks in 1 Corinthians 15:42–49 shed more light on the question of death and immortality. Here the apostle describes two modes of bodily existence diametrically opposed to each other. The first captures the frailties of life in a "natural" body, life that is perishable, dishonorable, weak, prone to decay and death. At the resurrection, we will receive what Paul calls the "spiritual" body, which will transform our lives into something imperishable, glorious, and powerful (vv. 42–44). It is noteworthy that Paul cites Genesis 2:7 (in 1 Cor. 15:45) in relation to this natural body, *not* Genesis 3 in the context of the fall. This striking allusion to creation implies that before his disobedience Adam had a natural body with all its fragility and vulnerability. Van den Brink seizes on this point as textual vindication of original mortality: "According to Paul, *we have been created* with a body that won't last forever and is vulnerable to weakness and decay."[108] Many recent biblical scholars agree with this interpretation.[109]

---

no. 4 (1998): 10–13. John C. Sanford posits "genetic entropy"—the idea that the human genome degenerates over successive generations—as the cause of the decreasing life spans in Genesis. John C. Sanford, *Genetic Entropy*, 4th ed. (Waterloo, NY: FMS, 2014).

106. As Herbert Leupold asserts, "Even under the curse of sin man's constitution displayed such vitality that it did not at first submit to the ravages of time until after many centuries had passed." Herbert Leupold, *Exposition of Genesis* (Grand Rapids: Zondervan, 1975), 234.

107. Commenting on 1 Cor. 15:56, Thomas Schreiner writes, "In saying that *the sting of death is sin*, the nexus between sin and death, which goes back to Eden, is uncovered." Thomas Schreiner, *1 Corinthians*, Tyndale New Testament Commentaries 7 (Downers Grove, IL: InterVarsity, 2018), 326.

108. Gijsbert van den Brink, *Reformed Theology and Evolutionary Theory* (Grand Rapids: Eerdmans, 2020), 202, emphasis original.

109. For example, see Heinrich August Wilhelm Meyer, *Critical and Exegetical Handbook to the Epistles to the Corinthians*, trans. D. Douglas Bannerman (New York: Funk & Wagnalls, 1890), 381. Jason Maston agrees that "Paul is describing Adam prior to his transgression" (Jason Maston, "Christ or Adam: The Ground for Understanding Humanity," *Journal of Theological Interpretation* 11, no. 2

Here we must tread carefully, for the ground is slippery. As we have noted already, theistic evolutionists and many old-earth creationists who affirm a historical Adam usually think that God created Adam with the natural disposition to age and eventually die.[110] I take this to mean that pre-fall Adam also had a natural disposition to conditions like chronic ischemic heart disease, congestive heart failure, atherosclerosis, cancers of various kinds, osteoarthritis, disability, and dementia.[111] Against this original mortality view, I have argued for original immortality—namely, that Adam and Eve were without any of the corruptions that come with disease, suffering, and death. They had no natural disposition to die. In the prelapsarian state, it was only possible for them to die *if they sinned*; the entrance of sin brought about divine judgment: the human constitution changed from a conditional immortality to the mortality that is now our common lot.

In Pauline eschatology, we can identify four modes of human existence: (1) Adam, pre-fall; (2) Adam and his descendants, post-fall; (3) Jesus incarnate, pre-resurrection; (4) Jesus incarnate, post-resurrection. The first three modes of existence fall under Paul's category of the natural body, while the resurrected Christ—and all those who will be resurrected in union with him—belongs to the final mode of existence, the spiritual body. Prelapsarian Adam was from the dust, perishable, and earthy, possessing a natural (or physical) body (1 Cor. 15:42–49).[112] The ontological structure of Adam's body—Adam as he came fresh from God's hands—was constituted in such a way that he would die physically if he sinned. Thus once Adam sinned, he and all his descendants became prone to death. Although fallen humanity and pre-fall Adam share the same material constitution that is inferior to the spiritual body of the resurrection (vv. 44–46), they also have differences. Fallen humanity is mortal by necessity, whereas pre-fall Adam only experienced death after he sinned. Unlike fallen humanity, diseases

---

[2017]: 281). Gordon Fee thinks that Adam received the natural body "at creation, a body subject to decay and death" (Gordon Fee, *The First Epistle to the Corinthians* [Grands Rapids: Eerdmans, 1987], 789). Even Ben Witherington, who once believed that mortality was triggered by Adam's sin in Gen. 3, now confesses that 1 Cor. 15:44–49 convinced him that "Adam was created mortal and so would naturally die." Ben Witherington, "Craig's Atonement and the Death of Christ—Part Sixteen," *The Bible & Culture*, April 6, 2021, https://www.patheos.com/blogs/bibleandculture/2021/04/06/craigs -atonement-and-the-death-of-christ-part-sixteen/.

110. Van den Brink, "Human Death in Theological Anthropology."

111. This point stands regardless of whether the ancient world had legitimate scientific views of the aging process. Cf. Laura Zucconi, *Ancient Medicine: From Mesopotamia to Rome* (Grand Rapids: Eerdmans, 2019).

112. I take the word "perishable" (translation of *phthora*) to connote mortality in the sense that prelapsarian Adam had the kind of physical body that could theoretically experience death, *not* that he had a natural disposition or tendency toward death (see my various definitions of mortality/immortality above).

like cancer, heart disease, dementia, and so on were foreign to prelapsarian Adam.[113] In his incarnation, the Son of God assumed the same material constitution—natural body—that is found in both unfallen and fallen humanity (John 1:14).[114] Only after his death and resurrection did Jesus the last Adam take on a spiritual body; the glory of the gospel is that Jesus dies as Adamic humanity and is raised as a new spiritual humanity. In doing so, he opened the door for us at the future resurrection to have our natural bodies transformed into spiritual bodies that are imperishable, glorious, and powerful. O felix culpa! As the hymn goes, "In Him the tribes of Adam boast more blessings than their father lost."[115]

In summary, arguing for prelapsarian mortality from 1 Corinthians 15:42–49 betrays a kind of atomistic exegesis that ignores the broader context of Paul's theology. Paul explicitly denies that death existed before the fall or that humans were created mortal. He also contradicts the post-Darwinian interpretation earlier in the same chapter: "For since death came through a man, the resurrection of the dead comes also through a man. For as in Adam all die, so in Christ all will be made alive" (15:21–22 NIV). Sin began with Adam, and death began with Adam's sin (Rom. 5:12–21, esp. v. 12). The causal link between sin and death suffuses Paul's theology with his constant refrain that death follows inexorably from sin (1:32; 6:16, 21, 23; 8:6, 13; 1 Cor. 15:56; Gal. 6:8).[116] Prelapsarian immortality was lost because of Adam's disobedience; now our bodies are mortal by necessity, and we await the resurrection when we will receive glorious, spiritual bodies that cannot die in principle.

Patristic Witness to Original Corruptibility

The church fathers often insisted that Adam and Eve were naturally corruptible and therefore *mortal*. "Corruptibility" is the idea, roughly, that the human body inevitably tends to deteriorate through fatigue, illness, suffering, and ultimately death; beyond that, our bodies are destined to dissolution into nothingness after death.[117] The great eighth-century systematizer of patristic theology, John of Damascus, defines corruptibility as "all the

113. For similar analyses of Paul's "natural" versus "spiritual" body that are consistent with original immortality, see Richard Gaffin, *Resurrection and Redemption: A Study in Paul's Soteriology*, 2nd ed. (Phillipsburg, NJ: Presbyterian and Reformed, 1987), 80–82; and Geerhardus Vos, "The Pauline Doctrine of the Resurrection," *Princeton Theological Review* 27, no. 1 (1929): 1–35.

114. The miraculous circumstances of his birth prevented him from inheriting original sin.

115. The hymn is by Isaac Watts (1674–1748), "Jesus Shall Reign Where'er the Sun."

116. Gaffin, *Resurrection and Redemption*, 81.

117. Jean-Claude Larchet, *The Theology of Illness*, trans. John and Michael Breck (Crestwood, NY: St. Vladimir's Seminary Press, 2002), 18n13.

human sufferings, such as hunger, thirst, weariness, the piercing with nails, death, that is, the separation of soul and body, and so forth. In this sense we say that our Lord's body was subject to corruption. For He voluntarily accepted all these things. But corruption means also the complete resolution of the body into its constituent elements, and its utter disappearance, which is spoken of by many preferably as destruction."[118]

As Athanasius explains, God's Word called humans into being, but their corruptibility returns them to non-being: "As [Adam and Eve] had come into being from non-existence, so also they might accordingly suffer in time the corruption consequent to their non-being."[119] He goes on to say that "man is by nature mortal in that he was created from nothing."[120] Gregory of Nyssa classifies man as a "mortal, passible, shortlived being," the inverse of the everlasting, impassible, and immortal God.[121]

However, those same fathers seemed to contradict themselves by also affirming original immortality. Athanasius, for example, believes that pre-fall Adam was able to "rejoice and converse with God, living an idyllic and truly blessed and immortal life."[122] Gregory pictures Adam as lacking "the elements of passion and mortality essentially and naturally in himself."[123] One can multiply similar witnesses ad nauseam of the fathers seemingly vacillating between two opinions.[124] (John Chrysostom, unlike many of his contemporaries, may have been the rare exception who consistently affirmed the original immortality of Adam.)[125]

118. John of Damascus, *Exposition of the Orthodox Faith* 28, in *The Nicene and Post-Nicene Fathers*, 2nd series, vol. 9, ed. Philip Schaff and Henry Wace, trans. S. D. F. Salmond (New York: Charles Scribner's Sons, 1908), 72.

119. Athanasius, *De Incarnatione* 4, in *Contra Gentes and De Incarnatione*, ed. and trans. Robert W. Thomson (Oxford: Clarendon, 1971), 143.

120. Athanasius, *De Incarnatione* 4 (*Contra Gentes and De Incarnatione*, 145). He writes in one of his letters that "it belongs to us all to be mortal, corruptible, capable of change, originated from nothing." Athanasius, *Ad Serapion* 2.3, in *The Letters of Saint Athanasius concerning the Holy Spirit*, trans. C. R. B. Shapland (London: Epworth, 1951), 155.

121. Gregory of Nyssa, *De Hominis Opificio* 16.4, in *Nicene and Post-Nicene Fathers*, 2nd series, vol. 5, ed. Philip Schaff and Henry Wace (New York: Charles Scribner's Sons, 1917), 404.

122. Athanasius, *Contra Gentes* 2 (*Contra Gentes and De Incarnatione*, 7).

123. Gregory of Nyssa, *On Virginity* 12, in *Saint Gregory of Nyssa: Ascetical Works*, trans. Virginia Woods Callahan (Washington, DC: Catholic University of America Press, 1967), 42. Gregory elsewhere says that Adam had "immortality in itself, so that by [this] inherent power one might both recognize the transcendent and desire the divine eternality." Gregory of Nyssa, *Catechetical Discourse* 5.6, in *Catechetical Discourse: A Handbook for Catechists*, trans. Ignatius Green (Yonkers, NY: St. Vladimir's Seminary Press, 2019), 74.

124. For helpful documentation, see Larchet, *Theology of Illness*, 17–26. On Irenaeus's view that humans are corruptible from creation, see M. C. Steenberg, *Irenaeus on Creation: The Cosmic Christ and the Saga of Redemption* (Leiden: Brill, 2008), 120–27.

125. E.g., Chrysostom assessed pre-fall Adam and Eve as naked, "incorruptible and immortal" (John Chrysostom, *Homilies on Genesis* 15.14, in *Homilies on Genesis 1–17*, trans. Robert Hill

These seemingly conflicting judgments about Adam reflect two distinct streams of thought that are in tension within the writings of the fathers—modern patristics scholars disagree on whether they are compatible, and if not, which is dominant.[126] In the first interpretation, the biblical story of salvation happens in two acts of *creation* and *elevation*. God created Adam imperfect and mutable—in the state of nature—with sin and mortality latent in the human condition. Redemption is the process by which God perfects man, elevating humanity to a supernatural mode of existence by which humanity gains sinlessness and immortality. In the second interpretation, the redemption story unfolds over three acts of *creation, fall,* and *restoration*. According to this three-act scheme, God creates humanity in a condition of immortality (creation), but the fall destroys that first condition and condemns the human race to sin and death (fall); God is now restoring his people "to the original condition of perfect fellowship" (restoration).[127] Both strands are present (and in tension with each other) in the writings of early theologians like Irenaeus and Origen, but most church fathers adopt one or the other scheme of salvation.

Donald Fairbairn argues that the creation-fall-restoration model was the majority view of the church, represented by the likes of Athanasius and Cyril of Alexandria, while creation-elevation was a minority report, represented by Theodore of Mopsuestia, Nestorius, and others. While I agree with Fairbairn's conclusions and have integrated them into my evaluation of patristic anthropology, opposing views among patristics scholars identify the creation-elevation scheme as the mainstream opinion. They adopt this latter approach, one suspects, because it resonates with evolutionary ideas of human progress; we have encountered this same dynamic repeatedly in this book among recent science-theology writers (and others like John Hick) who almost always prefer Irenaeus over their bête noire Augustine. Robert Brown, for example, in his study of Irenaeus, recognizes the two different streams within the church father

---

[Washington, DC: Catholic University of America Press, 1986], 203). Larchet interprets a comment by Chrysostom in Homily 17 as endorsing the intrinsic mortality of prelapsarian Adam (Larchet, *Theology of Illness*, 20n28). However, the translation that Larchet relies on ("clothed in a mortal body") reads too much into the original Greek. Instead, Chrysostom's view of pre-fall Eve is that despite her being corporeal or embodied—*not* mortal—God meant for her to lead a life free from pain or distress. A more accurate translation appears in *Homilies on Genesis* 17.30 (Chrysostom, *Homilies on Genesis 1–17*, 238): "My intention had been, [God] is saying, for you to have a life free of trouble and distress, rid of all pain and grief, filled with every pleasure and with no sense of bodily needs [*ton somatikon somaton*] despite your bodily condition [*soma perikeimenen*]."

126. I am indebted to the analysis in Donald Fairbairn, *Grace and Christology in the Early Church* (Oxford: Oxford University Press, 2003).

127. Fairbairn, *Grace and Christology*, 18.

and then, tellingly, gives his rationale for favoring the creation-elevation scheme:

> Interpreters of [Irenaeus's] Recapitulation (*anakephalaiosis*) doctrine routinely note that Christ's work brings two different benefits to the human race. First, humanity is restored to its status before the fall of Adam, thereby abolishing sin and its effects. Second, it is elevated or perfected to a higher form of being than that of the originally created human nature. Most commentators hold that Irenaeus intended his theological system to be structured around one of these themes as the central axis. Thus they relegate the other theme to a minor role. . . . A Christianity without a Pauline doctrine of Adam's original sin might have left room in the tradition for a full-scale development of Irenaeus' elevation theme as the main structure of the *Heilsgeschichte.* . . . *Irenaeus' elevation theme provides an interesting and worthy alternative to the prevailing Christian orthodoxy, but not at the price of embracing Pelagianism or any other major heresy. The doctrine of an original imperfection of human nature and its corollary implications also seems less incompatible with modern biological and anthropological knowledge about the human species, than does the traditional Adam-Christ anti-typology.*[128]

Emphasizing the same theme of elevation, Theodore believes that prelapsarian humanity was naturally prone to sin. The impulse to sin arises from human mutability, he argues, "so that by acquiring immutability we [become] free from sin."[129] By this logic, the first sin was inevitable because God himself created pre-fall Adam and Eve with an intrinsic corruptibility. But the God who reveals himself in Scripture is the pure and holy one who cannot be tempted by evil (James 1:13). Divine holiness implies that God is morally pure, ethically perfect, without stain or blemish (Lev. 11:44–45)—*nothing* God directly creates can be sinful or innately disposed to sin from the beginning. Since the creation-elevation scheme characterizes the prelapsarian situation as one of imperfection that will be resolved by redemption, sinfulness tends to be seen as already latent within the pre-fall state.

This notion that Adam is necessarily corruptible, mutable, and liable to dissipate to nothingness seems to be shaped as much by Platonic metaphysics as by Genesis.[130] Plato distinguishes reality into two principles of "Being"

128. Robert Brown, "On the Necessary Imperfection of Creation: Irenaeus' *Adversus Haereses* iv, 38," *Scottish Journal of Theology* 28, no. 1 (1975): 17, 24, 25, my emphasis.

129. Theodore of Mopsuestia, *Homiliae Catecheticae* 5.11, cited in Fairbairn, *Grace and Christology*, 32.

130. J. N. D. Kelly, *Early Christian Doctrines*, 5th ed. (New York: HarperCollins, 1978), 346. Some science-religion scholars want to retrieve this patristic anthropology as a way to reconcile evolutionary theory and Christian theology. For one such attempt focusing on Augustine, see Stanley P.

and "Becoming." The world of Becoming describes the physical material of nature, which is always in flux and subject to change. As Richard Norris maintains, "Nothing in it is permanent or stable. Consequently, nothing in it quite succeeds in *being* what it is, for the good reason that it is always in process of *becoming* something else."[131] The visible world is only a shadow of Being, the transcendent realm that Plato calls "Ideas" or "Forms." The unchangeable Truth lies beyond time and space in the invisible realm of the spiritual, intelligible, and eternal. This Platonic metaphysics "provided a language naturally adapted to express the majesty, the mysteriousness, and the absoluteness of the biblical Lord."[132] Thus, many early Christians embraced this distinction between Being and Becoming, identifying God as Being (or the Source of Being); all else was Becoming.

Despite being less influenced by Plato than by Scripture, the Greek fathers held a similar distinction between being and nonbeing. They affirmed the contingency of creaturely being, since God created heaven and earth out of nothing. Creation is inherently unstable, mutable, and corruptible, always tending toward nonexistence (nonbeing). They believed that this ontological instability applied to every aspect of creation—including humanity—even prior to the fall and was rooted in divine omnipotence expressed in creation from nothing.[133] This affirmation of creation from nothing seems to have led to the creation-elevation scheme in Theodore, Origen, and others. However, the two theological motifs are not inherently connected.

The mainstream patristic scheme of creation-fall-restoration clarifies some of the confusion surrounding what the church fathers believed about Adam before the fall. On the one hand, when they wrote that Adam was immortal and incorruptible in Eden, one might be tempted to interpret such statements in light of the Platonic idea that the human soul is *naturally* immortal and incorruptible. On the other hand, one might take their affirmations of Adam's mortality and corruptibility to mean that human beings would have died even if there had been no fall. However, not only are these two interpretations in awkward tension with each other, but they are also mistaken. Most church fathers were in fact theologically consistent: they held that Adam was corruptible by nature because he had been created from

Rosenberg, "Can Nature Be 'Red in Tooth and Claw' in the Thought of Augustine?," in *Finding Ourselves after Darwin: Conversations on the Image of God, Original Sin, and the Problem of Evil*, ed. Stanley P. Rosenberg (Grand Rapids: Baker Academic, 2018), 226–43.

131. Richard Norris, *God and World in Early Christian Theology: A Study in Justin Martyr, Irenaeus, Tertullian, and Origen* (London: Adam & Charles Black, 1966), 13.

132. Norris, *God and World*, 134.

133. See Joseph Torchia, *Creation and Contingency in Early Patristic Thought* (Lanham, MD: Lexington Books, 2019).

nothing, but since he had been created by God's special grace, he would be incorruptible so long as he remained in the grace he received at creation. In their view, God created Adam in a state of incorruptibility and immortality by filling him with his Spirit (Gen. 2:7). As J. N. D. Kelly remarks, "God showed Himself more generous to man than to the rest of creation. He enabled him to participate in His Word, thereby making him in His image. This communion with the Word bestowed supernatural knowledge upon him, made him rational, and gave him incorruption and immortality."[134] Adam in paradise was immortal while being sustained by God's supernatural grace.

The church fathers were right to emphasize the gratuity of creation. Human existence is a gift of God's grace. The doctrine of *creatio ex nihilo* led them to infer a latent corruptibility even in the prelapsarian state; just the same, Adam and Eve were, in fact, incorruptible because of divine grace. However, unlike the majority position, advocates of creation-elevation had no role for special grace at creation. As a result, the absence of special grace rendered sin inevitable in Eden, which in turn implicated God in the first sin. The logic of this minority interpretation left open the possibility that in the new heavens and new earth the fall could always happen again since even glorified saints are metaphysically dependent on God (though no church father actually drew that inference).[135] Happily, Scripture rules out this nightmare scenario since Adam and Eve were one of the wonders of Eden and part of the original goodness of creation, without any intrinsic deficiency or corruption. Their incorruptibility and immortality were concreated and not marred by any intrinsic defect within the creaturely order, which is why their subsequent fall remains a uniquely mysterious calamity.

Theodicy and the Shape of the Gospel

The doctrine of the fall serves notice that sin is not the core of what it means to be human. Men and women were not always sinners. Adam's fall, ironically, promises the hope of redemption, that "human beings can again become sinless without ceasing to be human."[136] But then how could sin possibly exist in a universe made by the triune God?

134. Kelly, *Early Christian Doctrines*, 346.

135. The tensions in the creation-elevation patristic anthropology reappear in the medieval concept of the *donum superadditum*, which the Reformed orthodox rejected in favor of the *donum concreatum*. On these two concepts, see Richard Muller, *Dictionary of Latin and Greek Theological Terms: Drawn Principally from Protestant Scholastic Theology*, 2nd ed. (Grand Rapids: Baker Academic, 2017), 97–99. See my discussion in chap. 7.

136. Anthony Hoekema, *Created in God's Image* (Grand Rapids: Eerdmans, 1986), 117.

Against Monism and Dualism

This puzzle of the origin of sin (or evil) has three possible solutions, two of which are heterodox: monism and dualism.[137] Monism traces the origin of evil and good to God or ultimate reality. Good and evil are swallowed up by the greater whole.[138] For example, Jakob Böhme (1575–1624), the German Lutheran mystic, believed that good and evil are opposing forces dueling within the very being of God. "God is all," he wrote. "He is darkness and light, love and wrath, fire and light." All the evil that afflicts this broken world springs from God himself, "for all things have their first beginning from the outflow of the divine will, be it evil or good, love or sorrow."[139] Baruch Spinoza, a seventeenth-century Jewish philosopher, defended a hard-boiled monism where everything, including evil, was one aspect of divine reality: "In nature there is nothing contingent, but all things have been determined from the necessity of the divine nature to exist and produce an effect in a certain way."[140] Evil is inseparable from the nature of God.

In the case of dualism, light and darkness are eternal forces in conflict with each other. Good and evil cannot be united in any way. Zoroastrianism is an ancient dualistic Persian religion, founded by Zoroaster around the late sixth century BCE.[141] The righteous god, Ahura Mazda, demands allegiance from humanity and fights against Angra Mainyu, the evil one who leads people astray. This dualism is an eternal battle between the god of darkness and the god of light.[142] Early Christians encountered dualism in Gnostic religions that privileged spirit over matter and disparaged physical embodiment as inherently evil. One example was a third-century religion

---

137. John Hick, *Evil and the God of Love*, rev. ed. (San Francisco: Harper & Row, 1978); Henri Blocher, *Evil and the Cross: An Analytical Look at the Problem of Pain* (Grand Rapids: Kregel, 1994). I have drawn from both works.

138. Monism can also refer to views of evil as unreal or fantasy. Certain forms of Hinduism or Buddhism take this line, as does Mary Baker Eddy's sectarian Christian Science. I shall ignore such varieties of monism.

139. Jakob Böhme, *The Way to Christ* (New York: London: SPCK, 1978), 199, cited in Grace Jantzen, "Action and Embodiment," in *Creation and Humanity: The Sources of Christian Theology*, ed. Ian McFarland (Louisville: Westminster John Knox, 2009), 418.

140. Baruch Spinoza, *The Ethics*, 1.29, in Benedict De Spinoza, *Ethics*, ed. and trans. Edwin Curley (New York: Penguin Books, 1996), 20.

141. Zoroaster's dates are contested by scholars of Zoroastrianism and are thought to range from roughly 1500 to 550 BCE. For the debate, see Gherardo Gnoli, *Zoroaster in History* (New York: Bibliotheca Persica, 2000).

142. Winfried Corduan explains, however, that Zoroaster's own teachings were likely *monotheistic*; Ahura Mazda is the supreme creator alone worthy of worship, whereas Angra Mainyu is an evil spirit, a creature derived from God. See Corduan *Neighboring Faiths: A Christian Introduction to World Religions*, 2nd ed. (Downers Grove, IL: IVP Academic, 2012), 189–90.

called Manichaeism, which was founded by Mani (216–77 CE) and had a marked influence on Augustine prior to his conversion. The Manichaeans carved up reality into two coeternal principles: God and matter, light and darkness, good and evil.[143] They taught that the powers of darkness created human beings as light (souls) trapped within matter (bodies), and salvation involves attaining the knowledge (*gnōsis*) that will liberate our souls from the evil of embodiment.

Christianity repudiates both monism and dualism. Believers worship the God of Abraham, Isaac, and Jacob, the triune God of bountiful goodness who is resplendent in holiness without any trace of evil. Clearly monism is unthinkable. This same God created and governs the whole cosmos teeming with all his creatures. Nothing exists independently of God, for every other reality derives its being from him. Any other so-called gods or eternal principles are the stuff of myth or demonic deceit. In the world of Scripture, dualism is as unthinkable as monism.

The only option left is a fall *in history*. Evil is something foreign and contingent that has defaced God's good creation.[144] This third solution is the genius of the Judeo-Christian tradition that evades the Scylla of monism and the Charybdis of dualism. Christian thinker C. S. Lewis understands this with great clarity: "[The fall] exists to guard against two sub-Christian theories of the origin of evil—Monism . . . and Dualism."[145] Henri Blocher hails the fall as an enduring insight of Christianity. "The myths," he says, "are forced to locate evil in God or else to opt for a dualism in which evil is equal with God, in an implicit or explicit polytheism."[146] In his 1924 Bampton Lectures, N. P. Williams concludes similarly: "It is impossible to lift the Fall out of the time-series without falling either into [dualistic] Manicheism or unmoral monism. . . . 'The Fall,' whatever else it may have been, *must have been* an event in time."[147]

A historical fall implies that sin originated with the creature, not the creator. Williams, however, was convinced that evolution falsifies a fall

143. Paul Mirecki and Jason DeBuhn, eds., *The Light and the Darkness: Studies in Manichaeism and Its World* (Boston: Brill, 2001).

144. In Paul Ricoeur's estimation, having evil originate in a historical fall "prevents it from being regarded as primordial evil. Sin may be 'older' than sins, but innocence is still 'older'" (Paul Ricoeur, *The Symbolism of Evil* [Boston: Beacon, 1967], 251). But Ricoeur interprets the fall mythically and denies that the events of Gen. 3 occurred in a specific place at some point in human history (Ricoeur, *Symbolism of Evil*, 235).

145. C. S. Lewis, *The Problem of Pain* (New York: Macmillan, 1962), 69.

146. Blocher, *In the Beginning*, 167.

147. Williams, *Ideas of the Fall*, xxxiii, my emphasis. See also T. A. Noble, "The Spirit World: A Theological Approach," in *The Unseen World: Christian Reflections on Angels, Demons, and the Heavenly Realm*, ed. Anthony N. S. Lane (Grand Rapids: Baker, 1996), 205.

in human history; he therefore theorized that humanity preexisted as disembodied souls who sinned against God and were then sentenced to embodiment on earth (i.e., they "fell").[148] The implications for soteriology are strange indeed as it would mean that our Savior should have become a disembodied soul in order to atone for sin. However, this speculative theory denies the clear witness of Hebrews 2:14 that the Messiah had to become flesh and blood like us. With its sheer desperation and implausibility, Williams's theory of a pretemporal fall refutes itself.

The Christian appeal to a historical fall to avoid monism and dualism is a kind of *theodicy*, an attempt to justify God from any charge of evil. Yet some theologians criticize the theodicy tradition as unproductive and even harmful to Christianity. Even Christian theodicies are judged as oppressive Enlightenment projects that are indifferent to the lived experiences of suffering people.[149] Instead of "explaining" evil and suffering, John Swinton writes that "evil and suffering can be *resisted* and *transformed* by the Christian community and in so doing, can enable Christians to live faithfully in the midst of unanswered questions as they await God's redemption of the whole creation."[150] I resonate with these concerns and the call for a practical theodicy that is tender, Christ-centered, and pastoral. God is displeased when we treat evil as merely an intellectual puzzle and overlook the suffering of real people (James 1:27). But forcing a choice between "intellectual" and "practical" approaches creates a false dichotomy.

In his review of Kenneth Surin's *Theology and the Problem of Evil*, Terrence Tilley comments, "Why write as if philosophers who professionally defend the coherence of Christian beliefs do not religiously seek to alleviate suffering? From the valid insight that one's material/ideal interests structure one's writings, [Surin] seemingly infers that what one writes reveals all

---

148. Williams, *Ideas of the Fall*, 489–530. For a similar pretemporal fall, see Julius Müller, *The Christian Doctrine of Sin*, trans. William Urwick, 5th ed., 2 vols. (Edinburgh: T&T Clark, 1868), esp. 2:357–401; Peter Green, *The Problem of Evil* (London: Longmans, Green, 1920), 108–52. In the third century, Origen argues that our lives on earth are the divine penalty for the fall of our preexistent souls (e.g., see *De Principii* I.4), a view condemned by the early church. For a different reading of Origen, see Marguerite Harl, "La Préexistence des Âmes dans l'Œuvre d'Origène," in *Origeniana Quarta*, ed. Lothar Lies (Innsbruck: Tyrolia, 1987), 238–58; Peter Bouteneff, *Beginnings: Ancient Christian Readings of the Biblical Creation Narratives* (Grand Rapids: Baker Academic, 2008), 108.

149. Kenneth Surin, *Theology and the Problem of Evil* (Oxford: Blackwell, 1986). Along similar lines, see Wendy Farley, *Tragic Vision and Divine Compassion: A Contemporary Theodicy* (Louisville: Westminster John Knox, 1990); Andrew Gleeson, *A Frightening Love: Recasting the Problem of Evil* (Basingstoke, UK: Palgrave Macmillan, 2012); and Elizabeth Johnson, *Ask the Beasts: Darwin and the God of Love* (London: Bloomsbury, 2014), 187.

150. John Swinton, *Raging with Compassion: Pastoral Responses to the Problem of Evil* (Grand Rapids: Eerdmans, 2007), 4.

one's material and ideal interests. But as people do more than write, inferring that theoreticians ignore suffering has an inadequate basis."[151] Quite right. The best theoretical and practical theodicies are complementary, not oppositional.

Something Like a Theodicy

In a stimulating essay titled "Theodicy and the Historical Adam," Patrick Franklin raises a different set of objections to the fall theodicy that I have been defending, and his arguments deserve attention.[152] Franklin reassures us that nonhistorical, non-lapsarian readings of Genesis 1–3 are wholly consistent with classical, orthodox, evangelical Christianity. Such readings emphasize the primary *theological* focus of the narrative, which most Christians agree with, without getting stymied by disputed questions around historicity. Against what he thinks is an Augustinian fixation on original sin and notions of universal corruption and guilt—doctrines widely rejected within Old Testament scholarship—Franklin argues that Scripture is largely mum on the ultimate origin of sin. The emphasis of the Bible lies in the fact *that* we are sinners needing redemption, not *how* we became sinful.

Franklin's main thesis is that the fall is *ineffective* as a theodicy. The irony, he says, is that belief in a historical fall doesn't even resolve the deepest riddle surrounding God and evil. Christians believe that after the resurrection we will be unable to sin. For the first time ever, we will know true freedom like that of the holy angels in heaven. But that raises a haunting question: *Why did God not create us sinless from the very beginning?* "Why did God not begin this way and so avoid all the sin, evil, pain, suffering, sickness, corruption, violence, destruction, and all other forms of ungodliness that human beings have caused and experienced?"[153] Theologians of course have pondered this question for millennia.[154] Franklin's issue, in particular, is that whether Adam fell or not, the problem remains with us.

Drawing on the seventeenth-century Reformed theological tradition, Donald Macleod argues that Adam committed the first sin in part because God withheld his efficacious or restraining grace. Macleod clarifies the

---

151. Terrence Tilley, review of *Theology and the Problem of Evil*, by Kenneth Surin, *Theological Studies* 48, no. 4 (1987): 748.

152. Patrick Franklin, "Theodicy and the Historical Adam: Questioning a Central Assumption Motivating Historicist Readings," *Perspectives on Science and Christian Faith* 74, no. 1 (2022): 39–53.

153. Franklin, "Theodicy and the Historical Adam," 42.

154. Classic responses include the free will defense and the supralapsarian "felix culpa" theodicy. For recent discussion, see W. Paul Franks, ed., *Explaining Evil: Four Views* (London: Bloomsbury Academic, 2019).

nature of this withheld grace by quoting the English Puritan William Ames: "The strengthening and confirming grace by which the act of sinning might have been hindered and the act of obedience effected was not given to him— and that by the certain wise and just counsel of God."[155] Troubled by Ames's explanation, Franklin responds: "God withholds the one thing necessary for them to succeed in arguably the most important aspect of being human, theologically speaking: the efficacious or restraining grace required to resist sin and to fully acknowledge and submit to the Creator God as Lord."[156] Why would a good God ever do such a thing? Franklin acknowledges there may be good reasons for God to withhold his grace, reasons that are beyond our ken, but the fall itself as a theodicy cannot resolve the issue.

Franklin's critique of Ames reminds us that the Reformed tradition some- times trips up when trying to explain what led Adam to sin in the first place.[157] But the first sin cannot be "explained" because it is ultimately inex- plicable. G. C. Berkouwer rejects the traditional language of a "probationary command" on precisely those grounds, for presupposing that in Genesis 2 God gave Adam the freedom to obey *or disobey*. But since true creaturely freedom—like the freedom of saints in glory or angels in heaven—would never choose disobedience, Berkouwer judges that tracing the origin of sin to human freedom merely rationalizes the fall.[158]

Building on Berkouwer, Blocher agrees that the concept of a probation- ary command "attenuates the scandalous originality of the fall, which is radically *other* than the good creation of God."[159] It might seem logical that the fall was the result of Adam and Eve abusing their God-given freedom, but Blocher asks, "Is it legitimate to apply *logic* here? It is legitimate to infer

155. Donald Macleod, "Original Sin in Reformed Theology," in *Adam, the Fall, and Original Sin: Theological, Biblical, and Scientific Perspectives*, ed. Hans Madueme and Michael Reeves (Grand Rapids: Baker Academic, 2014), 136. The Ames quote is from William Ames, *The Marrow of Theology*, trans. John Dykstra Eusden (Grand Rapids: Baker, 1997), 114 (originally published 1623).

156. Franklin, "Theodicy and the Historical Adam," 43.

157. Ames's suggestion that Adam sinned because God withheld his strengthening and confirm- ing grace is incautious. In Ames's defense, however, Franklin overstates his critique. In the original essay from which Franklin is quoting—indeed, in the same paragraph—Ames suggests that when Adam was created, "[he] had received in his creation sufficient grace to enable him to have remained obedient, had he chosen, and that grace was not taken from him *before he sinned*" (Macleod, "Original Sin in Reformed Theology," 114, my emphasis). Ames and other Reformed scholastics affirm that prelapsarian Adam had everything he needed to obey God perfectly. Indeed, sin was only external to pre-fall Adam, who had no sinful inclinations at all. That needs to be factored in when assessing Ames's further comment about a "strengthening and confirming grace"—in my judgment, it's an ill-judged attempt at explaining why Adam sinned despite his original righteousness. But Franklin misrepresents Ames's overall position by quoting this line without the broader context.

158. G. C. Berkouwer, *Man: The Image of God* (Grand Rapids: Eerdmans, 1962), 332–35.

159. Blocher, *In the Beginning*, 134.

A (created possibility) from B (actuality); but evil is an alien discontinuity."
He continues: "Unthinkingly applying the logic of inference to 'evil B' . . .
amounts to *surreptitiously* denying the otherness of evil by 'naturalizing'
it and giving it some kind of footing within the order of being."[160] Blocher
concludes that evil was not "possible" for Adam in Eden, but it was *"not
impossible."*[161]

These are subtle distinctions! Scripture, however, is plain in Genesis 2
and 3 that it was indeed possible for Adam to sin (after all, he did sin!). In his
state of innocence, Adam had the genuine ability not to sin (*posse non peccare*), and he was also somehow able to sin; thus we can affirm that Adam's
will and righteousness were "mutable" without denying the ultimate mystery of his fall.[162] Nevertheless, I accept Berkouwer's and Blocher's counsel
against naturalizing sin or reducing it to something essential to original
humanity. Even the Reformed colossus Francis Turretin stumbles when he
writes about Adam: *"Nor ought it to seem strange* that man (created capable
of falling and mutable) changed and fell, no more than that a beginning of
motion takes place in one perfectly at rest. For where there is a power to
change, the transition from power to act *is easy."*[163] I think not. Since Adam
was originally holy and righteous, it *should* seem strange, and it could not
possibly have been "easy" for him to sin. Turretin's logic strips away all the
mystery and scandal of the fall.

In the end, we simply do not know why Adam and Eve sinned (nor can
any other religious system adequately explain why evil exists). Certainly,
Eve ate from the forbidden tree because the serpent deceived her (Gen.
3:1–6), but *why* did she trust the serpent rather than God, and *why* did Adam
succumb as well? The first iniquity is shrouded in mystery, the impenetrable
obscurity of darkness, and the illogicality of evil.[164]

In response to an essay I co-wrote with Michael Reeves, Franklin accuses us of inconsistency because we treat Adam's fall as *mystery* but then
critique others who read "the Genesis 2–3 narrative as theologically and
existentially informative and authoritative though not explanatory in a

---

160. Blocher, "Theology of the Fall," 164.

161. Blocher, "Theology of the Fall," 164.

162. Systematic theologies commonly speak of Adam's prelapsarian will as "mutable." I am using
the term not to imply any Platonic notions of corruptibility or the like but simply to indicate that
when Adam received the commandment his will was sinless but not indefectible—that is, he could
persevere without ever sinning, or (mysteriously) he could do the unthinkable (i.e., sin).

163. Turretin, *Institutes of Elenctic Theology*, 1:607, my emphasis.

164. I am alluding to a line in Michael Reeves and Hans Madueme, "Threads in a Seamless Garment: Original Sin in Systematic Theology," in Madueme and Reeves, *Adam, the Fall, and Original
Sin*, 219.

literal, historical, or causal kind of way. The line [Reeves and I] draw to constrain the degree of allowable mystery is arbitrary."[165] In other words, if Reeves and I can explain the fall by appealing to mystery, then Franklin can do the same for the theological meaning of the Genesis 2–3 narrative without regarding it as literal or historical. Let me give two reasons why Franklin's criticism is misplaced.

First, he thinks non-lapsarian theology can make its own appeal to mystery: "A nonhistorical reading can still interpret the narrative as affirming that sin and evil are realities that emerge in human history (God does not create or initiate them), while admitting that the details remain mysterious."[166] However, given that Franklin denies a historical fall and accepts the standard evolutionary narrative, I do not see how his proposal can escape cosmological monism. In his account, God *does* create or initiate sin and evil in human history—appealing to "mystery" is trying to carry coals to Newcastle.

Second, the line Reeves and I draw is not "arbitrary" but guided by the Protestant Scripture principle. We locate the mystery at the point of Adam's sin precisely because we have no further revelation from Scripture and thus—due to our finitude and fallenness—are unable to discern *why* our first parents sinned. Adam's fall functions as a theodicy in a minimal sense only if sin entered the world through the free (i.e., unconstrained) disobedience of the creature, not the creator. The fall succeeds as a theodicy even if the first sin of Adam or of Lucifer before him is irreducibly mysterious. Furthermore, Paul reads Genesis 2–3 in a "literal" and "historical" way, and so should we. Franklin claims instead that "an evangelical theology of inspiration does not require us to believe everything that Paul believed, only what Paul intended to teach us."[167] Technically that is true, but then he approvingly cites Denis Lamoureux's advice that Christians should ignore the Bible's outdated cosmology and biology while affirming its theology; he can thus justify the nonhistoricity of Adam on the grounds that Paul did not "teach" the doctrine. Franklin's argument functions evidentially rather than dogmatically; it stands in the long tradition of Galileo and—by limiting the scope of what is epistemically binding in Scripture to areas outside the ambit of science—is a functional rejection of the authority of Scripture.

165. Franklin, "Theodicy and the Historical Adam," 43.
166. Franklin, "Theodicy and the Historical Adam," 48.
167. Franklin, "Theodicy and the Historical Adam," 53n52. See my discussion in chap. 4 under the heading "Apostolic Authority and the New Testament Dogmatic Rule," where I argue that the *assumptions* of the biblical authors can be just as important as their assertions.

The Shape of Redemption

The very shape of redemption hangs on whether there was a fall in our collective past. The purpose of the Son's incarnation and atonement was to rescue humanity from sin. Christ came into the world to save sinners (1 Tim. 1:15). In this "infralapsarian"[168] telling of the story, Christ atoning for Adam's sin gives a checkmark shape to redemptive history, "with the ending level of the narrative mounting far higher than the beginning point."[169] The fall in Genesis 3 ruins the shalom of Genesis 1–2 and its effects reverberate through history (Gen. 3 to Rev. 20); in Revelation 21–22, the new Jerusalem replaces the garden of Eden, and the new heaven and new earth are joined together forever—and the ending is far better than the beginning.[170] By contrast, Franklin argues that the incarnation and our union with Christ were always God's original plan for creation—the incarnation does not require the fall of Adam.[171] Franklin's "incarnation anyway" scenario moves like a forward slash from creation to consummation. Sin and redemption are "intervening acts" that are marginal to the primary plotline from creation to new creation. According to Franklin, the benefit in reshaping the plotline this way is that "human *sin/fallenness does not drive the logic of eschatological consummation*; creation does (along with incarnation, the divine assumption of humanity)."[172]

Franklin's argument coincides with other non-lapsarian evolutionary accounts that undo the checkmark shape of the gospel story.[173] In narrating the incarnation as the central purpose of creation, a "supralapsarian" Christology becomes an attractive way to tie the story together. The plot shifts from creation-fall-redemption-consummation (infralapsarian) to creation-incarnation-new creation (supralapsarian). This supralapsarian theology allows some theistic evolutionists to decouple the atonement from the fall:

168. I am using the terms "infralapsarianism" and "supralapsarianism" more loosely than their standard definitions in Reformed decretal theology. On the latter, see Bavinck, *Reformed Dogmatics*, 2:361–66.

169. Edith Humphrey, *And I Turned to See the Voice: The Rhetoric of Vision in the New Testament* (Grand Rapids: Baker Academic, 2007), 101.

170. Scholars often make the same point by appealing to the "U-shape" of the gospel story. See Northrop Frye, *The Great Code: The Bible and Literature* (New York: Harcourt Brace Jovanovich, 1982), 169; Cole, *Against the Darkness*, 83. However, the image of a checkmark is more accurate to the biblical story than the symmetry of the U-shape.

171. Franklin, "Theodicy and the Historical Adam," 45.

172. Franklin, "Theodicy and the Historical Adam," 47, emphasis original.

173. Although it is not my focus here, some have criticized the U-shape motif (and, by implication, the checkmark motif) for reasons unrelated to evolutionary theory. E.g., see Farley, *Tragic Vision*, 12–13; Paul Fiddes, *Freedom and Limit: A Dialogue between Literature and Christian Doctrine* (London: Macmillan, 1991), 47–62.

voilà, they bypass Adam's fall entirely. Thus, John Schneider replaces the paradise lost/regained metanarrative with a supralapsarian substitute: "God deliberately forging a world via the triumph over conditions of alienation and mortality for all creatures and things—a story of Christus Victor."[174] Similarly, Ron Cole-Turner writes: "God prepares the whole creation for the Incarnation by the emergence of life, mind, and consciousness, which (at least on earth) reaches its highest point in the human lineage."[175] Evolution with all its pain, suffering, and death is the providential mechanism God uses to prepare creation for the incarnation of his Son, who will usher us into the new creation.

The evolutionary supralapsarian framework is not limited to Protestants but has been taken up by Catholic and Eastern Orthodox theologians. As one Orthodox theologian explains, "Abandonment of the Fall does . . . infirm one line of reflection on the Incarnation: that the purpose of the Incarnation was to redeem 'fallen humanity' from its initial transgression of divine ordinance and to restore it to its initial perfect state of union with God in Paradise. The Incarnation is not oriented toward 'restoration' of a lost state of moral innocence, but rather to eschatology, to the full achievement of the Kingdom of God, the purpose of all creation: union with God."[176]

It is indeed a fascinating question whether Christ would have become incarnate had Adam not fallen, an issue that was debated in church history, especially among medieval theologians and into the early modern period.[177] Scripture does not tell us what would have happened had Adam not sinned since the whole focus of the biblical story is on what God has done for us in light of Adam's sin. However, we know that even in paradise Adam was an unfinished project; while he was able to sin and not sin (*posse peccare et posse non peccare*) and able to die and not die (*posse mori et posse non mori*), there remained the possibility outlined by Paul in 1 Corinthians

174. John R. Schneider, "The Fall of 'Augustinian Adam': Original Fragility and Supralapsarian Purpose," *Zygon* 47 (2012): 967. See also Schneider's "Recent Genetic Science and Christian Theology on Human Origins: An 'Aesthetic Supralapsarianism,'" *Perspectives on Science and Christian Faith* 62, no. 3 (2010): 196–212. In both essays, he invokes Irenaeus as an ancient precursor to his position. On the problems with this move, see n. 30 above.

175. Ronald Cole-Turner, "New Perspectives on Human Origins: Three Challenges for Christian Theology," *Theology and Science* 18, no. 4 (2020): 533.

176. Paul Ladouceur, "Evolution and Genesis 2–3: The Decline and Fall of Adam and Eve," *St. Vladimir's Theological Quarterly* 57, no. 1 (2013): 176. On the Roman Catholic side, see Johnson, *Ask the Beasts*, 222–26.

177. On the medieval debate, see Justus Hunter, *If Adam Had Not Sinned: The Reason for the Incarnation from Anselm to Scotus* (Washington, DC: Catholic University of America Press, 2020); for the modern resurgence of "incarnation anyway" Christology, see Edwin Chr. Van Driel, *Incarnation Anyway: Arguments for Supralapsarian Christology* (Oxford: Oxford University Press, 2008).

15:42–49 of an even greater perfection, of no longer being able to sin or die (*non posse peccare et non posse mori*). Thus, we can cautiously speculate that if Adam had persevered in the probationary period, God would have moved Adam from one degree of glory to a higher degree of glory (2 Cor. 3:18). At some point, God would likely have transformed his natural body into a spiritual body with an ontological structure designed for eternal life (*non posse mori*), the same spiritual body that all believers will have at the resurrection.

While it is true that the logic of 1 Corinthians 15:42–49 ties the spiritual body directly to Christ as the second federal head, that is because sin has in fact become a reality. As soon as Adam sinned, glorification was impossible *apart from* Christ's death and resurrection—yet the apostles never address what would have happened if Adam had remained upright. Like many past theologians, I do not think Scripture forbids such speculation (as long as we recognize it as such). For example, speaking about our first parents, Athanasius writes that "if they kept the grace and remained good they would enjoy the life of paradise, without sorrow, pain, or care, in addition to their having the promise of immortality in heaven."[178] Other church fathers share similar intuitions, suggesting that if Adam and Eve had not sinned they would have escaped death and been translated into heaven to be glorified.[179] Among the Protestant Reformers, John Calvin opines that if Adam had remained obedient in paradise, "he would have passed into heaven without death and without injury."[180] These motifs come together in Vos's dictum that eschatology precedes soteriology; the presence of the tree of life in Eden—the same tree that would appear again in Revelation 22:2, 14, and 19 (cf. Rev. 2:7)—invites the notion of a *preredemptive* eschatology that was already in place in Genesis 1–2. Adam and Eve would have experienced glorification had they persevered in paradise.[181]

At a superficial level, something similar seems to be happening with incarnation anyway Christologies as they suggest that if Adam and Eve had not sinned, the eternal Son would still have become incarnate, uniting himself to humanity and opening a path for us to be united with God—in a word,

---

178. Athanasius, *De Incarnatione* 3 (*Contra Gentes and De Incarnatione*, 141).

179. See Theophilus of Antioch, *Letter of Autolycus* 2.27; Augustine, *The Literal Meaning of Genesis* 6.23–28, in *The Works of Saint Augustine: On Genesis*, trans. Edmund Hill (Hyde Park, NY: New City, 2002), 320–23.

180. John Calvin, *Commentaries on the First Book of Moses Called Genesis*, trans. John King, 2 vols. (Grand Rapids: Eerdmans, 1948), 1:127.

181. See the writings of Geerhardus Vos: e.g., *The Pauline Eschatology* (Phillipsburg, NJ: P&R, 1994), 42–61 (originally published 1930); *The Eschatology of the Old Testament*, ed. James T. Dennison (Phillipsburg, NJ: P&R, 2001), 73–76.

glorified. Incarnation anyway theology is trying to glimpse God's eternal purpose in the incarnation. This kind of speculation can be ancillary to the explicit witness of God's ways in Scripture, except that in the case of *non-lapsarian* incarnation anyway theologies sin exists *apart from* the fall of Adam. Such accounts are difficult to reconcile with countless texts that consistently depict the incarnation as a response to human sin.[182] The eternal Son became incarnate to make atonement for our sins (Rom. 8:1–4). Because he took on human flesh, he can serve as our high priest and empathize with our sufferings (Heb. 4:14–16). He became sin for us so that we might become the righteousness of God (1 Cor. 5:21). Gentiles can be reconciled to the Father because his Son came down from heaven as a descendant of David and was raised from the dead (Rom. 1:3–6). These and other passages emphasize that God's purpose in the incarnation was to resolve the problem of sin and reunite humanity with himself (see also Gal. 4:4–6; 2 Cor. 8:9; 2 Tim. 1:9–10). I suspect that an obedient Adam could have gone straight to glorification apart from the incarnation and resurrection; there is no hint in Scripture, however, that the incarnation would have happened without sin.

In addition, Scripture never presents the resurrection of Christ as the solution to an originally defective creation, but as the solution to sin. The resurrection is the crux of God's plan of redemption (Rom. 4:24–25). Therefore, non-lapsarian incarnation anyway theologies not only violate the biblical witness, but they change the overall shape of the canonical story and distort the interrelations of the doctrinal loci. Cutting ties with the first Adam leads theistic evolutionists to redirect emphasis to the last Adam. Since the dogmatic pressure must be released somewhere, they compensate by overemphasizing Christology and soteriology.[183] As Ted

---

182. I like the moderation of Aquinas:

> For such things as spring from God's will, and beyond the creature's due, can only be made known to us through being revealed in the Sacred Scripture, in which the Divine Will is made known to us. Hence, since everywhere in the Sacred Scripture the sin of the first man is assigned as the reason of the Incarnation, it is more in accordance with this to say that the work of the Incarnation was ordained by God as a remedy for sin; so that, had sin not existed, the Incarnation would not have been. Although the power of God is not limited to this;—even had sin not existed, God could have become incarnate. (Thomas Aquinas, *Summa Theologica* III.1.3, trans. Fathers of the English Dominican Province, 22 vols. [London: Burns, Oates & Washbourne, 1911–25], 15:10)

183. For a striking example, Conor Cunningham writes, "We understand Adam only in virtue of the one true Adam, or, to put it more strongly, the *only* Adam. . . . It is folly to interpret the Fall or the existence of Adam in either positivistic terms or strictly historical terms, in the sense that there is no Fall before Christ. That is to say, there was but a glimmer of its occurrence, and this glimmer was only about Christ and not about some historical event of the same genus as the Battle of Trafalgar." Conor Cunningham, *Darwin's Pious Idea* (Grand Rapids: Eerdmans, 2010), 378, emphasis original.

Peters writes, "The paradise story and the concept of inherited sin are the dressing for the otherwise naked proposition that God and God alone is responsible for establishing a divine-human relationship that is *salvific*."[184] Who needs a historical fall if you can accentuate the need for salvation, the deeper meaning of the Adam story?

This distorting effect has eschatological implications. Once you play down the relevance of protology, the weight shifts disproportionately to eschatology. Eschatology is the new protology. David Fergusson sees this as a strength rather than a weakness: "By removing the distraction of a fall from a prior state of perfection, the theory of the atonement can be given greater Christological concentration and set in a stronger eschatological perspective."[185] In the same vein, Neil Messer advises that "there is no past golden age to which we can look back with longing, and to which we could be restored." Glorification is rooted in the future and "to the ultimate fulfillment of God's purposes for humans and the whole created order."[186] However, the biblical notion of eternal damnation loses coherence if one embraces non-lapsarian evolution. The teaching that sinners who never make peace with God will be condemned forever assumes that God is *just* to punish those outside Christ. But according to non-lapsarian theistic evolution, the sins we commit—and indeed our *sinfulness*—is a product of (evolutionary) creation. Since God made us this way from the beginning, he is responsible for sin that brings about everlasting damnation.[187]

I have been arguing that the fall of Adam is essential for a theodicy and for the very shape of the gospel. But Franklin is not convinced that an orthodox theology requires a literal, historical Adam. He holds up Dietrich Bonhoeffer as someone who rejects the historical Adam and fall but never concedes to theological liberalism. Bonhoeffer's theological and non-lapsarian reading of Genesis 1–3 enables him "to criticize Nazi ideology, German nationalism, anti-Semitism, and ecclesial corruption."[188] Yes, few of us reach such greatness. Bonhoeffer was a remarkable gift to the church,

---

184. Ted Peters, *Playing God? Genetic Determinism and Human Freedom*, 2nd ed. (New York: Routledge, 2003), 90, my emphasis.

185. David Fergusson, "Paradise Lost and Regained: An Ancient Symmetry Assessed," *Irish Theological Quarterly* 60, no. 2 (1994): 117.

186. Neil Messer, *Selfish Genes and Christian Ethics* (London: SCM, 2007), 203. See also Nicholas Lash, "Production and Prospect: Reflections on Christian Hope and Original Sin," in *Evolution and Creation*, ed. Ernan McMullin (Notre Dame, IN: University of Notre Dame Press, 1985), 273–89.

187. This alarming conclusion also applies to annihilationism, but to a lesser degree. For an interesting discussion of the evolutionary problem of damnation, see Daniel J. Pedersen, "Blame, Damnation, and Evolved Dispositions: A Dilemma," *Modern Theology* 37, no. 2 (2021): 458–75.

188. Franklin, "Theodicy and the Historical Adam," 49.

and I agree that rejecting a historical fall is not inevitably a slippery slope to theological liberalism. Happily, Christians are not always theologically consistent! Non-lapsarian theologians often affirm orthodox doctrines like divine holiness and the priority of Scripture, but the *theological logic* of their position undercuts those commitments.

We should not presume on God's grace preventing that logic from reaping its bitter fruit in later generations. If we can so easily set aside Scripture's witness to a golden age, why should we believe in the eschaton? If Scripture does not give us a reliable account of beginnings, why should we think it gives us a reliable account of endings? As Michael Lloyd remarks, "We cannot look forward to any golden age in the future, because we cannot now look back to any golden age in the past."[189] In fairness to those no longer convinced by the classical view of the prelapsarian state, they can still wholeheartedly accept the eschaton on the basis of God's promises. I am concerned, however, that the position lacks canonical consistency. The clear references to paradise in Revelation 2:7 and 22:1–5 at the end of the canonical story orient Christians to what our future holds: "They give the Christian canon a certain symmetry, balancing the account of the first paradise in Genesis 2–3 with a description of its recovered eschatological equivalent."[190] A supralapsarianism without a historical fall will preach poorly, if at all; it is a well-intentioned effort to alleviate tensions with conventional science, but its message is at odds with the consistent testimony of Scripture and generates notions of incarnation and atonement different from what the church has traditionally believed and what is taught in many pulpits across the world today.

Conclusion

Inspired by evolutionary biology, non-lapsarian theologians have retold the biblical story without Adam as the first protagonist. They lose the theological coherence of Scripture's redemptive-historical witness to Adam and Eve across the Testaments. They reject original righteousness such that redemption becomes a solution to a problem that God himself instigated. They present mortality and death as prelapsarian givens rather than postlapsarian

189. Michael Lloyd, "The Humanity of Fallenness," in *Grace and Truth in the Secular Age*, ed. Timothy Bradshaw (Grand Rapids: Eerdmans, 1998), 72n18.

190. Grant Macaskill, "Paradise in the New Testament," in *Paradise in Antiquity: Jewish and Christian Views*, ed. Markus Bockmuehl and Guy Stroumsa (Cambridge: Cambridge University Press, 2010), 80.

evils, and this in turn weakens the canonical testimony to God's originally good creation. As if these problems are not sobering enough, removing Adam from the redemptive story means that sin and evil have always been with us.

At first blush the story seems quintessentially modern. In the wake of Darwin, extratextual pressures have driven theologians to accommodate Scripture to the mental habits of post-Enlightenment thinking. However, these tensions between theology and science are symptomatic of a much older faith-and-reason dialectic. Some patristic theologians were not immune to cultural pressures, especially Neoplatonic assumptions, and tended to interpret reality theologically in dialogue with prevailing philosophies. The real question is not whether Christians should be in conversation with extratextual philosophies and ideas; given the contextual nature of theology, dialogue of that sort is inescapable. The question is how to navigate these areas critically in light of who God is and what he has revealed about himself and the world he made.

Adam's fall and Christ's atonement are the two unchangeable facts of redemptive history that hold all history together, from protology to eschatology. They also remind us that righteousness was once in our possession and will be again one day—this time forever—when the dwelling of God will be among the people (Rev. 21:3). Death is the normal experience in our broken world, but it was not always so. And because we know death came with Adam's fall, we have the firm hope that it will be put down decisively when the rider on a white horse appears in the clouds (19:11). Truly, the doctrine of Adam's fall preserves the goodness of God and the integrity of the biblical narrative. It is also, of course, essential to the doctrine of original sin, another area of tension between Christian doctrine and evolutionary biology. We turn to those matters next.

7

Original Sin and the Biological Problem

The traditional Christian dogma of original sin, its consequences and the mode of its transmission, as shaped in the West by St. Augustine, has always seemed to me . . . manifestly the most vulnerable part of the whole Christian account of the relations of God and man, and to call more imperatively than any other part of the theological system for reconstruction in light of philosophy and history.

—A. E. Taylor[1]

It is astonishing however that the mystery furthest from our understanding is the transmission of sin, the one thing without which we can have no understanding of ourselves!

—Blaise Pascal[2]

A similar cry of outraged indignation greeted Darwin's *The Descent of Man.* . . . The great theological doctrines of creation and fall, sin and redemption, with all the moral precepts hanging on them, seemed threatened by a preposterous theory that man was a cousin to the apes, if not of closer consanguinity.

—John Greene[3]

1. A. E. Taylor, *The Faith of a Moralist* (London: Macmillan, 1930), 165.
2. Blaise Pascal, *Pensées and Other Writings*, trans. Honor Levi (New York: Oxford University Press, 1995), 42.
3. John C. Greene, *Darwin and the Modern World View* (Baton Rouge: Louisiana State University Press, 1961), 14.

| n 1993, Han Brunner and his research team wrote up the case of an extended Dutch family with a strange affliction.[4] Eight of the men had a single genetic mutation that erased activity of monoamine oxidase, an enzyme that regulates the neurotransmitter serotonin. Each of them showed borderline mental retardation, antisocial behavior, and frequent aggressive outbursts. One of the men, imprisoned for raping his sister, ended up in repeated fights with inmates and later stabbed a warden in the chest. Another male relative, upset at being reprimanded for delinquent work, tried to flatten his boss with a car. In a separate case, the offender would visit his sisters' bedroom at night with a knife and coerce them to undress. At least two of the eight men were arsonists, while others were accused of voyeurism, exhibitionism, and groping of female relatives. Brunner and his coauthors concluded that these disquieting behaviors—dubbed "Brunner syndrome"—were caused by monoamine oxidase deficiency.[5]

Brunner syndrome raises difficult theological questions. On the one hand, the behaviors exhibited by these men seem to be clear instances of sinning against both God and his image bearers. On the other hand, it feels unfair or callous to blame them if these behaviors have biological causes. Scientific developments of this kind have led many to speculate that what we traditionally call "sin" is a fundamentally biological—not spiritual—problem. Evolutionary psychologists, for example, have reinterpreted behaviors like rape, war, and genocide as genetic adaptations resulting from natural selection.[6] Behavioral genetics is often seen as virtually eliminating a robust sense of free will.[7] In neuroscience, damage to areas like the ventral prefrontal cortex, angular gyrus, and amygdala has been shown to cause

4. H. G. Brunner et al., "X-Linked Borderline Mental Retardation with Prominent Behavioral Disturbance: Phenotype, Genetic Localization, and Evidence for Disturbed Monoamine Metabolism," *American Journal of Human Genetics* 52, no. 6 (1993): 1032–39.

5. See also H. G. Brunner, "MAOA Deficiency and Abnormal Behavior: Perspectives on an Association," in *Genetics of Criminal and Antisocial Behavior*, ed. Gregory Bock and Jamie Goode (New York: Wiley & Sons, 1996), 155–67. Since Brunner syndrome is inherited in an X-linked recessive pattern, the condition almost exclusively affects males. The MAOA gene is located on the X chromosome—recall that women have two X chromosomes, whereas men only have the one. A mutation in the gene will cause the condition in males; Brunner syndrome is highly unlikely in women because the mutation would have to affect both X chromosomes. However, the genetic causal link between MAOA deficiency and violence has not gone unchallenged. E.g., see E. Balaban, J. Alper, and Y. L. Kasamon, "Mean Genes and the Biology of Aggression: A Critical Review of Recent Animal and Human Research," *Journal of Neurogenetics* 11, nos. 1–2 (1996): 1–43.

6. David J. Buller, *Adapting Minds: Evolutionary Psychology and the Persistent Quest for Human Nature* (Cambridge, MA: MIT Press, 2005).

7. For a comprehensive analysis, see Denis Alexander, *Genes, Determinism and God* (Cambridge: Cambridge University Press, 2017).

psychopathic and antisocial behavior.[8] As E. O. Wilson declared in 1975, "The time has come for ethics to be removed temporarily from the hands of philosophers and biologicized."[9] Depending on who is calling the fight, biology has dealt sharp blows to the doctrine of original sin.

In its classical rendition, original sin identifies every descendant of Adam and Eve as born with disordered desires (original corruption) and guilty of Adam's first sin (original guilt). According to Augustinian realism, the entire human race existed seminally in Adam so that when Adam sinned we all sinned with him and thus incurred guilt and penal corruption. Reformed federalism—a broadly Augustinian tradition—roots original guilt and corruption in Adam's ordained role as the federal representative of the human race. In this chapter, I will take a Reformed approach that accepts this federalist Augustinian-Reformed account of original sin as the most biblical expression of the doctrine, a claim I have defended elsewhere.[10] (Readers from other traditions will not accept all of my theological assumptions in this chapter, but I hope they will still benefit from listening in.)

The main thesis of this chapter is that while original corruption is always expressed in and through embodied existence, sin itself is not—and indeed cannot be—biological. I use the phrase "biologizing sin" for the tendency to define sin as a fundamentally biological reality. The core question is whether biological realities can really capture the nature of sin; rightly answering that question was a struggle for the early church and is a struggle for us today.

Initially, I consider the challenges that evolutionary psychology and behavioral genetics pose for the idea of sin. I then review the main proposals from theistic evolutionists to revise the doctrine of original corruption in light of these challenges; I also give reasons why evolutionary doctrines of original sin are not convincing. Finally, I develop my own account of original sin that acknowledges the goodness of embodiment and the biological effects of the fall without biologizing sin itself.[11]

8. Adrian Raine, *The Anatomy of Violence: The Biological Roots of Crime* (New York: Pantheon Books, 2013).

9. E. O. Wilson, *Sociobiology: The New Synthesis*, 25th anniv. ed. (Cambridge, MA: Harvard University Press, 2000), 562.

10. Hans Madueme, "Mea Culpa: An Apology for Original Guilt," *Mid-America Journal of Theology* 32 (2021): 7–34; Hans Madueme, "The Drama of (Imputation) Doctrine: Original Guilt as Biblical and Systematic Theology," in *Hearing and Doing the Word: The Drama of Evangelical Hermeneutics*, ed. Daniel Treier and Douglas Sweeney (London: Bloomsbury T&T Clark, 2021), 253–69; Hans Madueme, "An Augustinian-Reformed View" and "An Augustinian-Reformed Response," in *Original Sin and the Fall: Five Views*, ed. J. B. Stump and Chad Meister (Downers Grove, IL: IVP Academic, 2020), 11–34, 127–39.

11. For the purposes of this chapter, I will be using the terms "original sin" and "original corruption" interchangeably.

Evolutionary Perspectives on Sin and Biology

Augustine describes our inborn, moral corruption as a disordered desire. Original sin is by generation, not imitation (he is fond of citing Rom. 5:12).[12] Throughout his long debate with Julian of Eclanum, his Pelagian nemesis, Augustine is adamant that original sin is transmitted from parent to offspring through sexual lust. Sin is propagated through the male coital act, the stain of original sin passed on through the man's vitiated seeds.[13] Even so, the core of Augustine's mature doctrine of original sin can logically be separated from his quasi-biological views on sin's transmission; biological transmission is not needed to affirm that all human beings are born morally degenerate because of their collective sin. The consequent necessity of sin is the essential idea of Augustine's doctrine of original sin—namely, that *after* Adam's fall everyone (except Jesus who was conceived miraculously by the Virgin Mary) is morally polluted and sins by necessity. This consequent necessity need not involve the genetic or biological transmission of sin.

Indeed, the two most common theories in church history for the transmission of original sin involve the soul. *Traducianism* maintains that original corruption is transmitted from parental souls to the souls of offspring, whereas *creatianism* is the idea that God creates each fresh soul individually before inserting it into the body at birth (or conception) where it contracts sin.[14] In church history, many were concerned about traducianism because, to their minds, it implied that the soul (and sin) are transmitted biologically rather than spiritually. Others worried that if creatianism is true, then sin originates from the body, or equally problematic, God directly implants sinful souls. Throughout his life Augustine vacillated between these two doctrines and set the terms of the debate for later Catholic and Protestant traditions. Even after the debates intensified among sixteenth- and seventeenth-century Roman Catholic and Protestant think-

12. E.g., Augustine, *Unfinished Work in Answer to Julian* 2.56, 2.83, 3.85, 3.88, etc.
13. As Elizabeth Clark concludes, "There can be no mistaking Augustine's meaning when he expresses himself so plainly and so often: the offspring contracted the original sin from Adam, the male who engendered; the woman receives the already vitiated seed from him, conceives, and gives birth." Elizabeth Clark, "Vitiated Seeds and Holy Vessels: Augustine's Manichean Past," in *Images of the Feminine in Gnosticism*, ed. Karen King (Minneapolis: Fortress, 1988), 387.
14. "Creatianism" often appears as "creationism" in theological writing, but I use the former term to avert any confusion with the creationism debate in science-theology settings. This distinction is usually present in French, German, and Dutch scholarship (*créatianisme; Kreatianismus*). See Lanier Burns, "From Ordered Soul to Corrupted Nature: Calvin's View of Sin," in *John Calvin and Evangelical Theology: Legacy and Prospect*, ed. Sung Wook Chung (Milton Keyes, UK: Paternoster, 2009), 82n92.

ers, the relationship between original sin and biology was never fully resolved.[15]

A new chapter in this debate over sin and biology emerged with the theory of evolution. Darwin's core thesis in *On the Origin of Species* is that any population of organisms will face limitations on food, water, and other resources, so that individuals with the most beneficial traits have a greater likelihood of survival and reproducing offspring. This "natural selection" was the mechanism by which living creatures evolved from a common ancestor. Darwin also describes a process he calls "sexual selection": individuals with physical traits that distinguish them from others of the same sex and species will have a reproductive advantage. The scientific community at the time accepted Darwin's theory of evolution, but they rejected natural selection because no one understood how hereditary information was transmitted.[16]

Everything changed at the turn of the twentieth century when scientists rediscovered Gregor Mendel's pioneering work on the laws of heredity. Mendelian heredity explains how advantageous traits could be naturally selected and persist through generations. By 1942, Julian Huxley developed a model that integrated Darwinian evolution, Mendelian genetics, and population genetics—he called it the "modern synthesis."[17] This neo-Darwinian synthesis became the dominant paradigm within biology and gave birth to evolutionary psychology, the study of human behavior from an evolutionary perspective.

Original Sin and Evolutionary Psychology

The story of evolutionary psychology begins with the study of instinct in the early to mid-twentieth century. Darwin thought instinct likely evolved under natural selection as the basis for more complex instincts.[18] Later theorists like James Mark Baldwin, William James, and William McDougall tried to develop this instinct idea, but the project collapsed for lack of

15. For a recent exploration of these themes, see Joshua Farris, "A Cartesian Exploration of the Soul's Origin, Original Sin, and Christology," in *The Soul of Theological Anthropology: A Cartesian Exploration* (New York: Routledge, 2017), esp. 119–26.

16. On how non-Darwinian evolutionary theories eclipsed Darwin's account in the early twentieth century, see Peter Bowler, *The Eclipse of Darwinism: Anti-Darwinian Evolution Theories in the Decades around 1900* (Baltimore: Johns Hopkins University Press, 1983), and Peter Bowler, *The Non-Darwinian Revolution: Reinterpreting a Historical Myth* (Baltimore: Johns Hopkins University Press, 1988).

17. Julian Huxley, *Evolution: The Modern Synthesis* (London: Allen & Unwin, 1942).

18. Charles Darwin, *On the Origin of Species by Means of Natural Selection, or the Preservation of Favoured Races in the Struggle for Life*, rev. ed., ed. Gillian Beer (Oxford: Oxford University Press, 2008), 155–81.

empirical evidence and the dominance of behaviorism in the early twentieth century.[19] The instinct theory was resuscitated in the mid-twentieth century by ethology, a branch of zoology that studies animal behavior in its native environment; its central figures were Konrad Lorenz (1903–89) and Nikolaas Tinbergen (1907–88).[20] In 1973, Lorenz, Tinbergen, and Karl von Frisch received the Nobel Prize for their work in ethology. In a controversial book, Lorenz had suggested that war and violence were inevitable expressions of the human instinct for aggression.[21] Ethologists argued that much of human sociality could be explained by our animal past and that human aggression was an evolutionary adaptation.[22]

In 1975, E. O. Wilson published his groundbreaking *Sociobiology: The New Synthesis*, which defined sociobiology as the "systematic study of the biological basis of all social behavior"—including human behavior.[23] The phenomenon of altruism has been a puzzle for evolutionary theory ever since Darwin and has been a special focus of sociobiology. Evolution by natural selection asserts that the traits of individuals with the most offspring will increase in subsequent generations, leading one to expect that altruistic traits would be eliminated and selfish behavior rewarded. But altruistic behavior permeates all creation, such as between sterile worker bees, soldier ants, parents and offspring, and relatives and nonrelatives. As William Rottschaeffer explains, "This apparent inconsistency between theory and data constitutes the biological problem of altruism."[24] The proposed solutions have included kin selection, reciprocal altruism, group selection, evolutionary game theory, and so on.[25] At any rate, the guiding principle

19. Henry Plotkin, *Evolutionary Thought in Psychology: A Brief History* (Malden, MA: Blackwell, 2004), 60–61.

20. Konrad Lorenz, *Evolution and Modification of Behavior* (Chicago: University of Chicago Press, 1965); Nikolaas Tinbergen, *The Study of Instinct* (London: Oxford University Press, 1951). Other important ethologists were Karl von Frisch, William Morton Wheeler, Karl Spencer Lashley, Bill Thorpe, and Robert Hinde.

21. Konrad Lorenz, *On Aggression* (London: Routledge, 1996) (originally published 1963).

22. For example, see Desmond Morris, *The Naked Ape* (New York: McGraw-Hill, 1967); Robert Ardrey, *The Territorial Imperative* (London: Collins, 1966); Lionel Tiger, *Men in Groups* (New York: Random House, 1969); and Lionel Tiger and Robin Fox, *The Imperial Animal* (New York: Holt, Rinehart, Winston, 1971).

23. Wilson, *Sociobiology*, 4.

24. William Rottschaeffer, "Naturalizing Ethics: The Biology and Psychology of Moral Agency," *Zygon* 35, no. 2 (2000): 264. On the problem with framing altruism as the central problem of evolutionary psychology, see Neil Messer, "Cognitive Science, Moral Reasoning, and the Theological Suspicion of Ethics," *Journal of the Society of Christian Ethics* 36, no. 1 (2016): 51–68, esp. 54–55.

25. For evolutionary theorizing about altruism and broader debates, see Philip Kitcher, *Vaulting Ambition* (Cambridge, MA: MIT Press, 1985); and Ullica Segerstråle, *Defenders of the Truth: The Battle for Science in the Sociobiology Debate and Beyond* (Oxford: Oxford University Press, 2000).

of sociobiology is that all behaviors, including most human behaviors, are genetic adaptations. Wilson claims that most forms of human aggression, like rape, war, and genocide evolved by natural selection.[26] As Robert Wright puts it, "We're all puppets, and our best hope for even partial liberation is to try to decipher the logic of the puppeteer."[27] Such controversial statements are only credible if genetic determinism is true.[28]

The most recent development is the shift from sociobiology to Evolutionary Psychology (capital E and P).[29] Sociobiology treats behavioral phenotypes as analogous to physiological phenotypes, but Evolutionary Psychologists criticize that approach for obscuring "a fundamental difference between them, for behaviors are *events*, which are the output of an information-processing brain reacting to informational input about the current conditions in both the environment and the brain itself."[30] They describe human psychology as having specific mechanisms that create and guide behavior. These mechanisms are adaptations that evolved to solve problems from our hunter-gatherer past.[31] In short, psychological mechanisms—not behavioral phenotypes—are the evolutionary adaptations.

According to Evolutionary Psychologists, human ancestors lived in hunter-gatherer groups during the Pleistocene epoch (2.6 million to twelve thousand years ago) and our psychological adaptations evolved to solve the problems we faced during that period. Cultural changes since the Pleistocene, they tell us, have occurred too rapidly for our brains to adapt: "The brain/mind mechanisms that constitute human nature were shaped by selection over vast periods of time in environments different in many respects from our own, and it is to these ancient environments that human nature is adapted."[32] Setting aside the in-house debates within Evolutionary

---

26. E. O. Wilson, *On Human Nature* (Cambridge, MA: Harvard University Press, 1978), 99–120.

27. Robert Wright, *The Moral Animal: The New Science of Evolutionary Psychology* (New York: Pantheon Books, 1994), 37.

28. E.g., Michael Ruse, *Sociobiology: Sense or Nonsense?* (Boston: D. Reidel, 1979); Richard Dawkins, *The Selfish Gene* (Oxford: Oxford University Press, 1977).

29. Here I am following David Buller who distinguishes "evolutionary psychology" (the broad discipline) from "Evolutionary Psychology" (a specific program *within* evolutionary psychology). See Buller, *Adapting Minds*.

30. David J. Buller, "Varieties of Evolutionary Psychology," in *The Cambridge Companion to the Philosophy of Biology*, ed. David L. Hull and Michael Ruse (Cambridge: Cambridge University Press, 2007), 259.

31. John Tooby and Leda Cosmides, "The Psychological Foundations of Culture," in *The Adapted Mind: Evolutionary Psychology and the Generation of Culture*, ed. Leda Cosmides, John Tooby, and Jerome Barkow (Oxford: Oxford University Press, 1992), 49–50.

32. Donald Symons, "On the Use and Misuse of Darwinism in the Study of Human Behavior," in Cosmides, Tooby, and Barkow, *Adapted Mind*, 138.

Psychology, theologians worry that evolutionary perspectives on behavior end up reducing human vice (and virtue) to biological forces that long predate the dawn of humanity.

Consider the book by primatologists Richard Wrangham and Dale Peterson, *Demonic Males: Apes and the Origins of Human Violence*. The authors chronicle violence, rape, and battering within chimpanzee communities: "The male violence that surrounds and threatens chimpanzee communities is so extreme that to be in the wrong place at the wrong time from the wrong group means death."[33] Wrangham and Peterson argue that chimpanzees and humans are violent by nature and share a "demonic" tendency to kill: "Our warring tendencies go back into our prehuman past."[34] Similar popularizations of evolutionary psychology are common,[35] and its insights have been applied further afield in political philosophy, criminology, and other disciplines.[36]

Frans de Waal, an ethologist, has criticized such evolutionary interpretations for their myopic emphasis on "selfish" genes that prevent us from seeing animals as empathetic and mutually cooperative. He calls this mindset a "Calvinist sociobiology" that treats morality as a thin veneer overlaid on a brutish and depraved animal nature.[37] De Waal argues instead that apes and other social animals show evidence of being morally good by nature.[38] Based on careful observation of primate communities, he contends that other animals, especially primates, have a form of morality or protomorality.[39] His research implies that morality is innate to human nature.

33. Richard Wrangham and Dale Peterson, *Demonic Males: Apes and the Origins of Human Violence* (New York: Houghton Mifflin, 1996), 21.

34. Wrangham and Peterson, *Demonic Males*, 22.

35. Wright, *Moral Animal*; Matt Ridley, *The Origins of Virtue: Human Instincts and the Evolution of Cooperation* (New York: Viking, 1996); Michael Shermer, *The Science of Good and Evil: Why People Cheat, Gossip, Care, Share, and Follow the Golden Rule* (New York: Times Books, 2004).

36. On political philosophy, see Larry Arnhart, *Darwinian Natural Right: The Biological Ethics of Human Nature* (Albany: State University of New York Press, 1998); on criminology, see Randy Thornhill and Craig Palmer, *A Natural History of Rape: Biological Bases of Sexual Coercion* (Cambridge, MA: MIT Press, 2000).

37. Frans de Waal, *Good Natured: The Origins of Right and Wrong in Humans and Other Animals* (Cambridge, MA: Harvard University Press, 1996), 13–20.

38. Frans de Waal, *Primates and Philosophers: How Morality Evolved* (Princeton: Princeton University Press, 2006); another primatologist doing similar work is Marc Bekoff, *The Emotional Lives of Animals* (Novato, CA: New World Library, 2007).

39. There is a lively debate in ethology over the evolutionary origins of animal morality. See Leonard D. Katz, ed., *Evolutionary Origins of Morality: Cross-Disciplinary Perspectives* (Thorverton, Exeter, UK: Imprint Academic, 2000); and Colin Renfrew and Iain Morley, eds., *Becoming Human: Innovation in Prehistoric Material and Spiritual Culture* (Cambridge: Cambridge University Press, 2009).

He writes, "One can consider humans as either inherently good but capable of evil or as inherently evil but capable of good. I happen to belong in the first camp."[40] Overall, de Waal offers a more optimistic picture of human nature in which virtue and vice both have a long evolutionary history. Since de Waal is a secular scholar and former Catholic, he does not interpret his research through the lens of Christian doctrine; by implication, however, even on his account, sin remains a biological phenomenon.

Aside from de Waal's concerns, many scientists criticize evolutionary psychology for sensationalizing and oversimplifying scientific research. Sociobiology is routinely lambasted for its reductionism and determinism.[41] Richard Lewontin and others fault it for ignoring holistic, social, and environmental modes of analysis.[42] Evolutionary Psychology is especially vulnerable to charges of determinism and reducing everything to an evolutionary adaptation.[43] One of the recurring problems in much of the literature in evolutionary ethics is the reliance on philosophical claims that are not supported by the scientific evidence. Even philosophers who endorse the broad project of evolutionary psychology have questioned various aspects of sociobiology and Evolutionary Psychology.[44] Christian scholars have raised parallel questions.[45]

Original Sin and Behavioral Genetics

Aside from the debates surrounding evolutionary psychology, people can be forgiven for thinking that original sin is merely a prescientific way of talking about behavioral genetics. After all, "hardly a month goes by without a media report that researchers have discovered the 'gene for' some

40. Frans de Waal, *The Bonobo and the Atheist: In Search of Humanism among the Primates* (New York: Norton, 2013), 38.

41. Sociobiology Study Group of Science for the People, "Sociobiology—Another Biological Determinism," in *The Sociobiology Debate: Readings on Ethical and Scientific Issues,* ed. Arthur Caplan (New York: Harper & Row, 1978), 280–90.

42. For example, see Richard C. Lewontin, Stephen Rose, and Leon J. Kamin, *Not in Our Genes: Biology, Ideology, and Human Nature* (New York: Pantheon Books, 1984).

43. For a trenchant critique of Evolutionary Psychology, see Buller, *Adapting Minds.* See Jonathan Marks's blistering critique of Wrangham and Peterson's book *Demonic Males* in *Human Biology* 71, no. 1 (1999): 143–46.

44. See Philip Kitcher, *In Mendel's Mirror: Philosophical Reflections on Biology* (Oxford: Oxford University Press, 2003); Stephen Clark, *Biology and Christian Ethics* (Cambridge: Cambridge University Press, 2000), 129–32, 176–86.

45. See Jitse van der Meer, "The Engagement of Religion and Biology: A Case Study in the Mediating Role of Metaphor in the Sociobiology of Lumsden and Wilson," *Biology and Philosophy* 15, no. 5 (2000): 669–98; Fraser Watts, *Theology and Psychology* (Burlington, VT: Ashgate, 2002), 17–31; David Fergusson, *Faith and Its Critics: A Conversation* (Oxford: Oxford University Press, 2009), 94–108.

complex human behavior or trait."[46] Our virtuous and vicious behaviors allegedly reveal the genetic hand we have been dealt. We wring our hands about the possibility of genetic fatalism and worry that traditional notions of moral responsibility are no longer trustworthy. These fears are not all baseless, but we must disentangle populist anxieties from what genetic scientists actually say.[47]

Let us review the basics. Humans have forty-six chromosomes consisting of extremely long sequences of nucleotides, or deoxyribonucleic acid (DNA). "Genes" are particular stretches of nucleotide sequences scattered throughout a chromosome and inherited from parent to offspring. The *genotype* is the sum of our genes. Although we all share the same basic set of genes, many different forms of the same gene (alleles) highlight individual differences between humans. The genotype generates the many proteins within the body that regulate our unique physical traits, such as eye color, hair type, and muscle mass. The manifestation of a physical trait (e.g., height) is the *phenotype* (e.g., tall or short). Some traits are "monogenic" because they are produced by a single gene (e.g., Marfan syndrome and sickle-cell anemia are monogenic diseases), but traits are usually polygenic, as they depend on multiple genes for their expression (e.g., diabetes and osteoporosis). In light of genetics, what is the status of human behavior? Should we think of behavior as a component of the phenotypic expression of our genotype? The discipline of behavioral genetics seeks to understand how genes and environment shape our behavioral traits.

The history of behavioral genetics falls into two phases: an earlier nonmolecular phase of research and a later molecular one.[48] In twin studies, which are the classic nonmolecular approach, identical—or monozygotic (MZ)—twins are thought to share 100 percent of their genetic inheritance, while fraternal—or dizygotic (DZ)—twins share roughly 50 percent of their genome. Early twin studies shared the *equal environments assumption*—that is, they assumed that MZ and DZ twins grow up experiencing the same environment. Based on this assumption, if MZ twins shared a phenotype with greater frequency than DZ twins, researchers could then calculate the degree of genetic inheritance based on the degree of difference in the shared

---

46. Nancy Press, Audrey Chapman, and Erik Parens, introduction to *Wrestling with Behavioral Genetics: Science, Ethics, and Public Conversation*, ed. Erik Parens, Audrey Chapman, and Nancy Press (Baltimore: Johns Hopkins University Press, 2006), xiii.

47. For helpful Christian perspectives on human genetic science, see Ted Peters, *Playing God? Genetic Determinism and Human Freedom*, 2nd ed. (New York: Routledge, 2003); and Robert Song, *Human Genetics: Fabricating the Future* (Cleveland: Pilgrim, 2003).

48. For a brief history of behavioral genetics, see John C. Loehlin, "History of Behavior Genetics," in *Handbook of Behavior Genetics*, ed. Yong-Kyu Kim (New York: Springer, 2009), 3–11.

phenotype. But critics argue that twin studies failed to fully disentangle the role of environmental and interpersonal factors (even in MZ twins).[49]

The adoption method is another nonmolecular approach that is more effective at separating genetic and environmental factors. The idea is that we can decipher the influence of genes and environment by examining behavioral differences between adopted children and adoptive parents, on the one hand, and adopted children and biological parents, on the other. Twin and adoptee studies indicate a significant genetic factor in individual intelligence and in conditions such as schizophrenia, but critical questions have been raised about methodological assumptions, the notion of heritability, interpretation bias, sampling issues, and so on.[50] In short, nonmolecular approaches to behavioral genetics disagree on the extent to which we can unambiguously separate environmental from genetic contributions.

Since the completion of the Human Genome Project, advances in molecular genetics have prompted the search for specific genes associated with behavioral traits.[51] This shift made sense given the relative success of twin and adoptee studies and what we already knew about genes associated with physical conditions. Linkage studies, which are the primary research strategy in molecular genetics, identify any correlations between a trait and a suspected genetic marker.[52] In the 1980s and 1990s, molecular genetic studies claimed genetic linkage with traits like schizophrenia, manic-depressive disorder, alcoholism, risk-taking, novelty seeking, homosexuality, and attention deficit hyperactivity disorder (ADHD). However, none of these genetic linkages have been widely confirmed. As one recent analysis concludes, "In nearly all of these cases, the claims were either subsequently retracted, were cogently criticized, or could not be replicated."[53] Rare cases like Brunner syndrome are the exceptions that prove the rule. Gene expression is

49. David M. Evans and Nicholas G. Martin, "The Validity of Twin Studies," *GeneScreen* 1, no. 2 (2000): 77–79; Evan Charney, "Behavior Genetics and Postgenomics," *Behavioral and Brain Sciences* 35, no. 5 (2012): 331–58.

50. In defense of twin and adoptee studies, see Michael Rutter, *Genes and Behavior: Nature-Nurture Interplay Explained* (Malden, MA: Blackwell, 2006); and Neven Sesardic, *Making Sense of Heritability* (Cambridge: Cambridge University Press, 2005). On the critical side, see the essays in David Wasserman and Robert Wachbroit, eds., *Genetics and Criminal Behavior* (Cambridge: Cambridge University Press, 2001).

51. I am following Jonathan Beckwith, "Whither Human Behavioral Genetics?," in Parens, Chapman, and Press *Wrestling with Behavioral Genetics*, 83–85.

52. Other methods that we cannot elaborate here include experimental crosses in animal systems, allele-sharing, and linkage disequilibrium methods. Stephanie Sherman and Irwin Waldman, "Identifying the Molecular Genetic Basis of Behavioral Traits," in *Behavioral Genetics: The Clash of Culture and Biology*, ed. Ronald A. Carson and Mark A. Rothstein (Baltimore: Johns Hopkins University Press, 1999), 35–60.

53. Beckwith, "Whither Human Behavioral Genetics?," 84.

an enormously complex process that involves the interplay of many genes and their environments. Genes never act alone, their action on behavior is indirect, and they act at different times during development.[54] In sum, genetic science data support the role of genetic *predispositions* in human behavior but not genetic *determinism.*

Evolutionary psychology and behavioral genetics raise important questions about the metaphysics of human sinfulness. Is the nature of sin biological, is sin a blend of the biological and spiritual, or does it somehow transcend those categories? Naturalistic evolutionary accounts of original sin collapse the distinction between "moral" and "natural" evil. As Ted Peters remarks, "By removing primary agency from the decisions of allegedly free human persons, what we previously thought was moral perversion becomes an expression of a more basic biological nature."[55] Evolutionary psychology renders talk about "sin" meaningless, for responsibility is a moot concept if all behavior has solely biological causes.

Conversely, some have argued that evolutionary psychology and behavioral genetics offer empirical scientific support for the doctrine of original sin.[56] Michael Ruse entertains just this possibility when he identifies original sin with the self-interested evolutionary struggle for existence. "Original sin," writes Ruse, "is part of the biological package. It comes with being human."[57] In his view, selfishness lies at the root of the natures we inherited biologically. Furthermore, de Waal and others claim that the moral experiences of animals and humans share hamartiological continuity, which is the context for the ongoing discussions about whether animals can sin against God.[58] These puzzles and questions underscore the daunting challenge theistic evolutionists face in their quest for a credible reinterpretation of original sin in light of evolutionary biology.[59]

54. For more holistic accounts of genetic science, see Alexander, *Genes, Determinism and God*; Mark L. Y. Chan and Roland Chia, eds., *Beyond Determinism and Reductionism: Genetic Science and the Person* (Adelaide, Australia: Australian Theological Forum, 2003).

55. Ted Peters, "The Evolution of Evil," in *The Evolution of Evil*, ed. Gaymon Bennett et al. (Göttingen: Vandenhoeck & Ruprecht, 2008), 21.

56. John Mullen, "Can Evolutionary Psychology *Confirm* Original Sin?," *Faith and Philosophy* 24, no. 3 (2007): 268–83.

57. Michael Ruse, *Can a Darwinian Be a Christian? The Relationship between Science and Religion* (Cambridge: Cambridge University Press, 2001), 210.

58. Michael Northcott, "Do Dolphins Carry the Cross? Biological Moral Realism and Theological Ethics," *New Blackfriars* 84, no. 994 (2003): 540–53.

59. Biologizing sin opens a Pandora's box:

We must . . . begin facing the real challenge that some parts of our sinful "natures" are indeed "natural" and not (or at least not merely) some postlapsarian corruption. Conversely, nature may have also graced us with good graces. It seems that evolution has conditioned

Original Sin and Theistic Evolutionists

Theistic evolutionists often depict human sinfulness as a primarily biological reality that originates in the genome. Violence and aggression, for example, are a normal part of human nature. Men and women are fundamentally similar to primates and other animals that manifest vices like violence, physical abuse, murder, and self-centeredness, and that manifest virtues like love, care, honesty, and guilt. Patricia Williams channels this position when she defends original corruption as an innate, evolved, inherited selfishness.[60] She embraces sociobiology but rejects genetic determinism in order to carve out space for freedom. Despite the constraints of biology, she thinks we can still exercise free will through reason, culture, and environment: "Human beings *can* act in contradiction to evolution's interest in survival and reproduction."[61] Still, she believes that conflict, violence, and selfish behavior are constitutive of human biology; our genome *necessarily* causes human conflict.[62] Williams's account epitomizes the biologizing of sin.

Daryl Domning likewise claims that selfishness is more evolutionarily basic than altruism.[63] Indwelling sin, he writes, "arose out of our animal nature itself."[64] Our sinful actions are experientially identical to the actions of our evolutionary ancestors who only experienced "selfishness" in a nonsinful or nonmoral sense. In our case, the evolution of consciousness and the ability to choose alternatives gave us the capacity for genuine selfishness toward other people: humans became selfish in a properly moral sense. Domning describes these different forms of selfishness as sharing historical and ontological continuity, but only the human form is properly

---

us for both antisocial and prosocial tendencies, which terribly muddies traditional theological distinctions between nature and grace. Put more simply and bluntly, if human sin is the direct result of a natural process, then what are we being held accountable for? Why the need for salvation? For atonement? For a cross? What is the gospel, the good news, for the human species? (Kenneth Reynhout, "Human Evolution and the Nature of Morality," *Theology Today* 72, no. 2 [2015]: 139)

60. Patricia Williams, *Doing without Adam and Eve: Sociobiology and Original Sin* (Minneapolis: Fortress, 2001).

61. Patricia Williams, "Sociobiology and Original Sin," *Zygon* 35, no. 4 (2000): 789, my emphasis.

62. Williams, "Sociobiology and Original Sin," 791: "Conflict . . . seems to be built into genetic structures. There are no specific genes for warlike behavior or for aggression. The genetic basis for conflict is more fundamental than this. It is based on diploidy. . . . It is fundamental to human nature."

63. Daryl Domning and Monika Hellwig, *Original Selfishness: Original Sin and Evil in Light of Evolution* (Burlington, VT: Ashgate, 2006). I will henceforth refer to Domning as the author since he wrote most of the book; Hellwig contributed fewer than twenty-five pages because she died tragically before the book was published.

64. Domning, *Original Selfishness*, 108.

sinful.[65] He identifies original sin with biological selfishness, "(the instinct for self-perpetuation) that is literally programmed into the genes of all living things—'the instinct of unlimited self-assertion,' our 'inheritance from the ancestors who fought a good fight in the state of nature,' in the words of T. H. Huxley."[66] This position renders humans *ontologically* sinful; from the very dawn of history, the material ingredients of sin have always inhered in humanity's biological constitution.

Such accounts that translate original corruption into a biological phenomenon end up naturalizing sin. They no longer recognize original sin as a sinful condition that is deeply internal to us, something morally awry at the very depths of our being, its guilt attributable to each of us in a just way. In the biblical witness, murder, adultery, sexual immorality, evil thoughts, and the like, arise from the moral center of our lives (the "heart"). They are not natural in a biological sense but are reflective of a deeper spiritual problem at the core of our human identity (Matt. 15:17–20; Jer. 17:9).

Many theistic evolutionists recognize the dangers in biologizing original sin and have been more careful to emphasize *nonbiological* themes like freedom, altruism, and culture. On these terms, original sin is simply another way to talk about how genes and cultural environment constrain human behavior.[67] Sinful predispositions and proclivities are passed down from evolution through our genome, but such factors are consistent with freedom and moral agency.

Enter Matthew Nelson Hill, who concedes that our sins are deeply rooted in our biology.[68] Yet even though genetics and environment constrain us, we are not genetically determined—indeed, humans enjoy genuine freedom. In Hill's estimation, humans are the only animals who can resist their biological constraints as they pursue the moral life. The freedom that is essential to any viable notion of moral responsibility "is made possible by the evolving human brain and developed cognitive and emotive faculties. Human consciousness plays a powerful role in giving the human the

65. Domning, *Original Selfishness*, 118.

66. Domning, *Original Selfishness*, 143. The Huxley quote is from Thomas H. Huxley, "Evolution and Ethics," in *Evolutionary Ethics*, ed. M. H. Nitecki and D. V. Nitecki (Albany: State University of New York Press, 1993), 49–50.

67. For a sample, see Helen De Cruz and Johan De Smedt, "Schleiermacher and the Transmission of Sin: A Biocultural Evolutionary Model," *TheoLogica* 7, no. 2 (2022), doi.org/10.14428/thl.v7i2.65763; Neil Messer, *Selfish Genes and Christian Ethics: Theological and Ethical Reflections on Evolutionary Biology* (London: SCM, 2007), 133–62; Ian Barbour, *Nature, Human Nature, and God* (Minneapolis: Fortress, 2002), 39–70; and John Polkinghorne, *Exploring Reality: The Intertwining of Science and Religion* (New Haven: Yale University Press, 2005), 41–45.

68. Matthew Nelson Hill, *Embracing Evolution: How Understanding Science Can Strengthen Your Christian Life* (Downers Grove, IL: IVP Academic, 2020), 110.

capacity to step beyond her or his own self and take on a new perspective."[69] Although Hill concedes the strong influence of genes and environment, he is also adamant that we are *whole persons* with the capacity for moral agency.[70]

According to Megan Loumagne Ulishney, much of the theorizing in evolutionary hamartiologies is stymied by a genes-environment (or nature-culture) dualism that inhibits holistic thinking. She applies insights from an approach called the "extended evolutionary synthesis," which includes epigenetics, to develop an updated evolutionary doctrine of original sin.[71] She agrees with Augustine (as she reads him) that sin is propagated biologically, but biology is always inseparable from culture: "From the moment of conception, we are formed within a dynamic matrix of biological and social/cultural forces. There is no time at which the biological is not also cultural, and there is no 'pure nature' that is later influenced by culture."[72] Biology and social culture are not only interdependent and interconnected, but they constitute "various webs of connection that have forming power over us, which we did not choose."[73] Therefore, original corruption is the dynamic interplay of our evolutionary past and our cultural inheritances.

Ronald Cole-Turner embraces evolutionary psychology but looks to behavioral genetics as a primary dialogue partner. In his view, behavioral genetics supports traditional notions of sin and responsibility: "In developing

---

69. Matthew Nelson Hill, *Evolution and Holiness: Sociobiology, Altruism and the Quest for Wesleyan Perfection* (Downers Grove, IL: IVP Academic, 2016), 126.

70. Hill, *Evolution and Holiness*, 130–33. Hill's account of freedom draws liberally from Stephen Pope, *Human Evolution and Christian Ethics* (Cambridge: Cambridge University Press, 2007), esp. 158–87.

71. The extended evolutionary synthesis approach is a recent conceptual framework that emphasizes how environmental factors play a sizeable role in evolutionary biology. Among its central research insights are evolutionary developmental biology, developmental plasticity, inclusive inheritance, and niche construction theory. For example, the phenotypic effects of specific genes are largely dependent on the environment; epigenetics reveals that parents pass on molecular switches to their offspring that determine which genes are expressed, yet those switches often depend on environmental factors outside the cell. See Megan Loumagne Ulishney, "Unity in the *Massa Peccati*: Original Sin and the Extended Evolutionary Synthesis," in *Emerging Voices in Science and Theology: Contributions by Young Women*, ed. Bethany Sollereder and Alister McGrath (New York: Routledge, 2022), 57–70, esp. 57–61; and, in detail, see Kevin N. Laland et al., "The Extended Evolutionary Synthesis: Its Structure, Assumptions and Predictions," *Proceedings of the Royal Society B: Biological Sciences* 282, no. 1813 (2015), doi.org/10.1098/rspb.2015.1019.

72. Ulishney, "Unity in the *Massa Peccati*," 63.

73. Megan Loumagne Ulishney, "Visiting Iniquity upon the Generations: Epigenetics, Systems Biology, and Theologies of Inherited Sin," *Philosophy, Theology and the Sciences* 7, no. 2 (2020): 223. For Ulishney's synthetic account of original sin, the evolution of sexual difference, and feminist philosophy, see her *Original Sin and the Evolution of Sexual Difference* (Oxford: Oxford University Press, 2023).

a theological understanding of the interplay between genes and environment, theologians should avoid thinking that there is no genetic basis for
behavior or personality type. It is equally mistaken, however, to think that if
there is a genetic basis to behavior, then behavior is genetically *determined*.[74]
In seeking a middle ground, Cole-Turner dismisses the strategy of invoking a soul as a way to escape the prison of genes and environment; rather,
disordered selves result from inherited genetic defects that affect body
and behavior.

In Cole-Turner's anthropology, the self is "genetically conditioned
through and through."[75] The evolutionary process, mediated by our genes,
conditions the neural complexity of our brains and thereby conditions culture, technology, religion, and morality. Cole-Turner thinks that behavioral
genetics invalidates libertarian notions of free will; rather, humans have
a more modest freedom of *self-determination*: "The human self or person
is the self-moved cause that determines human moral action. Such action
is free not because it is uncaused but because it is caused by the self as
moral agent."[76] The self is dependent on—but also transcends—our genes
and the environment.

In his perceptive analysis of genetic determinism, Ted Peters, a Lutheran
theologian, diagnoses two contrasting impulses in the gene myth: "puppet determinism" and "promethean determinism." On the one hand, we
see ourselves as reducible to DNA with all our vices and virtues mapped
out by a genetic fatalism. On the other hand, we also believe we can overcome our DNA, become Promethean masters of our genes, and control
our destiny.[77] Peters criticizes the fixed-pie assumption that "if our DNA
gets a bigger slice we get a smaller quantity of self-determining freedom."[78]
Our genes are merely one part of a greater reality that conditions our existence. As Peters remarks, "What we mean by freedom is the expression
of a self, a human person. Gene expression and human expression are not

74. Ronald Cole-Turner, *The New Genesis: Theology and the Genetic Revolution* (Louisville: Westminster John Knox, 1993), 87.

75. Cole-Turner, *New Genesis*, 88. The critique of dualism runs through his work. E.g., see Ronald
Cole-Turner, "Toward a Theology for the Age of Biotechnology," in *Beyond Cloning: Religion and the
Remaking of Humanity*, ed. Ronald Cole-Turner (Harrisburg, PA: Trinity Press International, 2001),
144–45.

76. Ronald Cole-Turner, "The Genetics of Moral Agency," in *The Genetic Frontier*, ed. Mark Frankel
and Albert Teich (Washington, DC: American Association for the Advancement of Science, 1994),
161–74, at 171.

77. Peters, *Playing God?*, passim. See also Ted Peters, "Genetics and Genethics: Are We Playing
God with Our Genes?," in *Science, Theology, and Ethics*, ed. Ted Peters (Burlington, VT: Ashgate,
2003), 139–63.

78. Peters, *Playing God?*, 195.

the same thing. Genes do not make decisions. Human beings do."[79] The human self is a whole that is greater than the parts of one's body. Freedom is not physical indeterminism but rather "is expressed and experienced by the whole person, not the person's individual parts."[80] Human freedom is a finite freedom. We are limited by our bodies and genes; but through language, thought, and imagination, the personal self gives us a measure of self-transcendence.[81] However, like most theistic evolutionists, Peters refuses to locate this transcendence in a metaphysical soul.[82]

Elsewhere Peters wrestles with the implications of evolutionary psychology and behavioral genetics for original sin.[83] Although he rejects the reductionistic aspects of sociobiology and the misleading popularizations of behavioral genetics, he thinks the core claims of sociobiology and Evolutionary Psychology resonate with Christian theology. Sociobiology, he notes, is consistent with the classical notion of sin as *bondage*. The focus of Scripture is on human *self*-determination, not some abstract notion of freedom—a self-determination consistent with determinism and moral agency.[84] For Peters, genetic and cultural determinism are compatible with moral responsibility. The mere fact that we can explain our actions in terms of genetic or environmental causes does not eliminate the reality of human agency; explanation does not imply exculpation.[85] Thus, he disagrees with the usual efforts by theistic evolutionists to safeguard free will. As long as humans have self-determination, Peters reassures us, then genetic and environmental determinism pose no threat. Even if original corruption is rooted in inherited biology, he concludes that the complexities of neural and genetic science rule out any kind of fatalism.

In summary, some theistic evolutionists emphasize the biological nature of original corruption and try to locate freedom in culture. Others recognize original sin as a complex synthesis of biology *and* culture and then try to preserve human freedom as something that transcends nature and culture. Much of the nuanced discourse on freedom is meant to make

79. Peters, *Playing God?*, 195.

80. Peters, *Playing God?*, 203.

81. Peters, *Playing God?*, 204.

82. Peters, *Playing God?*, 199. See also Ted Peters, *Anticipating Omega: Science, Faith, and Our Ultimate Future* (Göttingen: Vandenhoeck & Ruprecht, 2006), 129–53. While I disagree with the evolutionary aspects of Peters's doctrine of sin, there is much wisdom in his reflections on freedom.

83. Ted Peters, "The Genesis and Genetics of Sin," in *Sin and Salvation*, ed. Duncan Reid and Mark Worthing (Adelaide, Australia: Australian Theological Forum, 2003), 89–112.

84. Peters, "Evolution of Evil," 48.

85. Peters draws this insight from Steven Pinker, *The Blank Slate: The Modern Denial of Human Nature* (New York: Viking, 2002), 179 (cited in Peters, "Evolution of Evil," 48).

space for Christian altruism, which is a legacy of early debates within sociobiology.

The Problem with Evolutionary Hamartiology

Despite their theoretical differences, these evolutionary hamartiologies all end up grounding original sin in our biological condition. Evolutionary doctrines of original sin—particularly the ones that lack a point in history when the fall marred God's good creation—imply that God created a world in which human beings would inevitably sin given their evolved biological constitution. Such a quasi-Manichaean scenario defies the goodness and holiness of the Lord.[86]

Daniel Houck's book *Aquinas, Original Sin, and the Challenge of Evolution* does not biologize sin in quite the same way, but his proposal amounts roughly to the same conclusion.[87] In his account, Houck argues that God created Adam and Eve with disordered desires (concupiscence) which had to be kept at bay by his supernatural grace. Once the first couple sinned, they lost that sanctifying grace—this *absence of sanctifying grace* is Houck's definition of original sin. In the wake of the fall, all human beings are born with original sin—that is, without God's sanctifying grace.

The genius of Houck's proposal is that there is no need for a transmission theory of sin (e.g., creatianism or traducianism). All human beings suffer from original sin because God does not give us his supernatural grace. Original sin is the absence of that original grace. However, the immediate difficulty with this argument is that humans from the beginning had disordered desires; and if those desires are sinful, then God created the first humans in a state of sin, which would obviously violate the central truth of God's goodness. However, Houck defends the Anselmian position that even though concupiscence is not good, it is not *sinful* either. Thus, the first humans were not already sinful at creation.[88]

---

86. Nathan O'Halloran recognizes this problem and has suggested that a prior angelic fall "affected the contingent and imperfect natural order by wounding it, thereby transmitting to 'Adam' an already-wounded nature" (Nathan W. O'Halloran, "The Pre-human Biological and Cultural Transmission of the Effects of Originating Sin," *Contagion* 25 [2018]: 37). As I argued in chap. 5, this angelic fall theodicy lacks any valid exegetical support and contradicts Scripture's constant refrain about the goodness of primeval creation (Gen. 1:10, 12, 18, 21, 25, 31).

87. Daniel Houck, *Aquinas, Original Sin, and the Challenge of Evolution* (Cambridge: Cambridge University Press, 2020).

88. Daniel Houck, "Toward a New Account of the Fall, Informed by Anselm of Canterbury and Thomas Aquinas," *Pro Ecclesia* 29, no. 4 (2020): 441. Cf. Anselm, *De conceptu virginali et de originali peccato.*

Houck's rationale for this understanding of concupiscence turns on his reading of the book of James. The apostle seems to distinguish sin from temptation: "Blessed is anyone who endures temptation. Such a one has stood the test and will receive the crown of life that the Lord has promised to those who love him" (James 1:12 NRSV). (In the Christian tradition, temptation is often seen as a classic instance of concupiscence.) Not only is James talking about temptation as internal *desire*—and therefore not merely extrinsic to the individual—but he also (Houck notes) separates that desire from sin: "But one is tempted by one's own desire, being lured and enticed by it; then, when that desire has conceived, it gives birth to sin, and that sin, when it is fully grown, gives birth to death" (James 1:14–15 NRSV). Since sin arises later in the process, Houck concludes that concupiscence and sin are separate categories.

However, I doubt that James supports Houck's distinction between sin and disordered desires. As Douglas Moo notes, the context for what James says in 1:12 appears earlier in the chapter.[89] In verses 2–4, James writes: "Consider it pure joy, my brothers and sisters, whenever you face trials of many kinds, because you know that the testing of your faith produces perseverance. Let perseverance finish its work so that you may be mature and complete, not lacking anything" (NIV). God providentially allows us to experience all kinds of trials in order to test our faith. One problem is that Houck is using the Roman Catholic NRSV translation of verses 12–13, which gives the false impression that James is discussing temptation throughout those verses. In actuality, the same Greek word *peirazō* can also mean "test" (or "trial"). Therefore, given the broader context of James 1, the New Jerusalem Bible (another Catholic translation) offers a better rendition of verses 12–13: "Never, when you are being put to the *test* [not temptation], say, 'God is tempting me'; God cannot be tempted by evil, and he does not put anybody to the test." God tests his people throughout Scripture, allowing them to go through different trials (e.g., Israel in the wilderness [Deut. 8:2], Abraham and his only son [Gen. 22], Hezekiah's faithfulness [2 Chron. 32:31])—but God never tempts or induces anyone to sin.[90] In Moo's judgment, "despite the fact that the same Greek root (*peira-*) is used for both the outer trial and the inner temptation, it is crucial to distinguish them."[91]

89. I am indebted to the discussion in Douglas Moo, *The Letter of James*, Pillar New Testament Commentary (Grand Rapids: Eerdmans, 2000), 72–74.
90. For a helpful analysis of divine deception, including the problem passages, see Kevin Vanhoozer, "Ezekiel 14: 'I, the Lord, Have Deceived That Prophet': Divine Deception, Inception, and Communicative Action," in *Theological Commentary*, ed. Michael Allen (London: T&T Clark, 2011), 73–98.
91. Moo, *Letter of James*, 73.

Houck is also mistaken in drawing a hard line between sin and temptation based on the following verses in James 1:14–15.[92] We know from other
passages that many of our desires in and of themselves are already sinful
(e.g., "But I say to you that everyone who looks at a woman with lustful
intent has already committed adultery with her in his heart" [Matt. 5:28];
besides, James 1:14 explicitly describes the desires as *evil*—how could evil
desires *not* be sinful?). Thus, James is not presenting a different account
of sin; rather, Dan McCartney explains, James's purpose in laying out the
sequence from desire, to incipient sin, to "full-grown" sin, to death is "in
making it clear that the processes of sin do not originate with God."[93] After
all, incipient sin leads to death even if James 1:15 does not link the two directly (*all* sin leads to death! [Gen. 2:17; Rom. 6:23]); likewise, evil desires
are sinful even if the verse does not link them directly.[94]

Houck's overall thesis—that prelapsarian Adam had disordered desires
that inevitably lead to sin without God's sanctifying grace—derives from
the Roman Catholic notion that human beings lack the natural capacity
to have a relationship with God apart from supernatural grace. According
to the developed medieval position, "a direct and perduring relationship
with God surpasses human cognitive and affective capacities."[95] This idea
that the natural powers of humanity must be augmented by divine grace
made sense in light of Aristotelian assumptions.[96]

Aquinas accepted Aristotle's epistemology that all intuitive knowledge
implies an identity between the knower and the known. Thomas believed
that the highest intuition that our finite minds can achieve is an immediate awareness of self. Hence this dilemma: no finite mind can know God
directly or immediately, yet immediate knowledge of God is the highest

92. On a pastoral note, we should recall that not all temptation is sinful. The mere experience
of temptation does not mean I am already mired in sin; consider that "we do not have a high priest
who is unable to sympathize with our weaknesses, but one who in every respect *has been tempted
as we are, yet without sin*" (Heb. 4:15). If Jesus could be tempted, then all temptations are not sinful!
The debate over concupiscence concerns whether the narrower set of temptations that flow out
of evil desires are sinful.

93. Dan G. McCartney, *James*, Baker Exegetical Commentary on the New Testament (Grand Rapids: Baker Academic, 2009), 106.

94. The relationship between concupiscence and sin has been much debated in relation to the
moral status of same-sex sexual desires. For contrasting perspectives, see Denny Burk, "Is Homo-
sexual Orientation Sinful?," *Journal of the Evangelical Theological Society* 58, no. 1 (2015): 95–115; Karen
Keen, "Cultural Influences on Hermeneutical Frameworks in the Debate on Same-Sex Relationships,"
Interpretation 74, no. 3 (2020): 253–64. But I cannot pursue these matters here.

95. Stephen J. Duffy, *The Graced Horizon: Nature and Grace in Modern Catholic Thought* (Collegeville,
MN: Liturgical Press, 1992), 13.

96. I am following the helpful analysis in Duffy, *Graced Horizon*, 13–14.

blessing of existence (the beatific vision). Finite humanity by nature cannot commune with the infinite God. Roman Catholic theologians therefore concluded that "grace . . . is gratuitous not merely because of our sin, but primarily because of *the poverty of our being*."[97] Dubbed by the medievals as the *donum superadditum* ("added gift of grace"), it is God's supernatural grace that enables us to transcend our natural human powers and thereby attain direct communion with God.[98]

In Aquinas's doctrine of original righteousness, Adam's rectitude consisted in a perfect equilibrium within his spiritual, mental, and physical constitution. Reason submitted to God, lower powers submitted to reason, and body submitted to soul.[99] But this internal harmony was *not natural* to Adam, otherwise (Aquinas reasoned) it would have continued after the fall. Aquinas therefore infers that God must have given prelapsarian Adam "a supernatural endowment of grace" that would ensure harmony between all parts of his body and soul. As soon as Adam fell, God withdrew his supernatural grace and the inner moral equilibrium collapsed. Adam's mind was now set against God, his lower powers against reason, and his body against his soul. The human body inevitably became subject to death and "other bodily defects."[100]

Houck incorporates this Thomistic anthropology into his proposal, but it is defective on several counts. First, it implies that from creation—before the fall—Adam was already disposed to sin. His reason did not naturally submit to God, nor his lower powers to reason, nor his body to his soul. Moral instability was the created norm without the supernatural endowment from God (*donum superadditum*). Since God created Adam with an inherent instability in his moral architecture, Adam needed a *supernatural* gift from God to ensure that the proper hierarchy remain. That picture is hard to reconcile with the biblical witness: "God saw everything that he had made, and behold, it was very good" (Gen. 1:31).

Second, Houck's account depicts a primitive state in which the "higher" (reason, mind) and "lower" (emotions, appetites) elements of Adam's constitution are set against each other, the latter threatening to overpower the former unless the *donum superadditum* preserves order and balance.

---

97. Duffy, *Graced Horizon*, 14, my emphasis.

98. The *donum superadditum* also went under the name *gratia gratum faciens*; it received its mature formulation from Alexander of Hales (ca. 1170–1245). Cf. Reinhold Seeberg, *Text-Book of the History of Doctrines*, trans. Charles E. Hay, 2 vols. (Grand Rapids: Baker, 1952), 2:115.

99. Thomas Aquinas, *Summa Theologica* I.95.1, trans. Fathers of the English Dominican Province, 2nd ed., 22 vols. (London: Burns, Oates & Washbourne, 1911–25), 4:317–18.

100. Thomas Aquinas, *Summa Theologica* II–II.164.1 (13:262).

Setting aside the Platonic influences here, this scenario leaves the moral status of the body ambiguous: the body is intrinsically hostile to holiness and the life of the Spirit. Even Adam's reason on its own is unable to restrain the lower powers of the body. According to Aquinas, the only way Adam could live rightly before God was by receiving "a gratuitous strength superadded to natural strength."[101] As Herman Bavinck remarks about this view, "Matter is a power that stands over against God, one that is not per se sinful, as in Manichaeism, but nevertheless of a very low order; it moves totally in a direction of its own and automatically tempts man to engage in struggle and sin."[102]

In short, Houck's account of original sin as the absence of sanctifying grace implies the Aristotelian-Thomistic notion that eternal life as an end can only be attained by exercising powers that *exceed* the intrinsic capacities of human nature; thus, God must grant supernatural power commensurate with the goal of eternal life.[103] In addition, the *donum superadditum* comes with the assumption that the material dimension of the human being in and of itself is essentially disposed toward sin. This position ultimately detracts from the goodness of the original human constitution and functionally biologizes sin.

Evolutionary hamartiologies that transform sin into a biological problem put us on the horns of a christological dilemma: either Christ was fully human, fully participating in human biology, *and therefore* sinful; or Christ did not share a common biological nature with the rest of humanity and was therefore sinless. Either we deny that Christ was impeccable, or we embrace the heresy of docetism! One can try to escape the dilemma by appealing to Adam's disobedience: his free choice to disobey God polluted human biology all the way down to the genome, causing a corruption that extends all the way into our DNA. The biologizing of sin is thus postlapsarian.[104] But this solution violates the central canons of mainstream evolutionary biology and, in any event, would be cold comfort to theistic evolutionists who normally reject any notion of a cosmic fall.

101. Thomas Aquinas, *Summa Theologica* I–II.109.2 (8:327).

102. Herman Bavinck, *Reformed Dogmatics*, ed. John Bolt, trans. John Vriend, 4 vols. (Grand Rapids: Baker Academic, 2003–8), 2:547. Bavinck is commenting on Robert Bellarmine, *De gratia primi hominis* 5, but the same doctrine of *donum superadditum* is in view.

103. Cf. Seeberg, *Text-Book of the History of Doctrines*, 116.

104. This view implies that Christ assumed a fallen nature, a position first advanced by the nineteenth-century Scottish clergyman Edward Irving (1792–1834) and increasingly endorsed by modern theologians. On the flaws with this Christology, see Robert Letham, *Systematic Theology* (Wheaton: Crossway, 2019), 520–33; Stephen Wellum, *God the Son Incarnate: The Doctrine of Christ* (Wheaton: Crossway, 2016), 232–35.

Similar misgivings extend to soteriology. Before Christ returns in glory, God's remedy for sin is fundamentally spiritual (or nonbiological), and one therefore rightly expects that sin itself is a fundamentally spiritual or nonbiological problem. Justification by grace through faith is the "solution" to the "plight" of human sin. Biologizing sin puts evolutionary hamartiologies at cross-purposes with our union with Christ, justification, and sanctification.[105] To be sure, sin affects our biological bodies as well, but the solution to that problem awaits the resurrection of the body, when our very physicality will be transfigured at the end of the age.

Theologians and scientists who defend these evolutionary doctrines of original sin typically reject anthropological dualism in favor of Christian physicalism, but it is not clear that this materialistic framework can secure the moral responsibility that is a minimal requirement for any notion of sin.[106] The fundamental problem with biologizing accounts of sin is that they fail to capture the true nature of sin. Such concerns have led some theistic evolutionists to construe original corruption as something exclusively *nonbiological*.[107]

For example, Benno van den Toren defends original corruption as a "second nature" instead of a condition inherited biologically from our ancestors.[108] Given the freedom God has given us, we inherit sinful cultural practices as we exercise moral agency in the world. However, our sinfulness is not part of our biological nature but is transmitted culturally: "The cultural inheritance approach to original sin locates sin more strongly on the cultural side of the coevolution of genes and culture, thus locating sin in human action and history rather than in what is given with creation."[109] Van den Toren interprets the drives that we inherit from our evolutionary past as "not in themselves sinful." As he explains: "These biological drives only become sinful when they become integrated in a personal response to a God-given moral order. It is the integration of these desires in a life

105. See the relevant discussion in Ted Peters, "Holy Therapy: Can a Drug Do the Work of the Spirit?," *Christian Century* 120, no. 16 (August 9, 2003): 23–26.

106. Admittedly, while this claim is a reasonable generalization of the scholarship within the science-theology field, it does not hold for many philosophers and theologians outside this academic field who defend both evolutionary theory and anthropological dualism. See chap. 8.

107. Defending this position, John Haught concedes that we inherit aggressive and violent instincts from our evolutionary ancestors but says we should not attribute this fact to original sin. In his view, original sin is "the *culturally* and *environmentally* inherited deposit of humanity's violence and injustice that burdens and threatens to corrupt each of us born into this world." John Haught, *God after Darwin: A Theology of Evolution*, 2nd ed. (Boulder, CO: Westview, 2000), 139, my emphasis.

108. Benno van den Toren, "Human Evolution and a Cultural Understanding of Original Sin," *Perspectives on Science and Christian Faith* 68, no. 1 (2016): 12–21.

109. Van den Toren, "Human Evolution," 18.

characterized by a sinful rejection of God that makes them count as sin, and the solidification and accumulation of this rejection in human cultural history that counts as original sin."[110]

Denis Edwards defended the same position decades before van den Toren. He describes human beings as subjects of genetic and cultural forces that are often impulsive and disorderly. This experience is not sinful, however: "This experience is *intrinsic* to being an evolutionary human," he insists, "but it is *not* sin."[111] Edwards was borrowing a distinction from Karl Rahner—namely, sinful versus nonsinful concupiscence (as we saw with Houck's account of original sin, this distinction goes back to the medievals). Sinful concupiscence is original sin, the history of our rejection of God that conditions our lives and our free decisions. But Edwards recognizes a separate, morally neutral, nonsinful concupiscence, "which is not the result of sin but . . . is intrinsic to being a spiritual creature who is at the same time radically bodily and limited."[112] He classifies our finitude and physicality as fueling a disorder that is "intrinsic to the human," making it a nonsinful part of God's good creation.[113]

According to Edwards, culture tells a long story of inherited sinfulness involving countless personal and communal sins that are taken up into our inner selves to become part of our own moral story. "Original sin," he explains, "involves the inner effect on a person of the history of human rejection of God and of our creaturely status before God."[114] We should note that Edwards is using the language of "original sin" loosely. This "inherited sinfulness" that results from the sins of others is *not yet sin*, for sin itself is "personal and actual; it is the free and deliberate rejection of God. It is only for this kind of personal sin that we are morally responsible."[115] Only when we personally *choose* to disobey God can we speak of genuine sin.

---

110. Van den Toren, "Human Evolution," 18.

111. Denis Edwards, *The God of Evolution: A Trinitarian Theology* (Mahwah, NJ: Paulist Press, 1999), 65. See also Jerry Korsmeyer, who writes, "Humans are born into this state [of original sin], but are not actually sinners until they knowingly defy the divine call. The divine call to each individual is a call to transcend his or her predispositions, instincts, and social training. . . . Concupiscence, in this explanation, precedes sin." Jerry Korsmeyer, *Evolution and Eden: Balancing Original Sin and Contemporary Science* (New York: Paulist Press, 1998), 123.

112. Denis Edwards, "Original Sin and Saving Grace in Evolutionary Context," in *Evolutionary and Molecular Biology: Scientific Perspectives on Divine Action*, ed. Robert J. Russell, William R. Stoeger, and Francisco Ayala (Notre Dame, IN: University of Notre Dame Press, 1998), 384. See also Karl Rahner, "The Theological Concept of Concupiscentia," in *Theological Investigations*, trans. Cornelius Ernst, 23 vols. (Baltimore: Helicon, 1961), 1:347–82.

113. Edwards, "Original Sin and Saving Grace," 384.

114. Edwards, "Original Sin and Saving Grace," 385.

115. Edwards, *God of Evolution*, 67.

For Edwards, our inherited tendencies "are simply part of being a bodily, finite, and fallible creature."[116]

The shadow of Frederick Tennant looms large.[117] Edwards, like Tennant, has naturalized original corruption so that inherited tendencies are no longer sinful. According to Tennant, the property of "sinfulness" only applies to human free will. Evolutionary biology bequeaths all human beings with "perfectly non-moral antecedents of sin," and those antecedents form the material out of which the human will then freely chooses to sin.[118] Tennant and Edwards both reject the concept of inherited sin as ill-conceived, for they would say that anything inherited cannot be sinful. The Tennant-Edwards strategy of shielding free will from evolutionary determinism is the reincarnation of Pelagianism in a biological key. Edwards is right to distance the doctrine of original sin from the reductive grasp of evolution, but he has developed a reactionary, overinflated concept of free will that obscures Scripture's witness to original sin, a deeper moral corruption that is antecedent to our choices and actions.

The need to develop an evolutionary doctrine of sin becomes urgent if evolution is the truth about God's world. As we saw in earlier chapters, since the late nineteenth century Christians have devised all kinds of ways to reconcile evolution and Christian doctrine. While I cannot rehearse that long story here, I do not underestimate the magnitude of the questions raised (especially) by geology and evolutionary biology. However, earlier chapters in this book have argued at length in favor of such truths as biblical chronology, antediluvian life spans, monogenism, original goodness, a cosmic fall, and original immortality. And while my aim throughout this book has been to flesh out a dogmatic account of sin—not creation—in dialogue with science, each of these doctrines *individually* contradicts mainstream evolution. If we consider these doctrinal commitments *en masse*, then the mainstream story of evolution is doomed on theological grounds. And, of course, if evolution as such is implausible theologically, then the prospects for an evolutionary doctrine of original sin are very slim indeed.

At the same time, the different harmonizing strategies to biologize sin fail to capture the nature of sin. Human sinfulness as portrayed in Scripture and within the classical theological tradition is a problem that lies

116. Denis Edwards, *How God Acts: Creation, Redemption, and Special Divine Action* (Minneapolis: Fortress, 2010), 135.

117. See the beginning of chap. 6 above, where I introduced the work of Frederick Tennant.

118. Frederick R. Tennant, *The Origin and Propagation of Sin: Being the Hulsean Lectures Delivered before the University of Cambridge, 1901–02*, 2nd ed. (Cambridge: Cambridge University Press, 1906), 172–73.

deeper than our biology, and sin is not a problem that is intrinsic to our original human nature as created by God in Genesis 1 and 2. Theistic evolutionists who recognize these problems are forced to reinterpret sinful desires (i.e., concupiscence) as nonmoral biological drives inherited from an evolutionary past; as a result, "sin" becomes a limited notion exiled to the cultural and spiritual sphere. But since many Christian evolutionists hold to a nonreductive *physicalist* anthropology, this last strategy is really trying to run with the hare and hunt with the hounds. In short, evolutionary theories of original sin face insurmountable problems. For the remainder of this chapter I will therefore set evolution aside. That still leaves us with work to do as we think about the relationship between original sin and biology.

A Theology of Sin, Biology, and Embodiment

In the Calvinist tradition, compatibilism is the view, roughly, that divine determinism and moral responsibility are compatible.[119] While I accept divine determinism as faithful to Scripture, that is not my interest here; rather, I propose that we broaden Reformed compatibilism to include the additional claim that *biological embodiment* and moral responsibility are entirely compatible—thus, embodiment and original sin are compatible. Reformed compatibilism holds that human embodiment, behavioral genetics, and other biological facts about us are not a threat to responsibility but the very condition for its expression.

Reformed Compatibilism and Biology

Part of the problem in the West is that we live in an intellectual climate where biological concepts pervade our thinking about what we humans are and why we do the things we do. The history of psychiatry is the story of how moral and religious talk about sin was gradually replaced by scientific and biologically deterministic theories of human behavior.[120] Scientific criminology emerged in the wake of the eighteenth-century Enlightenment as long-standing medieval assumptions were discarded in favor of new

119. For example, see Guillaume Bignon, *Excusing Sinners and Blaming God: A Calvinist Assessment of Determinism, Moral Responsibility, and Divine Involvement in Evil* (Eugene, OR: Pickwick, 2018).

120. Janet Ann Tighe, "A Question of Responsibility: The Development of American Forensic Psychiatry, 1838–1930" (PhD diss., University of Pennsylvania, 1983). On controversies related to biological psychiatry, see Colin Ross and Alvin Pam, *Pseudoscience in Biological Psychiatry: Blaming the Body* (New York: Wiley & Sons, 1995).

biological theories.[121] The field of medical jurisprudence witnessed parallel developments.[122] Discourse about sin was secularized as older ways of thinking about human creatures conceded ground to newer biological and scientific horizons.

Nancy Press cautions that much of the research on the genetic bases of behavioral traits is socially constructed. Some behavioral patterns are not "concrete, bounded 'things in the world,'" but the scientific search for genetic underpinnings reifies those patterns of behavior and subjects them to the "medical gaze."[123] As soon as social scientists create a deviancy label, the classification itself reinforces or heightens the incidence of deviant behavior.[124] Ian Hacking terms this process *dynamic nominalism*: "Numerous kinds of human beings and human acts come into being hand in hand with our invention of the categories labeling them. . . . Our spheres of possibility, and hence ourselves, are to some extent made up by our naming and what that entails."[125] The medicalization of behavior *creates* a feedback loop or "looping effects."[126] Drawing on Hacking's work, Press writes, "The very process of looking for a 'gene for' a behavior reinforces the sense of the reality and medicalized nature of that behavior or disorder. In some cases, it may even help create a social role—a way for a person to *have* or to *be* that category. Once available, this role is easier to choose, and an individual, health care providers, a family, society, support groups, all may increasingly sort through feelings and behaviors in a way that reinforces and coalesces the 'syndrome.'"[127] Theologians need not endorse everything

121. Nicole Rafter, *The Criminal Brain: Understanding Biological Theories of Crime* (New York: New York University Press, 2008), 19.

122. James Mohr, *Doctors and the Law: Medical Jurisprudence in Nineteenth-Century America* (New York: Oxford University Press, 1993).

123. Nancy Press, "Social Construction and Medicalization: Behavioral Genetics in Context," in Parens, Chapman, and Press, *Wrestling with Behavioral Genetics*, 145. Some of these dynamics likely play into the disagreement within the American Psychiatric Association on how best to categorize personality disorders (categorical versus dimensional). The status quo (categorical) won the day, but they included the alternative dimensional classification in the section titled "Emerging Measures and Models." See American Psychiatric Association, *Diagnostic and Statistical Manual of Mental Disorders: DSM-5*, 5th ed. (Washington, DC: American Psychiatric Association, 2013), 761–806.

124. Ian Hacking, *The Social Construction of What?* (Cambridge, MA: Harvard University Press, 1999), 160.

125. Ian Hacking, "Making Up People," in *Forms of Desire: Sexual Orientation and the Social Constructionist Controversy*, ed. E. Stein (New York: Routledge, 1990), 87, cited in Press, "Social Construction and Medicalization," 145.

126. See also Ian Hacking, "The Making and Molding of Child Abuse," *Critical Inquiry* 17, no. 2 (1991): 253–88; and Ian Hacking, "The Looping Effects of Human Kinds," in *Causal Cognition: A Multidisciplinary Approach*, ed. Dan Sperber, David Premack, and Ann James Premack (Oxford: Clarendon, 1995), 351–83.

127. Press, "Social Construction and Medicalization," 145.

Press and Hacking are advocating; most of their critique applies especially
to journalists (and scientists acting like bad journalists!) who oversimplify
and misrepresent the scientific research. Serious geneticists and academic
psychiatrists recognize that most traits are influenced by multiple genes
(and epigenetic factors) rather than single genes causing discrete traits.

Nevertheless, nonspecialists are often biased toward genetic essentialism and think that genetics captures the essence of who human beings
are deep down.[128] The dictates of behavioral genetics are valorized as immutable, natural, and ultimate. But such notions are grossly misleading:
"When most people are thinking about genes, they are not really thinking
about genes in the complex ways that good scientists are—they are thinking about them in the simplistic ways that laypeople customarily think
about essences."[129] These looping effects widen the distance that people
feel between the biblical portrait of original sin and the medicalized image
of humanity.

In fact, sin is not physical or biological. Original sin is a *moral* quality of
someone separated from God, and thus it transcends our biological condition.[130] Herman Bavinck describes sin as the "ethical antithesis of the good"
that does not have its own independent existence. Sin is an ethical-spiritual
reality, not a physical-material one.[131] Our very existence as fallen creatures is conditioned by sin, antecedent to any actual sinful desires or deeds
(Rom. 5:12–21; 1 Cor. 15:21–22). In his riposte to Erasmus, Martin Luther
maintains that human wills are bound to sin and need transformation by
divine grace.[132] Beyond Luther, other magisterial Reformers agree that our
wills are fallen and conditioned by original sin. This Augustinian diagnosis
was enshrined as sober truth in Protestant confessional statements such as
these:

> It is taught among us that since the fall of Adam, all human beings who are
> born in the natural way are conceived and born in sin. This means that from
> birth they are full of evil lust and inclination and cannot by nature possess

128. Ilan Dar-Nimrod, Ruth Kuntzman, Georgia MacNevin, Kate Lynch, Marlon Woods, and
James Morandini, "Genetic Essentialism: The Mediating Role of Essentialist Biases on the Relationship between Genetic Knowledge and the Interpretations of Genetic Information," *European Journal
of Medical Genetics* 64, no. 1 (2021), doi.org/10.1016/j.ejmg.2020.104119.
129. Steven Heine, Benjamin Cheung, and Anita Schmalor, "Making Sense of Genetics: The
Problem of Essentialism," *Looking for the Psychosocial Impacts of Genomic Information*, special report,
Hastings Center Report 49, no. 3 (2019): S20–21.
130. Bavinck, *Reformed Dogmatics*, 3:116–17.
131. Bavinck, *Reformed Dogmatics*, 3:138.
132. E. Gordon Rupp, ed., *Luther and Erasmus: Free Will and Salvation* (Louisville: Westminster
John Knox, 2006).

true fear of God and true faith in God. Moreover, this same innate disease and original sin is truly sin and condemns to God's eternal wrath all who are not in turn born anew through baptism and the Holy Spirit.[133]

The condition of man after the fall of Adam is such, that he cannot turn and prepare himself, by his own natural strength and good works, to faith, and calling upon God: Wherefore we have no power to do good works pleasant and acceptable to God, without the grace of God by Christ preventing us that we may have a good will, and working with us when we have that good will.[134]

From this original corruption [of our first parents], whereby we are utterly indisposed, disabled, and made opposite to all good, and wholly inclined to all evil, do proceed all actual transgressions. . . . This corruption of nature, during this life, doth remain in those that are regenerated; and although it be, through Christ, pardoned and mortified, yet both itself and all the motions thereof are truly and properly sin.[135]

On the one hand, God condemns high-handed sins like adultery, murder, theft, bearing false witness, and the like (e.g., Deut. 5:6–21). One might thus infer that people have the capacity to avoid overt, deliberate rebellion against God; they can make a conscious choice for good. On the other hand, the voluntarist dimension to sin is only one side of the coin. Scripture also portrays sin as a deeper, more sinister reality. Sin is a slave master and we are its captives; rather than us controlling sin, it controls us. In the Pauline self-diagnosis, "I am unspiritual, sold as a slave to sin. I do not understand what I do. For what I want to do I do not do, but what I hate I do" (Rom. 7:14–15 NIV). Sin is inevitable, despite the best will to change.

Many reject this classical Augustinian picture as illogical: "That sin is *both* unavoidable *and* culpable is logically incoherent."[136] However, this inference is mistaken on two counts. First, each of us is born in a state of original guilt and corruption because all humanity was implicated in Adam's fall; that we

133. The Augsburg Confession (1531), in *The Book of Concord: The Confessions of the Evangelical Lutheran Church*, ed. Robert Kolb and Timothy Wengert (Minneapolis: Fortress, 2000), 37–38.

134. The Thirty-Nine Articles of the Church of England (1571), in *Creeds and Confessions of Faith in the Christian Tradition*, vol. 2, ed. Jaroslav Pelikan and Valerie Hotchkiss (New Haven: Yale University Press, 2003), 531. "Preventing grace" is God's prevenient grace (*gratia præveniens*) that inclines the will to conversion.

135. The Westminster Confession of Faith (1647), in Pelikan and Hotchkiss, *Creeds and Confessions of Faith*, 614.

136. Ian McFarland, "The Fall and Sin," in *The Oxford Handbook of Systematic Theology*, ed. John Webster, Kathryn Tanner, and Iain Torrance (Oxford: Oxford University Press, 2007), 145. McFarland himself does not think the Augustinian view is incoherent.

all invariably sin as a result is not incoherent or unfair.[137] Second, Scripture never endorses an autonomous free will, but instead depicts us as slaves to sin *and also* fully responsible. The biblical story falls apart without this latter notion of accountability.[138]

Scripture always attributes moral agency to the person *coram Deo* (before the face of God). "Against you, you only, have *I* sinned" (Ps. 51:4). *I* am guilty. Scripture never hints at causes or essences more basic than the person. Jesus says that evil thoughts, murder, adultery, and other such sins flow "out of the heart" (Matt. 15:19). Our sins arise from "the abundance of the heart" (Matt. 12:34)—the "heart" is what most fully discloses *me* (Gen. 6:5; Ps. 14:1–3; Mark 7:21; Rom. 3:9–20), embodied, to be sure, but not reducible to the body. The problem with biologizing sin is that it tends to conflate creation with sin; progressive sanctification then becomes a process more akin to overcoming genetic and environmental constraints.[139] But creation is fallen, *not* sinful. Our bodies are prone to suffering and death but are not ultimate sources of sin. Original sin itself tracks deeper than biology. Furthermore, divine forgiveness lies at the heart of soteriology, but biologized notions of sin threaten the biblical view of forgiveness. If sin is caused by biological forces that predate humanity by millions of years, then genuine culpability becomes elusive. Moral responsibility for sin is blunted, if not eviscerated, and the forgiveness of sins is no longer truly glad tidings for wayward sinners.

At the same time, original sin is always conditioned by embodiment. Sin reigns in our mortal bodies (Rom. 6:12). Scripture assumes close ties between the frailty of our bodies and our sinful condition.[140] "Though not the seat of sin," John Murray writes, "the body becomes depraved. It becomes the agent of sin and its members instruments of unrighteousness unto sin. The body is a sinful body and thus the body of sin (Rom. 6:6)."[141] Indwelling sin expresses its dominion over us *through* our bodies; it uses the body as an instrument of wickedness (Rom. 6:13). The glory of humanity is that we are embodied souls, higher than animals but lower than angels (Ps. 8:4–8). Embodiment gives a biological or "bodily" character to many of

137. I recognize these are contested claims—especially original guilt—but I have defended this position elsewhere. See references listed in note 10 above.

138. Scripture ties the reality of moral responsibility to the costly gift of redemption (e.g., Eph. 2:3–10; Col. 2:13–14). Bonnie Howe, "Accountability," in *Dictionary of Scripture and Ethics*, ed. Joel Green (Grand Rapids: Baker Academic, 2011), 37–39.

139. Hill defends this approach in *Evolution and Holiness*.

140. Bavinck, *Reformed Dogmatics*, 3:55.

141. John Murray, "Origin of Man," in *Collected Writings of John Murray*, 4 vols. (Edinburgh: Banner of Truth Trust, 1977), 2:15.

our sins that distinguishes us from fallen angels. As Bavinck says, "while the sensual nature of humans is not itself sin, nor the source or principle of sin, *it is its dwelling place*."[142] Sin is not physical, but it operates in and through the physical members of the body (Rom. 7:23)—"corporeal flesh is weak because of its physical needs and desires, and therefore easy prey for sin."[143] We serve our bodily appetites instead of the Lord Jesus (16:18). Our minds are distracted by earthly things and our stomach becomes our god (Phil. 3:19). Creaturely desires are a gift from God, but they are also expressed by "the deeds of the body" (Rom. 8:13).

In the context of original corruption, human genetics and the rest of our embodied nature are best seen as sources of *temptation*.[144] Temptation is the pull toward sin when we try to satisfy our perceived needs and desires in the context of our relationships with God, the external world, other people, and ourselves. Most of these desires are legitimate and God-given, but we try to satisfy them in the wrong ways; other temptations reflect corrupt desires rooted in original sin.[145] Everything in the world or in our very selves—indeed all of life—can be a source of temptation. We are tempted to turn against our Father. Our desires for food, drink, sex, friendship, pleasure, rest, and more are all sources of temptation. The list is endless.[146] As John McKinley reminds us, temptability to sin looks different for each person: "All temptations are related to the specific and subjective particularity of an individual person."[147] Behavioral genetics at its best describes the variability of each person *in their embodiment*—and that variability contextualizes the different ways we are tempted to sin.

This temptability is the pull to sin, *not* sin itself; it is a function of being human, something that was true of Adam and Eve before the fall and of Jesus during his incarnation.[148] This last point may seem to contradict the theological distinction between temptations that arise from outside the individual (the world; the devil) and temptations from within (sinful desires);

142. Bavinck, *Reformed Dogmatics*, 3:55, my emphasis.

143. Robert Gundry, *Sōma in Biblical Theology, with Emphasis on Pauline Anthropology* (Cambridge: Cambridge University Press, 1976), 137.

144. For my reflections here, I am indebted to John E. McKinley, *Tempted for Us: Theological Models and the Practical Relevance of Christ's Impeccability and Temptation* (Eugene, OR: Wipf & Stock, 2009), esp. 261–97.

145. Thus Jesus—the sinless God-man—experienced all kinds of temptation without any corrupt desires since he had no original sin (Heb. 4:15).

146. Not all temptation is connected to embodiment; for example, temptation by demons is often, but not always, parasitic on biological needs and desires.

147. McKinley, *Tempted for Us*, 275.

148. Will we be temptable in our glorified bodies in the new heavens and new earth? While I am not sure, I am inclined to say no (but see McKinley, *Tempted for Us*, 272n22).

the impeccability of Jesus implies that he experienced only *external* temptation without any of the sinful desires that are bound up with *internal* temptation.[149] However, my assertion that Jesus experienced temptability as a result of his genetic predispositions does not violate this conventional christological distinction. Here we need to nuance what we mean by "external" versus "internal" temptation. Jesus did not experience internal temptation if by "internal" we mean temptations that arise from moral corruption (i.e., original sin). But I have been arguing that genetic predispositions do *not* arise from our moral corruption at all; they are instead a function of our physical bodies given to us at creation—bodies that can certainly be affected by the fall (as we shall see below) but that are intrinsically part of the goodness of creation. Genetic predispositions are positionally internal to our bodies since they are located at the level of the genome, but hamartiologically they are external: such predispositions influence our personalities, temperaments, sensitivities, and the like, but these are not the stuff of original corruption. Sin arises from the soul and expresses itself in and through the variabilities of our embodiment. Genetic temptability as such does not threaten the sinlessness of Christ.

Temptation also has a dual teleology in that "a particular individual's circumstances may be simultaneously a *temptation* to sin and a *test* for sanctification."[150] The same dual teleology applies to genetic inheritances. Like the rest of God's good creation, our genetic predispositions are always potential sources of temptation and sanctification. Far from undermining moral responsibility, genetic predispositions are one of the primary settings God gives for our individual moral agency to find its full expression.

The Relationship between Biology and Sinfulness

I opened the chapter with Brunner syndrome, the case of a Dutch family where the affected males presented with unusually violent and impulsive behavior. Such behavior seems patently sinful. Something similar might be said for patients with the neuropsychiatric disorder Tourette's syndrome who sometimes manifest irresistible swearing and obscenities (coprolalia). In one case report, the individual shouted vulgarities at a frequency of fifty words per minute, including racial slurs and offensive words, only

149. This distinction goes back to early theologians like Augustine and Aquinas, who identified concupiscence as disordered desire and thus sinful; this temptation to sin (or temptability) is itself sinful. Anselm disagreed and argued that concupiscence is not sinful at all. For discussion, see Houck, "Toward a New Account of the Fall," esp. 441–44.

150. McKinley, *Tempted for Us*, 273.

to apologize right after.[151] Or consider the case of a man who had developed an insatiable appetite for sex and pedophilia; a persistent headache prompted an MRI, which led to the discovery of a tumor mass. The mass was removed and his symptoms vanished completely. Orbitofrontal tumors can apparently cause pedophilia and sex addiction.[152] What should we make of such cases? At the outset, it bears repeating that the ethical implications of many of these syndromes remain contested. For example, the published research on monoamine oxidase deficiency—the gene disorder thought to cause Brunner syndrome—is ambiguous if not contradictory.[153] Reflecting theologically on these data will require care.

In Jitse van der Meer's summary of the relevant mainstream science, he concludes that Adam's fall could not have changed the order of nature.[154] Ancient fossils, for instance, have left many traces of predator-prey interactions.[155] The fossil record also indicates fatal diseases in extinct organisms, including arthritis in dinosaurs and cancers dispersed throughout the animal kingdom.[156] Such widespread studies all date the evidence of past disease to millions of years before humanity ever existed. He also cites evidence that mutations causing genetic diseases long predate the fall. "This evidence," he writes, "has prompted a reinterpretation of the curses in Genesis 3:14–19, 4:11, 5:29, Deuteronomy 28:16–20."[157] Van der Meer concludes that genetic mutations are built into the very fabric of creation; thus, the scientific evidence falsifies the notion of a cosmic fall.

It follows from this post-Darwinian picture that Brunner syndrome, orbitofrontal tumors, and the like, are simply functions of God's good creation. Primeval sin, in this view, plays no causal role in these conditions. However, the doctrine of original goodness calls the scientific consensus at this point

151. Mouna Ben Djebara et al., "Aripiprazole: A Treatment for Severe Coprolalia in 'Refractory' Gilles de la Tourette Syndrome," *Movement Disorders* 23, no. 3 (2008): 438–40.

152. Jeffrey Burns and Russell Swerdlow, "Right Orbitofrontal Tumor with Pedophilia Symptom and Constructional Apraxia Sign," *Archives of Neurology* 60, no. 3 (2003): 437–40.

153. Alexander, *Genes, Determinism and God*, 162–84.

154. I am drawing my remarks (including secondary sources) from Jitse van der Meer, "Genesis, Science, and Theories of Origins," in *The Cambridge Companion to Genesis*, ed. Bill Arnold (Cambridge: Cambridge University Press, 2022), 244–47.

155. Patricia Kelley, Michal Kowalevski, and Thor Hansen, eds., *Predator-Prey Interactions in the Fossil Record* (New York: Kluwer Academic, 2003).

156. See, inter alia, Jennifer Anné, Brian Hedrick, and Jason Schein, "First Diagnosis of Septic Arthritis in a Dinosaur," *Royal Society Open Science* 3, no. 8 (2016), doi.org/10.1098/rsos.160222; Bruce Rothschild and Larry Martin, *Paleopathology: Disease in the Fossil Record* (Boca Raton, FL: Chemical Rubber Company, 1993); and Yara Haridy et al., "Triassic Cancer: Osteosarcoma in a 240-Million-Year-Old Stem-Turtle," *Journal of the American Medical Association Oncology* 5, no. 3 (2019): 425–26.

157. Van der Meer, "Genesis, Science, and Theories of Origins," 245.

into question (see chap. 5), which suggests the need for alternative scientific models that interpret the same empirical data without contradicting the Word of God. We need a different perspective on organic diseases that are associated with sinful behaviors.

To begin with, we sin because we are sinners; actual sins arise from original corruption. We are culpable for our inner depravity (original guilt) but are further culpable for sins we commit in thought, word, and deed. Syndromes like Brunner and Tourette's reveal a tragic effect of the cosmic fall—namely, that we can suffer genetic disorders that cause an unusual exacerbation and even disruption of the normal causal link between original corruption and actual sins. Affected individuals are blameworthy, but particular sins may involve a mitigated culpability.

Scripture lays out multiple scenarios in which culpability for sin is mitigated in some way. For example, the Old Testament groups sins in three categories as unintentional (Lev. 4:13; Num. 35), intentional but not high-handed (Lev. 5:1; 6:1–7; Num. 5:5–8), and high-handed (Num. 15:30–31).[158] Sacrificial atonement is possible for the first two kinds of sins but not the third.[159] By the time we reach the New Testament, this notion of different degrees of sin is not abrogated (e.g., see Heb. 6:4–6; 1 John 5:16). The presence (or absence) of intentionality plays a key role in how we ascribe moral culpability. Scripture usually considers us more blameworthy for sins committed with full intentionality versus sins committed unintentionally. Furthermore, culpability also depends on whether physical circumstances prevent one from obeying God's commandments. In Numbers 9:6–7, some men are unable to keep the Passover because they are ceremonially unclean, and they ask Moses for a ruling on their situation. After consulting with Yahweh, Moses rules that they are not culpable for breaking the Passover and should not be cut off from Israel (vv. 8–12).

In light of such passages, Reformed compatibilism has a disclosive notion of moral culpability that makes allowance for diminished culpability in certain situations (e.g., reduced intent; exculpating physical circumstances).[160] Specifically, culpability comes with what Jesse Couenhoven calls "deep

158. Jay Sklar, "Sin and Atonement: Lessons from the Pentateuch," *Bulletin for Biblical Research* 22 (2012): 469–85; Roy E. Gane, "Numbers 15:22–31 and the Spectrum of Moral Faults," in *Inicios, paradigmas y fundamentos: Estudios teológicos y exegéticos en el Pentateuco*, ed. Gerald A. Klingbeil (Libertador San Martín, Argentina: Editorial Universidad Adventista del Plata, 2004), 149–56; Mark J. Boda, *A Severe Mercy: Sin and Its Remedy in the Old Testament* (Winona Lake, IN: Eisenbrauns, 2009), 53–54.

159. However, nonsacrificial atonement was available for high-handed sins. See Sklar, "Sin and Atonement," 485–90.

160. For analysis of the relationship between sin and culpability, see Marguerite Shuster, *The Fall and Sin: What We Have Become as Sinners* (Grand Rapids: Eerdmans, 2004), 137–43.

responsibility," meaning that we are culpable for desires and actions that truly disclose our hearts. Deep responsibility, he explains, "is not so much self-making as self-disclosure."[161] We are deeply responsible for those things that disclose our hearts even if God is exhaustively sovereign over them (compatibilism)—libertarian freedom, the ability to do otherwise, is not necessary for deep responsibility.[162] We are morally responsible for desires and beliefs—and actions or inactions motivated by them—if they are produced in us when we are properly functioning or, more precisely, when they are produced in us in a way that *reliably discloses the heart*.[163] I suggest that individuals affected by the kinds of syndromes we have been discussing sometimes commit "sins" that are not reliably disclosing the heart. The link between original corruption and actual sins has been damaged.

I speculate that Brunner syndrome and similar disorders disrupt—in ways that I do not fully understand—the intimate union between soul and body. On the one hand, the affected person's outward behaviors *are* disclosing the moral corruption inherited from Adam. All of us have this moral corruption, and we sin because of it. In Brunner syndrome, Tourette's syndrome, and orbitofrontal sociopathy, the associated sins are indeed loathsome to God and the affected individuals are indeed culpable for them. Their outward sins disclose inner depravity, and if any of us were afflicted with the same condition, as fellow descendants of Adam with the condition of original sin (corruption), we would doubtless manifest the same behaviors. I am not therefore heaping condemnation on anyone with such struggles (cf. Luke 11:46; Matt. 23:4); my intention is to clarify the nature of sin.[164]

On the other hand, although sinful behaviors associated with these conditions disclose the heart, there are mitigating factors: these outward sins lack the normal tethering of God's common grace. While the sinful

---

161. Jesse Couenhoven, "What Sin Is: A Differential Analysis," *Modern Theology* 25, no. 4 (2009): 577.

162. Of course, many Christians hold that moral responsibility requires libertarian freedom (or incompatibilism). I cannot mount a defense here, but Bignon offers a Reformed account in his *Excusing Sinners and Blaming God*.

163. Couenhoven, "What Sin Is," 580. I am indebted to Couenhoven for this application of the proper function concept.

164. Since Brunner syndrome results from the fallenness of creation, I think it would have been impossible for Jesus to have suffered from this (or any other) genetic disease—given that the human nature he inherited was unfallen, not fallen. However, if the reader would allow me to engage in a hypothetical scenario (reverently!), what would have happened had Jesus developed Brunner syndrome during his earthly ministry? I speculate that his outward behaviors would have been unusual—repetitive, hyper-energetic, emotional, eccentric, flamboyant, and so on—but *not* sinful; it is impossible for Jesus to commit any sinful behaviors given his impeccability and the absence of internal moral corruption from which any sins could arise.

"quality" of their behaviors derives from the heart, the underlying condition seems to be amplifying the "quantity" of sinful behaviors expressed by the individual (and perhaps also distorting the quality of sins). In normal circumstances, original corruption does not manifest itself to the highest degree. In the Lord's kindness, much of our sinfulness remains below the surface at the level of the heart, or in our thought lives; as a result, we commit fewer behavioral sins and are thus presumably less culpable.[165] But in these rare cases, and for mysterious reasons, the link between original corruption and actual sins is functioning abnormally; inner depravity is not restrained in typical "common grace" ways, and intentionality is either absent or disordered. Taking all this together, I suggest that individuals affected by such conditions are less culpable and God thus judges their "untethered" sinful behaviors less severely.

Conclusion

In closing, it is worth summing up the argument of this chapter. Original sin is not biological but is conditioned by and acts through our biological constitution. In our post-Darwinian setting, evolutionary psychology and behavioral genetics raise questions about the relationship between original sin and biology. Evolutionary psychology—a group of controversial theories that try to explain human behavior from an evolutionary perspective—raises the possibility that original corruption is a biological reality that we inherit from our evolutionary ancestors. From a different perspective, behavioral genetics also prompts the question whether human sinfulness is ultimately rooted in genetic forces. These intellectual developments make it difficult to distinguish between "moral" and "natural" evil. Human sins now seem less about spiritual depravity than about the biological nature.

In light of these challenges from biology, theistic evolutionists have offered creative evolutionary accounts of original sin. Like the Manichaean theories of the ancient world, some of these proposals effectively transform sin into an ontological fact about human nature as such. Others try to carve out space for freedom and altruism to resist the biological pull of sin; on those accounts, original sin is the delicate interplay of biology and culture.

However, biologizing accounts of sin fail to capture the essence of sin as something irreducibly spiritual that is deeply internal to us. Evolutionary hamartiologies also imply that God is blameworthy since he created

---

165. Of course, I am not denying that God holds us accountable for sins of the heart (Matt. 5:27–30)! My only point is that we are *additionally* accountable for behavioral sins.

human beings using an evolutionary process that renders sin inevitable. A minority of Christian evolutionists insist that human sinfulness is not transmitted biologically in any sense, but culturally. The disordered desires that we inherit from evolution are part of the goodness of creaturely finitude. The theistic evolutionists who categorize sin as entirely nonbiological are somewhat successful in rescuing sin from biological reductionism, but they leave us with a hyperinflated concept of free will at odds with original corruption.

My constructive proposal expands the definition of Reformed compatibilism to include the full compatibility of physical embodiment and original corruption. The soul, not the body, is the source of sin. Original sin is not a biological but a moral quality signaling the absence of communion with God. Our very existence as fallen creatures is conditioned by sin, antecedent to any actual sinful desires or deeds. Moral agency, then, is more "self-disclosure" (compatibilist) than "self-making" (incompatibilist). Persons are culpable before God for internal desires and external actions that truly disclose their hearts.

Although original sin is not a physical-material reality, human sinfulness is always conditioned by our biological natures. Original corruption and our frail bodies interpenetrate in all kinds of ways; as Paul says, sin reigns in our mortal bodies (Rom. 6:12). Furthermore, Reformed compatibilism suggests that human genetics and other aspects of our embodied nature are often sources of temptation. Behavioral genetics describes individual variabilities rooted in our bodies that contextualize the different ways we can be tempted to sin. In the providence of God, genetic predispositions are potential sources of both temptation and sanctification. Biological embodiment is no threat to human responsibility but a central way that moral agency is expressed in God's world.

But this world suffers from the cosmic fall. One of the symptoms of fallen nature is that disorders like Brunner syndrome, Tourette's syndrome, and orbitofrontal tumors can disrupt the normal causal bond between original corruption and actual sins. Affected individuals sometimes present with sinful thoughts and behaviors that disclose the heart in a distorted hyperactive mode. Such individuals are culpable because these sins genuinely disclose original corruption; yet the disorder often enables their moral depravity to express itself in unusually prolific ways (and thus the grossly abnormal function suggests some degree of mitigated culpability).

One of the lingering questions in this chapter concerns the relationship between sin and anthropological dualism. Is it possible to make sense of the Christian doctrine of sin if the human constitution is physical without remainder? Or does the nature of sin require a dualist anthropology? I shall take up such questions in the following chapter.

In the meantime, the ground we have covered here impresses upon us the stark reality of original corruption. Yet the grim diagnosis brings the cure into sharp relief: "But God shows his love for us in that while we were still sinners, Christ died for us" (Rom. 5:8). Like the holy angels around heaven's throne, we can only fall down on our faces and worship God (Rev. 7:11–12 NIV):

> Amen!
> Praise and glory
> and wisdom and thanks and honor
> and power and strength
> be to our God for ever and ever.
> Amen!

8

Souls and the Nature of Sin

Souls are not fashionable, at present. People will listen with wondering acquiescence to scientific talk of such invisible entities as are said to be everywhere and very important, but they shy away from talk of souls. Souls have a bad name in the world of atomic energy.

—Robertson Davies[1]

One widespread tradition has it that we human beings are responsible agents, captains of our fate, *because* what we really are are *souls*, immaterial and immortal clumps of Godstuff that inhabit and control our material bodies rather like spectral puppeteers. . . . But this idea of immaterial souls, capable of defying the laws of physics, has outlived its credibility thanks to the advance of the natural sciences.

—Daniel Dennett[2]

Bible scholars generally have a phobia about "biblical anthropology," similar to the way a person might avoid a patch of highway years after having had a bad accident there.

—Jeffrey Boyd[3]

This chapter is a significant revision of my prior essay "From Sin to the Soul: A Dogmatic Argument for Dualism," in *The Christian Doctrine of Humanity*, ed. Oliver Crisp and Fred Sanders (Grand Rapids: Zondervan, 2018), 70–90 (used with permission).

1. Robertson Davies, *The Lyre of Orpheus* (New York: Penguin Books, 1992), 998.

2. Daniel Dennett, *Freedom Evolves* (New York: Viking, 2003), 1.

3. Jeffrey H. Boyd, "Losing Soul: How and Why Theologians Created the Mental Health Movement," *Calvin Theological Journal* 30, no. 2 (1995): 480.

T he opening quote from Daniel Dennett, one of the Four Horsemen
of New Atheism, challenges the idea that humans are embodied
souls. He thinks dualism is a lost cause; human beings are material organisms, plain and simple. Immaterial substances may serve as
grist for historians of antiquity but are hardly the sober truth about human
ontology. Since Dennett and fellow atheists do not believe in God, angels,
or any other supernatural entities, none of this is surprising—but atheists
do not have a monopoly on physicalist anthropologies.[4] They are joined by
Christian scholars who urge the death of dualism so that a better scientific
view of the person can rise from the ashes.

The Catholic theologian John Haught warns that dualism is "evasive, artificial, and theologically shallow."[5] The physicist-theologian John Polkinghorne remarks that "for many people [dualism] has become an extremely
problematic way of conceiving human nature."[6] Philip Hefner, a Lutheran
systematic theologian and founder of the Zygon Center for Religion and Science, claims that "dualism is foreign to the authentic Christian tradition."[7]
Although he gave that opinion in the 1960s, in many circles today he is
simply voicing a truism: the sky is blue; theologians are beautiful; Nigeria
will win the next World Cup.

Anti-dualism is not only rampant in the interdisciplinary field of science-
and-theology but is thriving among biblical scholars and theologians who
believe that Scripture best aligns with a physicalist anthropology.[8] Older
dualistic exegesis was allegedly forged in dialogue with Platonic and Aristotelian philosophies, the "sciences" of that day.[9] Given our current physical
understanding of the world, we are told, dualism is highly implausible.

4. In this chapter, I will use the term "physicalism" generically for any anthropology of human
beings as essentially physical-biological beings whose souls—if there are any—are necessarily dependent on their bodies. For my purposes, then, materialism, emergentism, nonreductive physicalism,
and dual-aspect monism would all count as physicalist anthropologies.

5. John Haught, *Making Sense of Evolution: Darwin, God, and the Drama of Life* (Louisville: Westminster John Knox, 2010), 46.

6. John Polkinghorne, *The God of Hope and the End of the World* (New Haven: Yale University
Press, 2002), 104.

7. Philip Hefner, introduction to *Changing Man: The Threat and the Promise*, ed. Kyle Haselden
and Philip Hefner (Garden City, NY: Doubleday, 1968), 12.

8. E.g., see Joel Green, "'Bodies—That Is, Human Lives': A Re-examination of Human Nature
in the Bible," in *Whatever Happened to the Soul? Scientific and Theological Portraits of Human Nature*,
ed. Warren Brown, Nancey Murphy, and H. Newton Malony (Minneapolis: Fortress, 1998), 149–73.
For a notable exception, see John W. Cooper, *Body, Soul and Life Everlasting: Biblical Anthropology
and the Monism-Dualism Debate*, 2nd ed. (Grand Rapids: Eerdmans, 2001). Cooper is a philosophical
theologian, not a biblical scholar.

9. On these developments, see LeRon Shults, *Reforming Theological Anthropology: After the Relational Turn* (Grand Rapids: Eerdmans, 2003), 163–88.

In theological discourse, relational and functional anthropologies have outstripped substantive ways of thinking about personhood; the image of God is seen as our capacity to relate to others or to enact the cultural mandate.[10] In a post-Darwinian age that places humanity in continuity with other living organisms, it seems false to say that *Homo sapiens* is ensouled. Physicalism looks eminently reasonable in light of neuroscience and the intimate connections between the mind and brain.

Nonetheless, these shifts away from dualism are mistaken. Recent biblical scholarship betrays a modern prejudice against substance ontology that in turn affects how scholars interpret anthropological biblical texts.[11] Among philosophers, ironically, dualism has grown in prominence in recent decades.[12] Many in the philosophical guild find physicalism unpalatable enough that exotic positions like panpsychism and idealism are gaining traction.[13] Some form of soul-body dualism was overwhelmingly the consensus of the church—Roman Catholic, Orthodox, and Protestant—either as substance dualism, which casts soul and body as distinct substances (with the soul permeating every part of the body), or as hylomorphism, which holds the soul as the form of the body (the soul organizes matter to be a living body).

This chapter argues that anthropological dualism makes the best sense of the human experience of sin (I use the term "dualism" to include substance dualism and Thomistic hylomorphism). I begin by describing the sort of moral responsibility that seems to be implied by the biblical narrative. Then I critically examine three noteworthy Christian physicalist proposals that have tried, and in my view failed, to offer an ontology of the human person that can account for moral responsibility. Based on the biblical presentation

10. See, e.g., Shults, *Reforming Theological Anthropology*; J. Richard Middleton, *The Liberating Image: The Imago Dei in Genesis* (Grand Rapids: Brazos, 2005).

11. Martine C. L. Oldhoff, "The Soul in the Bible: Monism in Biblical Scholarship? Analysing Biblical Studies from a Systematic Point of View," *European Journal of Theology* 27, no. 2 (2018): 147–61. In support of Oldhoff's argument, see Richard Steiner, *Disembodied Souls: The Nefesh in Israel and Kindred Spirits in the Ancient Near East, with an Appendix on the Katumuwa Inscription* (Atlanta: SBL, 2015); Richard Pleijel, "To Be or to Have a Nephesh: Gen. 2:7 and the Irresistible Tide of Monism," *Zeitschrift für die alttestamentliche Wissenschaft* 131, no. 2 (2019): 194–206.

12. See the contributions by Howard Robinson, John W. Cooper, J. P. Moreland, Stewart Goetz, Charles Taliaferro, Keith Yandell, and others. For a recent overview, see Andrea Lavazza and Howard Robinson, eds., *Contemporary Dualism: A Defense* (New York: Routledge, 2014).

13. For a sampling, see Joshua Farris and S. Mark Hamilton, eds., *Idealism and Christian Theology* (New York: Bloomsbury, 2017); Joanna Leidenhag, *Minding Creation: Theological Panpsychism and the Doctrine of Creation* (New York: Bloomsbury T&T Clark, 2021); Itay Shani, "Cosmopsychism: A Holistic Approach to the Metaphysics of Experience," *Philosophical Papers* 44, no. 3 (2015): 389–437; William Seager, ed., *The Routledge Handbook of Panpsychism* (New York: Routledge, 2020).

of sin, I suggest that the human person as embodied soul offers a stronger, more plausible ontological basis for moral responsibility and, therefore, sin. I also appeal to the nature of angelic sin as further evidence that the experience of sin presupposes immateriality. I conclude that dualism is more dogmatically coherent than physicalism.

Sin and Moral Responsibility

The Christian doctrine of sin implies that human beings are responsible creatures. This overwhelming truth so pervades every book and (possibly) every chapter of the Bible that it hardly needs defense. Sin, of course, is the very reason for the glad tidings of redemption. From the beginning, we sinned by disobeying God's commandments (Gen. 2:17; 3:1–6), a pattern that has repeated itself every day since that catastrophe in Eden; the apostle John describes sin as lawlessness (1 John 3:4). But elsewhere in the canon, sin is also couched as missing the mark (*hamartia*), unrighteousness (*adikia*), ungodliness (*asebeia*), transgression (*parabasis*), and so on.[14] Early theologians even tried locating the essence of sin in pride, greed, selfishness, unbelief, and other vices. Nevertheless, Scripture's different ways of talking about sin agree that it always involves culpability before God (Ps. 51:4). Cornelius Plantinga therefore rightly defines sin as "any thought, desire, emotion, word, or deed—or its particular absence, that displeases God and deserves blame."[15]

A theory of the person consistent with the doctrine of sin must include the capacity for what I call *moral transcendence*. Moral transcendence includes three interrelated features that encapsulate the theory of moral responsibility implicit in Scripture.

First, *all sin presupposes the baseline experience of the unity of consciousness and intentionality*. The unity of consciousness is my first-person experience of sinning against God: "Against you," says David, "you only, have I sinned" (Ps. 51:4). The experience of the Holy Spirit convicting of sin is not merely a series of neurons firing, or a complex sequence of brain function; rather, it is fundamentally a supernatural awareness of *personal* wrongdoing. The knowledge that I stand before God as his creature and that I have sinned

14. For a standard review of the biblical terms, see Thomas McCall, *Against God and Nature: The Doctrine of Sin* (Wheaton: Crossway, 2019), 33–39.

15. Cornelius Plantinga, *Not the Way It's Supposed to Be: A Breviary of Sin* (Grand Rapids: Eerdmans, 1995), 13. He goes on to say, "Let us add that the disposition to commit sins also displeases God and deserves blame, and let us therefore use the word *sin* to refer to such instances of both act and disposition" (13, emphasis original). I will address the dispositional element below.

against him is a first-person awareness of my unified self, an awareness that cannot be reduced to one or more parts of my body or brain.[16] Intentionality, on the other hand, is a technical philosophical term referring to one aspect of consciousness, the "of-ness" or "about-ness" that we associate with mental states (often referred to as "qualia" by philosophers).[17] Whenever I sin, there is always something I desire, want, or think that I need. Seconds before I decide to speak unkindly to my wife, I may feel the conviction of the Spirit urging me to desist because what I am considering saying to her will displease my heavenly Father. If I ignore that prompting and lash out verbally, I may later reflect on what I have done and feel remorse and perhaps repentance. Thus, every instance of human sinning involves intentionality, an array of mental acts directed at things, other people, and ultimately God.

Second, *all sin is responsive to reason, and that presupposes a (nonphysical) mind.* Sin always involves intellectual, emotional, or volitional aspects of the human person. We believe the wrong things, or the right things in the wrong ways; we desire things opposed to the will of God and we consciously disobey God even when we know that it displeases him. Scripture, in fact, gives a uniform depiction of human sinning: Eve sinned *because* "the tree was good for food and pleasing to the eye, and also desirable for gaining wisdom" (Gen. 3:6 NIV). Cain sinned against Abel *because* he was angry that God preferred Abel's sacrificial offering to his own (4:2–8). Aaron sinned by making a golden calf *because* he was persuaded by the Israelites and their desire to have gods like the other nations (Exod. 32:1–24). The Pharisees were hypocrites, not practicing what they preach, *because* "they love the place of honor at feasts and the best seats in the synagogues and greet-ings in the marketplaces and being called rabbi by others" (Matt. 23:6–7). Judas betrayed Jesus, at least in part, *because* there was money to be had (26:14–15).

Throughout Scripture people make moral choices in response to what they perceive as good reasons. The biblical attitude to sin assumes that people are morally responsible to the degree that they think, say, and do things for specific *reasons*—culpability holds as long as they sin for reasons that they think are compelling (even if divinely determined).[18] This model

16. On the unity of consciousness argument, see William Hasker, "Persons and the Unity of Consciousness," in *The Waning of Materialism*, ed. Robert C. Koons and George Bealer (New York: Oxford University Press, 2010), 175–90.

17. J. P. Moreland, *The Soul: How We Know It's Real and Why It Matters* (Chicago: Moody, 2014), 86–90.

18. My account here is consistent with the core idea of reasons-responsive compatibilism. See John M. Fischer and Mark Ravizza, *Responsibility and Control: A Theory of Moral Responsibility* (Cam-bridge: Cambridge University Press, 1993). However, I take no position on the extensive debates

fits the everyday, common-sense view of moral agency, and it seems extremely unlikely, if not impossible, that a physicalist account of the human person could account for such responsiveness to reasons.

Third, *all sin originates from the heart, the moral center of every person*. Everybody is guilty of sinning against God, but the doctrine of original corruption goes deeper. In addition to the inevitability of human sinning, Scripture also witnesses to the fact that we enter this world as *sinners*, each of us possessing a morally corrupt *condition* that precedes any sins we commit.[19] This original corruption starts from birth (Ps. 51:5; 58:3) and renders us full of evil and deception (Eccles. 9:3), dead in our transgressions and enemies of God (Eph. 2:1–3). Every facet of the human personality, from the soul and mind to emotions and desires, is tainted by depravity; every sinful thought and action is polluted (Matt. 15:16–20; Luke 6:43–44).[20] Furthermore, Scripture frequently locates the origin of sin in the *heart*—for example, Jeremiah testifies that "the heart is deceitful above all things, and desperately sick; who can understand it?" (Jer. 17:9). Jesus says, "A good man brings good things out of the good stored up in his heart, and an evil man brings evil things out of the evil stored up in his heart. For the mouth speaks what the heart is full of" (Luke 6:45 NIV).[21] Anthony Hoekema describes the heart as "a description of the inner core of the person; the 'organ' of thinking, feeling, and willing; the point of concentration of all of our functions. In other words, sin has its source not in the body nor in any one of man's various capacities, but in the very center of his being, in his *heart*. Since sin has poisoned the very fountain of life, all of life is bound to be affected by it."[22] According to the testimony of Scripture, we are culpable for any sin that *discloses* the inner corruption of our hearts.

This disclosive element reflects original sin. God can hold me accountable for a moral state over which I have no control (original corruption) as long as it accurately reflects *my* current spiritual condition.[23] This way of thinking about responsibility roughly lines up with what some philosophers

---

prompted by the reasons-responsive approach, because adjudicating the finer points is unnecessary for my project. For a recent discussion, see Michael McKenna, "Reasons-Responsiveness, Frankfurt Examples, and the Free Will Ability," in *The Oxford Handbook of Moral Responsibility*, ed. Dana Kay Nelkin and Derk Pereboom (Oxford: Oxford University Press, 2022), 27–52.

19. This section supplements my earlier remarks in chap. 7 on the notion of deep responsibility.

20. Robert Letham, *Systematic Theology* (Wheaton: Crossway, 2019), 397.

21. I will circle back to the biblical teaching about the heart below.

22. Anthony Hoekema, *Created in God's Image* (Grand Rapids: Eerdmans, 1986), 172. For a similar analysis of the heart, see Marguerite Shuster, *The Fall and Sin: What We Have Become as Sinners* (Grand Rapids: Eerdmans, 2004), 193–94.

23. While original guilt is relevant here, I can ignore that contested doctrine for the purposes of this chapter (see note 10 in chap. 7 above).

have dubbed "deep responsibility."[24] People are blameworthy (that is, deeply responsible) for dispositions and actions that reflect "robust" rather than "mere" ownership. Jesse Couenhoven is worth quoting at length:

> I mark the qualitative difference between the two kinds of ownership relevant to a discussion of deep responsibility by speaking of the difference between "mere" and "robust" ownership. Many things that are part of our identities, things that we own, are not attributable to us in such a way that it is fair to blame us for them. For instance, my pale skin might make it easier for me to be sunburned and perhaps to develop skin cancer, but I cannot be blamed for the paleness of my skin because it is a merely biological fact about me. The fact that I worry about giving my students grades they do not deserve reflects my character in a deep way, however, and it is robustly owned. . . . The idea that we are deeply responsible for what we robustly own, and that robust ownership is of the heart, and what comes from it, makes sense of the idea that only persons can sin: only persons have the hearts that make culpable evil a possibility. It also clarifies why biological conditions like leprosy are not sinful. A person should not be blamed for evils that are not evils of the heart; leprosy, cancer, and the like do not disclose a person's beliefs and desires, and so they are not things for which a person can be considered culpable (one might be responsible for somehow intentionally contracting leprosy, but that is a separate kind of case).[25]

Sin cannot be biological because we are not deeply responsible for biological facts that are true of us; such biological realities do not disclose our moral core (see chap. 7). Moral responsibility is a compatibilist (self-disclosure), not voluntarist (self-making), notion.[26]

Reflecting on the mystery of conscious experience, the late philosopher of mind Jerry Fodor confesses, "Nobody has the slightest idea how anything material could be conscious. Nobody even knows what it would be like to have the slightest idea about how anything material could be conscious. So much for the philosophy of consciousness."[27] David

24. Susan Wolf, *Freedom within Reason* (New York: Oxford University Press, 1990), 40–45. For an analytic theological defense of deep responsibility as disclosive, see Jesse Couenhoven, *Stricken by Sin, Cured by Christ: Agency, Necessity, and Culpability in Augustinian Theology* (Oxford: Oxford University Press, 2013), esp. 109–61.

25. Jesse Couenhoven, "What Sin Is: A Differential Analysis," *Modern Theology* 25, no. 4 (2009): 577–78.

26. Couenhoven, "What Sin Is," 577. Deep responsibility as *disclosive* corresponds roughly to "attributability" accounts of moral responsibility—e.g., see Gary Watson, "Two Faces of Responsibility," *Philosophical Topics* 24, no. 2 (1996): 227–48.

27. Jerry Fodor, "The Big Idea: Can There Be a Science of Mind?," *Times Literary Supplement* (July 3, 1992): 5.

Chalmers dubs this conundrum the "hard" problem of consciousness.[28] My argument is that moral transcendence—including intentionality and the unity of consciousness, responsiveness to reasons, and the moral centrality of the heart—is implied in the Christian notion of sin. This implication leads to a corresponding *hard problem of sin*—namely, can Christian physicalism fully account for the reality of sin? If it cannot, the stock value of dualism rises.[29]

Christian Physicalism and the Doctrine of Sin

Biblical Christianity collapses without a viable concept of moral agency, which is the hard problem of sin for Christian physicalists. They have responded along various lines, and I will now review three influential Christian physicalists: Joel Green, Nancey Murphy, and Philip Clayton.

Joel Green and the Biblical Witness

In his monograph *Body, Soul, and Human Life*, Joel Green devotes one chapter to analyzing the alleged conflict between the natural sciences and the doctrine of sin.[30] He opens his discussion with the case report of the patient with a right orbitofrontal tumor and impulsive pedophilia.[31] Green speaks for most of us when he observes, "Reports like this one are deeply disconcerting, harboring as they do the prospect of a loss of our sense of willful agency."[32] He categorizes the scientific challenge to conventional notions of free will in four ways that highlight the embodied nature of all decision-making: (1) studies from comparative psychology indicating human-like behavior from nonhuman animal species; (2) neuroscientific experiments that undermine our intuition that our actions are caused by conscious volition;[33] (3) case reports of people with impairment of the

28. David Chalmers, "Facing Up to the Problem of Consciousness," *Journal of Consciousness Studies* 2, no. 3 (1995): 200–219.

29. Dualism is not the only nonmaterialist option; for example, panpsychism and idealism are other contenders. But since I am making a hamartiological case for dualism, I largely ignore them in this chapter.

30. He titles the chapter "Sin and Freedom." Joel Green, *Body, Soul, and Human Life: The Nature of Humanity in the Bible* (Grand Rapids: Baker Academic, 2008), 72–105.

31. Jeffrey Burns and Russell Swerdlow, "Right Orbitofrontal Tumor with Pedophilia Symptom and Constructional Apraxia Sign," *Archives of Neurology* 60, no. 3 (2003): 437–40. See the earlier discussion of this case in chap. 7.

32. Green, *Body, Soul, and Human Life*, 74.

33. He particularly reviews the work by Benjamin Libet and Daniel Wegner, e.g., Benjamin Libet et al., "Time of Conscious Intention to Act in Relation to Onset of Cerebral Activity (Readiness-

frontal region of the brain who present with "disorders of volition"[34] (e.g., pathological lying and other forms of addiction, autistic behavior, inactivity); and (4) evidence that moral decision-making is tightly connected to brain processes. In light of these challenges, Green defends nonreductive physicalism as best able to account for sin and freedom.[35] He supports his position by drawing neurobiology into dialogue with the New Testament, specifically 1 Peter, James, and Romans.[36]

The epistle of 1 Peter portrays human lives enmeshed in sin. Christians used to live in a "former time of ignorance" (1:14), not realizing "the emptiness of [our] inherited way of life" (1:18). We were caught up in a "flood of unrestrained immorality" (4:4), living lives full of "acts of unrestraint, lust, drunkenness . . . and unseemly idolatry" (4:3).[37] Sin, Peter writes, pervades our lives and patterns of thought. Green highlights these features and insists that for Peter the pervasiveness of sin never excuses individual sin; it merely humbles us as we realize the extent to which our lives are socially conditioned. According to Green, "This perspective does not spell the loss of freedom to choose, but it does suggest the degree to which choices are circumscribed already by communities of formation, even formation along evil lines."[38] We are at God's mercy and therefore need a new vision of the world. If we follow the example of Christ in his suffering, then we too will be "finished with sin" (4:1).

Green is signaling points of convergence between neurobiology and biblical theology. In Peter's letter, human freedom is constrained, which is precisely what neurobiology is telling us. Green thus finds it ironic that free will is often seen as *the* point of tension between hamartiology and

---

Potential)," *Brain* 106, pt. 3 (1983): 623–42; Benjamin Libet, "Do We Have Free Will?," in *The Volitional Brain: Towards a Neuroscience of Free Will*, ed. Benjamin Libet et al. (Thorverton, Exeter, UK: Imprint Academic, 1999), 47–57; Daniel M. Wegner and Thalia Wheatley, "Apparent Mental Causation: Sources of the Experience of Will," *American Psychologist* 54, no. 7 (1999): 480–92.

34. For example, see Elkhonon Goldberg, *The Executive Brain: Frontal Lobes and the Civilized Mind* (Oxford: Oxford University Press, 2001). Phineas Gage is a famous historical example, a railroad worker whose life changed dramatically in 1848, after an explosion, when an iron rod penetrated his skull; remarkably, he survived, but his personality was permanently changed.

35. E.g., see Green, "Bodies—That Is, Human Lives"; Joel Green, "What Does It Mean to Be Human? Another Chapter in the Ongoing Interaction of Science and Scripture," in *From Cells to Souls—and Beyond: Changing Portraits of Human Nature*, ed. Malcolm Jeeves (Grand Rapids: Eerdmans, 2004), 179–98; Joel Green, "Restoring the Human Person: New Testament Voices for a Wholistic and Social Anthropology," in *Neuroscience and the Person: Scientific Perspectives on Divine Action*, ed. Robert J. Russell et al. (Notre Dame, IN: University of Notre Dame Press, 1999), 3–22.

36. My summary of Green's exegesis comes from his *Body, Soul, and Human Life*, 72–105.

37. For the sake of argument, I am using Green's translations of the cited passages in this section. His exegetical discussion is also far richer than I can capture in my exposition.

38. Green, *Body, Soul, and Human Life*, 91.

neurobiology. The misunderstanding, he suspects, lies in the fact that many Christians harbor naive notions of libertarian freedom and "self-conscious agency."[39] Drawing on Peter, Green argues instead that our freedom is always constrained by innate sinfulness and the sinful structures of society.

In James, human desire—not God—is the source of sinful temptation (1:13–14). Summarizing the apostle on temptation, Green writes, "Humans are characterized by an inclination toward evil, a predisposition toward sin, . . . [and they also] continue in at least some sense to bear the image of God in which they were made (3:9)."[40] Because sin arises from within, the gospel must be internalized, for it is the power of God for salvation. Once again, Green is shining the light on connections between neurobiology and biblical theology. The scientific evidence suggests that character and behavior are deeply shaped neurobiologically; similarly, the biblical evidence suggests that character and behavior are deeply shaped by sin.

In his treatment of Paul, Green focuses on Romans and its clear-eyed picture of our bondage to sin. "Indeed, the theme of Romans 6 is the inevitability of human slavery," observes Green, "with the only question being the identity of the master to whom one's life is presented."[41] We are either slaves to righteousness or slaves to iniquity (6:13, 16, 19). Green denies that Paul teaches a doctrine of original sin in Romans 5:12–21 (he blames Augustine for this misunderstanding based on his faulty Latin translation of 5:12). The true reason for the universality of sin, according to Green, is that "Adam's sin set in motion a chain of effects, one sin leading to the next, not because sin was an essential constituent of the human condition but because all humanity followed Adam in his sinfulness."[42] Furthermore, in Romans 1:18–32, Green takes sin to be an idolatrous *disposition*, not a set of individual *acts*. Since we are slaves to sin, it is not enough to speak of repentance or forgiveness of sins;[43] rather, we need something more

---

39. Green, *Body, Soul, and Human Life*, 103.

40. Green, *Body, Soul, and Human Life*, 96.

41. Green, *Body, Soul, and Human Life*, 99.

42. Green, *Body, Soul, and Human Life*, 100. Here Green cites favorably the discussion in Mark E. Biddle, *Missing the Mark: Sin and Its Consequences in Biblical Theology* (Nashville: Abingdon, 2005), 33–44.

43. According to Green, this explains why "forgiveness of sin" language is only found in very few of the letters attributed to Paul (i.e., Eph. 1:7 and Col. 1:14): "Sin needs to be addressed, but, given Paul's perspective on 'sin' as less 'act' and more 'disposition' or 'compulsion,' mere forgiveness or absolution is insufficient. Nor does Paul develop much the notion of 'repentance'; after all, the condition of enslavement is not mitigated by repentance on the part of the slave" (Green, *Body, Soul, and Human Life*, 102–3).

radical. We need God's grace, Green says, "through justification leading to eternal life through Jesus Christ our Lord" (5:21).[44]

The takeaway from Green's analysis of these three New Testament voices is that scientific and biblical pictures of freedom are consonant. He delivers a chastened account of human freedom that is more realistic than what is often assumed in popular discourse. However, Green's writing on anthropology assumes that the neuroscientific evidence fits most naturally with physicalism and then imposes that assumption on the exegetical data. The problem is that dualism and physicalism are both consistent with the neuroscientific data; theological anthropology is underdetermined by neuroscience.[45] Perhaps the empirical data from the neurosciences may rule out *some* forms of radical dualism, but they cannot in principle adjudicate between physicalism and dualism.

After all, most dualists have been interactionists who—millennia before the arrival of neuroscience—affirmed that the soul depends on the body in order to function. Ancients did not need modern science to recognize this relationship. Granted, the brain sciences have been able to link mental effects to specific parts of the brain, but since correlations between the mental and the physical can be local (as opposed to global), that fact alone does not count against dualism. Green and other Christian physicalists would likely grant these points but would still insist that what scientists have discovered about how closely the mental depends on the brain is more plausible with physicalism than dualism. But again, empirical science cannot deliver that kind of metaphysical conclusion. "Empirical questions about the nervous system are the province of neuroscience," J. P. Moreland explains, "but underlying issues about the nature of consciousness, self-consciousness, mind, thought, and the general nature of the relationship between mind and brain are the proper province of philosophy."[46] The neurosciences uncover the intricacies of embodiment but cannot resolve the debate between physicalism and dualism.[47]

The real issue is *reductionism*. Physicalism seems to reduce the mind to the smallest microparticles—conscious experience is "nothing but" the

44. Green, *Body, Soul, and Human Life*, 100.

45. My remarks here draw from C. Stephen Evans, "Separable Souls: Dualism, Selfhood, and the Possibility of Life After Death," *Christian Scholar's Review* 34, no. 3 (2005): 327–40, esp. 333–34.

46. J. P. Moreland, *Consciousness and the Existence of God: A Theistic Argument* (New York: Routledge, 2008), 159. Moreland also cites this book to support this argument for the autonomy of philosophy: M. R. Bennett and P. M. S. Hacker, *Philosophical Foundations of Neuroscience* (Oxford: Blackwell, 2003).

47. Even Nancey Murphy, a fellow physicalist, agrees that "science can never *prove* that there is no soul, a soul whose capacities are simply well *correlated* with brain functions." Nancey Murphy, *Bodies and Souls, or Spirited Bodies?* (Cambridge: Cambridge University Press, 2006), 112, emphasis original.

complex interactions of physical particles. Thus, it is difficult to see how Green's physicalism can yield the moral transcendence necessary for a feasible doctrine of sin.[48] At one point, he appeals to the "relative indeterminacy of human behavior" rooted in the complexity of brain states. The sheer complexity of neuronal processing rules out neurobiological determinism.[49] While this seems plausible, it offers nothing close to moral transcendence. More promising is top-down causation, but Green only mentions it in passing.[50] Furthermore, it is difficult to make sense of top-down causation within a physicalist paradigm (more below). Thus, Green's main contribution is to highlight the embodied nature of our mental lives; he does suggest top-down causation as a framework for moral transcendence, but he largely assumes it without defense.

Nancey Murphy and Nonreductive Physicalism

Nancey Murphy gives this missing defense in her account of moral responsibility under the auspices of nonreductive physicalism. She accepts ontological reductionism and describes reality as a hierarchy of levels that has no new metaphysical entities added as we move from the lower- to the higher-level processes, from atoms and molecules to cells and organisms. There are only physical substances (hence *physicalism*). But Murphy also accepts the reality of genuine mental properties that have intrinsic causal powers; the direction of causation does not run only bottom-up. The laws described in the higher-level sciences are not reducible to the laws of physics (hence *nonreductive*). But how does this work exactly?

In her early work, Murphy appealed to the concept of *supervenience* that allowed philosophers to move beyond the limited concepts of identity and causation to explain the relation between mind and brain: "Mental states or properties are *identical* with brain states or . . . they are *caused* by brain states."[51] Both options are reductionistic and thus inimical to a Christian physicalist. Therefore, "supervenience" emerged as a way to avoid reductionism; supervenience gave physicalists a way to remain *ontologically* re-

---

48. An additional problem with Green's position is that he eschews a historical fall of Adam—but theistic evolution without a historical fall implies that God created us *as sinners* from the beginning and is thus responsible for our depraved natures. See Joel Green, "'Adam, What Have You Done?': New Testament Voices on the Origins of Sin," in *Evolution and the Fall*, ed. William Cavanaugh and James K. A. Smith (Grand Rapids: Eerdmans, 2017), 98–116. (On these matters, see chap. 6 above.)

49. Green, *Body, Soul, and Human Life*, 104.

50. Green, *Body, Soul, and Human Life*, 104.

51. Nancey Murphy, *Anglo-American Postmodernity: Philosophical Perspectives on Science, Religion, and Ethics* (Boulder, CO: Westview, 1997), 193–94, my emphasis.

ductionist about human persons without succumbing to a *causally* reductive account of the mind's relation to the brain. The mental is dependent on the physical but not reducible to it.[52]

However, the supervenience relation is contested by philosophers, many of whom accuse it of trying to have its cake and eat it too. In several influential essays, Jaegwon Kim levels precisely that criticism: "If a relation is weak enough to be nonreductive, it tends to be too weak to serve as a dependence relation; conversely, when a relation is strong enough to give us dependence, it tends to be too strong—strong enough to imply reducibility."[53] The "physicalism" in nonreductive physicalism is doing all the work; the "nonreductive" part is impotent.[54] Murphy eventually recognized these problems and agreed that supervenience faces too many conceptual problems and is thus unable to resolve the challenge of reductionism.[55]

She therefore recruited a new concept of "downward" or "whole-part" causation. Downward causation implies that higher-level entities (e.g., mind) can have genuine causal powers without breaking causal closure at the micro level (e.g., brain). Murphy can thus affirm mental causation as real without having to invoke a nonphysical entity like the soul. Physical substances still have a complete monopoly over ontological reality, but the causal powers of the higher-level entities are not reducible to the properties of the constituent parts. Lower-level entities exist as part of a larger system, but that larger system can then exert downward constraints on the constituent parts. The broader system sets boundary conditions to constrain the parts *without* abrogating the laws of physics.

In Murphy's anthropology, human persons are not substances but complex, dynamic, nonlinear information-processing *systems*. Washing her hands of any reductive notions of mechanisms and aggregates, she shifts

52. For Murphy's defense of supervenience, see her "Physicalism without Reductionism: Toward a Scientifically, Philosophically and Theologically Sound Portrait of Human Nature," *Zygon* 34, no. 4 (1999): 551–72. She gives the following definition of supervenience: "Property S is supervenient on property B if and only if something's being B constitutes its being S under circumstance C." Murphy, "Physicalism without Reductionism," 558.

53. Jaegwon Kim, *Supervenience and Mind: Selected Philosophical Essays* (New York: Cambridge University Press, 1993), 276.

54. Murphy has challenged Kim's critique of nonreductive physicalism in Nancey Murphy and Warren Brown, *Did My Neurons Make Me Do It? Philosophical and Neurobiological Perspectives on Moral Responsibility and Free Will* (Oxford: Oxford University Press, 2007), 233–36.

55. She concedes this point in an exchange with Lindsay Cullen, who argues that Murphy's application of the supervenience relation is too idiosyncratic, "eccentric," and "unhelpful" (Lindsay Cullen, "Nancey Murphy, Supervenience and Causality," *Science and Christian Belief* 13, no. 1 [2001]: 39–50, at 39). Murphy's rejoinder is in "Response to Cullen," *Science and Christian Belief* 13, no. 2 (2001): 161–63.

the level of description from the atom to the organism; the properties of the constituents are dependent on their place in the larger system. Human beings are relations and processes that are subject to causal feedback loops. Organic systems grow in complexity as we move from prokaryotic to eukaryotic cells, and by the time we arrive at *Homo sapiens*, the level of information processing and self-recognition has become so complex that we are compelled to invoke the concepts of language, self-transcendence, and full-blown moral responsibility.[56]

Murphy offers a detailed metaphysical structure that can undergird Green's physicalist account of sin and freedom. On one level, Murphy's account does leave room for mental causation—the will, desire, and emotions—which comes close to the minimal conditions I laid out earlier for moral responsibility. However, some of her philosophical colleagues remain unpersuaded (Philip Clayton, for instance, does not think nonreductive physicalism is a coherent position).[57]

For my part, I do not think her view can really avoid causal reductionism; the "nonreductive" part is pulling a rabbit out of a hat.[58] First, her notion of whole-part causation works if human beings are a hierarchy of levels or systems, but "levels" or "systems" seem inadequate as descriptors of creatures morally accountable to the living God.[59] Since she accepts ontological reductionism, these higher levels must still be operating according to physical laws and therefore are not actually capable of genuine moral agency. Second, even though Murphy reinterprets humans as "relations" and "processes," such ideas only seem to capture (at best) a thin view of moral agency that is distant from the moral core of the person implied in the Christian doctrine of sin. It all feels too impersonal, almost mechanistic.

56. For detailed defense, see Murphy and Brown, *Did My Neurons Make Me Do It?*
57. In Philip Clayton's judgment, "Recent criticisms of nonreductive physicalism . . . raise serious doubts whether any version of physicalism other than reductivist physicalism is in the end coherent." Philip Clayton, *Mind and Emergence: From Quantum to Chaos* (Oxford: Oxford University Press, 2004), 124.
58. In dialogue with Murphy, William Hasker writes, "If the higher-level organization is to make a difference, it can only do this by *affecting the interactions of the constituents at the base level*—but this it is forbidden to do by the thesis of microdeterminism. Causal reduction has in no way been avoided." William Hasker, "On Behalf of Emergent Dualism," in *In Search of the Soul: Four Views*, ed. Joel Green and Stuart Palmer (Downers Grove, IL: InterVarsity, 2005), 89, emphasis original.
59. Perhaps downward causation is more plausible on the constitution view defended by Kevin Corcoran and Lynn Rudder Baker (e.g., see Kevin Corcoran, *Rethinking Human Nature: A Christian Materialist Alternative to the Soul* [Grand Rapids: Baker Academic, 2006]; and Lynn Rudder Baker, *Persons and Bodies: A Constitution View* [Cambridge: Cambridge University Press, 2000]). Although constitutionalism works as a theory of everyday objects—e.g., a golden rabbit is two distinct things (rabbit and gold) *constituted* by the same part, but once the gold is smelted, only one thing is left—the constitution relation fails as an account of the self in relation to the body.

In the end, I doubt that she has found a credible alchemy for changing neurobiology into the gold of moral agency.

Philip Clayton and Emergentism

Hunting for the same holy grail, Philip Clayton seeks a middle position between reductive physicalism and supernatural dualism. The operative category is *emergence*: "Although physical structures and causes may determine the initial emergence of the mental, they do not fully or solely determine the outcome of the mental life subsequent to its emergence."[60] According to Clayton, a viable notion of moral responsibility requires *strong* emergence— that is, the appearance of actual new entities. By "emergence," Clayton means more than whole-part causation; the emergent level should have distinct laws and causal activities, which in turn have real influence on the lower levels.

Clayton points to multiple cases of new and unpredictable phenomena that have emerged *naturally* during evolution as a result of increasing complexity in the biosphere. The natural world, he says, is full of new emergent levels of reality, such as eddies at the base of a waterfall, the formation of snow crystals and snowflakes, or the evolution of new organisms—we could not have predicted any of these phenomena from their constituent particles. Clayton chronicles countless examples of new emergent levels across a range of disciplines like physics, chemistry, and biology.[61] Admittedly not all of them are genuine instances of the *strong* emergence that Clayton thinks we need for moral agency.

But human consciousness is a clear instance. Clayton showcases the mind as strong emergence *par excellence*. This theory of emergence is not *dualism* by another name; rather, it is a thesis about *natural* history. Dualism implies that the world contains only physical and mental causes, but Clayton's notion of emergence—what he calls "ontological pluralism"—posits that there are many different levels of reality and many different kinds of causes. The human mind is only one of many emergent properties in the universe: natural emergentism replaces supernatural dualism. "Really distinct levels," Clayton writes, "occur within the one natural world and . . . objects on various levels can be ontologically primitive . . . rather than being understood merely as aggregates of lower-level, foundational particles."[62] This is not your old-fashioned dualistic kingdom; Clayton's proposal is a modern, democratic, pluralistic ontology.

60. Philip Clayton, "Neuroscience, the Human Person, and God," in *Bridging Science and Religion*, ed. Ted Peters and Gaymon Bennett (Minneapolis: Fortress, 2003), 108.

61. Clayton, *Mind and Emergence*.

62. Clayton, *Mind and Emergence*, 62.

All well and good, but Clayton thinks he needs the possibility of genuine freedom, an ontological level of reality that is not bounded by finite causal structures. We only seem to have an ontological horizon of *finite* causes, he argues, of which we humans are a part; that horizon cannot give us enduring spirit.[63] How do we know that our capacity for moral agency is not merely an evolutionary epiphenomenon? Clayton offers a transcendental argument—he posits an *infinite* ontological ground that renders real moral agency possible in the world. By positing God's existence, we create the possibility of other morally free agents existing in the world. God who possesses freedom preeminently *must* exist if we are to be truly free.

Clayton is searching for a notion of freedom that is not bounded by finite causal structures. Drawing on Karl Rahner, he reinterprets freedom as the "freedom of being," "the relationship of a finite being to its infinite ground."[64] "According to the hypothesis in its theistic form," Clayton explains, "God's overarching goal is that, given the total set of constraining conditions, a complex enough organism should emerge that it becomes capable of raising the question of the ultimate meaning of human existence and of freely entering into relationship with the ground of its existence."[65] God created the world so that human beings might emerge and freely seek a relationship with him, the "ground of their being." Only by positing the existence of a *panentheistic* God—a God who includes the finite world within himself but also extends beyond it and is not exhausted by it—can we then reason analogically to the existence of morally free creatures in the world who are biological but also reach beyond the biological.[66] The God of panentheism who possesses freedom par excellence must exist if *we* are to be genuinely morally responsible, and therefore, sinners.

But this subtle transcendental argument is limited. Yes, we all live *as if* we are free, but it does not follow that the "infinite horizon" of theism (or panentheism) is the right one. Perhaps we are self-deceived—maybe it *is* atoms and quarks all the way down. As one commentator writes, "That is why such arguments rarely, if ever, convince anyone; despite their usefulness as a 'rumor of angels,' transcendental arguments always leave one with the nagging doubt that the infinite horizon toward which we strain

63. Similar concerns apply to Timothy O'Connor's naturalistic emergentism in his *Persons and Causes: The Metaphysics of Free Will* (New York: Oxford University Press, 2002). If so-called emergent properties are causally dependent on the base properties, is a genuinely emergent moral freedom possible within a natural ontology?

64. Philip Clayton, *In Quest of Freedom: The Emergence of Spirit in the Natural World* (Göttingen: Vandenhoeck & Ruprecht, 2009), 147.

65. Clayton, *In Quest of Freedom*, 147.

66. Clayton, *In Quest of Freedom*, 137–41.

may, in the end, be more illusion than reality."[67] In Clayton's transcendental argument for moral agency, God does all the real metaphysical work. What is missing is an account of human freedom (and thus sinfulness) as a metaphysically dependent and yet genuine *creaturely* reality.

Clayton's emergentism fits within the larger context of evolution. The supervenience of mental experiences on physical brains is an instance of *evolutionary emergence*, which means there is a synchronic and diachronic element to Clayton's theological anthropology.[68] Human consciousness and our capacity to sin against God depend "upon the entire natural history [diachronic] that caused increasingly complex brains and central nervous systems to evolve, as well as on the physical state of the organism at a particular time [synchronic]."[69] Furthermore, Clayton rejects the idea of an originally sinless creation with the subsequent fall of Adam and Eve—yet if historical emergence is a completely *natural* process, without the historical entrance of sin into God's good creation, then sin as such is constitutive of being human.[70] Clayton's emergentism implies that our physical and moral constitution as human creatures is a direct ontological result of the increasing organic complexity from the evolutionary process. This kind of essentializing of sin is devastating because it renders sin the direct result of God's (evolutionary) process of creating the world. Human sinfulness becomes one of the necessary side-effects of evolution, which of course means that sin is a necessary side-effect of *creation*. In stark contrast, classical Christianity insists that sin is an ontological accident that is utterly foreign to the goodness of God's creation.

These three accounts of Christian physicalism, representative of recent proposals at the interface of science and theology, have notable strengths and weaknesses. Given that both nonreductive physicalism and emergence offer accounts of mental causation, they seem to provide some level of moral responsibility. In my judgment, however, as we review supervenience, top-down causation, emergence, and related concepts, none of these creative moves give satisfying resolutions to the hard problem of

---

67. Larry Chapp, review of *Is Nature Enough?*, by John Haught, *Modern Theology* 23, no. 4 (2007): 643. However, while I endorse Chapp's argument here, I make no claims that *all* transcendental arguments are illegitimate.

68. Clayton, *Mind and Emergence*, 127.

69. Clayton, *Mind and Emergence*, 127.

70. Cf. Philip Clayton, *God and Contemporary Science* (Edinburgh: Edinburgh University Press, 1997), 40–41: "Historical fallenness does not require a historical fall; it is sufficient if the doctrine expresses a basic feature or characteristic of human beings in the world, confirmed anew in the experience of each individual. . . . This interpretation of the doctrine of the fall may not make an original state of sinless existence and a subsequent historical fall essential to the theological narrative."

sin. I have certainly not reviewed every physicalist argument—Christian or otherwise—so my analysis is limited.[71] Perhaps a convincing solution will emerge in the future, but I remain a doubting Thomas. I am pessimistic that Christian physicalism can ever escape causal reductionism.[72]

Sin and the Soul in Canonical Perspective

These efforts to rescue moral responsibility within the bounds of physicalism reflect a broader discussion. Building on a free-will debate that stretches back to antiquity, much of the philosophical discussion focuses on whether human freedom is compatible with causal determinism. Compatibilists reply yes; incompatibilists say no. Contemporary philosophers have addressed these questions with a wide range of ingenious solutions, the various proposals swelling in erudition and complexity.[73] However, the core issue relating to moral agency between physicalism and dualism is reductionism, not determinism: the human person is morally transcendent. Furthermore, the scientific picture still sets the agenda for the debate. In the present milieu, a dualist anthropology may offer a corrective to the growing prevalence of Christian physicalism.

Anthropological Dualism in Scripture

Scripture presents a holistic picture of human persons. God created humanity to be embodied. Charles Taliaferro proposes helpfully that we think of embodiment as giving us a range of powers that are nonmoral virtues or excellences. "The power to see and to think are *good-making powers*," he writes. "While they are not like the moral virtues (such as courage), they are

71. For example, William Hasker's "emergent dualism" escapes most of the concerns I have raised about physicalism (see his *The Emergent Self* [Ithaca, NY: Cornell University Press, 1999]). He tries to combine insights from substance dualism with mainstream scientific perspectives on humanity (including evolution). I remain, however, skeptical that souls are the kinds of things that can emerge from matter; I also have theological objections to his evolutionary position (see the earlier chapters of this book). On philosophical objections to emergent dualism, see Brandan Rickabaugh, "Against Emergent Dualism," in *The Blackwell Companion to Substance Dualism*, ed. Jonathan J. Loose, Angus J. L. Menuge, and J. P. Moreland (Hoboken, NJ: Wiley-Blackwell, 2018), 73–86.

72. This chapter is a revision *and correction* of an earlier essay (Madueme, "From Sin to the Soul"), where I wrongly identified physical determinism as the core problem with Christian physicalism. Instead, I now believe that the central problem is *reductionism*, not determinism.

73. E.g., see Michael McKenna and Derk Pereboom, *Free Will: A Contemporary Introduction* (New York: Routledge, 2016); Robert Kane, ed., *The Oxford Handbook of Free Will*, 2nd ed. (New York: Oxford University Press, 2011).

essential in our fostering and pursuing moral virtues."[74] Furthermore, the wide range of anthropological terms in the Bible—such as *kardia, nephesh, ruach, psyche, nous,* and *pneuma*—often do not refer to isolated parts of the human constitution. As John Cooper admits, "Modern scholars largely agree [that these anthropological terms] pick out distinct but overlapping and interdependent aspects, powers, and functions that constitute an integral existential unity."[75] Cooper may be overstating the case given that Scripture's anthropological terms sometimes have dualistic implications.[76] But even if we accept his main point about the anthropological holism of Scripture—as we should—physicalism does not follow. Robert Gundry remarks, "It is not so much that the Bible teaches dualistic anthropology as it is that what it teaches on other matters often depends on the dualistic anthropology it presupposes."[77] Precisely so, the biblical depiction of sin takes dualism for granted.

I will defend this claim by examining four biblical texts: Matthew 5:27–30; Mark 7:19–23; Romans 2:28–29; and Ezekiel 36:26–27. They represent a range of texts throughout the Bible that contrast the "inner" and "outer" person, the material and the immaterial (e.g., 2 Cor. 4:16). While the biblical authors show no hint of Gnostic ideas that demonize the physical body, they present the inner person as the ultimate source of volition, will, and moral responsibility. This picture is most consistent with a dualistic anthropology.

The Sermon on the Mount warns that if you look at a woman lustfully you have already committed adultery with her in your heart (Matt. 5:28). Jesus explains that the inner thought, not the external act, is the ultimate origin of sin. He makes a distinction between adultery of the heart (cause) and physical adultery (effect). In the case of theft, for example, the act of stealing is the external manifestation; coveting what belongs to someone else is the root sin. As one commentator puts it, "The culprit lies elsewhere, in the heart, the inner person."[78] While Jesus does command us to gouge out the eye and to cut off the hand if they cause us to sin (Matt. 5:29–30),

74. Charles Taliaferro, "Substance Dualism: A Defense," in Loose, Menuge, and Moreland, *Blackwell Companion to Substance Dualism*, 45, emphasis original. See also Charles Taliaferro, "The Virtues of Embodiment," *Philosophy* 76, no. 1 (2001): 111–25.

75. John W. Cooper, "Scripture and Philosophy on the Unity of the Body and Soul: An Integrative Method for Theological Anthropology," in *The Ashgate Research Companion to Theological Anthropology*, ed. Joshua Farris and Charles Taliaferro (Burlington, VT: Ashgate, 2015), 31.

76. E.g., see Richard Pleijel, "Translating the Biblical Hebrew Word Nephesh in Light of New Research," *Bible Translator* 70, no. 2 (2019): 154–66.

77. Robert Gundry, *The Old Is Better: New Testament Essays in Support of Traditional Interpretations* (Tübingen: Mohr Siebeck, 2005), 192.

78. Donald Hagner, *Matthew 1–13*, Word Biblical Commentary 33a (Dallas: Word, 1993), 121. As Gundry remarks: "Against 'heart' stand 'eye', 'hand', 'members', and 'body' in verses 29–30." Robert

he is speaking in hyperbole since evil arises from the heart (Jer. 17:9). Amputation cannot ultimately resolve the sin problem. Jesus is cementing the point that "it is better to deal decisively with lust than be thrown into hell because of it."[79] The source of sin lies deeper than the body and its outward actions.

A similar dynamic appears in Mark 7:19–23 (// Matt. 15:17–19). The Pharisees thought that sin could be transmitted physically, by unclean hands contaminating the food, which would then contaminate the person. Jesus argues instead that sin is not fundamentally a problem of ritual uncleanness but a *spiritual* problem. Sin does not contaminate from the outside, for whatever enters the mouth passes through the stomach and is discharged from the body. Moral depravity arises from the nonphysical. "For from within, out of the heart of man, come evil thoughts, sexual immorality, theft, murder, adultery, coveting, wickedness, deceit, sensuality, envy, slander, pride, foolishness. All these evil things come from within, and they defile a person" (Mark 7:21–23). As Calvin puts it, "Man's heart is the seat of all evils."[80]

Consider Romans 2:28–29. The apostle Paul insists that being outwardly Jewish is inadequate; spiritual circumcision is not merely outward and physical (*en sarki*). "No," Paul writes, "a Jew is one *inwardly*, and circumcision is a matter *of the heart*, by the Spirit, not by the letter" (v. 29). This contrast between the inner and outer parts of the person is not just a perspective on a larger whole; it is best understood by a deeper immaterial versus material reality. True circumcision, H. C. G. Moule comments, is "a work *on the soul*, wrought by God's Spirit, not . . . a legal claim supposed to rest upon a routine of prescribed observances."[81] Certainly regeneration and human sinfulness apply to the *whole* person. Nonetheless, Paul's claims about the seat of sin and the object of regeneration presuppose an inner person who resides at a level deeper than material reality.

The ontological distinction between body and heart is also previewed, famously, in Ezekiel 36:26–27 (see also Jer. 31:31–34). The heart stands in for the inner person, the seat of the mind and thought, decision, and will.[82] Eze-

Gundry, *Sōma in Biblical Theology, with Emphasis on Pauline Anthropology* (Cambridge: Cambridge University Press, 1976), 111.

79. David Turner, *Matthew*, Baker Exegetical Commentary on the New Testament (Grand Rapids: Baker Academic, 2008), 171.

80. John Calvin, *A Harmony of the Gospels: Matthew, Mark and Luke*, trans. A. W. Morrison (Grand Rapids: Eerdmans, 1972), 165, commenting on Matt. 15:19.

81. H. C. G. Moule, *The Epistle to the Romans* (Fort Washington, MD: Christian Literature Crusade, 1975), 73, my emphasis.

82. Walther Eichrodt, *Ezekiel: A Commentary*, trans. Cosslett Quin, Old Testament Library (London: SCM, 1970), 499; Christopher Wright, *The Message of Ezekiel: A New Heart and a New Spirit*, Bible Speaks Today (Downers Grove, IL: InterVarsity, 2001), 296.

kiel promises that Yahweh will give his people a new heart and a new spirit, replacing the heart of stone with a heart of flesh (Ezek. 11:19; 36:26). These rich metaphors exclude physical realities, "for what could circumcision of the foreskin of the heart possibly mean unless the term 'heart' has lost its physical connotation?"[83] On the physicalist view, these divine promises merely refer to new spiritual desires and habits; while true as far is it goes, it misses the deeper anthropological assumptions in these texts. Ezekiel anticipates the inner-outer contrast in Mark 7:19–23 and Matthew 15:17–19—and in John 3:6 (NIV), Jesus signals this inner-outer contrast when he says, "Flesh gives birth to flesh, *but the Spirit gives birth to spirit*" (a hint here of anthropological dualism?). Human sinfulness is a problem that tracks deeper than our physical bodies. This problem inheres in our very souls.

My thesis is not that the catholic tradition is overwhelmingly dualist, although that is demonstrably true. As J. N. D. Kelly writes, "In both East and West alike it was taken for granted that man is a composite being made up out of body and soul. He is a 'rational animal' . . . with a foot in the higher, or intellectual, as well as the lower, or sensible, world."[84] Nor is my claim that dualism feels intuitively right to me and that I cannot conceive of what it would mean for physical things to have consciousness and reason (although that is also true). That argument only goes so far since we all have different intuitions.[85] Rather, my thesis is that Scripture's own theology of sin is implicitly dualist. Still, a physicalist might respond that these passages are merely describing the person that lies beyond the immediately perceptible physical body, someone with reason, will, and desire—but of course this view of the person is consistent with nonreductive physicalism and emergentism. Perhaps so, but dualism strikes me as a more plausible inference from these passages.

Furthermore, a physicalist might concede the Bible's implicit dualism yet respond that the biblical authors were merely reflecting their own limited (ancient) scientific views; now we know better. Here again the ground is slippery. Such appeals to divine accommodation are usually motivated by an undue confidence in current scientific, extrabiblical perspectives.[86]

---

83. Gundry, *Sōma in Biblical Theology*, 126.

84. J. N. D. Kelly, *Early Christian Doctrines*, 5th rev. ed. (New York: HarperCollins, 1978), 344. As one Christian physicalist concedes, "Most, if not all, orthodox Christian theologians of the early church were anthropological dualists." Kevin Corcoran, *Rethinking Human Nature: A Christian Materialist Alternative to the Soul* (Grand Rapids: Baker Academic, 2006), 121.

85. Sarah Lane Ritchie, "Wait, but Why? Challenging the Intuitive Force of Substance Dualism," *Scientia et Fides* 9, no. 1 (2021): 241–55.

86. See Vern Poythress, "Rethinking Accommodation in Revelation," *Westminster Theological Journal* 76, no. 1 (2014): 143–56; and, for historical background, Glenn Sunshine, "Accommodation

Besides, when Scripture makes assumptions about reality that are inseparable from its infallible teachings, then we should take those assumptions
as authoritative (as I argued in chap. 4). Our hermeneutics of Scripture
is narrow and reductive if we limit its authority to its explicit assertions.

At any rate, Jesus and the apostles did not engage in metaphysical speculation. Their teaching never lays out an explicit philosophical anthropology, but the biblical language has an *implicit* anthropology. If our only
contrasting terms were "inner" versus "outer," physicalists could perhaps
plausibly refer to them as merely aspects of an indivisible, physical whole,
or as vivid references to our corrupted desires. For example, James Dunn
argues that Greek thought viewed the human person "partitively" (made up
of distinct parts), whereas Hebrew thought viewed humans "aspectively" (a
whole person with different dimensions).[87] Dunn may be right about much
of Scripture, but I am not persuaded that his observation applies here. The
best explanation for the emphatic contrasts in the biblical texts (e.g., *not
heart . . . but* stomach, Mark 7:19; *not* outward and physical or flesh . . . *but*
inward, Rom. 2:28–29) is that the "inner" and "outer" parts are partitive and
not merely functional. This conclusion becomes especially compelling in
light of the biblical witness to their ontological *separability*.[88]

This separability is a refrain running through Scripture. Although the
Old Testament is often categorized as monistic, nothing could be further
from the truth. All human flesh returns to the dust, but their spirits persist ghostlike in Sheol. While Sheol often refers to the grave, it can also
signify the intermediate state between death and final judgment (e.g., Pss.
30:3; 49:15). The prophet Isaiah, for example, differentiates the entombed
corpses of kings from their spirits (*rapha*) eager to meet the Babylonian
king whose death brought him to the underworld (Isa. 14:9, 18–20). The
Old Testament laws against necromancy signal a widespread belief in the
spirits of the dead (Lev. 19:31; Deut. 18:11; Isa. 8:19). The clearest example
of Old Testament dualism is Saul's encounter with the medium at Endor
where the spirit of Samuel prophesies for God even though Samuel's body
has long been decomposing in the ground (1 Sam. 28:8–19).

In the New Testament, evidence for soul-body separability leaps off the
page. Jesus's promise to the penitent thief that they would see each other
again *that day*, in paradise, assumes that the Lord continued to exist in a

---

Historically Considered," in *The Enduring Authority of the Christian Scriptures*, ed. D. A. Carson (Grand
Rapids: Eerdmans, 2016), 238–65.

87. James D. G. Dunn, *The Theology of Paul the Apostle* (Grand Rapids: Eerdmans, 1998), 54. Dunn's
claim that Scripture views human persons aspectively is true for much of Scripture but not all of it.

88. I am drawing from Gundry, *Old Is Better*, 187–94.

disembodied state after death since his body would be buried in a tomb (Luke 23:39–56).[89] Earlier in his ministry, Jesus declares, "Do not fear those who kill the body but cannot kill the soul. Rather fear him who can destroy both soul and body in hell" (Matt. 10:28).[90] In 2 Corinthians 5:6–9, Paul's distinction between being at home in the body and away from the Lord versus being away from the body and at home with the Lord assumes the separability of soul and body (see also Phil. 1:20–24). Paul also thinks the spirit can be saved even if the body is destroyed (1 Cor. 5:3–5); and while recounting his experience of being caught up to paradise or the third heaven, he entertains the possibility that he was outside his body (2 Cor. 12:1–4). In Revelation 6:9–10, the souls of the martyrs in heaven poignantly attest that dead persons enter a disembodied state before the final resurrection.[91] And just before his martyrdom, Stephen offered this prayer: "Lord Jesus, receive my spirit" (Acts 7:59). The list goes on.[92] Given Scripture's pervasive assumption that the body and soul can be separated, the "inner" versus "outer" language surveyed earlier more likely indicates that the volitional, moral core of humanity transcends the physical.

In short, dualism makes better sense of human sin than physicalism. It is difficult to understand how moral responsibility can emerge from a material base. If physicalism is true and there are no immaterial entities, how would it be possible for an ontologically physical entity to sin? But some Christian physicalists respond with a "parity thesis"—namely, it is difficult to understand how moral responsibility can emerge from an *immaterial* base. *Tu quoque*: the shoe is on the other foot.[93] In other words, if it is mysterious to imagine matter engaging in thought and moral reasoning,

89. For discussion, see Cooper, *Body, Soul and Life Everlasting*, 139–45.

90. While Luke's parallel account does not mention the soul, it is not incompatible with Matthew's explicit dualism (Luke 12:4–5).

91. The Pharisees agreed with Jesus and the apostles on this point. See N. T. Wright, *The Resurrection of the Son of God* (Minneapolis: Fortress, 2003), 131–34, 190–206, 366–67, 424–26. On Wright's later wobbling on dualism, see Stewart Goetz, "Is N. T. Wright Right about Substance Dualism?," *Philosophia Christi* 14, no. 1 (2012): 183–91; Brandon Rickabaugh, "Responding to N. T. Wright's Rejection of the Soul," *Heythrop Journal* 59, no. 2 (2018): 201–20. Even if one questions whether Rev. 6:9–10 gives an "empirical" account of the martyred souls—since we are dealing with a vision—my main point is that the text assumes dualism and the intermediate state.

92. For more examples with discussion, see Cooper, *Body, Soul and Life Everlasting*. See also John W. Cooper, "'Absent from the Body . . . Present with the Lord': Is the Intermediate State Fatal to Physicalism?," in *Christian Physicalism? Philosophical Theological Criticisms*, ed. R. Keith Loftin and Joshua Farris (Lanham, MD: Lexington Books, 2018), 319–39.

93. See Clifford Williams, "Christian Materialism and the Parity Thesis," *International Journal for Philosophy of Religion* 39, no. 1 (1996): 1–14, which triggered a protracted exchange with J. P. Moreland. The parity thesis is deployed in Peter van Inwagen, *Metaphysics*, 4th ed. (New York: Westview, 2015), 234–37; and Corcoran, *Rethinking Human Nature*, 61–63.

then it is just as mysterious to imagine nonmatter engaging in thought and moral reasoning. Here, I think, we have help from an unexpected place: fallen angels.

Demonology and the Metaphysics of Sin

Demonology gives us a clue into the essence of sin. In the first place, that demons are creatures that *sin* hardly needs defense. Scripture calls them *"evil* spirits" (e.g., Luke 7:21; 8:2; Acts 19:12–16), agents of idolatry (1 Cor. 10:20–21; Rev. 9:20), and the spring of false doctrine (1 Tim. 4:1), among other things. The devil himself is the father of lies and the ultimate origin of sin (John 8:44); his certain fate is eternal damnation (Rev. 20:7–10). In the second place, the Old and New Testaments present demons (and angels) as *immaterial* creatures. Scripture consistently employs the same ontological terminology to describe both God, on one side, and angels and demons, on the other. The numerous references to God as "spirit"—using terms like *ruach* and *pneuma*—serve to indicate his immaterial essence. Since the Bible describes angels and demons using identical words for "spirit," we can assume that the angelic nature is likewise immaterial (e.g., 1 Sam. 16:14–15; Judg. 9:23; Matt. 8:16; Mark 5:12–13).[94]

On this latter question about the immateriality of angels, we should pause to consider the witness of church history. Scripture, of course, is the *norma normans* (the norming norm) and therefore has supreme authority over other authorities, including church tradition, experience, and reason—these latter authorities function as *norma normata* (ruled norms). Nevertheless, reading Scripture with the tradition promotes exegetical honesty. This is true especially when we are forced to wrestle with why past interpreters often understood the meaning of particular canonical texts differently—as was the case prior to the twelfth century when theologians believed that the nature of angels lay somewhere between material and immaterial.[95]

They knew God had already made the angels before he created the physical world, so they could not be physical beings—but most concluded that angels and demons must have spiritual *bodies* since only God is incor-

---

94. As Ingolf Dalferth says about classical angelology, "Angels are understood to be spiritual substances in accordance with Scripture (Ps 104:4; Heb 1:14); that means that like humans, they are *created* and therefore *finite* beings; but unlike humans, they are (put positively) entirely *spiritual* and *intelligent* beings and thus (put negatively) are *non-corporeal* beings." Ingolf Dalferth, *Malum: A Theological Hermeneutics of Evil*, trans. Nils F. Schott (Eugene, OR: Cascade Books, 2022), 204, emphasis original.

95. I am indebted to Shandon L. Guthrie, *Gods of This World: A Philosophical Discussion and Defense of Christian Demonology* (Eugene, OR: Pickwick, 2018), esp. 39–66, 151–81.

poreal.[96] As fallen angels, demons were seen as spiritual beings composed of a material-like, aerial substance.[97] Considering demons as possessing light bodies clarified how they could interact with the physical world even though they were invisible, and this angelology seemed consistent with biblical accounts of angels who sometimes manifest physically and can even eat food (Gen. 18:18).[98] But the notion of spirits as material or quasi-material substances—an ontology inherited from the early Greeks—was not a fully coherent position, since spirit and matter are metaphysically different kinds of things.[99] The Greeks had not yet understood "the antithesis between spirit and matter," as Frederick Copleston remarks. "They were not fully conscious of the distinction, or at least they did not realise its implications."[100] In patristic and early medieval theology, demons were both spiritual and material, lying somewhere between the immaterial God and the material world around us.

By the twelfth century, the consensus on angelic corporeality had shifted decisively. Angels and demons as purely spiritual, immaterial, incorporeal

96. John Cassian (d. ca. 433) was typical in his defense of angelic corporeality. John Cassian, *Collationes* 7.13, in *The Conferences*, trans. Boniface Ramsey (New York: Paulist Press, 1997), 256–57. He cites 1 Cor. 15:40 and 15:44.

97. Advocates of demonic corporeality include Tertullian (*On the Flesh of Christ* 6) and Augustine (*The City of God* 10.13). Although patristic views on the corporeality of demons cited biblical proof texts, pagan philosophers shared similar views of the spirit world. See Valery V. Petroff, "Eriugena on the Spiritual Body," *American Catholic Philosophical Quarterly* 79, no. 4 (2005): 600–601. For other patristic witnesses from the sixth to the ninth century, see Isidore of Seville (*Etymologiae* 8.11.16), John of Damascus (*De Fide Orthodoxa* 2.3), and Bernard of Clairvaux (*De Consideratione* 5.4). For the same doctrine in John Scotus Erigena and Florus (ninth century) and in Honorious of Autun (twelfth century), see Louis Coulange, *Life of the Devil*, trans. Stephen Haden Guest (New York: Alfred A. Knopf, 1930), 51. Coulange is a pseudonym for Joseph Turmel.

98. Clement of Alexandria describes manna as "the celestial food of angels" (Clement of Alexandria, *Paed.* 1.6.41, in *Christ the Educator*, trans. Simon P. Wood [New York: Fathers of the Church, 1954], 39). For the same view in Justin Martyr, see *Dial.* 57.2, in *Dialogue with Trypho*, trans. Thomas B. Falls, rev. ed. (Washington, DC: Catholic University of America Press, 2003), 88. Origen believes that demons gorge themselves on burnt offerings, "always on the lookout for the smoke and steam and blood and incense of sacrifice." Origen, *Mart.* 45, cited in Gregory A. Smith, "How Thin Is a Demon?," *Journal of Early Christian Studies* 16, no. 4 (2008): 483.

99. Shandon L. Guthrie, "Christian Demonology: A New Philosophical Perspective," in *Philosophical Approaches to Demonology*, ed. Benjamin McGraw and Robert Arp (New York: Routledge, 2017), 60.

100. Frederick Copleston, *A History of Philosophy*, vol. 1 (New York: Doubleday, 1993), 20 (originally published 1946), cited in Guthrie, "Christian Demonology," 60. On related medieval debates over whether and how angelic spirituality should be understood in relation to Aristotelian hylomorphism, see David Keck, *Angels and Angelology in the Middle Ages* (Oxford: Oxford University Press, 1998), 93–99; and Travis Dumsday, "Angels, Principalities, and Powers," in *Neo-Aristotelian Metaphysics and the Theology of Nature*, ed. William M. R. Simpson, Robert C. Koons, and James Orr (New York: Routledge, 2021), 267–90.

beings became the orthodox position in Western medieval theology.[101] The seeds for this change had been planted centuries earlier by Pseudo-Dionysius the Areopagite (fifth to sixth century). Because angels are beyond our ken, we naturally depict them physically even though they are immaterial spirits.[102] But it was Hugh of Saint Victor (ca. 1096–1141) who disseminated the Areopagite's ideas in the West. Hugh argued that angels and demons are not created from any preexisting matter and have a "simple and immaterial substance."[103] In 1215, the immateriality of angels would become Catholic dogma at the Fourth Lateran Council when its first canon described God creating "from nothing both spiritual and corporeal creatures, that is to say angelic and earthly, and then created human beings composed as it were of both spirit and body in common."[104] The view that angels are purely incorporeal and immaterial spirits became normative after the thirteenth century.[105]

The immateriality of angels is in fact the sober truth of Scripture. The triune God is the paradigm case of spirit, and demons are spiritual in a derivative sense. God is spirit (*pneuma*) and enjoys immateriality in an infinite and unlimited sense (John 1:18; 4:24; 1 Tim. 1:17; 6:15–16), whereas fallen (and holy) angels are immaterial in a finite and limited sense.[106] The canonical witness repeatedly testifies that demons are "spirits" (e.g., 1 John 4:1, 3, 6), "evil spirits" (Matt. 12:45; Luke 7:21; 8:2; 11:26), "unclean spirits"

101. Nonetheless, a bewildering plurality of views on angels and demons has flourished since the medieval period. See Peter Marshall and Alexandra Walsham, eds., *Angels in the Early Modern World* (New York: Cambridge University Press, 2006); Isabel Iribarren and Martin Lenz, eds., *Angels in Medieval Philosophical Inquiry: Their Function and Significance* (Burlington, VT: Ashgate, 2008). Theology in the Orthodox East never settled on the issue of angelic corporeality and remains a topic of (limited) debate to this day.

102. According to Dionysius, "We lack the ability to be directly raised up to conceptual contemplations. We need our own upliftings that come naturally to us and which can raise before us the permitted forms of the marvelous and unformed sights" (Dionysius, *The Celestial Hierarchy* 2.2, in *Pseudo-Dionysius: The Complete Works*, trans. Colm Luibheid [New York: Paulist Press, 1987], 149). See also *Celestial Hierarchy* 2.3, 4.2.

103. Hugh of Saint Victor, *De Sacramentis* 1.5.8, in *Hugh of Saint Victor on the Sacraments of the Christian Faith*, trans. Roy J. Deferrari (Cambridge, MA: Medieval Academy of America, 1951), 78.

104. "Fourth Lateran Council (1215)," in *Decrees of the Ecumenical Councils*, ed. Norman Tanner, 2 vols. (Washington, DC: Georgetown University Press, 1990), 1:230.

105. Thomas Aquinas defended this view in his *Summa Theologica* I.50.1–2. By the time of the early scholastic period (ca. 1130–ca. 1230), the pure spirituality (or incorporeality) of angels was the consensus position. For example, William of Auxerre (1150–1231) and Alexander of Hales (ca. 1170–1245) both defended this view. Marcia Colish, "Early Scholastic Angelology," *Recherches de Théologie ancienne et médiévale* 62 (1995): 80–109.

106. As Herman Bavinck notes, "[Angels] do not transcend all space and time as God does, for they are creatures and therefore finite and limited." Bavinck, *Reformed Dogmatics*, ed. John Bolt, trans. John Vriend, 4 vols. (Grand Rapids: Baker Academic, 2003–8), 2:457.

(Matt. 10:1; Mark 1:23, 26; 3:11; 6:7; Luke 4:33, 35, 41; 6:18), and so on. The textual evidence overwhelmingly supports the Fourth Lateran Council's judgment that angels are spiritual and immaterial.

Angels certainly manifest themselves physically throughout the biblical narrative (e.g., Gen. 18–19; Num. 22:22–35; Luke 1:11–12; Acts 5:19–20), usually in human, sometimes in nonhuman form—but such appearances are instances of God accommodating transcendent spiritual realities to finite humans. We should not infer from such passages that angels are *literally* physical creatures.[107] However, for all the faults of the patristic belief in angelic corporeality, those fathers rejected any notion that angels have physical bodies akin to those of humans; angelic "corporeality" denoted an aerial substance, much lighter than human flesh, and devoid of any neurology, genetics, physiology, cardiology, and so on. Even from the perspective of angelic corporeality, angels are not biological creatures.[108]

Demons are not only immaterial but they have moral agency and are therefore blameworthy before the triune God. The serpent's presence in Genesis 3 reveals that sin itself began with a fallen angel.[109] The devil and the other fallen angels were sinning before God had created Adam and Eve.[110] They have the monopoly on sin and are guilty of capital vices like vainglory, envy, sloth, avarice, wrath, and lust. Indeed, pride is usually considered the root sin and the one that church fathers most associated with the devil's fall—for example, Paul cautions that a church elder should not

107. On angelophanies, see Graham Cole, *Against the Darkness: The Doctrine of Angels, Satan, and Demons* (Wheaton: Crossway, 2019), 76–78.

108. But what about the account in Gen. 6:1–4 of the "sons of God" marrying the "daughters of men"? If the passage is about fallen angels, then it implies some kind of angelic corporeality given the ability to have sex with humans. At the outset, we should recognize the exegetical difficulties here. As David Albert Jones says, "This short paragraph from the book of Genesis is possibly the strangest passage in the entire Hebrew Bible" (David Albert Jones, *Angels: A Very Short Introduction* [Oxford: Oxford University Press, 2011], 110). Interestingly, some church fathers thought demons are not strictly fallen angels, but rather wandering souls of dead Nephilim—that is, the departed spirits of hybrid offspring of women and evil angels who were killed in the flood (cf. Gen. 6:1–4). For a defense of this view, see Michael Heiser, *Demons: What the Bible Really Says about the Powers of Darkness* (Bellingham, WA: Lexham, 2020), esp. 127–44. At any rate, while it is textually possible that fallen angels were having sexual intercourse with women, other interpretations are available—for example, that godly Sethites ("sons of God") were marrying worldly Cainites ("daughters of man"), or that wicked male princes were marrying female commoners (see Graham Cole's discussion in *Against the Darkness*, 114–20, 138–40). Given the obscurity of the passage, we should not invoke it dogmatically for establishing an angelic ontology; we also note that the fallen angels view seems to contradict Matt. 22:30, where Jesus says that angels in heaven—like resurrected believers—do not marry and presumably do not (or cannot?) have sexual intercourse.

109. Biblical scholars may resist identifying the serpent with Satan, but that identification is standard in the catholic tradition and warranted by the rest of the canon. Cole, *Against the Darkness*, 87–89.

110. See my brief discussion of the fall of Satan in chap. 6.

be a recent convert "or he may become conceited and fall under the same judgment as the devil" (1 Tim. 3:6 NIV). Angelic sin is irreversible without the possibility of grace and redemption.[111] The ultimate penalty for sin is eternal damnation in hell, the certain fate of the devil and his demonic entourage (Matt. 25:41; Rev. 20:7–10).

In short, demons personify the very essence of sin; they are creatures without biological structure or form—indeed without material constitution. They are morally responsible because they have angelic minds that give them unity of consciousness, intentionality, and a moral core—that is, moral transcendence. Since the conditions for moral agency are the same for human and angelic creatures, it appears that being embodied is not necessary for moral agency; fallen angels exemplify my claim that moral transcendence requires immaterial mind.[112] This conclusion is consistent with my central thesis that a dualist anthropology makes the best sense of the human experience of sin, and that human beings have the capacity to sin because they have immaterial souls. Therefore, demonology invalidates the parity thesis, the idea that moral responsibility is just as difficult to understand for dualists as it is for physicalists. No, it is not; the fact that *demons are creatures that sin* offers a clear case of moral responsibility emerging from an immaterial base—yet it remains difficult, if not impossible, to understand how moral responsibility can emerge from a material base. No parity here.

Drawing all the threads together, Scripture offers a picture of human persons as culpable before God for internal desires and external acts that truly disclose their hearts. The moral agency implied in the doctrine of original corruption reflects the principle of self-disclosure over self-making. I have genuine moral agency when my moral states and actions are properly functioning—that is, they are produced in me in a way that reliably discloses the heart: "For out of the heart come evil thoughts, murder, adultery, sexual immorality, theft, false witness, slander" (Matt. 15:19).[113] Human sinning is "by *my* fault, by *my* own fault, by *my* own most grievous fault," as the Lutheran liturgy avows.[114] This notion of original sin implies a robust sense of moral agency, something close to what philosophers call agent causation.

---

111. Origen, Clement, and others in church history believed that the devil and the other fallen angels will eventually be saved, but this idea has no basis in Scripture.

112. See Martyna Koszkało and Robert Koszkało, "What the Fall of Angels Tells Us about the Essence of Morality," *Religions* 12, no. 11 (2021), doi.org/10.3390/rel12110920.

113. See chap. 7 for this aspect of Reformed compatibilism.

114. *Lutheran Book of Worship* (Minneapolis: Augsburg, 1978), 155, my emphasis.

In a helpful essay, Meghan Griffith defines agent causation as *"irreducible substance causation.* The agent, the person, is a metaphysical substance whose causal activity grounds autonomous agency (and responsibility)."[115] *I* am an agent-cause of a desire or action if I am the cause of that desire or action; or, to state it differently, I am an agent-cause if a desire or action properly discloses *my* heart rather than something external to or more fundamental than me as a moral agent. The Christian practice of confessing sin assumes something like agent causation: "We confess that we have sinned against you in thought, word, and deed." The view of responsibility in Scripture and the tradition is consistent with agent causation. Sin, by definition, implies guilt—personal guilt that each of us bears because of our covenantal relation to Adam (Rom. 5:12–21; 1 Cor. 15:21–22) and guilt for our own individual sins (Prov. 24:12; 2 Cor. 5:10). Sinners are morally accountable as agent-causes before God.

Most philosophers who defend agent causation do so in order to preserve incompatibilism (or indeterminism). They take the agent-causal theory to be an incompatibilist theory. However, agent causation is actually motivated by *anti-reductionism* and is thus separable from the determinism-versus-indeterminism debate. As Christopher Franklin writes, "The reason to accept the agent-causal theory of free will is that neither is the agent himself reducible to states and events nor is his role in self-determination reducible to the causal activities of states and events. The real issue motivating acceptance of this theory concerns neither determinism nor indeterminism, but reductionism."[116] My thesis is that Scripture affirms an agent-causal theory of responsibility and that the dualist assumptions of Scripture, together with the insights from angelic sin, suggest that dualism makes the best sense of agent causation.

Conclusion

The debate between Christian physicalists and dualists turns on two principal questions: (1) Does my anthropology resonate with current scientific plausibility structures? (2) Does my anthropology enjoy dogmatic fit with other deliverances of Scripture? Typically, Christian physicalists privilege scientific consonance while Christian dualists favor dogmatic fit. Science

---

115. Meghan Griffith, "Agent Causation," in *The Routledge Companion to Free Will*, ed. Kevin Timpe, Meghan Griffith, and Neil Levy (New York: Routledge, 2017), 73.

116. Christopher Evan Franklin, "If Anyone Should Be an Agent-Causalist, Then Everyone Should Be an Agent-Causalist," *Mind* 125, no. 500 (2016): 1125–26.

itself can neither prove physicalism nor falsify dualism. The relation between neural firings and the mind is consistent with *correlation* without causation; if the human soul is immaterial, then it is inaccessible to empirical science. Therefore, since our anthropology is underdetermined by the natural sciences, dualism strengthens its case by making better sense of sin and yielding a tighter correspondence with other areas of Christian doctrine.

On this latter point, considering again the intermediate state (see above), dualism is congruent with Christology while physicalism is not. If it is not true that our lives continue after physical death, then Christ's divine and human natures must have been separated between his death and resurrection. Such a scenario violates the Council of Chalcedon, which insists that the person of Jesus is "to be acknowledged in two natures, inconfusedly, unchangeably, indivisibly, inseparably." Furthermore, our union with Christ is everlasting and indestructible (Rom. 8:38–39). If Christian physicalism is true, then our lives do *not* continue between death and resurrection, and Christ failed to keep his promise to abide with us always.[117] Likewise, dualism fits well with the doctrine of the image of God. "If God is eternal and immortal spirit," writes John Cooper, "then it is not surprising that the human spirit which images God is everlasting, immortal, and capable of perpetual bodily life."[118]

Let us return in conclusion to Philip Clayton's emergentism, arguably the strongest account of Christian physicalism. He thinks that modern physics and the scientific method raise difficult questions for special divine action. Clayton observes that modern thinkers rely on theories about human mental causation in order to understand divine causality. This leads him to the following thesis: "The question of God's relation to the world, and hence the question of how to construe divine action, should be controlled by the best theories we have of the relationship of *our* minds to our bodies—and then corrected for by the ways in which God's relation to the universe must be *different* from the relation of our mental properties to our brains and bodies."[119] The result is Clayton's panentheistic analogy—just as the human mind is to the body, so God is to the world. "God is analogous to the mind which dwells in the body," Clayton writes, "though God is also more than the

117. I am drawing from Mary Vanden Berg, "The Impact of a Gap in Existence on Christology and Soteriology: A Challenge for Physicalists," *Calvin Theological Journal* 49, no. 2 (2014): 248–57.

118. Cooper, "Absent from the Body," 326. For the same judgment among premodern theologians, see, inter alia, Augustine, *De anima et ejus origine*, 4.14.20; John Calvin, *Institutes of the Christian Religion*, 1.15.2–3.

119. Clayton, *God and Contemporary Science*, 233.

natural world taken as a whole."[120] Since his emergence thesis implies that human mental causation breaks no natural laws, so too his panentheistic argument reconceives divine action without breaking any natural laws. Notice the method: start with what our best sciences say about human persons (emergentism), then use that picture to solve the problem of divine action. Call this approach *scientific faith seeking biblical understanding*.

This is theologically misguided. Our triune God is ontologically and epistemologically fundamental. As immaterial spirit, this God sustains creation providentially and sometimes intervenes in the world supernaturally. Our knowledge of God should control how we understand ourselves—call this approach *biblical faith seeking scientific understanding*.

Despite the perennial objections of philosophers, there is therefore nothing mysterious in the claim that the immaterial acts in and through the material world. As creatures fashioned in the image of the immaterial God, it is perfectly natural to ground human moral agency in a dualistic anthropology. Christians should not despise the astonishing world uncovered by neuroscience and the other scientific disciplines, but we also know that this visible world is enfolded in a richer cosmos bursting with unspeakably glorious things, the rumor of angels, and indeed the inbreaking of the eschatological kingdom of God (John 18:36). At the resurrection, our bodies will be glorified to reunite with our souls forever, and—that day cannot come any sooner—we will never ever sin again.

120. Philip Clayton, *Adventures in the Spirit: God, World, Divine Action* (Minneapolis: Fortress, 2008), 128.

Conclusion

Science and an Evangelical Dogmatics of Sin

> The number one reason young Christians leave the faith is the conflict between science and faith, and that conflict can be narrowed to the conflict between evolutionary theory and human origins as traditionally read in Genesis 1–2. It works like this: many Christians grow up with a view of Scripture as inerrant, and that means for them . . . that it is not only true but also more or less magically true, true beyond its time, true when everything else says something else. . . . One's interpretations of Scripture become as infallible as the Bible itself, and since everything interlocks, giving in one inch is the first step toward apostasy. One of those interpretations is that the Bible teaches science in Genesis 1–2. When the evangelical student marches off to university, takes a biology class from an able-minded, rhetorically skilled, and atheistic/agnostic professor who makes it more than clear that the earth is not 6,000–10,000 years old but is in fact closer to 4.5 billion years old . . . a student's faith can be more than shaken. Many walk away or, more significant today, embrace an ironic faith.
>
> —Dennis Venema and Scot McKnight[1]

The above concern reminds us that questions about the interaction between science and the doctrine of sin are not merely academic but are inevitably spiritual. The perception that the Bible and science are in deep conflict can sometimes lead to people losing their faith.

---

1. Dennis Venema and Scot McKnight, *Adam and the Genome: Reading Scripture after Genetic Science* (Grand Rapids: Brazos, 2017), 104–5.

Such alarming "deconversion" narratives are on the rise and, unsurprisingly, are often used rhetorically to score points in the origins debate (e.g., "*your* theology leads Christians to deconvert when they encounter science"). Behind all the rhetoric, however, are the anxieties and doubts of real people who are trying to make sense of faith in a world of scientific wonder.

Imagine a believer who has recently been convinced by mainstream evolution and now thinks she must reject original goodness and monogenism, doctrines she previously accepted as true. Imagine, further, that these two beliefs are bound up with her conception of what it means to be a genuine believer—the only choice, she concludes, is to give up her faith. Her decision strikes most of us as tragic, not merely because of the high stakes but because she ignored other, less drastic options. Christians, after all, always find new ways to interpret Scripture that can harmonize with the scientific consensus (as we have seen throughout this book).

In addition, Christian piety does not demand we always pit Scripture against the natural sciences; that kind of antagonistic attitude brings disrepute to the faith. Even Augustine raised this concern in the patristic era. "Now it is quite disgraceful and disastrous, something to be on one's guard against at all costs," he wrote, "that they should ever hear Christians spouting what they claim our Christian literature has to say on [scientific issues], and talking such nonsense that [non-Christians] can scarcely contain their laughter."[2] Likewise, in recent decades we have seen immense intellectual energies devoted to reducing conflict between science and theology. Such efforts are a form of apologetics—"external" apologetics to persuade unbelievers that Christian faith is reasonable, and "internal" apologetics to reinforce the faith of believers.[3]

The idea seems to be that Christians can disagree about the scientific implications of different areas of Christian doctrine so long as they do not strike at essential elements of the faith. In terms of dogmatic rank, views on the age of the earth or Noah's flood do not have the same level of importance as Christ's bodily resurrection or justification by grace through faith. Mature Christians, so the argument goes, must therefore engage in

2. Augustine, *The Literal Meaning of Genesis* 1.19.39, in *The Works of Saint Augustine: On Genesis*, trans. Edmund Hill (Hyde Park, NY: New City, 2002), 186. I gave the broader context of the quote in chap. 1. The "scientific" issues that Augustine refers to include "knowledge . . . about the earth, about the sky, about the other elements of this world, about the movements and revolutions or even the magnitude and distances of the constellations, about the predictable eclipses of moon and sun, about the cycles of years and seasons, about the nature of animals, fruits, stones and everything else of this kind." Augustine, *On Genesis*, 186.

3. For the distinction between internal and external apologetics, see James Beilby, *Thinking about Christian Apologetics: What It Is and Why We Do It* (Downers Grove, IL: InterVarsity, 2011), 27–28.

theological triage which allows them to distinguish between primary, secondary, and tertiary doctrines.[4] Primary doctrines are essential, but getting tertiary doctrines wrong will condemn no one to hell. Most of the doctrines that are contested in the science-theology literature are usually ranked at a tertiary level—they are seen as relatively unimportant; good Christians can agree to disagree.

Taking Dogmas Seriously

However, this book tells a more complex story. Biology and other sciences have been instrumental in how the doctrine of sin is articulated among many academics today. Aside from the confession that humans are *sinners*, much of the classical doctrine has been stripped away. The early chapters of Genesis are apparently no longer historically informative. The historical Adam and his fall into sin are gone. The idea of a once-sinless world and original righteousness have lost credibility. Original sin has been refashioned in biological categories, and moral corruption is understood without reference to the soul. While these examples represent extreme revisions to the doctrine of sin, there are other less radical models (e.g., Adam and Eve reconfigured as members of an original population of early humans). In either case, whether the strategy is radical or minor revision, our current picture of the world shapes how theologians think about sin.

The first worry stirred by this situation concerns Holy Scripture. The central principle of biblical realism—the methodology laid out in chapter 2—is that Scripture is the infallible Word of God. Given the nature of divine discourse, when the biblical account addresses areas of history that overlap with the conclusions of natural science, it does so with complete epistemological authority. God's version of reality is necessarily more reliable than any scientific theory. Central doctrines, moreover, are not warranted on scientific or evidential grounds but are authorized by inerrant Scripture.

The second worry arises in response to the tendency to treat doctrines like original goodness, monogenism, and dualism as somewhat marginal to the biblical story. Christian doctrines are never isolated beliefs but are integrated components within a theological system—not skeins of thread, but seams in a garment. Lesser doctrines often have significant theological

4. Albert Mohler, "A Call for Theological Triage and Christian Maturity," AlbertMohler.com, July 12, 2005, http://www.albertmohler.com/2005/07/12/a-call-for-theological-triage-and-christian -maturity/. Mohler may not intend to use theological triage as a means of prioritizing doctrines, but that is in fact how the concept functions in many Christian circles.

ties to core aspects of the biblical story; denying the one will imply denial of the other. Original goodness, for example, is a corollary of the holiness of God; without a historical fall, we implicate God in creating a world of natural evil (at least) and moral evil (at worst). Furthermore, the gospel story becomes incoherent. The logic of a God who redeems sin and death and promises that everything will be made right in the new heaven and new earth falls apart if he created the world with evil and suffering from the beginning. Original goodness is merely one of many doctrines that may seem marginal but that, in fact, are doctrinally inseparable from what is central to the biblical narrative.

This is the nature of Christian dogmatics; doctrines interconnect and must maintain inner coherence. In the words of Herman Bavinck, "Even in his system a theologian's sole responsibility is to think God's thoughts after him and to reproduce the unity that is objectively present in the thoughts of God and has been recorded for the eye of faith in Scripture."[5] The doctrine of sin has internal bearing on doctrines about other realities—like creation, humanity, Christ, and salvation. Even a well-established scientific theory should not easily displace a doctrine that is clearly taught in Scripture, widely held in the tradition, and central to the redemptive-historical story.

Taking Science Seriously

Some readers will still object that biblical realism seems ad hoc and does not take science seriously. This objection allows me to clarify some potential misunderstandings. First, biblical realism engages science dogmatically rather than evidentially. As a result, scientific theories cannot overturn central doctrines, nor can they overturn "lesser" doctrines that are theologically connected to core teachings—Scripture cannot be broken (John 10:35). Such dogmatic beliefs enjoy an intrinsic warrant that is greater than any potential scientific defeater. However, doctrines that are not clearly attested in Scripture or central to the biblical story can be overturned by scientific theories that are well confirmed.

---

5. Herman Bavinck, *Reformed Dogmatics*, ed. John Bolt, trans. John Vriend, 4 vols. (Grand Rapids: Baker Academic, 2003–8), 1:44. Trevor Hart writes, "Faith in God as the sort of Creator to which Scripture testifies compels us, I think, to make the presumption that, finally, things hold together, that 'reality' is orderly and meaningful, a genuine universe rather than a 'pluriverse'; and this presumption places us under a moral obligation to approach it on these terms, seeking the unitive form or forms which hold it together, seeking links, connections, pattern." Trevor Hart, "Systematic—in What Sense?," in *Out of Egypt: Biblical Theology and Biblical Interpretation*, ed. Craig Bartholomew, Mary Healy, Karl Möller, and Robin Parry (Grand Rapids: Zondervan, 2004), 344.

Second, if the doctrine of sin contradicts established scientific conclusions, it is not because we do not take science seriously. It happens because the historical sciences assume methodological naturalism; they operate with a limited evidence base that excludes anything supernatural. Biblical realism, by contrast, draws on a wider evidence base that includes all the events revealed by Scripture, including original creation, Adam's fall, the global flood, and more. Since methodological naturalism rules out any evidence from special revelation, a biblical realist will find many of the conclusions from the historical sciences regarding human origins epistemologically suspect.

Although this book has been largely critical of scholars working in the field of science-and-religion, I applaud them for taking on the most difficult questions that Christians face today. Confessional believers need to make their own distinctive contributions to the conversation; critique is not enough. We need more natural scientists working from an explicitly confessional framework with the widest possible evidence base. In the Western context, a kind of scientific pluralism is inevitable among Christians—that is, believers will have different perspectives on how science should interact with faith, and they will pursue scientific research in light of those assumptions (the more, the merrier).

However, there should be *some* Christian academic journals that are less resistant to publishing research from the perspective of theistic science. Such research would never be published by the mainstream establishment, but Christian scientific journals should allow competent research that draws on evidence from special revelation. Dismissing such perspectives merely allows the more reckless exemplars to dominate the landscape through their own publishing channels. Rather than trying to limit controversy by sidelining legitimate Christian approaches to natural science, we can improve the dialogue by publishing the best examples of various positions.

A Closing Pastoral Note

As for young Christians struggling with the conflicts between science and faith, what are the pastoral implications of my argument? Given that I have taken a dogmatic position often in tension with the canons of science, some will accuse me of making matters worse. I disagree. In the short term, I think many Christians can endorse sub-biblical doctrines of sin while at the same time accepting the main lines of theological orthodoxy. Happily, Christians often live with theological inconsistency and a dogmatically jumbled faith without knowing it. However, while I am no prophet, in the long term I suspect that the doctrine of sin (and possibly other related doctrines) will continue to degenerate with subsequent generations. Nothing good comes from allowing bad theology to fester. We should keep teaching the full-orbed, robust doctrine of sin because it is nothing less than mainstream, classical, Christian orthodoxy. The tensions with mainstream science will be unavoidable but can be handled with wisdom and pastoral care.

Our Lord said to his disciples, "If the world hates you, keep in mind that it hated me first. If you belonged to the world, it would love you as its own. As it is, you do not belong to the world, but I have chosen you out of the world" (John 15:18–19 NIV). As believers we live—and we die—by the message of the cross, the foolishness of God that is wiser than man's wisdom. The cross is the weakness of God and yet is stronger than man's strength (1 Cor. 1:25). In this holy paradox, "God chose what is foolish in the world to shame the wise; God chose what is weak in the world to shame the strong" (1:27). Far from being a sacrifice of the intellect, biblical realism is a discipleship of the mind. In an increasingly post-Christian world, following Christ will sometimes mean physical and intellectual martyrdom for the faith, which is a daunting prospect.[6] Still, what is impossible with man is possible with God.

Lest we forget, natural science falls under the ambit of the Lordship of Christ. As Abraham Kuyper said, "There is not a square inch in the whole domain of our human existence over which Christ, who is sovereign over all, does not cry 'Mine!'"[7] It's no wonder, for Jesus is the author of creation (John 1:3) and crafted the universe by his powerful word (Heb. 1:2–3). All things came into existence by him and hold together in him (Col. 1:16–17). Scientific research is therefore a privilege God grants us to investigate the endless intricacies of his creation, regardless of whether individual scientists recognize this reality. Nevertheless, even as we labor this side of the eschaton, our scientific pursuits will always see through a glass darkly (cf. 1 Cor. 13:12).

Special revelation gives us clarity of vision and thus will sometimes challenge the scientific consensus. Such tension often walks hand in hand with faith (cf. Heb. 11). Consider the many historical episodes in the life of God's people: the genesis of languages at the tower of Babel (Gen. 11:1–9), the

6. Kevin Vanhoozer, "The Trials of Truth: Mission, Martyrdom, and the Epistemology of the Cross," in *To Stake a Claim: Mission and the Western Crisis of Knowledge*, ed. J. Andrew Kirk and Kevin Vanhoozer (Maryknoll, NY: Orbis Books, 1999), 120–56.

7. Abraham Kuyper, "Sphere Sovereignty," in *Abraham Kuyper: A Centennial Reader*, ed. James Bratt (Grand Rapids: Eerdmans, 1998), 488.

exodus and the parting of the Red Sea (Exod. 14), the fall of Jericho as the walls tumbled down (Josh. 6), Jonah's sojourn in the belly of a great fish (Jon. 1–2), Jesus's miracles during his earthly ministry (e.g., Matt. 4:24; Mark 1:34), the marvel of Pentecost and speaking in tongues (Acts 2). Such historical events, which are major plotlines in the biblical story, stand in stark contrast to the prevailing beliefs of cultures at the time—and today.

However, they pale in comparison to the resurrection of Christ. Here is an event that turned the world upside down, the climactic redemptive act toward which all other miracles had been pointing all along. Orthodox Christianity holds that the Son of God became man, lived a sinless life, proclaimed the kingdom of God, performed miraculous wonders, died, made atonement for our sins, rose again after three days, and ascended into heaven. Yet these glad tidings clash with most everything that naturalistic science tells us about the world we live in. If Christians can embrace the reality of the resurrection, then nothing within this book should trouble the thoughtful believer. If this colossus of a miracle stands at the very core of biblical Christianity, then a full-throated doctrine of sin is not only what we would expect but precisely what we need—now more than ever.

Author Index

Scripture Index

Subject Index

Promethean determinism, 262
propositional revelation, 32–34
providence, 50, 60, 66, 84–85, 105–6, 112–13, 214, 221
Prozac, 3
Pseudo-Dionysius, 187, 310
psychiatry, 3
Ptolemy, 14
puppet determinism, 262

racism, 139–40
Rahner, Karl, 127, 142–43, 270, 300
Rankine's thermodynamic theory, 57
reason, 11–12, 13, 23, 289–90
redemption, 156–57, 211–12, 229, 240–45
reductionism, 295–98, 302
Reformation, the, 15, 49, 68, 92
regeneration, 50, 304
responsibility, 128, 189, 256–58, 260, 261, 263, 269, 272, 276, 280–81, 288–92, 312–13
restoration, 163–69, 229, 231–32, 241
resurrection and immortality, 215, 225–27
resurrection of Christ, 50, 147, 323
revisionist theology, 44
righteousness. *See* original righteousness
Robertson, James Burton, 28–29
Roman Catholicism, 28, 203–4

sacrificial system, 172, 211, 222
salvation, 211–12, 243–44, 269
sanctification, 50, 276–78
Satan, 113, 141, 155n12, 160, 207, 214n69, 311nn109–10
Scaliger, Joseph Justus, 94–95
science
  conflict thesis and, 38–41
  estimation of, 320–21
  faith and, 317–19, 321–23
  Galileo's impact, 14–21, 23, 24
  and Whig theology, 24–31
  See also natural science
science-and-religion, 36–38, 48, 80–87, 321
scientific fallibilism, 44–45, 56–67, 87, 193
scientism, 38, 47, 51
Scofield, C. I., 160
"scriptural" geologists, 26n69
scriptural limitation, 20–22
Scripture, authority of
  after Barbour, 36–38
  Calvin's view, 194–95

conflict thesis, 38–41
  eclipse of, 16–25
  epistemological priority over creation, 66
  and New Testament dogmatic rule, 149–50
  primary function of, 66–67
  rise of modern theology, 32–36
  scriptural limitation, 20–22
secondary fundamental articles of doctrine, 71
secularization thesis, 39
Sedgwick, Adam, 27
self-determination, 262–63
selfishness, 258–60, 288
Sermon on the Mount, 303
Sextus Julius Africanus, 93
Sheol, 306
Siger of Brabant, 13, 48
Silliman, Benjamin, 27
Simon, Richard, 99
Simpson, Richard, 28
sin
  Adam and, 127, 129–30
  angelic sin, 141, 214n69, 312–13
  anthropological dualism and, 281, 283, 296, 302–8
  biologizing of, 260, 264, 269–72
  as bondage, 263
  Christian physicalism and, 292–302
  and concupiscence, 264–66, 270, 272, 278n149
  critique of fall theodicy, 236–39
  culture and, 261, 269–71
  definition of, 274
  degrees of, 280
  demonology and metaphysics of, 308–13
  as idolatrous disposition, 294
  evolutionary theory and, 202–3
  fall theodicy as origin of, 234–36
  human mutability and, 230–31
  mitigated culpability, 280–82
  modernity and, 1–2
  and moral responsibility, 288–92
  and original righteousness, 208–13
  origin of, 205, 207–8, 232–36
  and physical death, 223–25
  redemption and, 240–45
  Reformed compatibilism and biology, 272–78
  and temptation, 265–66
  transmission of, 250, 264
  See also atonement; biology and sin; forgiveness of sin

Smith, George, 109, 121
Smith, James K. A., 143, 148–50
Smith, John Pye, 27
Smith, Robert Payne, 27
Smith, W. Robertson, 53, 101
Sober, Elliott, 77–78, 193–94
social culture and sin, 261
Socinianism, 216
sociobiology, 252–53, 255, 263
soft concordism, 26n68, 81–82
sola scriptura, 24, 75
soul, the, 50, 215, 250, 262
  anthropological dualism in Scripture, 302–8
  demonology and, 308–13
  moral responsibility and, 288–92
  physicalism, sin and, 292–302
Sparks, Kenton, 107, 144–45
special creation, 50, 50n31, 69, 129
special revelation, 62, 66, 83, 114–17, 195, 321, 322–23
Spinoza, Baruch, 25, 99, 233
spiritual death, 215, 217, 220, 222
Starry Messenger, The (Galileo), 14, 15n16
Suarez, Antoine, 128
substance dualism, 287, 302n71
suffering and death, 154–55, 157–59, 161–62, 165, 167–68
supernaturalism, 44, 45–52, 50n28
supervenience, 296–97, 301
Swamidass, Joshua, 130–31
Symeon the New Theologian, 186–87

taxonomy, biological, 124n7
Tempier, Étienne, 13
Templeton Foundation, 4
temptation, 265–66, 277–78, 283, 294
Tennant, Frederick, 202–3, 205, 271
Tertullian, 12, 179, 309n97
theistic evolutionists, 7–8, 145, 226, 243, 259–64, 268–69, 272
theodicy, 232
  "aesthetic" theodicy (Schneider), 155
  cosmological monism, dualism, and, 232–36
  critique of fall theodicy, 236–39
  and evolutionary proposals, 154–62
  fall theodicy, 234–36
  redemption and, 240–45
Theodore of Mopsuestia, 229–30

theology
  after Barbour, 36–38
  conflict thesis, 38–41
  liberal, 33, 35
  modernizing, 44
  neo-orthodoxy, 34–36
  rise of modern, 32–36
Theophilus of Antioch, 12, 93, 178
Thomas Aquinas, 13, 23, 48, 94, 128, 188–89, 196, 243n182, 266–68, 278n149, 310n105
Tindal, Matthew, 99
Tourette's syndrome, 278–80, 281, 283
tower of Babel, 85, 116, 322
traducianism, 250, 264
tree of life, 217–18, 242
Trinity, the, 55, 68, 70n103, 73–74
twin studies, 256–57

unconceived alternatives, 58–59, 61
United Free Church College (Glasgow), 1
United Presbyterian College (Edinburgh), 1
unity of consciousness, 288–89, 292, 312
University of Paris, 13, 48n19
unwritten special revelation, 114–17
Urmonotheismus, 119
U-shape motif of the gospel, 240n170, 240n173
Ussher, James, 95, 101n53

vegetarianism, original, 166, 172, 175–79, 181–83, 185, 189, 190, 191. *See also* animal suffering and death
Vincent of Lérins, 68
violence, 157, 236, 248n5, 252–54, 259, 269n107
  absence of, 162, 164, 166, 169
  animal, 154, 183, 188
Voltaire, 99
Vossius, Isaac, 99

warfare metaphor, 38, 38n122, 38n123, 39–41
Warfield, B. B., 30–31n86, 102, 127n17, 142n77
Westcott, B. F., 53
Westminster Confession of Faith, 5, 7, 9, 68, 71n104, 208
Westminster Larger Catechisms, 5
Westminster Shorter Catechisms, 5
Westminster Standards, 5
Whig history, 26n67
Whig theology, 24–31